Broadband Integrated Networks

Broadband Integrated Networks

Mischa Schwartz

Department of Electrical Engineering
Columbia University
New York, N.Y.

For book and bookstore information

http://www.prenhall.com

Prentice Hall PTR
Upper Saddle River, New Jersey 07458

Library of Congress Cataloging-in-Publication Data

Schwartz, Mischa.
    Broadband integrated networks / Mischa Schwartz.
        p.   cm.
    Includes bibliographical references and index.
    ISBN 0–13–519240–4
    1. Integrated services digital networks.   2. Broadband
communication systems.   3. Asynchronous transfer mode.   I. Title.
TK5103.75.S38   1996
004.6′6—dc20   95–48184
                                                                                CIP

Acquisitions editor: Paul Becker
Cover designer: Talar Agasyan
Cover design director: Jerry Votta
Manufacturing buyer: Alexis R. Heydt
Compositor/Production services: Pine Tree Composition, Inc.

© 1996 by Prentice Hall PTR
Prentice-Hall, Inc.
A Simon & Schuster Company
Upper Saddle River, New Jersey 07458

The publisher offers discounts on this book when ordered in bulk quantities.

For more information contact:
        Corporate Sales Department
        Prentice Hall PTR
        One Lake Street
        Upper Saddle River, New Jersey 07458

        Phone: 800–382–3419
        Fax: 201–236–7141
        email: corpsales@prenhall.com

Printed in the United States of America
10 9 8 7 6 5 4 3 2 1

ISBN: 0-13-519240-4

Prentice Hall International (UK) Limited, *London*
Prentice Hall of Australia Pty. Limited, *Sydney*
Prentice Hall Canada, Inc., *Toronto*
Prentice Hall Hispanoamericana, S.A., *Mexico*
Prentice Hall of India Private Limited, *New Delhi*
Prentice Hall of Japan, Inc., *Tokyo*
Simon & Schuster Asia Pte. Ltd., *Singapore*
Editora Prentice Hall do Brasil, Ltda., *Rio de Janeiro*

*To the memory of my
parents, Bessie and
Isaiah Schwartz*

Contents

Preface

Activity in the area of broadband integrated networking has been expanding at a rapid rate. Commercial ATM switches, particularly for the LAN market, have gained wide-spread acceptance and have been deployed in many laboratories and other establishments. The ATM Forum has been attempting to expedite the development of standards for ATM-based networks so that vendors can produce products that will interwork compatibly with one another. The volume of papers published, covering everything from traffic characterization for this new field to performance studies of proposed control mechanisms to proposals for improved ATM switch designs, appears to be increasing as well. This makes it difficult for newcomers to the field to quickly become familiar with, or master, aspects of the field of interest to them.

Survey and tutorial papers, covering various aspects of broadband ISDN and ATM technology in a descriptive and qualitative manner, have appeared in technical journals and magazines from time to time. Books on the subject, written in a similar descriptive manner, have begun to appear as well. These books and survey papers can be used to address the problem noted above. There is still a need, however, for a textbook that provides an introductory, quantitative approach to the study of broadband integrated networks. This book is designed to fill this need. Its focus is on modeling and performance analysis in the high-speed ATM networking environment. As noted above, the literature covering quantitative design and performance issues in ATM is vast and is growing rapidly. A reader mastering the material presented here should have no difficulty understanding literature in the field. It is the author's firm belief that with the quantitative understanding comes a much better appreciation of the design issues involved in developing new products or deploying them, when available. This has always been the case for new technology, and the ATM networking world is no exception.

Because the book stresses modeling and performance issues, it requires some knowledge of elementary queueing theory. (More advanced concepts are introduced within the text where needed.) For those readers not familiar with the basic aspects of queueing theory, or those requiring a quick review, an appendix is provided that introduces the reader to the material needed to begin studying the quantitative portions of the book.

Most of the book has been tested in class. It is based on, and is an outgrowth of, a set of notes developed for a graduate course on broadband integrated networks taught at Columbia University for a number of years. The notes were also used by the author to present a series of weekly lectures on the subject during a sabbatical with the Electronic and Electrical Engineering Department of University College London.

The course given at Columbia had, as a prerequisite, an introductory quantitative course on computer networks, which introduced the student to the necessary queueing theory and analysis noted above. In universities where no such prior course is given, or where a prior course in queueing theory is not required, a course covering the material in this book could be offered with the material in the appendix presented first. The book thus lends itself to a variety of courses. Because of the quantitative nature of much of the material, however, a working knowledge of probability theory is a definite prerequisite.

The book begins with an overview of the types of services expected to be provided over ATM networks, and the resultant traffic types that might be expected to use these networks. These include voice, video, images, files, and bursty data, among other types. It then discusses the ATM protocol model, with emphasis given to the ATM layer and the various ATM Adaptation Layer (AAL) types designed to fit above it. This descriptive introduction to broadband ISDN and ATM in Chapter 2 is followed by the first quantitative chapter, Chapter 3, which provides an introduction to traffic characterization. Two types of models used to represent traffic are stressed in this chapter: fluid source modeling and the Markov-modulated Poisson Process (MMPP). Packet-voice modeling, using these two techniques, is introduced first because of its relative simplicity and because packet voice is relatively well understood. The same techniques are then applied to modeling variable bit rate (VBR) video sources. These two types of models are then combined in presenting the well-known cell and burst regions occurring in determining buffer loss probability as a function of traffic load. The chapter concludes with a brief discussion of the two-state Markov process, a special case of the Markov-modulated process, as a useful way of representing image traffic or intermittent file transfers.

Note that the stress here is not on providing an encyclopedic overview of various models proposed for different traffic types. The field of traffic characterization is, by itself, a very active and vital one, with the number of papers on the subject proliferating rapidly. The treatment here is introductory and tutorial only. The author has, of course, demonstrated a certain personal bias in selecting models with which he is familiar, or which he has personally found interesting and useful. Workers in the field may feel their favorite models have been slighted. The only answer the author can give is that a reader following the discussion here should have no difficulty reading the current literature and deciding for himself/herself which particular model should be most appropriate for some particular purpose. Much of the rest of the book follows the same pattern. The author has selected studies or topics of most interest to him. Collectively, however, they do provide a thorough introduction to the quantitative design and performance issues arising in broadband ATM networks carrying integrated traffic. A reader should thus have no problem continuing with self-study in the area.

Chapter 4 uses the two models mentioned (with particular stress on the two-state Markov process for simplicity) to study admission and access control in broadband networks. Access control here is limited to the leaky bucket technique which has become almost a classic control procedure. A reader absorbing this material should again have no problem in studying and evaluating other control techniques proposed in the literature. Chapter 5, on ATM switches, stresses the significance of using output queueing where possible, and develops the now-classic penalty introduced by using input queueing. It provides examples of shared memory, shared medium, multistage space, and self-routing switches. Comparisons are given where possible.

Chapters 3 through 5 focus on performance analysis at one node in an ATM network. Chapters 6 and 7 attempt to expand the performance study to a path in the network. This is an extremely difficult area of study, with much research currently underway. For this reason, Chapter 6 covers bounds of performance only. As a byproduct, the concept of effective capacity, currently a very "hot" topic, falls out very nicely. There are tradeoffs in the use of this concept: The impact of sources on admission control can be evaluated simply and additively, but the resultant control policies are quite conservative, with the advantage gained by statistically multiplexing sources in a network often absent. Finally, Chapter 7 discusses and analyzes feedback control of congestion in a high-speed network. One section is devoted to the ATM Forum proposal for a rate-based control mechanism; another section covers an interesting proposal for window control in a large delay-bandwidth environment, characteristic of the wide-area, high-speed ATM networks coming in the not too distant future.

The field covered here is vast. As already noted, much selectivity had to be exerted to keep this book at a reasonable size. Important topics had to be left out out of necessity. Rapid improvements in the technology and better understanding of the characteristics of the traffic transmitted over broadband integrated networks once deployed may change some of the conclusions described in the book. But the main point, as already noted, is not to provide an encyclopedic description of models and techniques, possibly useful in the design of these networks, but to provide a clear, tutorial introduction to modeling and performance analysis, so that a reader will be able to understand and keep up with new developments as they arise. The author can only hope he has been successful in this goal.

Mischa Schwartz
New York

Acknowledgments

As is always the case with writing textbooks of a more advanced nature, such as this one, there are many individuals whose help the author must acknowledge. First and foremost are the students who took the graduate course for which the book was developed. Their questions and responses to queries, as well as projects carried out as part of the course requirements, forced the author to think issues through clearly and present ideas and concepts in an understandable way. He has found, over the years, that presenting this type of material to a discerning audience is the best way of gaining a clearer understanding of the subject for himself. Two of his doctoral students, Paul Skelly, now at GTE Laboratories, and Ness Shroff, now at Purdue University, carried out original research reflected in a number of the sections in this book. Regular interactions and discussions with them also forced the author to come to a better understanding of much of the material presented here. He thanks both of them for the use of material appearing in their doctoral theses.

Keeping up with the rapidly changing standards and standards proposal discussions at the ATM Forum and ITU-T, as well as keeping abreast of products reaching the marketplace, is very time-consuming and difficult for an academic to carry out. One must thus rely heavily on input from individuals in industry for this information. The following individuals were particularly helpful in answering questions and providing material to use in various places in the book: Wai Chen and Faramak Vakil of Bellcore; Kai Eng, Xiaoqiang Chen, and Carolyn Ngueyen of AT&T Bell Laboratories; and Giovanni Pacifici, of the Center for Telecommunications Research (CTR) at Columbia.

A pioneering project on a light-wave-based, very high-speed network of the future called Acorn (carried out at CTR some years ago jointly between CTR students, staff, and faculty, and many industrial representatives) stimulated the author into thinking much more deeply about the area of high-speed integrated networks. This project was conceived by Professor Anthony Acampora, the then-Director of CTR. The author had the fortunate opportunity to head up the Network Management and Control Group for this project, and thanks members of that group for the many discussions of control issues arising at meetings of the group. Subgroups led by industrial representatives were organized to suggest ways of implementing access and admission control on the Acorn testbed.

The author would also like to acknowledge support for his research on broadband integrated networks from the U.S. Office of Naval Research (ONR) and from the National Science Foundation through its support of CTR, one of the original Engineering Research Centers. This support was absolutely essential in setting the groundwork for developing the graduate course for which this book was written. Finally, the author again thanks Mrs. Betty Lim, Editorial Assistant of the Electrical Engineering Department at Columbia, for preparing and producing the text and accompanying figures for, first, the notes, and then the book manuscript. Her unfailing help has been invaluable.

Chapter 1

Introduction

Most existing telecommunication networks encompass either one of two types: the ubiquitous circuit-switched networks (characteristic of telephony) carrying principally voice traffic; packet-switched networks used primarily to transmit data of various types [SCHW 1987]. Telephone networks have been with us for over a hundred years. The packet-switched data or computer communication networks are much more recent, having first been deployed in the late 1960s.

The digitization of most of the public telephone networks worldwide, as well as the concurrent deployment of optical fiber, now allow potentially much wider bandwidths (higher bit rates) to be used than has previously been the case for the voice and data networks mentioned above. This has, in fact, been universally recognized by the adoption of worldwide standards for very high bandwidth digital transmission over optical fibers. The standards define a hierarchy of synchronous time-multiplied transmission, compatible with optical transmission [ANSI 1991a] [SCHW 1990]. In North America, the digital hierarchy, called SONET, ranges from 51.84 Mbps to 2.48832 Gbps (and poten-

[SCHW 1987]   Schwartz, M., *Telecommunication Networks: Protocols, Modeling and Analysis,* Reading, MA: Addison-Wesley, 1987.

[ANSI 1991a]   *American National Standard for Telecommunications Digital Hierarchy Optical Interface Rates and Formats Specifications,* ANSI T1.105-1991, New York: American National Standards Inst., 1991.

[SCHW 1990]   Schwartz, M., *Information Transmission, Modulation, and Noise,* 4th ed. New York: McGraw-Hill, 1990.

tially even higher) in multiples of 51.84 Mbps. The equivalent CCITT[1] international recommendation for a Synchronous Digital Hierarchy (SDH) joins SONET at the higher transmission rates, but differs somewhat at the low end of the hierarchy because of the need for compatibility with existing digital telephone transmission systems at 50 Mbps and below.

With such bit rates as 155 Mbps, 622 Mbps, and 2.4 Gbps becoming available, it is natural to start planning new user services that would make use of these bandwidths. Prime candidates include applications involving high-resolution images and video. In addition, it becomes natural to start thinking of merging services currently provided by different networks (e.g., voice and packet data) onto one common network. This desire to *integrate* services is being pushed, as well, by the computer venders' move toward multimedia workstations and the transport capability needed to support multimedia communications.

Activity has thus begun in earnest, worldwide, to develop *B*roadband *I*ntegrated *S*ervices *D*igital *N*etworks (B-ISDN) capable of carrying out the functions just described. This activity is taking different forms. The International Consultative Committee on Telephony and Telegraphy (CCITT), now renamed the International Telecommunications Union-Telecommunication Standardization Sector (ITU-T), has issued a number of Recommendations (its terminology for standards documents) concerning B-ISDN. Since much of the traffic projected to be deployed over these networks is new and not yet supported over any digital network, the potential traffic must be characterized in order to properly design such integrated networks. Much research in the past few years has in fact been devoted to studying and characterizing the potential video and image traffic, as well as studying ways of controlling its impact on networks. Finally, manufacturers have been developing and have begun to provide switches capable of being deployed in broadband integrated networks.

Actively involved in standards development worldwide is the ATM Forum, a voluntary group of several hundred manufacturers, vendors, communication carriers, and other organizations with interests in seeing ATM standards development speeded up to expedite the delivery of ATM products to the marketplace. Since the ATM Forum has no official status with the ITU-T the standards recommendations made by this body can be unofficial only. However, because of the worldwide influence of the companies participating in its activities, its recommendations are equivalent to defacto standards. We shall have occasion to refer to some of the ATM Forum recommendations in this book.

---

[1]CCITT was renamed ITU-T, the International Telecommunications Union-Telecommunication Standardization Sector, in 1993. Both terms will be used in the material following, since reference will be made to older CCITT documents as well as to newer ITU-T Recommendations.

In this book we first summarize the current state of the CCITT Recommendations for B-ISDN. We focus principally on *ATM* (Asynchronous Transfer Mode), a cell-based (short, fixed-length packet) mode of transmitting integrated traffic through broadband networks. We then move to the topic of traffic characterization in Chapter 3 and study, comparatively, a number of models proposed for characterizing traffic. We begin with voice, since this traffic type is well understood, although its representation in packet form is relatively recent. Some of the models proposed for packet voice are then carried over to video characterization, an area still under intense study. We conclude the topic of traffic characterization by briefly introducing one model often used to represent image or data file traffic in an interactive mode.

The discussion in Chapter 3 is quantitative and relies on some prior knowledge of elementary queueing theory. A brief introduction to this subject appears in the Appendix for those readers not familiar with the subject or for those desiring a review. More advanced topics are introduced both in this chapter and later in the book when needed. The analytical techniques and traffic models developed in this chapter are also used in later chapters when needed.

Given a number of ways of characterizing the traffic that might be deployed over broadband networks, it is then natural to use these models to study traffic control into, and across, the network. Control is required because of limited capacity within the network. It is thus important to ensure that no one user dominate the network, that each user traffic source be provided the appropriate quality of service required, and that the aggregate traffic not congest the network. The Quality of Service (QoS) defined for each traffic class is, in these networks, a multidimensional performance objective function including such parameters as delay (mean and/or specified quantile), call blocking probability, cell (packet) dropping probability, end-to-end time jitter, throughput, and the like.

Traffic control takes at least three forms. First, there is admission control—a decision must be made whether a user, desirous of establishing a connection (call) over the network, can be accommodated. This is based on some estimate of the characteristics of the traffic to be transmitted. Second, once a call is admitted, control must be maintained at the entrance (access) to the network to ensure the traffic entering the network receives its negotiated quality of service and does not adversely affect other traffic. This is done by appropriately scheduling the different traffic classes and elements within them and by maintaining a so-called "policing" function to ensure each user abides by its traffic estimate. Admission and access control are discussed in Chapter 4.

Third, control must be maintained throughout the network and at the various traffic destinations to ensure network and receiver congestion does not develop, or, if it starts developing, to quench it as quickly as possible. Network congestion control mechanisms are not new. They have been studied and used for years in both circuit-switched and packet-switched networks [SCHW 1987]. What makes the admission, access, and congestion control problem particularly different in the broadband integrated environment is the variety of traffic types (classes) to be accommodated (each to be provided with a potentially different quality of service) and the very high transmission bandwidths (bit rates) of these networks. Because of the high bit rates, the transmission times of cells (packets) being switched through the network are very short. Thousands of them may thus potentially be enroute between any two source-destination points in even a moderately sized, wide-area network. The problem of preventing or responding to congestion in a network thus takes on dimensions never before encountered in telecommunication networks. This is a point we will be particularly stressing in our discussion of congestion control later in Chapter 7.

Following the discussion of network traffic control in Chapter 4 we move into the realm of switching for B-ISDN in Chapter 5. A number of high-speed ATM switches have been proposed; some are available in the market. They can be categorized in a number of ways. We carry out a comparative study of simple models of some of these in Chapter 5, focusing on their complexity and throughput/delay characteristics.

The traffic characterization and admission/access control studies in Chapters 3 and 4, respectively, focus on representation at one point in a network, normally at the entrance point, or user-network interface. The characteristics of a given traffic stream change, however, as the stream progresses through a network, due to queueing and interaction with other traffic streams at switching and buffering points. This makes the study of traffic end-to-end across a network quite complex. In addition, admission control, as we shall see, should be carried out considering the impact of a newly admitted call of any type on previously established connections along its entire proposed path end-to-end. The end-to-end properties of traffic are thus vital to a realistic analysis of its impact on a network.

In Chapter 6 we introduce this subject by summarizing work on end-to-end performance bounds that has appeared in the literature. This study leads quite naturally, as we shall see, to a concept called the *equivalent* or *effective capacity* of a given traffic source that has received a lot of attention. This property of a source is additive, enabling us to easily estimate the effect of a given source on other sources already present at a given multiplexing point in a network. This in turn simplifies the admission control problem at a given entrance point. The use of this property does result in an overly conservative control in some cases since the statistical multiplexing or smoothing advantage known to occur when sources are combined at a point is ignored.

Chapter 7 returns to the problem of network control, focusing on feedback control mechanisms devised to control network and receiver congestion. Both window and rate control techniques are discussed, with prime consideration given to the impact of high-speed transmission on the control mechanisms. The distinguishing characteristic here, as contrasted to lower-speed packet switching, is that the propagation delay from source to destination plays a key role. Questions of stability arise in wide-area broadband networks, particularly where the propagation delay is many times the packet or cell length. Alternately put, the control in this case has to be designed with the knowledge that many packets may be enroute over a given path end-to-end, and cannot simply be dropped when congestion is encountered.

Chapter 2

Broadband Services and ATM

As noted in the introduction, the basic concept behind Broadband Services Integrated Digital Networks (B-ISDN) is that of supporting a wide range of audio, video, and data services within the same network. To cover the widest range of applications possible, B-ISDN should support both switched and non-switched connections and be able to provide both circuit mode and packet mode services. The framework for this concept has been established internationally by the CCITT [CCITT 1992a], [CCITT 1992b], [BELL 1990].

ATM (Asynchronous Transfer Mode) has been designated as the target transfer mode approach to providing the desired integration of the various traffic types to be supported by B-ISDN. It is essentially a packet-switched mode of transfer through the network, using short, fixed-length, 53-octet (byte) packets called cells. The cells are assigned on demand at the user-network interface (UNI).

The services to be provided by B-ISDN may be grouped essentially into two categories: interactive services and distribution services. Interactive services include such categories as conversational services, store-and-forward messaging, and message retrieval services. Examples include video and multimedia conferencing, transmission of high-resolution images, archiving services, document browsing, as well as a host of other possible applications. Some of these were mentioned earlier. The emphasis is, as already noted, on

---

[CCITT 1992a]   Recommendation I.121, Broadband Aspects of ISDN, CCITT, Geneva, 1992.

[CCITT 1992b]   Recommendation I.362, Adaptation Layer (AAL) Functional Description, CCITT, Geneva, 1992.

[BELL 1990]   Preliminary Report on Broadband ISDN Transfer Protocols, Special Report SR-NWT-001763, Issue 1, Bellcore, Morristown, NJ, Dec. 1990.

the transmission of video and images. Distribution services involve the distribution, from centralized service providers to network users, of files, books, documents, stored video clips, movies, images, and the like.

Some simple calculations indicate why wideband networking is required for many of these services and applications. Consider a black-and-white X-ray to be transmitted from a medical file to a radiologist, for example. Say the vertical and horizontal axes of a single image are each broken into 2000 lines, or levels, to ensure the high resolution required of the image to be read. This is referred to as 2000×2000 resolution, giving rise to 4,000,000 picture elements (pixels) per image. (To put this in perspective, TV sets in the United States currently provide a resolution per frame, or picture, of approximately 500×500, or 250,000 pixels). If 8-bit gray scale quantization per pixel is used (this provides $2^8 = 256$ levels of intensity), and a picture is to be transmitted in less than 1 sec, the bandwidth required turns out to be more than 32 Mbps. If a three-color picture with the same specifications is to be transmitted, 96 Mbps capacity is required. (Compression could, however, be used to reduce this number considerably).

Consider color television now, transmitting 30 frames/sec. In the United States, this translates to 7.5 million pixels/sec. Intra- and interframe coding techniques can be used to compress the bandwidth to 7.5 Mbps or less. (VCR-quality video can be transmitted at rates as low as 1.5 Mbps.) High-definition TV, under development, would require much higher bandwidths, however. A 1000×1000 frame, with 24 bits/pixel used, requires 720 Mbps of capacity. With compression, this could be brought down to less than 100 Mbps. These bandwidths required to transmit video and images are substantially higher than those currently available for end-user usage in public-switched communication networks.

For this reason, B-ISDN rates have initially been chosen as 155.52 Mbps and 622 Mbps (two of the SONET rates mentioned earlier), with the possibility of eventually reaching 2.4 Gbps and above. An ATM-based 155.52 Mbps user-network interface (UNI) would thus be handling 367,000 cells/sec in either direction across the interface. At 622 Mbps, this represents 1.467×10^6 cells/sec! Much of the traffic would be expected to be video or images. (Current digitized voice requires 64 kbps per voice channel. One voice source at a UNI would thus use only 1 cell in 2400, on the average, at the 155 Mbps rate!)

The CCITT and other standard bodies have identified five generic service classes among the various services and applications that an ATM B-ISDN might support [CCITT 1992a]. These are listed in Table 2–1. Both voice (audio) and video are examples of real-time traffic, in which bits are periodically generated, providing a constant flow (stream) of data. If uncompressed, this is generically termed constant bit rate (CBR) traffic. Voice sources are sampled periodically, once every 125 μsec, with 8 bits used to represent each sample. This provides the continuous (constant) bit rate of 64 kbps mentioned earlier [SCHW 1990]. Video is initially generated at a con-

TABLE 2–1 ■ B-ISDN Service Classes

Class	Bit Rate	Timing Relation*	Connection Mode	Example
A: stream	constant (CBR)	R	Connection-oriented	voice
B: stream	variable (VBR)	R	Connection-oriented	video
C: data	variable (VBR)	NR	Connection-oriented	bursty data
D: data	variable (VBR)	NR	Connectionless	data
X: data	variable (VBR)	NR	Connection-oriented	data

*between source and receiver
R = required; NR = not required

stant rate as well. Compression converts it to a variable bit rate traffic type (VBR), however. Video and voice, being real-time traffic, cannot incur too much jitter during their journey from source to destination. This is the reason why a timing relation is listed in Table 2–1 as being required. Both also require connections to be set up to ensure cells arrive in proper sequence.

Image traffic, on the other hand, might not require strict timing: short delays of less than a second, say, should not be noticeable to a human observer. File transfers do not normally require strict timing either. A sequence of images or a relatively long file transfer presumably require a connection to be set up, however. The image bit rate might be expected to be variable, either because a sequence of images is transmitted in random fashion, or because a given image might require variable numbers of bits for different portions of its scanned area if compression is used.

More specifically, class-A service traffic, with voice as the obvious example, is assumed to be generated in an uninterrupted flow, at a constant bit rate. It requires a guaranteed transmission capacity, with small average cell delay as well as small cell delay variation across the network. Some cells may be lost during transmission end-to-end, with the probability of loss to be constrained below some specified small value. Class-B service traffic, with compressed video as an example, is also assumed to be generated in an uninterrupted (real-time) fashion, but requires a variable bit rate channel, between specified minimum and maximum values. It too has a strict cell delay constraint as well as small cell delay variation and cell loss requirement end-to-end. Classes C and D represent bursty data traffic, delivered in connection-oriented or connectionless form, respectively, with mean and/or cell delay percentile specified. A very low data loss rate is required end-to-end.

Examples of applications that might require the connection-oriented class-C service include TCP/IP over ATM and Frame Relay service. SMDS over ATM is an example of a connectionless data service that might use class-D service. Frame Relay and SMDS are mentioned briefly in the following discussion of ATM adaptation layers.

Class X is a service class designed for data traffic that might just require raw cell delivery service using proprietary, nonstandardized protocols. Although the timing relation is shown in Table 2–1 as not being required for this class of service, this condition is really application-dependent. Another service class, class Y, is under discussion as well. This class is similar to class X, with the major difference being that its bit rate characteristics might be expected to vary during a communications session, while the class X characteristics are presumed to be defined at the session initiation. It is important to note at this point that these service classes and their distinctions may be expected to change as recommendation and standards discussions continue, and as ATM networks begin to be deployed. As an example, there were originally four classes defined, labeled 1–4. A fifth class, class 5, was subsequently proposed by computer manufacturers to cover the case of applications generating inter-LAN traffic. The numerical designations were then changed to the corresponding letter ones described here.

To provide these classes of service a layered protocol model has been developed for B-ISDN, and is shown in Figure 2–1 [CCITT, 1992a]. The ATM layer shown here is responsible for generating the (asynchronous) 53-octet cells mentioned earlier. This layer is also responsible, within the network, for carrying out cell routing, for multiplexing (and demultiplexing) user traffic over a given link or path within the network, for verifying cell header integrity, and for providing, at the user-network interface, a limited flow control capability. These functions will be discussed briefly later on.

Returning to Figure 2–1, the physical layer shown here is medium dependent. As an example, SONET would presumably provide the physical layer capability for optical fiber in North America. Since the five classes of B-ISDN traffic listed in Table 2–1 arise from very different sources, traffic from each class must be handled differently in preparation for generating its corresponding ATM cells. For this reason an ATM adaptation layer (AAL) has been defined to generate 48-octet segments from user information passed down from the higher layers. These segments, in turn, have five header (control) octets added at the ATM layer to form the 53-octet ATM cells transmitted out over the network using the physical layer.

Consider the ATM layer in more detail. Figure 2–2 shows the format of the 53-octet cells formed at that layer. The basic cell format shown in Figure 2–2a consists of the 48 octets of AAL information plus 5 octets of header

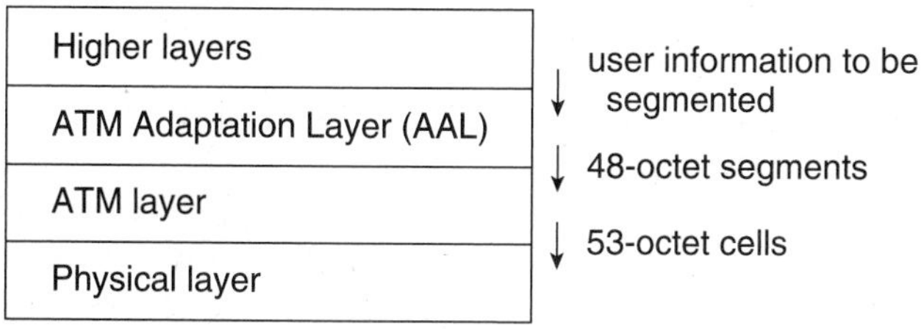

| Higher layers |
| ATM Adaptation Layer (AAL) |
| ATM layer |
| Physical layer |

↓ user information to be segmented

↓ 48-octet segments

↓ 53-octet cells

FIGURE 2–1 ■ ATM protocol model.

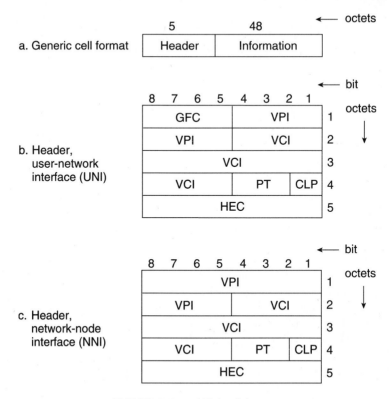

FIGURE 2–2 ■ ATM cell format.

added at the ATM layer, as noted above. Two types of ATM cells have been defined. One type (Figure 2–2b) corresponds to cells generated on either side of the user-network interface (UNI), the access to the network. The asynchronous cell transmission across the UNI is portrayed in Figure 2–3. The other type of cell represents cells switched at a network-node interface (NNI) (Figure 2–2c). Both types of cells carry the 5-octet header; they differ only in the last four bits of the first octet (byte) of the header. These four bits in the UNI cell format (Figure 2–2b) are labeled GFC, for generic flow control. They are used to control multiple traffic streams across the interface. In a later chapter we will discuss the concept of traffic shaping, to be carried out at the access to the network. "Shaping" information could be conveyed by these four bits.

Most of the 5-octet header is devoted to providing a routing or connection id: ATM is designed primarily as a virtual circuit-type, or connection-oriented service. End-to-end connections, or virtual circuits, are defined in terms of two identifiers, a virtual path id (VPI) and a virtual connection id (VCI). As shown in Figure 2–4, a virtual path (VP) represents a network-defined, end-to-end connection. It is defined to follow a specific route or path, and provides a specified quality of service (QoS). This quality of service could include such

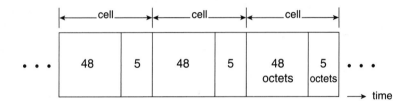

FIGURE 2–3 ▪ ATM cell transmission across UNI.

parameters as bandwidth (transmission capacity) available over that path (minimum/maximum bandwidth, average/peak bandwidth, or some other bandwidth descriptors); constraints on time delay (average, maximum, specified quantile, etc.) and on time jitter; cell loss probability, and so on. A given virtual path is presumed to have been set up permanently (permanent VP) or could be set up dynamically using some signaling channel.

Each VP has multiple VCs within it. This concept of end-to-end virtual paths, each carrying a large number of virtual connections, is very similar to the explicit route (ER)/virtual route (VR) concept pioneered with IBM's SNA (System Network Architecture) [SCHW 1987, Section 5.3]. Cells are routed on the basis of the VPI/VCI pair. Although ATM has been designed as a connection-oriented service, many applications including single message delivery do not require connections to be set up. Service class D includes such applications. A connectionless service then has to be built on top of the ATM layer.

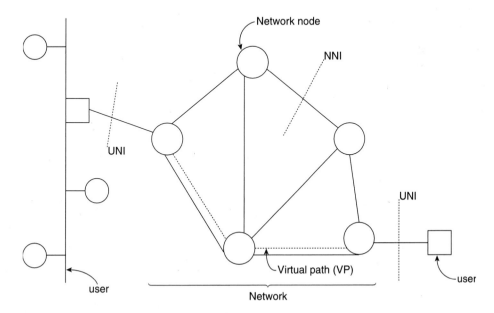

FIGURE 2–4 ▪ B-ISDN.

Consider now the VPI/VCI portion of the ATM cell header in more detail. The 8 bits allocated to the VPI in the UNI cell header of Figure 2–2b indicate that up to 256 virtual paths may be multiplexed at one user access point, with $2^{16} = 64,000$ virtual connections associated with each. (Note that a "user" in B-ISDN terminology could be a single host or data source, a LAN, a large private network connecting to an ATM-based public network, a large number of customer terminals/workstations accessing a given network port, etc.) Figure 2–2c indicates that at any NNI, $2^{12} = 4096$ virtual paths may be multiplexed together. This number can be increased substantially by VPI/VCI swapping: At each incoming link to a network node (see Figure 2–4), a given VPI/VCI pair may be swapped to a specified outgoing link VPI/VCI pair using a network node table lookup. VPI/VCI pairs can thus be reused on each network link. This is very similar to virtual-circuit swapping used for many years in packet-switched networks [SCHW 1987].

Now consider the other bits in the ATM cell: the three-bit payload type (PT) is used to designate the type of information, user or operations/management data, being carried in the 48-octet cell information field. It is also used to designate whether or not congestion has been experienced. The CLP bit, if set to 1, indicates a lower-priority cell that can be dropped in the event of network traffic congestion. (This subject will be discussed in a later chapter). Finally, the 8-bit HEC field is used to provide error checking of the 5-octet header. This is used to correct single-bit errors and/or detect multiple errors (see [PRYC 1991] and [HAND 1994] for more discussion of this subject).

A number of adaptation layer types have been defined, to correspond generally to the B-ISDN service indicated in Table 2–1 [CCITT 1992b], [CCITT 1992c]. Although it is expected that most service classes will map directly to a specified ATM adaptation layer (AAL) type, this is not generally required. One AAL type could conceivably serve a number of classes of user. It might be desirable, for example, to have one AAL type serve both connectionless and connection-oriented data traffic.

The prime purpose of the ATM adaptation layer (AAL) at the access point of a network is to segment user information into ATM cells; at the destination it reassembles the ATM cells transmitted across the network into the original user information. Depending on the service class to be handled, additional, service-dependent, functions may be required as well. This is also carried out by the adaptation layer. To distinguish between these two functions, the adaptation layer is divided into two sublayers, a convergence sublayer

---

[PRYC 1991]   de Prycker, M., *Asynchronous Transfer Mode Solution for Broadband ISDN*, Chichester, England: Ellis Norwood, 1991.

[HAND 1994]   Händel, R., M. N. Huber, and S. Schröder, *ATM Networks, Concepts, Protocols, Applications*, 2nd ed. Wokingham, England: Addison-Wesley, 1994.

[CCITT 1992c]   Recommendation I.363, Broadband ISDN Adaptation Layer (AAL) Specifications, Geneva, 1992.

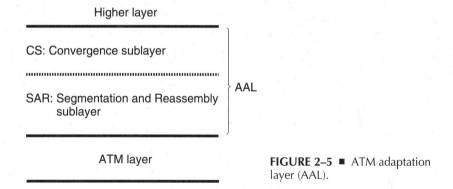

Higher layer

CS: Convergence sublayer

SAR: Segmentation and Reassembly
        sublayer

AAL

ATM layer

FIGURE 2–5 ▪ ATM adaptation layer (AAL).

(CS) resting just below the higher (user) layer and a segmentation and re-assembly (SAR) sublayer. These are shown schematically in Figure 2–5. Four different types of AAL have been proposed or defined. These are labeled AAL Types 1, 2, 3/4, and 5.

AAL Type 1 has been designed to handle continuous bit rate (CBR) services and hence corresponds most closely to B-ISDN service class-A. The 48-octet segment handed down to the ATM layer in this case (Figure 2–1) consists of a 47-octet information field (payload) preceded by an 8-bit header (Figure 2–6). The segment is termed an SAR-PDU.[1] The header has two parts, as shown in Figure 2–6. The 4-bit SN field contains a 3-bit sequence number plus a CSI (convergence sublayer indication) bit with default value of zero. The sequence number enables the AAL to detect lost or misinserted cells. The SNP field has a 3-bit CRC designed to protect the SN field against errors. The even parity bit will, in turn, detect an odd number of errors in the preceding 7-bit code word. In normal, default mode, the SNP field will correct single header errors.

Sequence count processing is carried out by the convergence sublayer (CS) of AAL Type 1. At the transmitting end, the CS provides the segmentation-and-reassembly (SAR) sublayer below with the sequence count number, modulo 8, in addition to the 47-octet payload. At the receiving end, it receives the sequence count and CS indication (CSI) bit from the SAR, in addition to the 47-octet payload, and uses these to detect any cell loss or misinsertion of a cell. In addition to sequence number processing, the AAL Type 1 CS handles cell delay variation and provides timing (clock) information to the destination. (Recall from Table 2–1 that CBR services involve stream type traffic that require a timing relation to be maintained between source and destination).

The AAL Type 1 SAR sublayer in turn forms the 48-octet SAR-PDU from the 47-octet payload plus sequence count information passed down from the CS. It computes the 3-bit SRC and parity check bit noted above.

---

[1]Segmentation-and-Reassembly Protocol Data Unit.

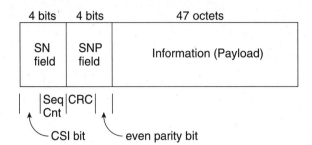

FIGURE 2–6 ■ Format, AAL Type 1 SAR-PDU.

AAL Type 2 has been proposed to handle connection-oriented variable bit rate (VBR) services such as video. It has not been fully defined as of yet because of a lack of consensus on the video coding algorithms to be supported.

AAL Types 3/4 and 5 are designed to handle bursty data, whether network-layer protocol data units (packets) or MAC-sublayer frames. The AAL Type 3/4 protocol is based upon the IEEE 802.6 MAN protocol (DQDB), around which Bellcore has designed SMDS, a high-speed connectionless data service used for interconnecting local area networks (LANs) [IEEE 1991]. Type 3/4 was originally two separate AAL Types, 3 and 4, as the designation indicates. They were later merged because of the similarity in their functions and design. Type 5 provides a much simpler ATM Adaptation Layer, with fewer functions and resultant lower overload in ATM usage. It developed out of proposals made by the LAN and computer industries.

In both AAL Types 3/4 and 5, the convergence sublayer (CS) of the ATM adaptation layer (Figure 2–5) is further split into two parts, a higher service-specific convergence sublayer (SSCS) and a lower common part convergence sublayer (CPCS). The resultant AAL for both has the form of Figure 2–7 [CCITT 1992c].

The service-specific convergence sublayer may in some cases be null, in which case the adaptation layer reverts back to the form of Figure 2–5. A frame relaying SSCS associated with AAL Type 5 is one example of a service-specific function that has been proposed for the SSCS [ITU-T 1993a]. FR-SSCS provides the core frame relay service. Its association with AAL Type 5 allows broadband ISDN (B-ISDN) to emulate frame relaying service or to connect to (interwork with) a frame relaying network.

AAL 3/4 and AAL 5 both provide two modes of service: a message mode service and a streaming mode service. In the message mode, the higher layer above the AAL passes an AAL service data unit (a packet or frame, for example) as one atomic unit across the higher layer AAL interface to the SSCS. In

[IEEE 1991]   IEEE Standard 802.6, Distributed Queue Dual Bus (DQDB), Subnetwork of a Metropolitan Area Network (MAN), New York: IEEE, 1991.

[ITU-T 1993a]   Frame Relaying Service Specific Convergence Layer (FR-SSCS), Draft Recommendation I.365, COM 13-10-E, ITU-T, Geneva, March 1993.

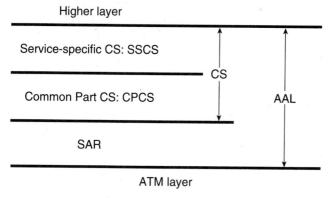

Higher layer

Service-specific CS: SSCS

CS

Common Part CS: CPCS

AAL

SAR

ATM layer

FIGURE 2–7 ▪ AAL, types 3/4 and 5.

the streaming mode service the AAL-SDU is transferred across the interface as one or more units called AAL interface data units (AAL-IDU). The transfers may occur separated in time. Once transferred to the SSCS, multiple message mode AAL-SDUs, if small and of fixed size, may be assembled or blocked into one SSCS-PDU. (The reverse procedure, disassembly or deblocking, is then carried out at the destination AAL). A long, variable length AAL-SDU in the message mode may be segmented in the SSCS and transferred in one or more SSCS-PDUs. Reassembly is then carried out at the destination.

In the streaming mode case, all the AAL-IDUs corresponding to a single AAL-SDU may be transferred in one or more SSCS-PDUs, with the reverse procedure being accomplished at the destination. A pipelining procedure may be applied in which the sending (source) AAL entity starts the transfer before it has received the complete AAL-SDU. In this case one or more of the AAL-IDUs may be transferred in successive SSCS-PDUs, as they arrive across the interface.

Both AAL 3/4 and AAL 5 offer an assured or nonassured service. In the assured case retransmission of missing or corrupted SSCS-PDUs ensures the AAL-SDU is delivered to the destination user exactly the way it was sent. Assured service requires the existence of an SSCS sublayer to carry out this function. In the nonassured case AAL-SDUs may be lost or corrupted. The CPCS sublayer provides nonassured data transfer only. Both AAL types carry out some form of error detection and error indication (both bit error and cell loss) to the layer(s) above. Both attempt to maintain CPCS-SDU sequence integrity on each CPCS connection.

In what way, then, do AAL Type 3/4 and AAL Type 5 differ? It was noted earlier that Type 5 is a much simpler protocol, with less control overhead, and correspondingly less functionality. It has less ability to maintain sequence integrity, for example. This is shown by spelling out in more detail the functions and corresponding data units for each AAL type in both the CPCS and SAR sublayers. Consider AAL Type 3/4 first. The formats of the CPCS-PDU and the 48-octet SAR-PDU containing portions of the CPCS-PDU appear in Fig-

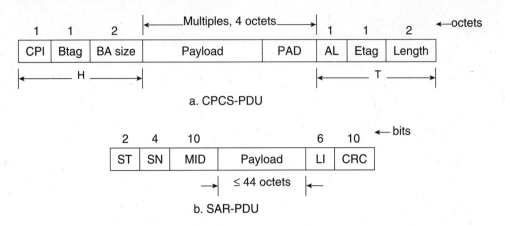

FIGURE 2–8 ■ PDU formats, AAL type 3/4.

ures 2–8a and b, respectively [CCITT 1992c]. The CPCS-PDU is designed to fit into multiples of 4-octet words (32 bits) to simplify and speed up processing. The PAD field shown is thus adjusted to have the payload or information field appear as multiples of 4 octets as well. The actual length of the payload is provided by the 2-octet length field appearing in the 4-octet trailer T.

The 1-octet common part indicator (CPI) in the 4-octet header H of the CPCS-PDU is used to establish "counting units" in all the fields following. (These could be 4-octet units, or others, if desired). The 2-octet BA size field in the heads is a buffer allocation field. The Btag and Etag fields, in the header and trailer, respectively, carry the same information. Finally, the 1-octet alignment (AL) field is simply a sequence of all 0s to align the entire CPCS-PDU to the desired 4-octet word format.

These various fields in the CPCS-PDU format are used by the CPCS sublayer to detect and handle any CPCS-PDU corruption. (A faulty CPCS-PDU can either be discarded, or delivered corrupted, to the layer above the SSCS sublayer, if operational, or any other layer above the CPCS sublayer). Examples of errors that can be detected include Btag/Etag mismatch, actual received length and CPCS-PDU length indicator mismatch, buffer overflow, improperly formatted CPCS-PDU, as well as errors indicated by the SAR sublayer below.

Now consider the AAL Type 3/4 SAR sublayer and the 48-octet SAR-PDU it generates, as shown in Figure 2–8b. The function of the sending SAR sublayer is to accept variable-length SAR-SDUs containing the CPCS-PDUs from the CS sublayer, and to segment them into 48-octet SAR-PDUs, containing up to 44 octets of data (payload) each. AAL Type 3/4 provides for the multiplexing (and subsequent demultiplexing at the receiving AAL) of multiple CPCS connections onto one SAR sublayer. Preservation of an SAR-SDU (or the corresponding CPCS-PDU) is maintained, despite possible segmentation

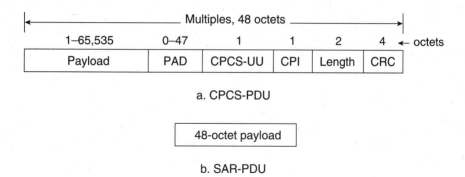

a. CPCS-PDU

b. SAR-PDU

FIGURE 2–9 ▪ PDU formats, AAL type 5.

into multiple SAR-PDUs, by means of a 2-bit segment type field ST, shown in Figure 2–8b. A "10" in this field indicates the beginning (BOM) of a message (SAR-SDU); "00" signifies continuation of message (COM); and "01" indicates end of message (EOM). A "11" in this field means the message consists of only one segment that is less than or equal to 44 octets in length. The 6-bit length indicator (LI) field is used to indicate the actual size of the payload, in octets.

The 10-bit MID field ("mux id" field) is used for the multiplexing function noted above. Each CPCS connection carries a different MID number. (All 0s implies no multiplexing). Segment sequence integrity is maintained for each CPCS connection (MID) by associating with each a 4-bit sequence number field SN. Finally, a 10-bit cyclic redundancy check field (CRC) is used to detect bit errors and/or lost or gained SAR-PDUs.

Now contrast these Type 3/4 operations and PDU formats with those of AAL Type 5. The CPCS-PDU and SAR-PDU formats for AAL Type 5 are shown in Figures 2–9a and b, respectively, and correspond to the formats for AAL Type 3/4 appearing in Figure 2–8 [ITU-T 1993b]. Note how much simpler both of these formats are, compared to those for the corresponding Type 3/4 PDUs.

The 1-octet CPCS user-to-user indication (CPCS-UU) field of the CPCS-PDU is used to transparently transfer information from one user to another, without being monitored by the network. (Recall that ATM switches in a network only have access to, and carry out their switching and congestion control functions on the basis of the 5-octet header of the 53-octet ATM cell. Adaptation layer functions are carried out at the network source and destination points only). The 1-octet CPI (common part indicator) field has as its prime function that of aligning the CPCS-PDU trailer to 64 bits. (Other functions are left for future study). The PAD field is used, as the name indicates, and as was noted in discussing the Type 3/4 CPCS-PDU format, to pad the payload

[ITU-T 1993b]   Section 6 of Recommendation I.363-Framework of AAL Type 5, COM 13-9-E. ITU-T, Geneva, March 1993.

(the CPCS-SDU) up to a desired length: All Type 5 CPCS-PDUs are prescribed to have lengths that are multiples of 48 octets. This simplifies constructing the 48-octet SAR-PDU of Figure 2–9. The SAR-PDU carries payload, only with no control information (header or trailer) added. It is obtained by just segmenting the CPCS-PDU of Figure 2–9a into 48-octet blocks. (Note that the CPCS-PDU is passed down to the SAR sublayer as an SAR-SDU).

The length field in Figure 2–9a indicates the length of the CPCS-PDU payload (the embedded CPCS-SDU), in octets. An all-zero length field is used to indicate a partially-transmitted payload (CPCS-SDU), to be aborted at the destination if desired. Finally, the CRC field is used for error detection.

Delineation of consecutive CPCS-PDUs (or the equivalent SAR-SDUs) is accomplished by using bit number 2 in the 3-bit PT field of the ATM cell header (Figure 2–2). A "0" in that bit denotes the beginning or continuation of an SAR-SDU. A "1" indicates the end of the SAR-SDU. This method of marking an ATM cell (and hence the SAR-PDU carried as its payload) is quite simple. It also implies breaking the usual rule of maintaining strict separation of protocol layers: The header at the ATM layer is used to carry information about the AAL layer embedded as the data (payload) portion of the ATM cell. This procedure is obviously required since the 48-octet SAR-PDU of Figure 2–9b has no control (header or trailer) information added at the SAR sublayer. The SARs sole function is then that of segmentation and reassembly.

Comparing Figures 2–8 and 2–9, it is obvious that AAL Type 5 provides much less functionality and, hence, is a much simpler protocol than AAL Type 3/4. Type 5 has no provision for multiplexing, has no sequencing function, and provides no error detection capability at the SAR level. Where the Type 3/4 SAR-PDU carries an error-checking field, AAL Type 5 carries out error detection at the CPCS sublayer (Figure 2–9a). The 32-bit CRC field of the CPCS-PDU is thus used to detect bit errors and segments out of sequence. (The CRC field will detect missing or added segments—SAR-PDUs—as well, but those corresponding to the CPCS-PDU payload will be detected by the length field of the CPCS-PDU).

The various AAL types just discussed were designed by the ITU-T to cover the B-ISDN service classes of Table 2–1. The ATM Forum has, in turn, recommended a set of five ATM layer service classes to cover the QoS service requirements of the various types of traffic expected to utilize ATM network facilities. These requirements include cell loss ratio (CLR), the fraction of cells lost in a number generated (this is comparable to probability of cell loss to be discussed in chapters following), cell delay variation (CDV) and cell transfer delay (CTD), peak cell rate (PCR) and cell delay variation tolerance (CDVT), sustainable cell rate (SCR) and burst tolerance (BT), and minimum cell rate, among others. An ATM call would be admitted under a traffic contract consisting of a subset of these parameters. Note that most of these parameters are among those mentioned earlier in discussing, generically, various QoS parameters.

Table 2–2 shows the five ATM layer service classes and the corresponding distribution of service requirements or attributes for each. These obviously represent a much more detailed set of requirements than the three attributes—bit rate, connection mode, and timing requirement—of the B-ISDN (AAL type) service classes of Table 2–1.

We have already mentioned, briefly, the continuous bit rate (CBR), real-time, type of traffic, such as voice, which has tight constraints on end-to-end transfer delay and delay jitter (variation), as well as a relatively tight constraint on cell loss. In this type of application it is assumed that a cell delivered later than the CTD transfer delay constraint is generally useless and would presumably be dropped. Variable bit rate (VBR) traffic can be further subdivided into real-time and nonreal-time traffic, however, with correspondingly different service requirements. The ATM Forum has thus specified a service class for each, designated, respectively, as the RT-VBR and NRT-VBR classes. They are so indicated in Table 2–2. We have previously mentioned real-time VBR traffic with compressed video as the key example. Real-time voice could similarly be delivered as variable bit-rate traffic if compression techniques were used. This type of traffic has QoS requirements similar to those of real-time CBR traffic: there are tight constraints on end-to-end transfer delay, delay jitter (variation), and cell loss ratio (or probability of loss). The nonreal-time VBR service, however, is designed to accommodate applications that are bursty in nature, have some cell transfer delay bound, and a low cell loss rate. These applications, unlike real-time traffic applications, have no delay variation requirement. Their burstiness and rate of transmission into the network, as covered by the burst tolerance and sustainable cell rate attributes of Table 2–2, are assumed to be controllable by a technique called the "leaky bucket" or Generic Cell Rate algorithm (GCRA) to be de-

TABLE 2–2 ■ ATM Layer Service Classes

Attribute	CBR	RT-VBR	NRT-VBR	ABR	UBR
Cell Loss Ratio (CLR)	S	S	S	S	U
Cell Delay Variation (CDV) Cell Transfer Delay (CTD)	S	S	S	U	U
Peak Cell Rate (PCR) CDV Tolerance (CDVT)	S	S	S	S	S
Sustainable Cell Rate (SCR) Burst Tolerance (BT)	—	S	S	—	—
Minimum Cell Rate (MCR)	—	—	—	S	—

S = Specified
U = Unspecified

scribed in Chapter 4. Transmission of a set of images would be one example of such an application.

All other data traffic applications are taken to be covered by either one of the two remaining service classes listed in Table 2–2. These are the unspecified bit rate (UBR) and available bit rate (ABR) classes. The UBR service is designed to have ATM networks accommodate some of the current common computer-communication applications, such as file transfers, that occur in spaced bursts of cells and have relatively few service requirements. It provides no QoS guarantees at the ATM level, and, in turn, is not subject to a guaranteed bandwidth allocation that would be provided by the end-to-end VC setup noted earlier. Higher protocol layers, above the AAL layer, would presumably be required to provide any performance guarantees such as probability of loss. Statistical multiplexing of many traffic sources is supported by this service.

The available bit rate (ABR) service shown in Table 2–2 was established to accommodate nonreal-time data traffic that requires a specific guarantee of the cell loss ratio (probability of cell loss), but has only *vague* requirements as to throughput and delay [BONO 1995]. (Many data users would be hard-pressed to specify delay and throughput requirements.) Applications using this service require a minimum guarantee of cell transmission rate (minimum cell rate MCR) but are otherwise able to vary their transmission rate to accommodate conditions existing in the network. They thus lend themselves to flow control. The ATM Forum has therefore adopted a rate-based flow control mechanism, discussed in Chapter 7, for ABR traffic, that is designed to overcome possible congestion in the network. The words "available bit rate" come from the fact that the traffic source rate of this type of traffic is adjustable, using whatever rate is available, above the specified minimum.

[BONO 1995] Bonomi, F., and K. W. Fendick, "The Rate-Based Flow Control for the Available Bit Rate ATM Service," *IEEE Network*, 9, 2 (March/April 1995): 25–39.

Chapter 3

Traffic Characterization for Broadband Services

3.1 ▪ INTRODUCTION

In both preceding chapters we have stressed the fact that the broadband networks of the future, based on ATM cell transmission, are expected to carry a variety of traffic types in integrated fashion. This differs considerably from the case of the century-old, ubiquitous, circuit-switched telephone networks designed primarily to handle voice, and the much more recent packet-switched networks designed to handle data. Traffic models have played a significant role in the design and engineering of both of these network types. In particular, Poisson arrival and exponential call-holding time statistics have served as excellent models for almost a century in carrying out both the engineering and performance evaluation of circuit-switched voice telephony. Poisson arrival and relatively simple, packet-length models have been used extensively in studying the performance of packet-switched networks as well. It is not at all clear, however, that these older, well-established models will suffice in carrying out the design of the broadband integrated networks of the future. In fact, quite the contrary may be true. It appears that the integration of packetized voice, packet video, packetized images, and computer-generated data traffic (whether brief bursts or much longer file transfers), each with its own multi-objective quality of service (QoS), requires the development of rather sophisticated traffic models to carry out accurate design and performance evaluation.

The material in this chapter as well as those following assumes some prior acquaintance with the elements of queueing theory. For those readers lacking this knowledge, or those wishing to refresh their background in queueing analysis, we have provided a brief introduction to the subject in the

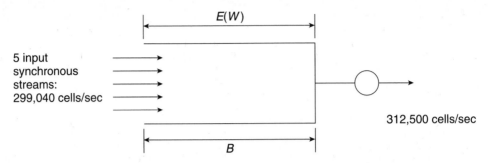

FIGURE 3–1 ■ Model, ATM multiplexing-buffering.

Appendix to this book. The material presented there should be sufficient to provide the background necessary to follow the discussion in this chapter. More advanced topics not treated in the Appendix are developed when needed, both in this chapter and elsewhere in the book.

Consider the following simple example that indicates the need for detailed traffic studies and modeling [GECH 1988]. Say five synchronous traffic streams of B-ISDN service class-A (Table 2–1) are multiplexed and buffered at a user-network interface (UNI) port for transmission through an ATM network. Each continuous bit rate (CBR) stream delivers one 53-octet ATM cell to the multiplexing buffer periodically, every 16.72 µsec. The total cell arrival rate of the five synchronous streams is thus 299,040 cells/sec. The transmission capacity across the interface, into the network, is 312,500 cells/sec. (This corresponds to a 132.5 Mbps capacity for 53-octet cells). Cells are delivered to the network in FIFO (FCFS) order. Figure 3–1 portrays the multiplexing-buffering function graphically. The problem is to determine the buffer size B required, in units of cells, and the average time $E(W)$ a typical cell must wait in the multiplexing queue before delivery to the network. The wait time is one possible measure of the multidimensional quality of service (QoS) mentioned briefly in our discussion of B-ISDN in Chapter 2.

The buffer size B for this example is easily found by inspection: Although each stream is individually defined to be periodic in nature, the five streams in this example are assumed independently generated. The aggregate (multiplexed) arrival rate, as already noted, is 299,040 cells/sec, just below the service rate of 312,500 cells/sec. The utilization defined as the ratio of the net arrival rate to the queue to the service rate is thus $\rho = 0.957$. (Since the concept of utilization occurs frequently throughout this book, readers not familiar with the term, or requiring some review, are referred to the Appendix of this book). A little thought will indicate that a buffer size of four cells, not including one in service, will suffice to handle the cell arrivals. (While one cell

[GECH 1988]   Gechter, J., and P. O'Reilly, "Standardization of ATM," *Proc. IEEE Globecom '88*, 4.3.1–4.3.5., Dec. 1988.

from one of the streams is being transmitted, at most four other cells from the other streams may arrive).

The average wait time $E(W)$ in the buffer requires a more sophisticated analysis. Since fixed-length cells are being read out at a uniform rate of 312,500 cells/sec, the queueing model of Figure 3–1 is seen to be that of a $G/D/1/B$ queue.[1] More specifically, if the five streams are taken to be uniformly distributed in arrival time with respect to one another, as is the case from the independent assumption noted above, the queueing analysis becomes that of the $nD/D/1$ queue, with $n = 5$ here. An analysis of this model with $\rho = 0.957$, the utilization chosen for this example, turns out to give $E(W) = 2.7$ μsec [ECKB 1979]. (The worst-case wait time is 12.8 μsec, since each cell takes 3.2 μsec to be transmitted.)

So far so good. But now take the same problem and let the composite cell arrival process be Poisson with the same average arrival rate of 299,040 cells/sec. The average wait time is just the wait time of the $M/D/1$ queue [SCHW 1987]:

$$E(W) = \frac{\rho m}{2\,(1-\rho)} \tag{3–1}$$

Here $m = 3.2$ μsec is the cell service (transmission) time. For $\rho = 0.957$ we get $E(W) = 35.6$ μsec, more than ten times the previous synchronous traffic, result! Further, the buffer size B required for a loss (blocking) probability less than 10^{-9} turns out to be $B = 249$! [GECH 1988]. Recall that $B = 4$ for the synchronous arrival case resulted in zero blocking probability. It is thus apparent that the Poisson arrival model and the synchronous traffic model lead to vastly different results in this simple example.

The moral of this example is, of course, quite simple: The Poisson arrival process, used so extensively in network performance analysis, doesn't always work, particularly when dealing with stream-type, continuous bit rate, traffic. (Actually, by the law of large numbers, multiplexing many independent streams of traffic would give rise to a composite Poisson arrival process. The problem is with the word "many". It can require as many as twenty or more multiplexed streams to begin to approach Poisson arrivals for the example shown here). Another example, that involving the multiplexing of multiple bursty sources, leads to results that are vastly different from the Poisson model result as well [DAIG 1992]. Bursty sources have

---

[1]This queueing notation is often referred to as the Kendall notation, after the statistician D. G. Kendall. See the Appendix for the meaning of the notation.

[ECKB 1979] Eckberg, Jr., A. E., "The Single Server Queue with Periodic Arrival Process and Deterministic Service Times," *IEEE Trans. On Commun., COM-27*, 3 (March 1979), 556–562.

[DAIG 1992] Daigle, J. N., *Queueing for Telecommunications*, Reading, MA: Addison-Wesley, 1992.

been used as models for data traffic file transfers and image transmission. B-ISDN service classes C and D correspond to this type of traffic. We shall have occasion later to discuss this traffic model in somewhat more detail. Suffice it to say, at this point, that this type of traffic is characterized by alternating, randomly varying periods of inactivity and activity. A bursty source is usually one for which the period of inactivity is much longer than the time during which it is active and transmitting cells (see Figure 3–2c). In a particular model analyzed by Daigle, the buffer occupancy distribution deviates more from the Poisson, $M/D/1$, result as the number of sources multiplexed increases! [DAIG 1992, Figure 5–2]

Measurements of both LAN and wide-area TCP (Internet) traffic indicate that the Poisson model breaks down in a number of real-life application

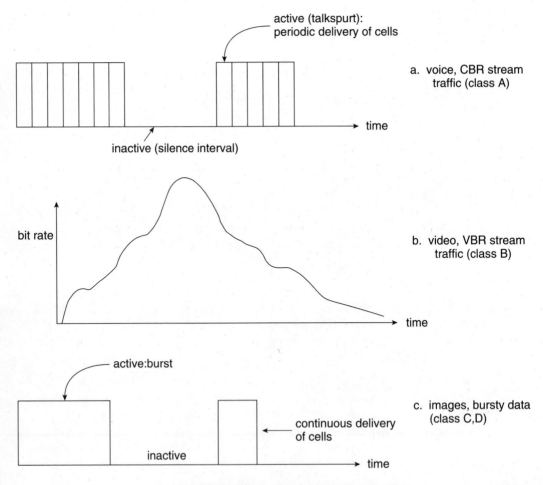

FIGURE 3–2 ■ Traffic characteristics, B-ISDN.

areas [LELA 1994], [PAXS 1994]. Statistical studies of these measurements indicate that the traffic is *self-similar* or *fractal-like* in nature. The term self-similar means that the statistical characterization of the traffic is essentially invariant with the time scale; the same statistical properties are observed as the time scales change from hundreds of seconds to seconds to milliseconds. This phenomenon of self-similarity was first described by B. Mandelbrot, who found this type of behavior appearing not only in time series generated by traffic, but in many natural phenomena as well [MAND 1983]. The implication, thus, is that one has to be very careful in basing design of high-speed networks on traditional traffic models.

Despite this warning about the use (or overuse) of Poisson arrival statistics, we shall have occasion, later in this book, to invoke the Poisson arrival assumption. The purpose of the examples cited here is not to propose dispensing with this model. It is still an extremely useful one, and can often lead to powerful and significant results. We must, however, be careful in its use. It is important to carefully characterize the traffic under study to ensure the models used do lead to useful network performance results. Our main point is that this is particularly important when dealing with relatively new sources such as packet (cell-based) video, packetized images, and multimedia traffic. Traffic characterization is not only important when designing buffers for multiplexers, the example used here, but in studying admission, access, and flow control (topics to be explored later in this book). In all of these topics and other areas related to network performance management in broadband ISDN—ensuring all traffic types receive the appropriate quality of service (QoS)—good models of integrated traffic are required. This is why we stress traffic characterization in this chapter.

The three types of traffic on which we shall focus in this chapter correspond to the three basic B-ISDN service classes discussed in Chapter 2 and tabulated in Table 2–1; continuous bit rate (CBR) voice (class-A), video as representative of variable bit rate (VBR) stream traffic (class-B), and variable bursty data (classes C and D). These are represented schematically in Figure 3–2. We shall describe methods proposed to characterize both individual sources and multiplexed sums of sources of each type, using the models obtained to determine buffer occupancy statistics, queue wait times, and blocking probabilities, among other QoS parameters. These models will then be applied in the chapter following to study admission and access control.

It should be stressed that the models we discuss are only selected examples of such models proposed in the literature. There has literally been an outpouring of models designed to represent different types of traffic. The models

[LELA 1994]   Leland, W. E., et al., "On the Self-Similar Nature of Ethernet Traffic (Extended Version)," *IEEE/ACM Trans. On Networking, 2,* 1 (Feb. 1994): 1–15.

[PAXS 1994]   Paxson, V., and S. Floyd, "Wide-Area Traffic: The Failure of Poisson Modeling," *Proc. SIGCOMM '94,* London, Aug. 1994: 257–268.

[MAND 1983]   Mandelbrot, B., *The Fractal Geometry of Nature,* NY: Freeman, 1983.

we use are representative and should serve to introduce the reader to this area. We shall, in fact, have very little to say about self-similar (fractal) models, even though, as noted earlier, studies indicate that some very significant traffic types appear to have the self-similar property. This is an active area of current research, and the impact of self-similarity, both in modeling and on system design and performance, remains to be assessed.

3.2 ■ PACKET VOICE MODELING

We begin by discussing a number of models described in the literature for representing the statistical multiplexing of packet voice sources. These models predate the ATM cell-based environment, but they capture properties of the multiplexing process that are useful for design purposes: They provide fairly good design estimates, for example, of buffer sizes required to maintain a specified packet (cell) loss probability as a function of outgoing link utilization and number of sources multiplexed. In addition, the modeling and analysis techniques used have been adapted to video traffic characterization and modeling and so will be useful in discussing video traffic later.

It has been known for many years that a single voice source is well-represented by a two-state process: Human speech consists of an alternating sequence of active, or *talk spurt,* intervals, typically averaging 0.4–1.2 sec in length, followed by silence (inactive) intervals averaging 0.6–1.8 sec in length. This phenomenon has long been used in analog telephony to pack multiple calls into smaller numbers of telephone circuits (trunks). A system using this technique is called a time-assigned speech interpolation (TASI) system. The same technique applied to digital telephony is called *digital speech interpolation* (DSI) [CAMP 1976], [SCHW 1990]. Figure 3–2a, referred to briefly in the previous section, portrays this phenomenon.

To a reasonably good approximation, the states may be assumed to be exponentially distributed in length [BRAD 1969]. (The talk spurt duration is well-approximated by the exponential distribution; the silence interval is less well-represented by this distribution. Added states have been proposed to improve the model, but this complicates the representation). This gives rise to the two-state birth-death model of Figure 3–3.[2] The parameter λ represents

---

[2] Birth-death processes are discussed briefly in [SCHW 1987, Chapter 2]. They are discussed in more detail in [KLEI 1975], as well as in other books on queueing and stochastic processes. See the Appendix to this book as well.

[CAMP 1976]   Campanella, S. J., "Digital Speech Interpolation," *Comsat Tech. Rev., 6,* 1 (1976): 127–158.

[BRAD 1969]   Brady, P. T., "A Model for Generating On-off Speech Patterns in Two-way Conversations," *Bell System Tech. J., 48* (Sept. 1969): 2445–2472.

[KLEI 1975]   Kleinrock, L., *Queueing Systems, Vol I: Theory,* New York: John Wiley, 1975.

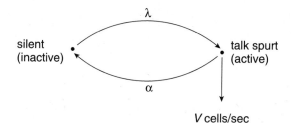

FIGURE 3–3 ▪ Two-state model, voice source.

the rate of transition out of the silent state; α is defined to be the rate of transition out of talk spurt. The average talk spurt is thus 1/α sec in length. The average silence interval is 1/λ sec in length. It is left for the reader to show that the probability a speaker is active (in talk spurt), the speaker activity factor, is λ/(α + λ). If the average talk spurt is 1/α = 0.4 sec and the average silence interval is 1/λ = 0.6 sec, the activity factor is 0.4. This implies that for large numbers of users a circuit-switched network could accommodate close to 1/0.4 = 2.5 as many users as circuits (trunks) available. The reciprocal of the activity factor is often called the *TASI advantage*.

Now consider the talkspurt interval in more detail. With normal speech encoding, the voice process is sampled every 125 μsec, with samples encoded into 8 bits (256 levels) [SCHW 1990]. Each sample thus constitutes an ATM octet, and 47 samples would make up the 47-octet ATM Type-1 payload discussed in Chapter 2 (Figure 2–6). During talk spurt an ATM cell would thus be generated every 5.875 msec. Alternately said, each voice source generates a periodic stream of $V = 170$ ATM cells/sec while in talk spurt. This is shown in Figure 3–3.

The composite model for N such independent voice sources multiplexed together can now be found quite simply. Consider Figure 3–4, which shows N sources multiplexed at a network access buffer. Each source generates V cells/sec while in talk spurt, as noted above. Because of the statistical multiplexing advantage, the output link capacity, into the network, can be less than NV, the maximum number of cells/sec that can be generated. It is useful to let the link capacity be written as VC cells/sec [STER 1983]. C is a dimensionless parameter in this case. Because of statistical multiplexing we should have $C < N$. How much less than N can C be? It is left to the reader to explain that the average rate of generation of cells is $VN\lambda/(\alpha + \lambda)$. It is thus clear that the parameter C must satisfy the lower bound inequality given by

$$\left(\frac{\lambda}{\alpha + \lambda}\right)N < C \tag{3–2}$$

[STER 1983] Stern, T. E., "A Queueing Analysis of Packet Voice," *Proc. IEEE Globecom '83*, San Diego, CA., Dec. 1983: 2.5.1–2.5.6.

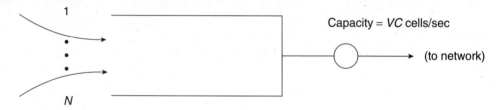

FIGURE 3–4 ■ Access buffer model, N voice sources, V cells/sec each, when in talk spurt.

For an infinite buffer, this represents the condition for stability. Dividing equation (3–2) through by C we can define the utilization ρ to be the resultant left-hand side of the inequality and get

$$\rho \equiv \left(\frac{\lambda}{\alpha+\lambda}\right)\frac{N}{C} < 1 \qquad (3\text{–}2a)$$

We shall return to this definition of utilization later.

As an example, if $\lambda/(\alpha+\lambda) = 0.4$, with the TASI advantage at 2.5, C must be somewhat greater than 0.4 N. The utilization is then $\rho = 0.4\ N/C$. Specifically, say a bandwidth of 3000 cells/sec (1.272 Mbps) at an ATM access port is set aside to accommodate voice traffic. Since $V = 170$ cells/sec is the cell generation rate of each voice source while in talk spurt, $C = 3000/170 \doteq 17.6$ in this case. For an activity factor of 0.4, this system could accommodate between 18 and $(2.5 \times 18) = 45$ users.

Given this model of packet voice multiplexing, it is of interest to use it to find such performance and design parameters as queue-occupancy statistics, delay statistics (required as part of the voice QoS), and the size of the buffer required to ensure an acceptable cell loss probability. (This is also a significant QoS parameter for voice traffic). In the next chapter we extend the use of models such as this one to the analysis of admission and access control procedures proposed for B-ISDN.

It is left to the reader to show that the N multiplexed independent voice sources of Figure 3–4, each represented by the two-state model of Figure 3–3, give rise to the composite traffic model of Figure 3–5. This model can be seen, by inspection, to be an $(N+1)$-state birth-death model. The state here represents the number of sources active. At state i, for example, i sources are active, and the average rate of delivery of cells to the buffer is then iV cells/sec. (Although each source generates V cells/sec periodically while in talk spurt, the sum of the independent, nonsynchronized sources, gives rise to a random input process, with an average value of iV cells/sec.)

Two specific states, J_u and J_o, have been singled out in Figure 3–5 [STER 1983]. J_u, called the underload state, is defined to be the integer part or floor of the capacity C:

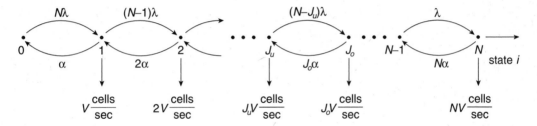

FIGURE 3–5 ■ Composite model, N voice sources of Figure 3–4.

$$J_u = \lfloor C \rfloor \qquad (3\text{--}3)$$

In the example cited previously, with the actual capacity taken as $VC = 3000$ cells/sec, and $V = 170$ cells/sec, $C = 17.6$, and $J_u = 17$.

Similarly, J_o, called the *overload* state, is the ceiling function of C, the integer just above C:

$$J_o = \lceil C \rceil \qquad (3\text{--}4)$$

For the same example, $J_o = 18$.

Why single these two states out? It is apparent that when the state $i > C$, the composite traffic source is causing the queue of Figure 3–4 to fill. When $i < C$, the queue is tending to empty. J_u thus represents the state below which the queue is emptying; J_o represents the state above which the queue is filling. Alternately said, when state $i > C$, the queue is filling and the system is said to be in *overload;* when $i < C$, with the queue emptying, the system is said to be in *underload*. The rate of change of the queue of Figure 3–4, when in state i, is $V(C - i)$ cells/sec.

The steady-state probability π_i that the composite source is in state i, is easily written by noting that it is just the (binomial) probability that i of N two-state sources are active (in talk spurt), while the remaining $(N - i)$ are inactive (silent). Since the probability that each source is active is $\lambda/(\lambda + \alpha)$, the probability π_i is written, by inspection, as

$$\pi_i = \binom{N}{i}\left(\frac{\lambda}{\lambda + \alpha}\right)^i \left(\frac{\alpha}{\lambda + \alpha}\right)^{N-i} \qquad (3\text{--}5)$$

with $\binom{N}{i}$ the usual representation of the number of combinations of N things, taken i at a time. This expression is also readily rewritten in the following equivalent form:

$$\pi_i = \binom{N}{i}\left(\frac{\lambda}{\alpha}\right)^i \left(1 + \frac{\lambda}{\alpha}\right)^{-N} \qquad (3\text{--}6)$$

An alternative derivation of equation (3–6), using birth-death analysis, is also useful, particularly in connection with some of the analysis to follow. Consider the general, state-dependent, birth-death process of Figure 3–6. The parameter λ_i represents the rate of transition up from state i to state $i + 1$; μ_i is the rate of transition down from state i to $i - 1$. Then it is well-known that the steady-state probability π_i of being in state i is given by

$$\pi_i = \frac{\lambda_0 \lambda_1 \lambda_2 \ldots \lambda_{i-1}}{\mu_1 \mu_2 \ldots \mu_i} \pi_0 \qquad (3\text{–}7)$$

with π_0 found by summing over all the states and setting $\Sigma_{i=0}^{N} \pi_i = 1$ (see Appendix). It is left to the reader to show that for the special case of Figure 3–5, the state probability π_i is, in fact, found to be given by equation (3–6).

Another representation of the birth-death process of Figure 3–5 will be found to be useful in the work following as well. Using Figure 3–5, we set up the balance equations at each state (see Appendix) as follows:

$i = 0$: $\quad N\lambda\pi_0 = \alpha\pi_1$

$1 \le i \le N - 1$: $\quad \pi_i[i\alpha + (N - i)\lambda] = [N - (i - 1)]\lambda\pi_{i-1} + (i + 1)\alpha\pi_{i+1} \qquad (3\text{–}8)$

$i = N$: $\quad N\alpha\pi_N = \lambda\pi_{N-1}$

We rewrite these equations in an equivalent form by moving the left-hand terms to the right-hand side:

$$-N\lambda\pi_0 + \alpha\pi_1 = 0$$

$$N\lambda\pi_0 - [\alpha + (N - 1)\lambda]\pi_1 + 2\alpha\pi_2 = 0$$

$$\vdots \qquad\qquad (3\text{–}8a)$$

$$[N - (i - 1)]\lambda\pi_{i-1} - [i\alpha + (N - i)\lambda]\pi_i + (i + 1)\alpha\pi_{i+1} = 0$$

$$\vdots$$

$$\lambda\pi_{N-1} - N\alpha\pi_N = 0$$

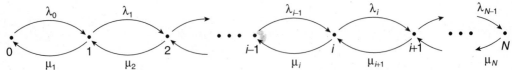

FIGURE 3–6 ■ General birth-death process.

Now define an $(N + 1)$-element row vector $\boldsymbol{\pi}$ as the vector containing the $(N + 1)$ values of π_i:

$$\boldsymbol{\pi} \equiv [\pi_0, \pi_1, \pi_2 \ldots \pi_N] \tag{3-9}$$

It is left to the reader to show that the set of equations (3–8a) can be written in the compact matrix equation form as

$$\boldsymbol{\pi} M = 0 \tag{3-10}$$

The $(N+1) \times (N+1)$ matrix M, with row elements summing to 0, is then given by

$$M = \begin{bmatrix} -N\lambda & N\lambda & 0 & \cdots \\ \alpha & -[\alpha + (N-1)\lambda] & (N-1)\lambda & \cdots \\ 0 & 2\alpha & -(N-2)\lambda - 2\alpha & \cdots \\ 0 & 0 & 3\alpha & \cdots \\ \vdots & \vdots & \vdots & \end{bmatrix} \tag{3-11}$$

(The reader is invited to complete this matrix, particularly the last two rows).

The matrix equation (3–10) is a special case of the same equation obtained more generally for *continuous-time Markov chains,* of which the birth-death process and, more specifically, the model here of N multiplexed voice sources are special cases [KLEI 1975]. The matrix M whose elements represent the transition rates between states, with row elements summing to 0, is termed the *infinitesimal generating matrix* of the underlying Markov chain. (The continuous-time Markov chain can generally make all transitions between states rather than the special case of the birth-death process of Figure 3–6, with transitions possible to adjacent states only. In general, then, all elements of the matrix M could be nonzero. The form of M in this more general case will be discussed in section 3.4)

Given the model of Figure 3–5 of N statistically multiplexed, packet voice sources, with its analytical representation of equations (3–8) to (3–11), how do we now use it to study the access multiplexer of Figure 3–4? Specifically, how do we calculate the performance and design parameters such as delay and loss statistics and buffer size required, noted previously?

Three approaches have been analyzed and compared by Daigle and Langford [DAIG 1986]. One, which attempts to capture the periodic arrival process at rate V of each source, leads to a semi-Markov process model to be analyzed. It is based on the work presented earlier by Stern [STERN 1983]. This model is found to provide reasonable agreement with simulation. Be-

[DAIG 1986]   Daigle, J. N., and J. D. Langford, "Models for Analysis of Packet Voice Communication Systems," *IEEE JSAC, SAC-4,* 6 (Sept. 1986): 847–855.

cause of the comparative complexity of this approach we shall not outline it here, but leave it to the reader to pursue if inclined, using [DAIG 1986] and the references contained therein to study the approach in detail. We will focus on the two other approaches.

The second model Daigle and Langford analyze approximates the generation of cells (packets) by a source in the active state as a Poisson process producing packets exponentially-distributed in length. This is an example of a Markov-modulated Poisson process (MMPP), one in which the underlying system generates packets at Poisson rates, the actual rate changing from state to state. Transitions between states are governed by an underlying continuous-time Markov chain, as already described here. This model turns out to be the poorest of the three, compared to simulation. We shall discuss it here, however, because it has been used successfully in modeling various types of traffic (an application to video traffic will be provided later in this chapter). In addition, it enables us to introduce a useful technique for solving continuous-time Markov chain models that appear in various traffic models.

The third model assumes each active source transmits information uniformly, with the transmitting link, the server, also operating in the same manner. Such a model is called a *fluid flow* model and has been applied successfully to a variety of problems in communication networks as well as other applications. This model will be used in characterizing multiplexed video sources later in this chapter. It will also be used to study access control in B-ISDN in the next chapter. In the problem under study here, this model turns out to give results comparable to those of the first model, that is, reasonable agreement with simulation.

Because of the importance and general usefulness of the fluid flow approach to traffic characterization and modeling, we begin our discussion with this model. We devote the next section to this model, focusing on the packet voice application, but generalizing the results where possible. (These more general results will then be applied to video traffic characterization later in this chapter.) We will then follow with a discussion of the Markov-modulated Poisson process (MMPP) model.

3.3 ■ FLUID SOURCE MODELING OF PACKET VOICE

We refer again to the basic two-state model of a voice source as shown in Figure 3–3. The fluid flow model arises by assuming that the number of cells generated during a talk spurt is so large that it appears like a continuous flow of fluid. As applied to the statistical multiplexer of Figure 3–4, this approach is particularly valid if the number of sources N and the capacity VC are so large that the discreteness of the buffer, due to cells arriving and leaving (being transmitted), may be neglected. The buffer occupancy thus becomes a *continuous* random variable x. This is the "fluid" referred to in using the ex-

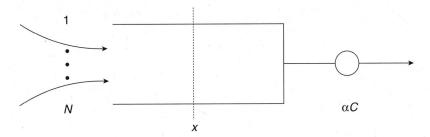

FIGURE 3–7 ▪ Access buffer of Figure 3–4, N voice sources, stochastic fluid model.

pression fluid flow analysis. The units of x are defined to be the number of cells arriving during a talk spurt. One voice source, generating cells at the rate of V cells/sec during a talk spurt of average length $1/\alpha$ sec, will, on the average, increment x by V/α cells during a talk spurt. Call this a "unit of information" [ANIC 1982]. A system with capacity VC cells/sec will thus have an equivalent capacity of $VC/(V/\alpha) = \alpha C$ "unit of information" per sec. The access buffer model of Figure 3–4, with N voice sources multiplexed, can thus be replaced by the equivalent fluid-based model of Figure 3–7. The buffer occupancy x is a random variable whose statistics are to be found.

Once we find the probability distribution of x, we can relate this back to the original problem of finding the buffer occupancy distribution in actual units of cells. This is done as follows. Let l be the state of the buffer in units of cells. Since x increments by V/α cells during an average talk spurt, we must have $l \equiv xV/\alpha$ as the appropriate conversion between "units of information" and cells. The probability $P[l > i]$ that the buffer occupancy l exceeds some number i must thus be given by

$$P[l > i] = P[x > \alpha i/V] \qquad (3\text{--}12)$$

where $P[x > x_0]$ is the probability x exceeds x_0. As an example, consider the numbers developed earlier for voice. We found for voice that the rate of cell generation was $V = 170$ cells/sec during a talk spurt. If the average talk spurt length is $1/\alpha = 1.25$ sec ($\alpha = 0.8$), $V/\alpha = 212.5$ cells. This is the "unit of information" in this case. Then

$$P[l > i] = P[x > i/212.5]$$

For example,

$$P[l > 1000 \text{ cells}] = P[x > 4.7]$$

[ANIC 1982]   Anick, D., et al., "Stochastic Theory of a Data-Handling System with Multiple Sources," *Bell System Tech. J., 61,* 8 (Oct. 1982): 1871–1894.

Thus, given the distribution of x, we can convert this to the initial problem of finding the buffer cell distribution, assuming the fluid model is accurate.

To find the distribution of x, we use the approach pioneered by Anick, Mitra, and Sondhi in their classic paper [ANIC 1982]. Refer to Figure 3–7. Say there are i sources in talk spurt. They are "pumping" αi "units of information" per second into the buffer. The buffer is at the same time emptying at the rate of αC. Just as before, in discussing the model of Figure 3–4 in section 3.2, using the composite traffic model of Figure 3–5, the buffer is filling if $i > C$ and emptying if $i < C$. The difference is that the buffer occupancy x is now a continuous random variable.

Now define $F_i(t,x)$, $0 \le i \le N$, as the cumulative probability distribution, at time t, with the system in state i (that is, the probability that the buffer (queue) occupancy is less than or equal to x with i sources on). We assume at this point that the queue is infinite. In the next chapter, in applying the fluid approach to access control, we consider the finite buffer case as well. To find $F_i(t, x)$, we proceed by setting up a generating equation for $F_i(t + \Delta t, x)$ at an incremental time Δt later in terms of the probabilities at time t. This equation makes use of the buffer filling/emptying rates indicated above. It also makes use of the two-state source model of Figure 3–3. Specifically, it is left to the reader to show that $F_i(t + \Delta t, x)$ is given by the following equation:

$$F_i(t + \Delta t, x) = [N - (i - 1)]\lambda\Delta t F_{i-1}(t, x) + (i + 1)\,\alpha\Delta t F_{i+1}(t, x)$$
$$+ \{1 - [(N - i)\lambda + i\alpha]\Delta t\}F_i[t, x - (i - C)\alpha\Delta t] + o(\Delta t) \quad (3\text{–}13)$$

Here $o(\Delta t)$ implies that other terms are higher order in Δt and go to zero more rapidly than Δt as $\Delta t \to 0$. It is also assumed that $F_{-1}(\ )$ and $F_{N+1}(\ )$ are set equal to zero.

We now expand $F_i(t + \Delta t, x)$ and $F_i(t, x - \Delta x)$ ($\Delta x \equiv (i - C)\alpha\Delta t$) in their respective Taylor series, assuming appropriate continuity conditions are met, and let $\Delta t \to 0$. It is again left to the reader to show that equation (3–13) simplifies to the following equation:

$$\frac{\partial F_i(x, t)}{\partial t} = [N - (i - 1)]\,\lambda F_{i-1}(t, x) + (i + 1)\,\alpha F_{i+1}(t, x)$$

$$- [(N - i)\lambda + i\alpha]\,F_i(t, x) - (i - C)\,\alpha\frac{\partial F_i}{\partial x}(t, x) \quad (3\text{–}14)$$

We now assume stationarity conditions hold; that is, as time goes on the system settles down to statistical equilibrium so that $\partial F_i(x, t)/\partial t = 0$ and $F_i(t, x) \to F_i(x)$, the stationary probability that the buffer occupancy is less than or equal to x, given i sources in talk spurt. Equation (3–14) then becomes the set of equations

$$(i - C)\alpha \frac{dF_i(x)}{dx} = [N - (i - 1)]\lambda F_{i-1}(x) - [(N - i)\lambda + i\alpha]F_i(x)$$
$$+ (i + 1)\alpha F_{i+1}(x) \tag{3-15}$$

Here $0 \le i \le N$, with $F_{-1}(x) = F_{N+1}(x) = 0$. It is this set of equations that we have to solve for $F_i(x)$. Note that we must have $C < N$, as noted in section 3.2, so that there are both emptying states ($i < C$) and filling states ($i > C$). (To reader—Why is this necessary?)

The solution of this set of equations is readily obtained by first writing them out in their complete form:

$$-C\alpha \frac{dF_0(x)}{dx} = -N\lambda F_0(x) + \alpha F_1(x)$$

$$(1 - C)\alpha \frac{dF_1(x)}{dx} = N\lambda F_0(x) - [(N - 1)\lambda + \alpha]F_1(x) + 2\alpha F_2(x)$$

$$(2 - C)\alpha \frac{dF_2(x)}{dx} = (N - 1)\lambda F_1(x) - [(N - 2)\lambda + 2\alpha]F_2(x) + 3\alpha F_3(x) \tag{3-15a}$$

$$\vdots \qquad\qquad \vdots$$

$$(N - C)\alpha \frac{dF_N(x)}{dx} = \lambda F_{N-1}(x) - N\alpha F_N(x)$$

If we define the $(N + 1)$ – element row vector

$$\boldsymbol{F}(x) \equiv [F_0(x), F_1(x), \ldots, F_N(x)],$$

a little thought will indicate that equation (3–15a) may be written in the compact matrix equation form

$$\frac{d\boldsymbol{F}(x)}{dx} D = \boldsymbol{F}(x)M \tag{3-15b}$$

with D an $(N + 1) \times (N + 1)$ diagonal matrix defined as

$$D = \text{diag} \, [-C\alpha, (1 - C)\alpha, \ldots, (N - C)\alpha] \tag{13-16}$$

and the $(N + 1) \times (N + 1)$ matrix M precisely the infinitesimal generating matrix previously defined by equation (3–11) in section 3.2! Alternately, one can rewrite equation (3–15b) in a more compact form by dividing equation (3–15) through by $(i - C)$, thus obtaining

$$\frac{d\boldsymbol{F}(x)}{dx} = \boldsymbol{F}(x)M' \tag{3-15c}$$

Clearly we must have C a noninteger. The specific form of M' is left up to the reader to write out.

Equations (3–15a), or the equivalents (3–15b) and (3–15c) in matrix-vector form, represent a set of first-order linear differential equations for which the solution is well-known to be a sum of exponentials. More specifically, if we focus on the matrix-vector form equation (3–15b), the solution is the weighted sum of exponentials in the eigenvalues of the matrix MD^{-1} or, equivalently, M' of (3–15c) [NOBL 1977]. Since the matrices M and D are of order $(N + 1)$, there are $(N + 1)$ eigenvalues, and the general solution of (3–15b) is given by

$$F(x) = \sum_{i=0}^{N} a_i F_i e^{z_i x} \tag{3–17}$$

with z_i the ith eigenvalue, $\mathbf{\Phi}_i$ the corresponding eigenvector given as the solution to the eigenvector equation

$$z_j \mathbf{\Phi}_j D = \mathbf{\Phi}_j M \tag{3–18}$$

and the $\{a_i\}$ a set of undetermined coefficients. The reader is left to show that equations (3–17) and (3–18) are the solutions to equation (3–15b). More specifically, recall our definition of $\mathbf{F}(x)$ as the row vector whose jth component $F_j(x)$ is the probability that the buffer occupancy is less than or equal to x, given j sources on, that is, in talk spurt. Then we have

$$F_j(x) = \text{Prob. } [j \text{ sources on, buffer occupancy} \le x]$$

$$= \sum_{i=0}^{N} a_i \Phi_{ij} e^{z_i x} \qquad\qquad 0 \le j \le N \tag{3–19}$$

with Φ_{ij} the jth component of eigenvector $\mathbf{\Phi}_i(x)$:

$$\mathbf{\Phi}_i(x) = [\Phi_{i0}, \Phi_{i1}, \ldots \Phi_{ij}, \ldots, \Phi_{iN}]$$

To complete the solution, we must now find the $(N + 1)$ eigenvalues z_i of the matrix MD^{-1}, the corresponding eigenvectors $\mathbf{\Phi}_i$, and the $(N + 1)$ coefficients a_i. We proceed for the special case of an infinite buffer. This simplifies the problem somewhat and allows us to draw directly on results in [ANIC 1982]. (The more general case of a finite buffer is considered in the next chapter in discussing access control in broadband networks). For the infinite buffer case the terms in the sum of equation (3–17), and hence in equation (3–19), corresponding to positive eigenvalues, must all be set to zero: since the buffer size $x \ge 0$ and the probability distribution $F_j(x)$ is always bounded to at most 1, any positive eigenvalues must be ruled out on physical grounds as

[NOBL 1977] Noble, B., and J. W. Daniel, *Applied Linear Algebra*, Englewood Cliffs, NJ: Prentice-Hall, 1977.

$x \to \infty$ in the case of an infinite buffer. The corresponding set of a_i's are then zero. We can thus write, for the infinite-buffer case,

$$F(x) = \sum_{i:\mathrm{Re}[z_i \leq 0]} a_i \Phi_i e^{z_i x} \tag{3–17a}$$

Continuing further for this case, we note immediately that one of the eigenvalues must have the value zero, for, from equation (3–18), letting $z_0 = 0$ be that eigenvalue, we get $\Phi_0 M = 0$. But recall from equation (3–10) that $\pi M = 0$ is the relation satisfied by the matrix M, with π the vector representing the probabilities of state of the underlying Markov chain. Since the eigenvector Φ_0 is only known to within a constant we can write $\Phi_0 = \pi$, showing $z_0 = 0$ is one of the eigenvalues. As a check, let $x \to \infty$ in equation (3–17a). But $F_j(\infty)$ is just the probability that j sources are in talk spurt which is precisely π_j. Thus, $F(\infty) = \pi = a_0 \Phi_0$. Since, as noted above, the eigenvector Φ_0 is only known to within a constant, we can set $a_0 = 1$ and get $\Phi_0 = \pi$, as already shown.

Equation (3–17a) now simplifies to

$$F(x) = \pi + \sum_{i:\mathrm{Re}[z_i < 0]} a_i \Phi_i e^{z_i x} \tag{3–17b}$$

In their paper, Anick et al show that the number of negative eigenvalues for this problem is just $N - \lfloor C \rfloor$ [ANIC 1982]. This is therefore the number of values of a_i that have to be found. But this is also the number of overload states $i > C$ of the driving Markov chain, the composite model of the N multiplexed voice sources (Figure 3–5). This observation enables us to set up the appropriate number of equations from which to find the remaining unknown a_i's. Specifically, if the system is in overload (more than C sources are in talkspurt), the buffer in Figure 3–7 is tending to *fill*. As a result, the buffer cannot be empty while in this state. Since $F_i(0)$ is the probability the buffer is empty, we immediately have

$$F_i(0) = 0 \qquad i > C \tag{3–20}$$

This provides the appropriate number of equations from which to find the a_i's.

As an example, say $N = 10$ and $C = 5.5$. Then $J_o = \lceil C \rceil = 6$, and there are 5 overload states, $i = 6$–10. There are the same number of negative eigenvalues z_i. From equations (3–17b) and (3–20), we write, replacing i by j in equation (3–20) to avoid confusion,

$$F_j(0) = 0 = \pi_j + \sum_{i=6}^{10} a_i \Phi_{ij} \qquad 6 \leq j \leq 10$$

This gives us the necessary five equations from which to find the five values of a_i in this case. More generally, we would have

$$F_j(0) = 0 = \pi_j + \sum_{i=J_o}^{N} a_i \Phi_{ij} \qquad J_o \le j \le N \qquad (3\text{--}21)$$

Given π_j and Φ_{ij}, we can solve these equations simultaneously to find the $N - \lfloor C \rfloor$ values of a_i.

Anick et al [ANIC 1982] have derived two specific equations from which to find the eigenvalues in the general case of N sources (see their equations. (22a) and (22b)). (A word of caution: They work with a normalized version $\alpha = 1$, of our basic equation (3–15). Alternatively, their λ is equivalent to our λ/α). They have also found explicit expressions for the eigenvectors and the coefficients $\{a_i\}$ for an equivalent formulation of the problem in which $F(x)$ and Φ_i are defined as column vectors (their matrix M is thus the transpose of our matrix M). These eigenvectors are called the left eigenvectors. They show how the right eigenvectors (our formulation) may be obtained from the left eigenvectors. They also provide a useful asymptotic solution to which we will return after first working out the simple example of one voice source, that is, $N = 1$.

For this case the matrix M, from equations (3–10) and (3–11), is the 2×2 matrix

$$M = \begin{bmatrix} -\lambda & \lambda \\ \alpha & -\alpha \end{bmatrix} = \begin{bmatrix} -\gamma & \gamma \\ 1 & -1 \end{bmatrix} \qquad \gamma \equiv \lambda/\alpha \qquad (3\text{--}22)$$

It is simpler here to work with the reduced matrix M' [equation (3–15c)]:

$$M' = \begin{bmatrix} \dfrac{\gamma}{C} & \dfrac{\gamma}{1-C} \\ \dfrac{-1}{C} & \dfrac{-1}{1-C} \end{bmatrix} \qquad (3\text{--}23)$$

The eigenvalues are then given by solving the matrix equation

$$zI - M' = 0 \qquad (3\text{--}24)$$

with I the identity matrix and z the set of eigenvalues to be found. It is left for the reader to show that the solutions turn out to be $z = 0$, as expected, and

$$z = \frac{\gamma}{C} - \frac{1}{1-C} \qquad (3\text{--}25)$$

Since we have shown that we must have $z < 0$, the capacity parameter C is immediately seen to be bounded by

$$\frac{\gamma}{1+\gamma} < C < 1 \qquad (3\text{--}26)$$

This is precisely what was stated much earlier in equation (3–2). There are two states of the birth-death model in this example: the underload state $i = 0$ and the overload state $i = 1$. For the fluid approximation to be applicable we must have the parameter C set at a value between the two. When the source moves to the silent (underload) state, the buffer tends to empty at the rate of C unit/sec. When the source is in talk spurt (overload), the buffer tends to fill at the rate $\alpha(1 - C)$ unit/sec. The equivalent utilization ρ is just

$$\rho \equiv \left(\frac{\gamma}{1+\gamma}\right)\frac{1}{C} < 1 \tag{3–27}$$

An alternate expression for the negative eigenvalue may be written, using equation (3–27):

$$z = -\frac{(1-\rho)(1+\gamma)}{(1-C)} \tag{3–25a}$$

This shows specifically that to have $z < 0$, we must have both $\rho < 1$ and $C < 1$.

Since there is only one negative eigenvalue in this case, the solution for the desired vector $\boldsymbol{F}(x)$ is given simply by

$$\boldsymbol{F}(x) = \boldsymbol{\pi} + a\boldsymbol{\Phi}e^{zx} \tag{3–28}$$

where we have dropped the subscripts on a_i and $\boldsymbol{\Phi}_i$ in equation (3–17b) since there is only one term in the sum. To find the eigenvector $\boldsymbol{\Phi} = [\Phi_0, \Phi_1]$ we use the eigenvector equation (3–18) or its equivalent

$$z\boldsymbol{\Phi} = \boldsymbol{\Phi}M' \tag{3–29}$$

with z, in this case, given by equation (3–25) and M' by equation (3–23). It is left to the reader to show that the solution to (3–29) is given by

$$\Phi_1/\Phi_0 = C/(1 - C) \tag{3–30}$$

Since the eigenvectors can only be found to within a constant (how can this be explained from equation (3–28)?), we choose

$$\Phi_0 = (1 - C) \quad \text{and} \quad \Phi_1 = C \tag{3–31}$$

arbitrarily. We thus have

$$\boldsymbol{F}(x) = \boldsymbol{\pi} + a[(1 - C), C]e^{zx} \tag{3–28a}$$

To find the remaining unknown parameter a, we use equations (3–20) and (3–21). In this case of one source, we have the one equation

$$F_1(0) = 0 = \pi_1 + a\Phi_1 \tag{3–32}$$

with π_1 the probability the source is in talk spurt (on) and $F_1(0)$ the probability the buffer is empty, given the source is in talk spurt. This latter probability is zero, from our previous discussion. For the single source case, the probability the source is in talk spurt, using our model (Figure 3–3), is just

$$\pi_1 = \frac{\lambda}{\alpha + \lambda} = \frac{\gamma}{1 + \gamma}, \qquad \gamma \equiv \lambda/\alpha \qquad (3\text{--}33)$$

This is the speaker activity factor (discussed earlier in this section) and left to the reader to derive. It was the value used in the N-speaker (source) model of equation (3–5). Using equations (3–33) and (3–31) in equation (3–32), the parameter a is readily found to be given by

$$a = -\pi_1/\Phi_1 = -\gamma/C(1 + \gamma) \qquad (3\text{--}34)$$

Finally, using these results, the solution for the probability distribution vector is given by equation (3–28a).

The individual components of $\boldsymbol{F}(x) = [F_0(x), F_1(x)]$ are, respectively,

$$F_0(x) = \pi_0 + a(1 - C)e^{zx}, \qquad (3\text{--}35)$$

the probability the buffer occupancy is less than x, given the source is silent, and

$$F_1(x) = \pi_1 + aCe^{zx}, \qquad (3\text{--}36)$$

given the source is in talk spurt. The probability $F(x)$ the buffer occupancy is less than or equal to x is just

$$F(x) = F_0(x) + F_1(x) = 1 + ae^{zx} \qquad (3\text{--}37)$$

(Why? More generally, for N sources explain why $F(x) = \Sigma_{i=0}^{N} F_i(x)$). The complementary probability distribution function $G(x)$, the probability that the buffer occupancy *exceeds* x is $1 - F(x)$. In this case, it is thus given by

$$G(x) = 1 - F(x) = -ae^{zx}$$
$$= \rho e^{-\frac{(1-\rho)(1+\gamma)}{(1-C)}x} \qquad (3\text{--}38)$$

with $\rho \equiv (\gamma/1 + \gamma)\ 1/C < 1$ the utilization defined previously in equation (3–27), and $\gamma \equiv \lambda/\alpha$. $G(x)$ is also called the *survivor function* and is often used as a measure of the probability of loss for x large. It can thus be used to find the buffer size required for a given loss probability. Note that $G(x)$ decreases exponentially with x, the buffer size (here given in "units of information"). The rate of decrease increases as C approaches 1; it decreases as the utilization ρ approaches 1.

We can now convert this probability of loss or buffer overflow to buffer size, in cells, by using equation (3–12). Specifically, the probability $P[l > i]$ that the buffer occupancy will exceed i cells is given, using equation (3–12), by

$$P[l > i] = G[\alpha i/V]$$

$$= \rho e^{-\frac{(1-\rho)(1+\gamma)}{(1-C)}\alpha i/V}$$

(3–39)

This expression implies that the larger the rate V of producing cells for a given capacity C, the larger the overflow (loss) probability will be. Alternatively, the buffer size i has to increase in proportion to V to keep the loss probability fixed. The probability of buffer overflow increases as well, with average talk spurt length $1/\alpha$.

Consider some examples. Say $\gamma = \lambda/\alpha = 2/3$. Then the speaker activity factor $\lambda/(\alpha + \lambda) = \gamma/1 + \gamma = 0.4$, the example cited earlier in this chapter. Let $1/\alpha = 1.25$ sec, the number used earlier as well. We also noted that $V = 170$ cells/sec for standard 64-kbps digital speech segmented into 53-octet ATM cells. Then $V/\alpha = 212.5$ cells. Say $C = 0.5$, that is, the transmission capacity devoted to the voice input is $VC = 85$ cells/sec (Figure 3–4). Then $\rho = \gamma/(1 + \gamma)\ 1/C = 0.8$. From equation (3–39), then,

$$P[l > i] = 0.8\ e^{-0.003i} \qquad C = 0.5 \tag{3–40}$$

To have $P[l > i] \doteq 10^{-4}$, equation (3–40) says that $i = 3000$ cells! This is clearly a large buffer required to handle one voice source. We now increase the capacity parameter to $C = 0.8$, keeping all other parameters fixed. Then $\rho = 0.5$, and equation (3–39) becomes

$$P[l > i] \doteq 0.5\ e^{-0.02i} \qquad C = 0.8 \tag{3–41}$$

For the same probability $P[l > i] = 10^{-4}$, the buffer size i required is now reduced to somewhat fewer than 450 cells, a considerable reduction in buffer size. This indicates the sensitivity of the overflow probability to the transmission capacity, because of the exponential dropoff in that probability.

What is the effect now of multiplexing multiple sources? One would expect an improvement in the behavior of the system; that is, a relative reduction in buffer size required, if the capacity C is scaled up according to the number of sources multiplexed. Anick et al have provided an asymptotic result for the probability $G(x) \equiv 1 - F(x)$ that the buffer occupancy exceeds x [ANIC 1982, equation (52)]. This result is obtained by noting that since the probability distribution is, in general, given by the sum of negative exponentials (equation (3–17b)), the exponential with the smallest negative eigenvalue will dominate. Using the symbol $-r$ to represent this eigenvalue, they show that

$$r = \frac{(1-\rho)(1+\gamma)}{1-C/N} \tag{3–42}$$

with the parameter ρ the utilization defined here, as an extension of equation (3–27), to be

$$\rho \equiv \left(\frac{\gamma}{1+\gamma}\right)\frac{N}{C} < 1 \qquad (3\text{--}27a)$$

[ANIC 1982, equation (51)]. (Note that equation (3–27a) is precisely the definition introduced earlier in this chapter in equation (3–2a)). This is precisely the solution we obtained for the case of $N = 1$! (See equation 3–25a). The probability $G(x)$ that the buffer occupancy exceeds x is then shown to be given approximately by

$$G(x) \sim A_N \rho^N e^{-rx} \qquad (3\text{--}43)$$

with A_N explicitly given [ANIC 1982, equation (52)]. Note that this is again in the form of equation (3–38), our own solution for the case of $N = 1$ source. The dominant behavior of $G(x)$ is determined by the exponential term and is modified somewhat by the multiplicative parameters ρ^N and A_N.

Equations (3–42) and (3–43) indicate that the asymptotic exponential term e^{-rx} of the buffer overflow probability $G(x)$ is independent of the number of sources N multiplexed, if the capacity is scaled up correspondingly; note that the asymptotic exponential parameter r depends only on the ratio C/N. (Recall that $\rho \equiv (\gamma/1 + \gamma)N/C$ depends only on C/N as well). Converting the probability $G(x)$ that buffer overload exceeds the value x, in units of information, to the desired probability $P[l > i]$, that the buffer overload exceeds i cells, we have, again using equation (3–12),

$$P[l > i] \sim A_N \rho^N e^{-r\alpha i/V} \qquad (3\text{--}44)$$

with r given by equation (3–42). To a first approximation, then, the buffer size i required to keep the buffer overflow probability to some desired probability is independent of the number N of sources multiplexed, providing the capacity C is scaled accordingly. This says that the number of buffers *per source*, i/N, decreases as N increases. Actually, because of the concurrent reduction in $P[l > i]$, due to the ρ^N parameter, the buffer size required reduces even more. (This assumes the parameter A_N doesn't change very much with N). This also says that the queueing delay *decreases* as the number of sources multiplexed increases. As the transmission capacity VC, in units of cells/sec, increases, with the buffer size kept fixed, or even decreased somewhat, the wait time in the buffer decreases correspondingly. Statistically multiplexing N sources thus provides an improvement in both the buffer size per source required and in the total queueing time in the buffer.

How valid are the asymptotic approximation of equation (3–44) and the comments just made, based on this approximation? Daigle and Langford have carried out the complete fluid-flow calculations for some examples, comparing them to simulation. Some of their results are reproduced in Figures 3–8 to 3–10 [DAIG 1986, Figures 6-8]. The curves shown are plots of $G(\alpha i/V)$, the buffer overflow (loss) probability, or survivor function, versus buffer size i, in

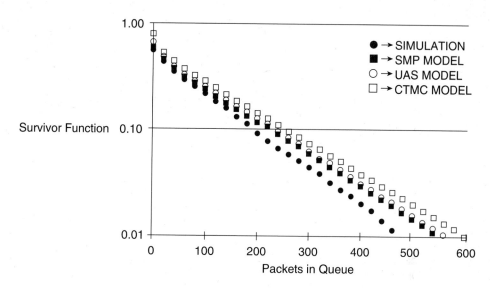

FIGURE 3–8 ■ Queue length survivor function, $N = 8$, server utilization $= 0.85$ (from [DAIG 1986], Figure 6. © 1986 IEEE).

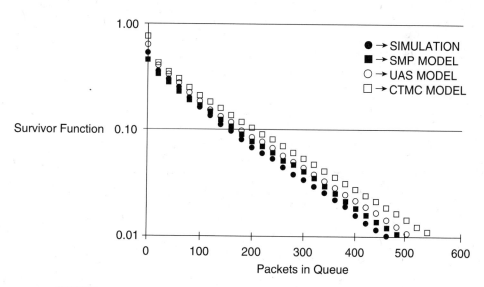

FIGURE 3–9 ■ Queue length survivor function, $N = 15$, server utilization $= 0.85$ (from [DAIG 1986], Figure 7. © 1986 IEEE).

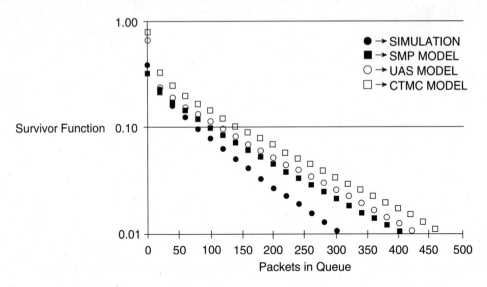

FIGURE 3–10 ▪ Queue length survivor function, $N = 30$, server utilization $= 0.85$ (from [DAIG 1986], Figure 8. © 1986 IEEE).

packets (cells in our notation). These curves have been calculated for the case of $V = 62.5$ cells/sec, average talk spurt $1/\alpha = 1.35$ sec, average silence interval $1/\lambda = 1.65$ sec, and $\rho = 0.85$. The ratio λ/α is then 0.82, and the speaker activity factor $\gamma/(1 + \gamma) = 0.45$. The curves labeled UAS in these figures are those for the fluid-flow approach (called the Uniform Arrival and Service model in the notation of the paper). The SMP model results in Figures 3–8 to 3–10 refer to the Semi-Markov model mentioned earlier in this section. The CTMC model corresponds to the Markov-modulated Poisson process approach to be discussed in the next section.

For the numbers chosen above, the parameter r in equation (3–44) is calculated to be 0.58. The exponent appearing in equation (3–44) is then $r\alpha/V = 0.0069$. Note that the curves in Figures 3–8 to 3–10, drawn on a logarithmic scale to the base 10, tend to be almost linear as predicted by equation (3–44). The slope of the UAS curve turns out to be approximately −0.003. This is exactly what is predicted by equation (3–44) in this example, on writing $\log_{10} P[l > i]$: The slope of the resultant linear equation is just

$$-\frac{r\alpha}{V} \log_{10} e = 0.0069 \times 0.434 = -0.003$$

The single exponent of equation (3–44) thus provides an accurate measure of the slope of the analytical curves in Figures 3–8 to 3–10. The actual value of the overflow probability for a given buffer occupancy i or, conversely, the buffer size i required for a given overflow probability is not as accurate, however: In the case of $N = 8$ multiplexed sources (Figure 3–8), equation (3–44) provides a value of $i = 480$ cells for $P[l > i] = 0.01$ with A_N arbitrarily set equal to 1. Figure 3–8 has $i = 570$ for this value of $P[l > i]$. If the number of multiplexed sources is increased to $N = 15$ (Figure 3–9), equation (3–44) predicts $i = 313$ cells in queue with A_N again taken equal to 1. Figure 3–9 has the value $i = 500$ at this point. Presumably the combination of the variation in A_N and added eigenvalue terms required to calculate $P[l > i]$ more accurately give rise to this difference. Note also that equation (3–44) is an *asymptotic* result for *small* values of $P[l > i]$. The curves of Figures 3–8 to 3–10 only go as low as 0.01. But the simple form of equation (3–44) can still be quite useful in providing first-order buffer design results.

Figures 3–8 and 3–9 indicate that the fluid-flow model (the UAS model in these figures) approximates the simulation results fairly well in the case of $N = 15$ sources, somewhat less well for $N = 8$ sources, and differs substantially from simulation results for $N = 30$ sources. It does provide conservative design results in all cases, however. (In practice, much smaller values of buffer overflow probability, of 10^{-6} or even less, might be chosen for design purposes.) The fluid-flow model and approximation equation (3–44) obtained from it, can thus provide useful "back of the envelope" results in sizing buffers for statistically multiplexed sources. We shall return to the fluid-flow model later in characterizing video sources.

The Markov-modulated Poisson process model, the CTMC model in these figures, provides results that differ even more from simulation. Other cases discussed in [DAIG 1986] indicate that this model is always less accurate than the fluid-flow model for this problem of multiplexed voice sources. Nonetheless, we describe this model in the next section, since we will find it useful later as one possible model of video sources. As noted, we will return to the fluid-source model in discussing video traffic modeling, and shall use it in the next chapter in discussing traffic control in the broadband ATM environment.

3.4 ■ MARKOV-MODULATED POISSON PROCESS: APPLICATION TO VOICE MULTIPLEXING

The Markov-modulated Poisson process (MMPP) has been used extensively in the representation and study of a variety of traffic models. In this section we apply this process to the same problem discussed in the last section: the statistical multiplexing of N voice sources. We shall use this process again later, to model video traffic.

The Markov-modulated Poisson process (MMPP) is defined to be one having n states in general, with the process, while in any state i, $1 \leq i \leq n$, behaving as a Poisson process with a state-dependent rate parameter λ_i. Transitions between states are governed by an underlying continuous-time Markov

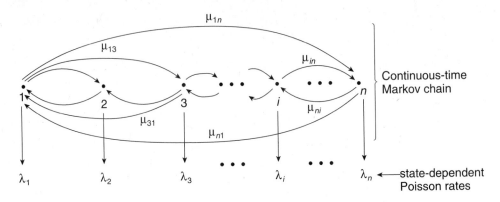

FIGURE 3–11 ■ Markov-modulated Poisson process (selected transitions only shown).

chain. An arbitrary example appears in Figure 3–11, with only a few of the possible state transitions shown.

Our emphasis, in past sections, on the continuous-time Markov chain, was on the special case of the birth-death model, with state transitions limited to adjacent states only. Our discussion in this section, and those following, will continue to focus on this special case. More generally, however, transitions to nonadjacent states could be present, as indicated in Figure 3–11. The parameter μ_{ij} would then represent the rate of transition between states i and j, as shown in Figure 3–11. It is left to the reader to show, in this more general case, that the n-element row vector

$$\boldsymbol{\pi} = [\pi_1, \pi_2, \ldots \pi_i \ldots, \pi_n] \tag{3–45}$$

representing the n stationary state probabilities, again satisfies the matrix equation

$$\boldsymbol{\pi} M = 0 \tag{3–46}$$

with the $n \times n$ matrix M given, in general, by

$$M = \begin{bmatrix} \mu_{11} & \mu_{12} & \mu_{13} & \cdots & \mu_{1ij} & \cdots & \mu_{1n} \\ \mu_{21} & \mu_{22} & \mu_{23} & \cdots & \mu_{2j} & \cdots & \mu_{2n} \\ \vdots & \vdots & \vdots & & \vdots & & \vdots \\ \mu_{i1} & \mu_{i2} & \mu_{i3} & \cdots & \mu_{ij} & \cdots & \mu_{in} \\ \vdots & \vdots & \vdots & & \vdots & & \vdots \\ \mu_{n1} & \mu_{n2} & \mu_{n3} & \cdots & \mu_{nj} & \cdots & \mu_{nn} \end{bmatrix} \tag{3–47}$$

The diagonal rate parameter μ_{ii} is here given by

$$\mu_{ii} = -\sum_{\substack{j=1 \\ j \neq i}}^{n} \mu_{ij} \qquad 1 \leq i \leq n \tag{3–48}$$

The matrix M is the infinitesimal generating matrix for the general continuous-time Markov chain. Equations (3–45) to (3–48) extend the earlier analysis of equations (3–9) to (3–11) for the special case of N multiplexed voice sources to the more general case of the continuous-time Markov chain. The derivation of equation (3–46) is carried out the same way equation (3–10) was previously: by setting up the balance equations for the chain in Figure 3–11, as done previously in equations (3–8) and (3–8a), and then showing that they may be represented by the compact matrix form of equation (3–46).

We have shown briefly above how the statistically-multiplexed voice source model of the past sections may be extended to incorporate a general continuous-time Markov chain as the basic transition mechanism between states. The fluid-flow analysis of the previous section may be similarly generalized, giving rise to a more general form of equation (3–15b) as well. This will become apparent later, after our discussion of the application of the stochastic flow model to video sources.

Rather than proceed with the general MMPP analysis at this point, however, we return to the problem described in the past sections: the characterization, modeling, and analysis of N voice sources multiplexed at a buffer. This enables us to apply the MMPP analysis to a problem with which we are already familiar. It also serves as an introduction to the use of the technique in video modeling later, as already noted. We again follow the approach of [DAIG 1986].

We proceed as previously, by first modeling each voice source as being in two states, talk spurt and silence, with the rate λ, again representing the rate of transition from the silent state to talk spurt, and α the rate in the reverse direction. The difference between this model and the earlier one, however, is that while a source is in talk spurt, its voice packets are assumed to be transmitted randomly, obeying a Poisson process with average rate β. This assumption gives rise to the MMPP model.

The single voice-source model is now the one shown in Figure 3–12. This is clearly not an accurate model of a voice source. It replaces the source's periodic generation of packets (cells) while in talk spurt by a random (Poisson) arrival process. We have already seen, from Figures 3–8 to 3–10, that this model provides the poorest results of the three shown there, in comparison

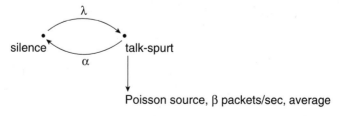

FIGURE 3–12 ■ Poisson model, single voice source.

with simulation. But, as we shall see, the model lends itself quite readily to analysis and can be extended to handle various service strategies. The MMPP model will be seen later to be particularly applicable, as already noted, to the modeling of video traffic. The analysis here thus serves as an introduction to the use of the MMPP model in a variety of other telecommunications traffic situations.

Now consider the statistical multiplexing of N voice sources such as that of Figure 3–12. With $i \leq N$ voice sources in talk spurt it is apparent, from the additive property of Poisson sources, that the composite source in this case is also Poisson, with an arrival rate parameter $i\beta$ cells/sec, on the average. This gives rise to the special type of MMPP model shown in Figure 3–13. This is to be compared to the model of Figure 3–5, which was previously used to represent N multiplexed voice sources. The Poisson arrival rate $i\beta$ cells/sec with i sources in talk spurt, corresponds to the parameter iV cells/sec used previously in describing the multiplexed source output. The previous model, while capturing the periodic arrival of cells, had all i sources synchronized. The model here does capture the randomness in cell generation among the i sources, but cannot capture the periodicity in cell arrivals of any source in talk spurt.

We now apply this MMPP model to the buffering of the N voice sources at a statistical multiplexer. This is the same problem to which the fluid-flow analysis was devoted in the last section. To carry out the analysis of statistical multiplexing using the MMPP model of Figure 3–13, we must define the cell (packet) length distribution or, equivalently, the multiplexer service-time distribution. We choose the time-honored exponential distribution, with average cell length $1/v$ sec, since this enables the analysis to proceed fairly systematically. This is, of course, not realistic for ATM multiplexers, where cells are of fixed length. It does render the analysis easier to carry out. It does of course provide another reason as to why analytical results may differ from simulation, as shown by Figures 3–8 to 3–10.

An average cell length of $1/v$ corresponds to an average cell service rate of v cells/sec. This must then be the capacity of the multiplexer and is so shown in the buffer model of Figure 3–14. This is to be compared to the previous model of Figure 3–4. As in that model, we may define a utilization para-

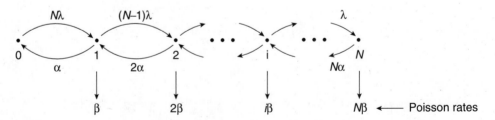

FIGURE 3–13 ■ MMPP model, N multiplexed voice sources.

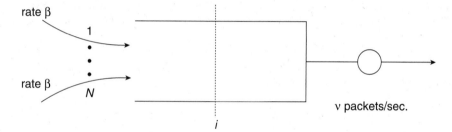

FIGURE 3–14 ■ Statistical multiplexer for input model of Figure 3–13.

meter ρ or, equivalently, the condition the capacity ν must satisfy to ensure a stable solution in the case of an infinite buffer. Specifically, with each source delivering an average of β cells/sec when in talk spurt, the average number of cells/sec entering the queue of Figure 3–14 is just $N\beta(\lambda/\alpha + \lambda)$. This must be less than the capacity ν, so that we have

$$N\beta\left(\frac{\lambda}{\alpha + \lambda}\right) < \nu \tag{3–49}$$

or, equivalently,

$$\rho \equiv N\beta\left(\frac{\lambda}{\alpha + \lambda}\right)/\nu < 1 \tag{3–50}$$

for an infinite buffer. These inequalities are to be compared with equations (3–2) and (3–2a), or (3–27a), the capacity and utilization expressions introduced earlier in this chapter.

The objective now is to, again, find the probability distribution of buffer occupancy. Recall that in the fluid-flow model of the previous section we did this by first finding the joint (two-dimensional) cumulative probability distribution $F_j(x)$, the probability that the buffer occupancy is less than or equal to x with j sources on. We use a similar approach here, since the buffer occupancy (a random variable) is dependent on the number of sources in talk spurt (itself a random variable). We didn't mention this point earlier, but it is the reason we conditioned on the number of sources j in talk spurt, in finding $F_j(x)$ in the previous section.

We let the integer value $i \geq 0$ again represent the queue state; j is, as already noted, the number of sources in talk spurt. We then define p_{ij} as the joint probability that the queue length is i with j sources on:

$$p_{ij} = P[\text{queue length} = i, j \text{ sources on}] \tag{3–51}$$

This quantity is analogous to the function $F_j(x)$ appearing in the fluid-flow model. This is the probability for which we have to solve to find all quantities of interest. The marginal probability p_i, that the queue length is i, is then given of course by

$$p_i = \sum_{j=0}^{N} p_{ij} \qquad (3\text{–}52)$$

The doublet (i, j) defines a two-dimensional state space. A finite buffer of maximum value B would then mean this state space ranges from 0 to N in the j direction; from 0 to B in the i direction. To simplify the analysis we assume the buffer is infinite. The resultant two-dimensional state space, with transitions between states superimposed, appears in Figure 3–15. Note that the two-dimensional birth-death representation of Figure 3–15 is made possible precisely because of the assumption of Poisson arrivals at a rate β, for each voice source when in talk spurt, as well as exponential service-time distribution with parameter ν. Details are left to the reader.

There are a number of ways of solving for p_{ij} using the two-dimensional state space of Figure 3–15. Employing moment-generating functions (transforms of the probabilities) is one possibility [SCHW 1987], [DAIG 1992]. We

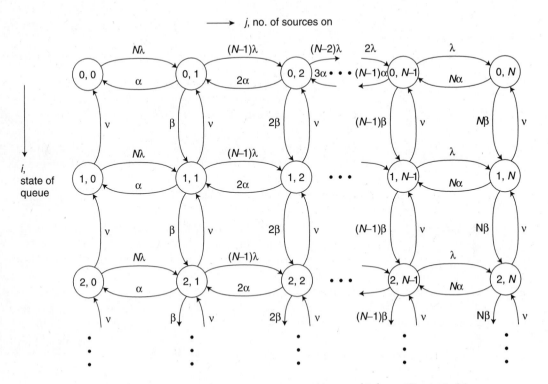

FIGURE 3–15 ■ State space representation, multiplexer, Figure 3–14.

focus here on an algorithmic technique called the *matrix geometric* approach [NEUT 1981], [DAIG 1992]. We shall mention as well, a simple approximation technique that is useful under conditions in which the two random variables i and j may be decoupled. This approach turns out to be particularly applicable in the case of video sources, as we shall demonstrate later.

All the solution techniques rely on setting up two-dimensional balance equations for the two-dimensional state space of Figure 3–15. We do this for the first, $i = 0$, row of Figure 3–15. The writing down of the remainder of the equations is left as an exercise for the reader. As is the case with one-dimensional balance equations, we equate the rate of leaving a state to the rate of entering it. We then get first, for $j = 0$,

$$i = 0, j = 0: \qquad N\lambda p_{00} = \alpha p_{01} + \nu p_{10} \qquad (3\text{–}53)$$

We choose to rewrite this in an alternate form suitable for the matrix geometric solution technique:

$$p_{00} = (1 - N\lambda)p_{00} + \alpha p_{01} + \nu p_{10} \qquad (3\text{–}53a)$$

Continuing for other values of j, the general balance equation for $1 \leq j \leq N - 1$ is readily shown to be given by

$$i = 0, 1 \leq j \leq N - 1: \quad [(N - j)\lambda + j\alpha + j\beta]p_{0j} = [N - (j - 1)]\lambda p_{0j-1} \\ + (j + 1)\,\alpha p_{0j+1} + \nu p_{1j} \qquad (3\text{–}54)$$

Rewriting this equation as in the case above of $j = 0$, we get

$$p_{0j} = [N - (j - 1)]\lambda p_{0j-1} + [1 - (N - j)\lambda - j\alpha - j\beta]p_{0j} + (j + 1)\alpha p_{0j+1} + \nu p_{1j} \qquad (3\text{–}54a)$$

Finally, to complete the case for $i = 0$, we write the boundary equation for $j = N$:

$$i = 0, j = N: \qquad (N\alpha + N\beta)p_{0N} = \lambda p_{0N-1} + \nu p_{1N} \qquad (3\text{–}55)$$

Again, rewriting this in an alternate form, we have

$$p_{0N} = \lambda p_{0N-1} + [1 - N\alpha - N\beta]p_{0N} + \nu p_{1N} \qquad (3\text{–}55a)$$

The set of equations (3–53a), (3–54a), and (3–55a) may be written concisely in matrix form. To do this define a set of $(N + 1)$-element row vectors $\boldsymbol{p}_i$:

$$\boldsymbol{p}_i \equiv [p_{i0}, p_{i1}, p_{i2}, \ldots, p_{iN}] \qquad (3\text{–}56)$$

It is then left to the reader to show that the set of equations (3–53a), (3–54a), and (3–55a) may now be written in the equivalent compact matrix-vector equation

$$\boldsymbol{p}_0 = \boldsymbol{p}_0 B_0 + \boldsymbol{p}_1 B_1 \qquad (3\text{–}57)$$

[NEUT 1981] Neuts, M. F., *Matrix-Geometric Solutions in Stochastic Modeling: An Algorithmic Approach*, Baltimore, MD: Johns Hopkins University Press, 1981.

The $(N + 1) \times (N + 1)$ matrices B_0 and B_1 are readily shown to be given by

$$B_0 = \begin{bmatrix} (1-N\lambda) & N\lambda & 0 & \cdots & 0 \\ \alpha & [1-\alpha-(N-1)\lambda-\beta] & (N-1)\lambda & \cdots & 0 \\ 0 & 2\alpha & [1-2\alpha-(N-2)\lambda-2\beta] & \cdots & 0 \\ 0 & 0 & 3\alpha & \cdots & 0 \\ \cdot & \cdot & 0 & \cdot & \cdot \\ \cdot & \cdot & \cdot & \cdot & \cdot \\ \cdot & \cdot & \cdot & \cdot & \cdot \\ \cdot & \cdot & \cdot & \cdots & \lambda \\ 0 & 0 & 0 & \cdots & (1-N\alpha-N\beta) \end{bmatrix} \quad (3\text{--}58)$$

and

$$B_1 = \text{diag}[v, v, \ldots, v] \quad (3\text{--}59)$$

It is now left to the reader to show that the complete set of balance equations for the entire two-dimensional chain, for all values of i, may be written in terms of one (infinite-dimensional) matrix equation:

$$\boldsymbol{p} = \boldsymbol{p}\,P \quad (3\text{--}60)$$

Here

$$\boldsymbol{p} = [\boldsymbol{p}_0, \boldsymbol{p}_1, \boldsymbol{p}_2, \ldots \boldsymbol{p}_i, \ldots] \quad (3\text{--}61)$$

with the $(N + 1)$-element vector $\boldsymbol{p}_i$, the vector defined previously by equation (3–56). An equation of the form of (3–60) serves as the defining equation in discrete-time Markov chains with the matrix P there called the transition probability matrix [KLEI 1975], [KARL 1975]. Just as in that case, the infinite-dimensional matrix P here is a *stochastic* matrix, with each of its rows summing to 1. The matrix P in equation (3–60) is found to be representable as a number of repetitive $(N + 1) \times (N + 1)$ submatrices as follows:

$$P = \begin{bmatrix} B_0 & A_0 & 0 & 0 & \cdots \\ B_1 & A_1 & A_0 & 0 & \cdots \\ 0 & A_2 & A_1 & A_0 & \cdots \\ 0 & 0 & A_2 & A_1 & \cdots \\ 0 & 0 & 0 & A_2 & \cdots \\ \cdot & \cdot & \cdot & \cdot & \cdots \\ \cdot & \cdot & \cdot & \cdot & \cdots \\ \cdot & \cdot & \cdot & \cdot & \cdots \end{bmatrix} \quad (3\text{--}62)$$

[KARL 1975]   Karlin, S., and H. M. Taylor, *A First Course in Stochastic Processes,* 2nd ed. San Diego: Academic Press, 1975.

B_0 and B_1 are of course the two matrices defined by equations (3–58) and (3–59). It is left as an exercise for the reader to specify the three additional matrices A_0, A_1, A_2.

It is apparent from equations (3–60) and (3–62) that equation (3–57) is contained within equation (3–60). From equation (3–60), using equation (3–62), it is also apparent that $\boldsymbol{p}_i$, $i \geq 1$, may also be represented by the (finite-dimensional) matrix equation

$$\boldsymbol{p}_i = \boldsymbol{p}_{i-1}A_0 + \boldsymbol{p}_i A_1 + \boldsymbol{p}_{i+1} A_2 \qquad i \geq 1 \tag{3–63}$$

The matrix-geometric solution technique utilizes the repetitive structural form of equation (3–62) and matrices like this to provide algorithmic solutions to equation (3–60) [Neuts, 1981].

Rather than focus on equation (3–60) at this point, we detour somewhat to summarize the matrix-geometric solution technique in a more general context. We follow the approach of [NEUT 1981]. Consider a matrix equation of the form

$$\boldsymbol{x} = \boldsymbol{x}P \tag{3–64}$$

with $\boldsymbol{x}$ an infinite-valued row vector in general, whose elements x_i sum to l:

$$\sum_i x_i = 1 \tag{3–65}$$

Alternately, we may write

$$\boldsymbol{x}\, \boldsymbol{e}^T = 1 \tag{3–65a}$$

with $\boldsymbol{e}^T$ a unit column vector. The matrix P is a stochastic matrix, with rows summing to 1.

To apply the matrix-geometric solution technique we assume P has a repetitive structure of the form

$$P = \begin{bmatrix} B_0 & A_0 & 0 & 0 & \cdots \\ B_1 & A_1 & A_0 & 0 & \cdots \\ B_2 & A_2 & A_1 & A_0 & \cdots \\ B_3 & A_3 & A_2 & A_1 & \cdots \\ \cdot & \cdot & \cdot & \cdot & \cdots \\ \cdot & \cdot & \cdot & \cdot & \cdots \\ \cdot & \cdot & \cdot & \cdot & \cdots \end{bmatrix} \tag{3–66}$$

with the A_i's and B_i's all $m \times m$ nonnegative matrices. (Note then that equation (3–62) is a special case of equation (3–66) incorporating only two and three B_i and A_i matrices, respectively). Such matrices occur in the representation of Markov chains, as already noted.

The solution technique for the vector $\boldsymbol{x}$ proceeds as follows: Partition $\boldsymbol{x}$ as the vector

$$x = [x_0, x_1, x_2, \dots] \tag{3–67}$$

with x_k an m-element row vector. Then we have, from equations (3–64) and (3–66),

$$x_0 = \sum_{v=0}^{\infty} x_v B_v \tag{3–68}$$

$$x_k = \sum_{v=0}^{\infty} x_{k+v-1} A_v, \qquad k \geq 1, \tag{3–69}$$

with

$$\sum_{k=0}^{\infty} x_k\, e^T = 1 \tag{3–70}$$

and e^T again a unit column vector. (Note how the partitioning of x and the resultant set of equations (3–68) and (3–69) parallel and generalize our own set of equations (3–57), (3–61), and (3–63).) Neuts has shown that the desired solution for the m-element row vector x_i is found to be given by

$$x_{i+1} = x_i R \qquad i \geq 0 \tag{3–71}$$

with R an $m \times m$ matrix. The matrix R is itself found as the minimal, nonnegative solution to the matrix equation

$$R = \sum_{k=0}^{\infty} R^k A_k \tag{3–72}$$

(In our special case, we have $R = A_0 + RA_1 + R^2A_2$).

The solution x to the initial equation (3–64) is then replaced by that of finding the matrix R.

Before proceeding further with this solution approach, two problems with the method should be pointed out. First, for this method to be applied, the eigenvalues of the matrix R must lie *inside* the unit disk; that is, its spectral radius must be less than 1. This poses a problem with *finite* chains (as obtained with finite buffers, for example), for which the eigenvalues may lie *outside* the unit disk. Hajek has extended Neut's technique to include this case [HAJE 1982]. Second, computational experience indicates that the algorithms used to find R (we shall mention two such algorithms shortly) converge rather

[HAJE 1982]   Hajek, B., "Birth-Death Processes on Integers with Phases and General Boundaries," *J. Appl. Prob., 19* (1982): 488–499.

slowly, leading to difficulties in solving problems with large m (N in our case). Ye has developed an efficient algorithm for dealing with both problems [YE 1991].

These caveats aside, we now return to the matrix-geometric solution approach. As noted, the problem of finding x_i has now switched to that of finding the matrix R, the minimal nonnegative solution to equation (3–72). It is also clear from equation (3–71) that the m-element vector x_0 must be separately found as well. Consider the solution for x_0 first. We assume R has already been found. Note from equation (3–68) that x_0 is itself given in terms of the other vectors x_v and the known matrices B_v. Substituting the solution equation (3–71) for x_v into equation (3–68), we obtain

$$x_0 = x_0 \sum_{v=0}^{\infty} R^v B_v$$

$$= x_0 \, B(R) \tag{3–73}$$

with

$$B(R) = \sum_{v=0}^{\infty} R^v B_v \tag{3–74}$$

It turns out that the matrix $B(R)$ is itself a stochastic matrix. The vector x_0 is, from equation (3–73), the left eigenvector of this matrix. (In our special example, we have, from equation (3–57), $B(R) = B_0 + R\, B_1$).

The vector x_0 is not completely specified by the solution to the eigenvector equation (3–73). It must also be chosen such that all the x_k's satisfy the normalization condition of equation (3–65).

There are a number of ways of carrying out the normalization. One may find x_0 from equation (3–73) to within some arbitrary constant, and find the other x_i's using equation (3–71) and sum all the elements x_j. The sum will turn out to equal some value K, say. Dividing all elements x_j through by K provides the desired normalization. Alternately, focus on the normalization condition of equation (3–65), or its equivalent, equation (3–65a). Define an m-element unit column vector $e_m{}^T$. We can then write

$$x e^T = \sum_{i=0}^{\infty} x_i e_m{}^T = 1 \tag{3–65b}$$

[YE 1991]   Ye, J., "Analysis of Multimedia Traffic Queues with Finite Buffer and Overload Control—the Folding Algorithm," *Ph.D. dissertation,* Columbia University, 1991.

Replacing x_i by the value $x_0 R^i$ from equation (3–71), we get

$$xe^T = x_0 \sum_{i=0}^{\infty} R^i \, e_m^{\ T}$$

(3–65c)

$$= x_0 [I - R]^{-1} e_m^{\ T} = 1$$

with I the $m \times m$ identity matrix. (Note that $|R| < 1$ is required in general for this representation to converge, just the problem raised earlier). Requiring x_0 to satisfy equation (3–65c) provides another way of normalizing x_0.

The matrix-geometric approach may be summarized thus far as follows:

1. Find R by solving the equation (3–72).
2. Find the vector x_0 by solving the eigenvector equation (3–73).
3. Normalize x_0 by either using equation (3–65c), or, as noted earlier, by finding all x_i and normalizing the sum of all elements x_j.
4. Finally we have, from equation (3–71),

$$x_i = x_0 R^i$$

We have left for the end, the remaining problem of finding the matrix R. There are a number of ways one can solve equation (3–72) for R. Neuts has suggested two possible recursive techniques [NEUT 1981]. One approach is to start with the basic equation

$$X = \sum_{k=0}^{\infty} X^k A_k$$

(3–75)

Let $X(0)$ be an initial trial solution. Keep iterating, using $X(l - 1)$ to find $X(l)$. As an example, one can select $X(0) = 0$, in which case the next, iterated, solution, would be $X(1) = A_0$. Then $X(2) = A_0 + X(1) + X^2(1)A_2 + \ldots$ Neuts has shown that $\{X(l)\}$ converges monotonically to the desired minimal nonnegative solution $X^* = R$.

A second suggested recursive solution is obtained by rewriting equation (3–72) as

$$R[I - A_1] = \sum_{\substack{k=0 \\ k \neq 1}}^{\infty} R^k A_k$$

(3–76)

Here, I is again the $m \times m$ identity matrix.

Post-multiplying both sides of equation (3–76) by $[I - A_1]^{-1}$, we get

$$R = \left[\sum_{\substack{k=0 \\ k \neq 1}}^{\infty} R^k A_k \right] [I - A_1]^{-1}$$

(3–77)

We now start with a trial solution such as $R = 0$, and again iterate.

In the problem with which we are dealing, we have, as special cases of equations (3–75) and (3–76),

$$X = A_0 + XA_1 + X^2A_2 \tag{3-78}$$

and

$$R = [A_0 + R^2A_2][I - A_1]^{-1} \tag{3-79}$$

Either one of these two equations is to be solved iteratively for R.

As a simple, almost trivial, example of the use of the matrix-geometric method, consider the infinite $M/M/1$ queue. Its state diagram is shown in Figure 3–16. In this case the A and B matrices of equation (3–62) become scalars:

$$A_0 = \lambda \qquad A_1 = 1 - \lambda - \mu \qquad A_2 = \mu \tag{3-80}$$
$$B_0 = (1 - \lambda) \qquad B_1 = A_2 = \mu$$

The infinite-dimensional P matrix of equation (3–62) is then given by

$$P = \begin{bmatrix} 1-\lambda & \lambda & 0 & 0 & \cdots \\ \mu & 1-\lambda-\mu & \lambda & 0 & \cdots \\ 0 & \mu & 1-\lambda-\mu & \lambda & \cdots \\ 0 & 0 & \mu & 1-\lambda-\mu & \cdots \\ \cdot & \cdot & \cdot & \cdot \\ \cdot & \cdot & \cdot & \cdot \\ \cdot & \cdot & \cdot & \cdot \end{bmatrix} \tag{3-81}$$

Note that the matrix is stochastic (its rows sum to 1) as expected. Note also, as a check, that this resultant P matrix could have been written down by inspection.

The equation to be solved for R is then just

$$R = A_0 RA_1 + R^2A_2$$
$$= \lambda + (1 - \lambda - \mu)R + \mu R^2 \tag{3-82}$$

R is, itself, just a scalar. The quadratic equation (3–82) may thus be solved directly for R, yielding the well-known result that $R = \lambda/\mu \equiv \rho$. (A second root, $R = 1$, is not acceptable. Recall we stipulated that the spectral radius of R must be less than unity). Hence we immediately have, from equation (3–71),

$$x_{i+1} = \rho x_i$$

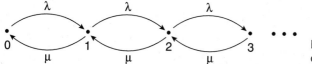

FIGURE 3–16 ▪ $M/M/1$ queue state diagram.

and

$$x_i = \rho^i x_0 \qquad (3\text{–}83)$$

the standard solution for the $M/M/1$ queue.

Daigle and Langford have applied the matrix-geometric technique to the statistical multiplexing problems of Figures 3–14 and 3–15, as already noted [DAIG 1986]. They have used this technique to calculate the complementary probability distribution function of the cells in the statistical multiplexer queue of Figure 3–14. As noted in the previous section, this function is also called the queue length *survivor function* and can be used to approximate the cell loss probability for finite queues. Their results appear in Figures 3–8 to 3–10 for the case of $v = 62.5$ cells/sec, an average talk spurt of $1/\alpha = 1.35$ sec, average silence intervals of $1/\lambda = 1.65$ sec, and a utilization $\rho \equiv N\beta \, (\lambda/\alpha + \lambda)/v = 0.85$ [equation (3–50)]. The plots are for $N = 8$, 15, and 30, respectively. The MMPP results are labeled CTMC model (for continuous-time Markov chain). Note, as already pointed out in the previous sections, that this model provides the least accurate results of the three models analyzed.

The purpose of introducing the MMPP model here, however, was not solely to check its utility for voice sources. We have already noted that voice sources produce a periodic stream of cells during talk spurt. The MMPP model assumes cells are generated at varying random, Poisson, rates in the various states. Thus, the relative inaccuracy of the model for the multiplexed voice source case was to be expected. We shall find, in discussing video traffic modeling in the sections following, that the MMPP model *does* provide useful results in that case. We shall, in fact, develop a simple approximation for the calculation of buffer statistics in the statistical multiplexer model of Figure 3–14, using the MMPP model, that provides accurate results in the case of video, and that obviates the need to use the matrix-geometric approach introduced here.

3.5 ■ VIDEO TRAFFIC CHARACTERIZATION

Recall that in Chapter 2 we discussed the various service classes defined to be covered by broadband ISDN (B-ISDN). Voice traffic, discussed in detail in this chapter, provides the prime example of class-A stream traffic with constant bit rate. Video traffic, in compressed form, is expected to be the prime example of class-B, stream traffic with variable bit rate (see Table 2–1). As already noted in Chapters 1 and 2, video and high-resolution images represent the prime candidates for the use of the high-capacity capability to be provided by B-ISDN.

In its raw, uncompressed form, a video signal is representative of continuous bit-rate traffic: Video frames to be transmitted at the common rate of 30 frames/sec are sampled and quantized, picture element (pixel for short) by picture element, providing a constant number of bits/frame, and hence bits/sec. As an example, consider the North American standard of approximately 500×500 or 250,000 pixels per frame. If an 8-bit gray scale is used (256 levels of amplitude), this gives rise to a rate of 2 Mbits/frame, or a 60 Mbits/sec signal. For three colors to be transmitted, this means 180 Mbits/sec capacity is required. Compression, using a variety of coding techniques, can reduce these values considerably. With 0.5 bit/pixel transmission attained, on the average, through the use of compression, for example, this reduces the transmission rate for a video signal to 3.75 Mbits/sec for monochrome video or 11.25 Mbits/sec for color signals. Elsewhere in the world, Europe in particular, higher resolution signals are used (more pixels/frame), and the transmission rates required are increased correspondingly.

If we now go to digital, high-definition television (HDTV), using, say, 10^6 pixels/frame, the uncompressed transmission rate also rises correspondingly. In this case 720 Mbits/sec capacity would be required per TV channel! Recent gains in compression techniques have brought this number down considerably to an expected value of the order of 50 Mbits/sec or less. Examples of coding techniques adopted are DPCM, DCT (discrete cosine transform), and subband coding for intraframe compression [IEEE 1989]. Interframe coding and motion compensation techniques are also required to provide the compression desired. A broadcast TV standard designated MPEG-2 has been developed for that application.

MPEG-2 coding is one of several coding standards being developed by the Moving Pictures Experts Group (MPEG), a working group of ISO and IEC, designated ISO/IEC JTC1/SC29/WG11. MPEG-1, operating at 1.5 Mbps, deals with the compression of video signals for digital storage media such as CD-ROMs. MPEG-2 involves higher-quality coding, including that for HDTV. The MPEG coding standards use interframe, as well as intraframe, coding to achieve exceptionally high compression characteristics. But because MPEG was developed originally for the storage and retrieval of digitally-compressed video, as noted above, the coding characteristics do not take wide-area network transmission characteristics into account. As a result, typical MPEG sequences exhibit quasi-periodic peaks in their bit-rate characteristics which require relatively high peak rate capacity, although the *average* capacity required is quite low. Studies are ongoing to adapt the MPEG standard for transmission over high-speed networks. One possibility under consideration is to transmit coded MPEG as a continuous bit rate (CBR) stream, at a lower bit rate than the original uncompressed CBR stream, using a smoothing

[IEEE 1989]   *IEEE J. on Selected Areas in Communications,* Special Issue on Packet Speech and Video, 7, 5 (June 1989).

buffer. The problem with this approach, however, is that the resultant traffic output varies in quality. Discussions of the MPEG standard and its adaptation for high-speed ATM networking appear in [LEGA 1991], [PANC 1994], [CHIA 1994], and [SHRO 1995], among numerous publications. Since this whole area of MPEG transmission over high-speed networks is under study, we focus in this book on variable bit rate (VBR) video, using intraframe discrete-cosine transform (DCT) coding only, as incorporated in another standard, called the JPEG standard.

The bit rate as a function of time or frame number of a typical compressed video signal appears in Figure 3–17. Different compression algorithms or coders provide different bit rate characteristics, but all are of this general form. (The bit rate, as indicated, could be given in terms of bits/pixel, bits/frame, or bits/sec. Each is simply a scale-factor change from the others). Several characteristic properties of this signal are worthy of notice. First is the relatively slow variation of the signal. Video signals, despite the heavy compression, typically manifest high correlation from frame to frame (most often the frame contents do not change very much from frame to frame). A typical correlation measure is 10–20 frames or 300–600 msec. This property will be found useful in developing models of video signals. A second characteristic feature of a video signal, emphasized in Figure 3–17, is that occasionally the bit transmission rate is found to increase dramatically for a brief interval of time (at most 1–2 frames) and then drop down to a more normal range. This is attributed to scene changes, with correspondingly large changes in the picture content. The coder then takes a brief interval of time to adapt to the change and resume its normal compression process. Such scene changes may occur anywhere from 100–150 frames, and even more, apart. The traffic models we shall be discussing ignore scene changes, although we shall refer, in passing, to some attempts to include this phenomenon in the modeling process.

A bit rate histogram, or probability distribution function, serves as one useful measure of the bit rate signal variation with time. Examples of probability distribution functions for three types of video service as measured in Europe—videophone, video conference, and studio TV scene—appear in Figure 3–18 [VERB 1989]. The compressed TV scene covers the widest range of

[LEGA 1991]   LeGall, D., "MPEG: A Video Compression Standard for Multimedia Applications," *Comm. of the ACM, 34,* 4 (April 1991): 305–313.

[PANC 1994]   Pancha, P., and M. El Zarki, "MPEG Coding for Variable Bit Rate Video Transmission," *IEEE Comm. Mag., 32,* 5 (May 1994): 54–66.

[CHIA 1994]   Chiang, T., and D. Anastassiou, "Hierarchical Coding of Digital Television," *IEEE Comm. Mag., 32,* 5 (May 1994): 38–45.

[SHRO 1995]   Shroff, N. B., "Traffic Modeling and Analysis in High-Speed ATM Networks," *Ph.D dissertation,* Columbia University, 1995.

[VERB 1989]   Verbiest W., and L. Pinnoo, "A Variable Rate Codec for Asynchronous Transfer Mode Networks," *IEEE JSAC, 7,* 5 (June 1989): 761–770.

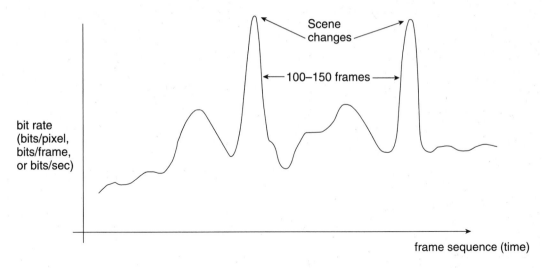

FIGURE 3–17 ■ Typical compressed video bit rate.

bit rates, followed by the videoconference. The videophone covers the smallest range of bit rates. Note that both the videoconference and TV scene histograms appear Gaussian in their shape. This property has been noted in a number of measured cases.

A number of traffic models incorporating these characteristics of VBR (compressed) video have been proposed. We shall discuss some of them in this chapter. It is to be noted that some properties of self-similar traffic, noted earlier with respect to LAN data traffic and TCP traffic, appear in video traffic as well [GARR 1994]. In particular, it has been found that there is long-range dependence over many frames of a video sequence and relatively heavy tails of the bandwidth distribution. These are not accounted for in the models we shall be discussing.

A number of these models involve autoregressive stochastic models that attempt to capture the frame correlation as well as the Gaussian probability property noted above. These models are useful in characterizing the variation of bit rate with time, as in Figure 3–17. They are less useful in studying statistical multiplexing, cell loss, admission and access control, and other features of ATM-based B-ISDN networks. We focus on the simplest form of this model in this section. Two other proposed models that we discuss in the sections following, mirror the models discussed previously in connection with packet (cell-based) voice. These are the Markov-modulated fluid flow-based model of section 3.3 and the MMPP model of section 3.4. In the next chapter

---

[GARR 1994]   Garrett, M. W., and W. Willinger, "Analysis, Modeling, and Generation of Self-Similar VBR Video Traffic," *Proc. SIGCOMM '94,* London (Aug. 1994): 269–280.

Probability (1E-3)

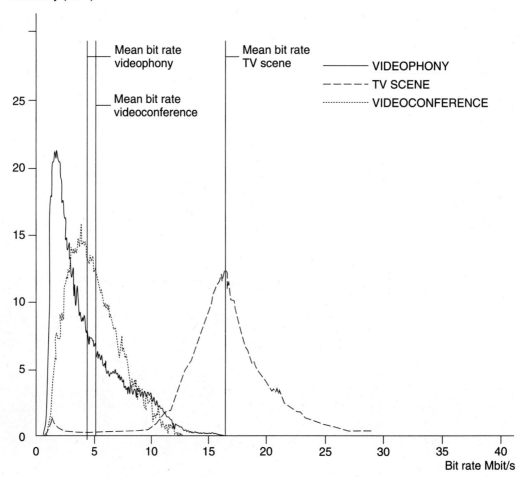

FIGURE 3–18 ■ Bit rate pdf (from [VERB 1989], Figure 11. © 1989 IEEE).

we again use the fluid flow approach, this time to study a form of access control proposed for ATM networks.

In discussing these models we first follow the work of B. Maglaris and co-authors, who were among the first to study video models in the context of statistical multiplexing—the same buffer design problem we explored earlier in sections 3.2 to 3.4. Maglaris and his co-authors describe two modeling approaches, one using the autoregressive model mentioned above, the other the Markov-modulated fluid-flow approach. In both cases they propose matching first- and second-order statistics of the models to measured signal characteristics [MAGL 1988]. These models turn out to capture the effects of coded

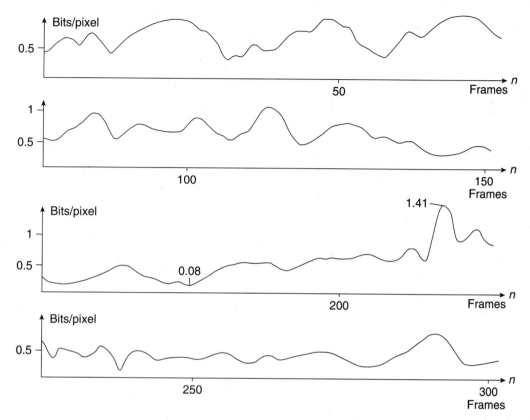

FIGURE 3–19 ■ Coding bit rate of the captured sequence (in bits/pixel) (from [MAGL 1988], Figure 3. © 1988 IEEE).

video *within* a scene fairly well; they do not attempt to resolve the effect of scene changes. We shall reference some work proposed to model scene changes later.

The work by Maglaris et al. described here, uses one sample coded video sequence 300 frames long to test the two models discussed. The corresponding bit rate sequence, $\lambda(t)$, is reproduced here as Figure 3–19. The test sequence is that of a head of a talking person. This sequence may be representative of videophone signals, but clearly not that of broadcast TV. (Later in this chapter we use other sequences appropriate for TV). The bit rate units used in Figure 3–19 are bits/pixel, as indicated. The minimum and maximum bit rates, indicated in the third strip of Figure 3–19, are 0.08 bit/pixel and 1.41

[MAGL 1988]   Maglaris, B. et al., "Performance Models of Statistical Multiplexing in Packet Video Communications," *IEEE Trans. on Commun., 36,* 7 (July 1988): 834–844.

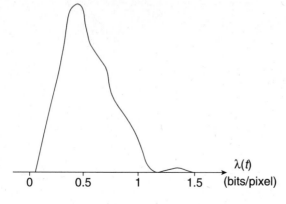

FIGURE 3–20 ◾ Bit rate histogram (from [MAGL 1988], Figure 4. © 1988 IEEE).

bits/pixel, respectively. The corresponding bit rate histogram appears in Figure 3–20. Note its rough resemblance to a normal distribution. The average value $\bar{\lambda}$ is 0.52 bit/pixel; the standard deviation is $\sigma = 0.23$ bit/pixel.

Consider now the autocovariance function for the process (signal) of Figure 3–19. This is the autocorrelation function less the first-moment squared and is a measure of the correlation between frames. This may be defined either in terms of continuous time or discrete time (frames) [PAPO 1990]. In terms of continuous time this is given by

$$C(\tau) = E[\lambda(t)\,\lambda\,(t + \tau)] - E^2\,(\lambda) \tag{3–84}$$

In terms of discrete time one can write

$$C(n) = E[\lambda(m)\,\lambda\,(m + n)] - E^2(\lambda) \tag{3–85}$$

Here, m is the frame number; $m + n$ represents a frame n units (frames) away. Since frames are generated at a rate of 30 frames/sec, it is clear that the two representations of correlation may be connected together by writing the parameter τ as $\tau = n/30$, in sec. Measurements made on the video sequence of Figure 3–19 indicate that the covariance function for that sequence is approximated fairly well by an exponential for values of $n \leq 10$ frames or $\tau \leq 300$ msec. In that range, the covariance function is then given by

$$C(\tau) = \sigma^2\,e^{-K\tau} \tag{3–84a}$$

in continuous-time form, or

$$C(n) = \sigma^2\,e^{-Kn/30} \tag{3–85a}$$

in discrete-time form. From the measurements, the parameter K is found to be $K = 3.9$/sec, so that for the test sequence of Figure 3–19,

[PAPO 1990] Papoulis, A., *Probability, Random Variables, and Stochastic Processess,* 3rd ed. New York: McGraw-Hill, 1990.

$$C(\tau) = 0.0536 \, e^{-3.9\tau} \qquad\qquad (3\text{–}84\text{b})$$

or

$$C(n) = 0.0536 \, e^{-0.13n} \qquad\qquad (3\text{–}85\text{b})$$

(Since $\sigma = 0.23$ bit/pixel, $\sigma^2 = 0.0536$.)

The exponential form of the covariance function suggests that the bit-rate sequence may be represented by a first-order autoregressive process. This is the rationale behind the use of the first model. This is the one we now describe in more detail. Using the discrete form of the autoregressive process, and letting n now be the frame number, $\lambda(n)$ is represented, in this model, by

$$\lambda\,(n) = a\,\lambda(n-1) + bw(n) \qquad |a| < 1 \qquad\qquad (3\text{–}86)$$

The function $w(n)$ is taken to be a stationary Gaussian white noise (i.i.d.) process with unit variance and average value $E(w) = \eta$. The covariance function for this process is readily shown to be exponential, precisely the reason why this model has been adopted. Specifically, it is left for the reader to show, using both equation (3–86) and the defining relation equation (3–85), for the discrete-time covariance function $C(n)$, that one gets

$$E(\lambda) = b\eta/(1-a) \qquad |a| < 1 \qquad\qquad (3\text{–}87)$$

$$C(n) = \sigma_\lambda^2\,|a|^n \qquad n \geq 0 \qquad\qquad (3\text{–}88)$$

and

$$\sigma_\lambda^2 = C(0) = E(\lambda^2) - E^2(\lambda)$$
$$= b^2/(1-a^2) \qquad\qquad (3\text{–}89)$$

(In deriving equation (3–89) we have used the fact that σ_w^2, the variance of the white-noise process $w(n)$, is assumed to be unity. In deriving equation (3–88), the integer n is again taken to be the displacement between frames, as indicated earlier in equation (3–85). The frame number n in equation (3–86) is then simply replaced by m, to avoid confusion.)

Note that $C(n)$ in equation (3–88) does, in fact, turn out to have a geometically-decaying form, the equivalent of the exponentially-decaying form in the continuous-time case. This result is well known for the first-order autoregressive stochastic process of equation (3–86) [PAPO 1990]. Equations (3–87) to (3–89) can now be matched to the equivalent time (frame) averages of the actual video time samples. Specifically, for the video sample appearing in [MAGL 1988] the time-averaged covariance function $C(n)$ was given by equation (3–85b). Comparing with equation (3–88), we then have

$$\sigma_\lambda^2 = \frac{b^2}{1-a^2} = \sigma^2 = 0.0536$$

and

$$a = e^{-0.13} = 0.878$$

For this same video strip, we noted earlier that $\overline{\lambda} = 0.52$ bit/frame is the average bit rate (see Figures 3–19 and 3–20). Equating these measured numbers to the equivalent values in equations (3–87) to (3–89), it is left for the reader to show that the two additional parameters in the autoregressive model of equation (3–86) are $b = 0.11$ and $E(w) = \eta = 0.58$.

These numbers then provide the fit of the first-order autoregressive model to the actual video strip of Figure 3–19. Other video samples would be handled similarly, assuming the first-order autoregressive model provides a reasonable fit to the samples.

As noted earlier, the autoregressive model for video cannot readily be applied to the analytical determination of buffer sizes or the equivalent delay determinations in broadband, cell-, or packet-based networks. Other models such as the fluid-flow or MMPP models, to be discussed shortly, must be introduced to analyze the impact of video traffic on networks. However, the autoregressive model *is* useful in providing a simple representation of coded video source statistics for simulations of network behavior with video traffic applied [MAGL 1988].

It was also noted earlier that the simple autoregressive model does not capture the effect of a scene change in a video sequence. This effect manifests itself in a sudden but brief increase in the encoded bit rate statistics as the video coder adapts to a new scene. A number of proposals of models capturing this effect have appeared in the literature. Ramamurthy and Sengupta, in particular, have proposed augmenting the autoregressive model by adding one or more very high bit rate states to which the process moves quickly and from which it drops back within one or two frames to the original system. This captures the effect of the brief interval in which the encoder has to adapt to a new scene change [RAMAM 1990]. This augmented model is, again, particularly useful for representing video traffic in network simulation studies.

Note that none of these models captures the self-similarity effect found in some video signals studies [GARR 1994]. The exponentially varying autocovariance function model of equations (3–84a) and (3–85a) was specifically noted to be limited to small numbers of frames only. Despite the limitations of these models, they are relatively simple, and have been found useful in practice.

In the next section we focus on the second video traffic model proposed in [MAGL 1988]. It uses an $(M + 1)$-state, voice source-like model to represent

[RAMAM 1990]   Ramamurthy, G., and B. Sengupta, "Modeling and Analysis of a Variable Bit Rate Video Multiplexer," Paper 8.4, 7th ITC Specialist Seminar, Morristown, NJ, Oct. 1990.

the combined (multiplexed) sum of N video sources, with $M \gg N$. This model representation combined with the fluid-flow analysis approach of section 3.3 enables us to determine the loss probability and buffer occupancy statistics of a statistical multiplexer in a manner similar to that described earlier, for voice, in section 3.3.

In section 3.7 we describe a Markov-modulated Poisson process (MMPP) model for a *single* video source and show how loss probability and buffer occupancy statistics may be obtained quite readily, at a B-ISDN access port, using this model. It turns out that for the case of video, the matrix-geometric method of analysis described in section 3.4 is not necessary. An approximate, histogram, method of analysis is found to suffice in this case.

3.6 ▪ FLUID SOURCE MODELING OF A VIDEO MULTIPLEXER

We continue the presentation of the work of Maglaris et al [MAGL 1988] in this section, focusing on their second model. Unlike the first autoregressive model, discussed in the preceding section, which is designed to capture the first and second order statistics of a single video source, the second model described here is designed to study the effects of video statistical buffering at an access port of a broadband network. It parallels the approach used previously in section 3.3 in studying packet voice modeling.

Specifically, say N independent video sources are multiplexed together. Each source is characterized by its first- and second-order statistics, the average bit rate λ_i (per frame or per second, as the case may be), and autocovariance function $C_i(n)$ for source i, as discussed in the previous section. The statistical multiplexer to be analyzed appears in Figure 3–21a. This is similar to the statistical multiplexer figures presented previously. Note that the access port transmission capacity is written here, for simplicity, as C bits/pixel. It could be equally well-defined in terms of bits/frame, bits/sec (after multiplying by the number of pixels/sec), or in terms of cells/sec.

To analyze the multiplexer and, more specifically, to find the multiplexer buffer occupancy statistics and, from these, an approximation to the buffer loss probability, we now follow Maglaris et al. in representing the multiplexed process by an *equivalent* process. This equivalent process is identical to the one used in sections 3.2 and 3.3 to discuss the multiplexing of voice sources. The equivalent process will be defined to be the sum of M identical two-state "minisources", each moving back and forth exponentially between an "off state" and an "on state" in which A bits/pixel are offered to the access buffer. The minisource model appears in Figure 3–21c. The multiplexed minisource source appears in Figure 3–21b. (Note that the minisource model is precisely that used to describe a single voice process in section 3.2).

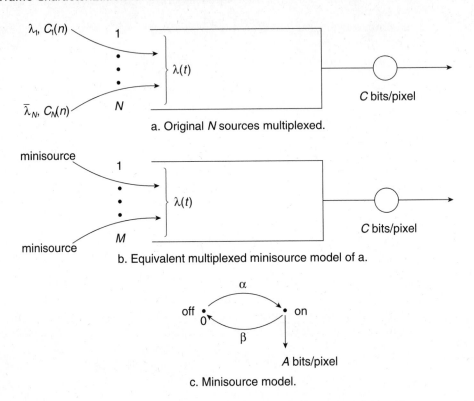

a. Original N sources multiplexed.

b. Equivalent multiplexed minisource model of a.

c. Minisource model.

FIGURE 3–21 ■ Statistical multiplexer, N video sources ($M \gg N$).

The composite (time varying) rate, in units of bits/pixel, is labeled $\lambda(t)$ in Figure 3–21. Note that this rate will actually change at frame intervals (30 frames/sec) rather than continuously, as shown in Figure 3–21. Note also that we have used $\lambda(t)$ to represent the multiplexed rate in both Figures 3–21a and b, even though the model in Figure 3–21b can only produce an approximation to the measured rate $\lambda(t)$. We have done this for tutorial reasons, to show that the model of Figure 3–21b is to be designed to represent the real multiplexed process of Figure 3–21a.

It is now clear, from our previous discussion of multiplexed voice sources, that the composite minisource process of Figure 3–21b is represented by an $(M + 1)$-state Markov chain with state-dependent transition rates, just like the one sketched in Figure 3–5 previously. This chain is sketched here in Figure 3–22. It should be apparent to the reader, both from the minisource model of Figure 3–21c and from the Markov chain representation of Figure 3–22, that the equivalent multiplexed source model of Figure 3–21b is a quantized version of the original multiplexed source. The time-varying bit rate $\lambda(t)$ has been quantized to have the values 0, A, 2A, . . . , MA bits/pixel only. One

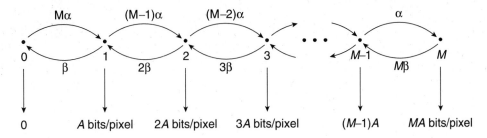

FIGURE 3–22 ▪ Markov chain representation, equivalent process, Figure 3–21b.

can hope to reduce the effect of quantization in the model by increasing M, the number of minisources summed. This is why we indicated earlier that we should have $M \gg N$.[3]

Now how does one choose the three minisource model parameters α, β, and A of Figure 3–21c? The approach is to, again, match first and second moments of the composite Markov chain model and the measured statistics. Specifically, let $\lambda_i(t)$ represent the sample bit rate of video source i. The multiplexed signal $\lambda(t)$ is then of course given by

$$\lambda(t) = \sum_{i=1}^{N} \lambda_i(t) \tag{3–90}$$

It is then left to the reader to show that the covariance $C(\tau)$ of the composite process is also the sum of the individual covariance functions:

$$C(\tau) = \sum_{i=1}^{N} C_i(\tau) \tag{3–91}$$

Here $C_i(\tau)$ is the autocovariance function of source i, defined by equation (3–84) with λ_i used in place of λ there. The multiplexed signal bit rate λ is of course used in calculating $C(\tau)$. (It is more convenient to use the continuous-time form of the covariance function, as defined by equation (3–84), because of the continuous-time Markov-chain model.)

From elementary probability we also have

$$E(\lambda) = \sum_{i=1}^{N} E_i(\lambda_i) \tag{3–92}$$

---

[3]The single-source MMPP model of video, to be discussed in section 3.7 following, will also require quantization. There, the single source, not the composite source, is quantized. It will be shown there that eight levels of quantization provide accurate results in that case.

and

$$\sigma^2 = \sum_{i=1}^{N} \sigma_i^2 \tag{3-93}$$

The parameter σ_i^2 represents the variance of video source i, while σ^2 is used to represent the variance of the composite signal. (Recall that in the previous section we used $E(\lambda)$ and σ^2 to represent the single source statistics). Note also that $C_i(0) = \sigma_i^2$ and $C(0) = \sigma^2$, checking equation (3-93).

For the special case of N independent sources with identical moments, the case assumed here, we than have

$$C(\tau) = N \, C_i(\tau) \tag{3-91a}$$

$$E(\lambda) = N \, E(\lambda_i) \tag{3-92a}$$

and

$$\sigma^2 = N \, \sigma_i^2 \tag{3-93a}$$

These parameters are to be matched to those of the measured statistics, again equating ensemble (statistical) averages and time (sample) averages. They are then, in turn, matched to the equivalent parameters of the Markov chain of Figure 3-22. We use the video conferencing example of the previous section (Figures 3-19 and 3-20) to demonstrate the procedure [MAGL 1988]. Recall that for that example, $E(\lambda_i) = \overline{\lambda}_i = 0.52$ bit/pixel. We also had $\sigma_i^2 = 0.0536$ and $C_i(\tau) = \sigma_i^2 \, e^{-3.9\tau}$. The N-source parameters are then found using equations (3-91a) to (3-93a).

Now consider the multiplexed minisource model of Figure 3-21b whose parameters are to be matched to those of the N multiplexed video sources of Figure 3-21a.

It may be shown that the autocovariance function of the two-state minisource model of Figure 3-21c is given by

$$C_i(\tau) = A^2 \frac{\alpha\beta}{(\alpha+\beta)^2} e^{-(\alpha+\beta)\tau} \tag{3-94}$$

(This model is precisely that of a two-state continuous-time Markov chain, switching randomly at the rates α and β, between the two values 0 and A. It has also been called the "random telegraph signal." See [PAPO 1990] and [SCHW 1970] for derivations of the autocorrelation function of this signal type). This may be written in simpler form if we let $p \equiv \alpha/(\alpha + \beta)$ be the probability the minisource is in the "on" state, and $(1 - p)$ the probability it is in the "off" state. We then have

$$C_i(\tau) = A^2 p(1 - p)e^{-(\alpha+\beta)\tau} \tag{3-94a}$$

[SCHW 1970]   Schwartz, M., *Information Transmission, Modulation and Noise,* 2nd ed., New York: McGraw-Hill, 1970.

The important point to note is that the two-state covariance of the two-state minisource exhibits the desired exponential behavior. The "time constant" of this function is just $1/(\alpha + \beta)$. (The exponential behavior of the covariance is, in fact, a general property of Markov processes [PAPO 1990]). The M multiplexed minisources must then have the composite autocovariance function

$$C(\tau) = MC_i(\tau) = MA^2 p(1 - p)e^{-(\alpha+\beta)\tau} \tag{3–95}$$

In addition, since the average number of minisources "on" is just $M\,\alpha/(\alpha + \beta) = Mp$, the average bit rate of the equivalent minisource model is

$$E(\lambda) = MpA \tag{3–96}$$

We now use equations (3–95) and (3–96) to match the M-minisource model to the N multiplexed video sources. In particular, for the video conferencing example under discussion here, we have three equations from which the three parameters A, α, β, of the minisource model, may be found:

1. $E(\lambda) = MpA = 0.52\,N$
2. $\sigma^2 = C(0) = MA^2\,p(1-p) = 0.0536\,N$
3. $(\alpha + \beta) = 3.9$

It is left to the reader to show that for these particular measured values, we have

1. $\beta = 3.9/(1 + 5.05\,N/M)$
2. $\alpha = 3.9 - \beta = 19.7\,N/M(1 + 5.05\,N/M)$
3. $A = 0.4/\beta = 0.1 + 0.52\,N/M$

Note that the ratio N/M has been left undetermined. Maglaris et al., in their work, have found that $M = 20\,N$ provides results that agree with simulation. (We shall see in the next section, as already noted, that a direct approximation of one source by an MMPP requires only eight quantized levels. This is far fewer than the twenty levels per source specified here, found by using the two-state minisource approximation).

Letting $M/N = 20$ in this example, we have

1. $\beta = 3.12$
2. $\alpha = 0.78$
3. $A \doteq 0.13$ bit/pixel

Hence $p = \alpha/(\alpha + \beta) = 0.2$ and $(1 - p) = 0.8$. (The composite minisource model representing the N multiplexed video sources is thus quantized to a spacing of 0.13 bit/pixel, to a maximum bit rate of 0.13 M bit/pixel).

With the composite minisource model for video determined, we now re-turn to the statistical multiplexer of Figure 3–21 to see how one uses this video source model and the fluid-flow approach to calculate parameters of interest. Conversely, with the queueing model of Figure 3–21 representing the buffer at the access port to a network, we use the model and the fluid-flow technique, as was done in section 3.3 for multiplexed voice sources, to design the access buffer to provide a specified probability of cell loss, and to deter-mine the resultant video access delay.

Specifically, let the queue occupancy in Figure 3–21b be a *continuous* random variable x, given directly in units of bits. (We now deviate somewhat from the definition of the queue occupancy variable x in section 3.3, which was given as the number of cells arriving during a talk spurt). Since the buffer sizes found will always be large numbers of bits, the distinction be-tween the usual integer values of bits, and the continuous values appearing here, will be negligible. This further motivates the use of the fluid-flow ap-proach. We then define the probability distribution function $F_i(x)$ as the joint probability that the buffer occupancy is less than or equal to x, with i mini-sources "on." This is essentially the same definition used in section 3.3, with the one distinction that we are considering minisources "on," rather than ac-tual voice sources in talk spurt, as was the case in section 3.3. We also define the *steady-state* joint probability directly here, rather than first starting with the time-varying probability function $F_i(x,t)$, as was done in section 3.3. By de-finition then,

$$F_i(x) \equiv P[\text{queue} \leq x, i \text{ sources on}]$$

$$= P[\text{queue} \leq x, \lambda = iA]$$

(3–97)

With our minisource model equivalent, each minisource producing A bits/pixel when on, the input rate to the statistical multiplexer is thus $\lambda = iA$ bits/pixel when i sources are "on." As a special case of equation (3–97), and in agreement with the equivalent statement made in section 3.3, we also have

$$F_i(\infty) = P[\lambda = iA] = \pi_i$$

$$= \binom{M}{i} p^i (1-p)^{M-i}$$

(3–98)

$p \equiv \alpha/(\alpha+\beta)$. We have again defined π_i as the probability i sources are "on." This is just the binomial probability presented earlier as equation (3–5), with the notation changed somewhat to accommodate the parameters defined here.

We now follow the same procedure used in section 3.3 in deriving the set of first-order differential equations for $F_i(x)$, $0 \leq i \leq M$. The only difference, as already noted, is that here we deal directly with x in units of bits; in section 3.3 information units (cells in a talk spurt interval) were used. Recall (from section 3.3) that in going from equation (3–13) to (3–14), and then, finally, to the set of stationary (steady-state) equations (3–15), for $F_i(x)$, we defined the quantity $\Delta x \equiv (i - C)\alpha\Delta t$ as the change in buffer size over an interval Δt sec long when the system is in state i. A little thought will indicate that we must use the equivalent expression $\Delta x = (iA - C)K\Delta t$, with K the number of pixels (picture elements) per second required to transmit a video signal. As an example, if a video frame contains 250,000 pixels, and the system transmits 30 frames/sec, as in the North American TV standard, $K = 7.5 \times 10^6$ pixels/sec. As a check of the expression for Δx, note that when i minisources are on, the buffer is tending to fill at a rate of KAi bits/sec. It is tending to empty at the transmission capacity rate KC bits/sec, with C the capacity in bits/pixel. The net change in buffer size in a Δt sec interval, in bits, is thus $\Delta x = (iA - C) K\Delta t$, as indicated.

With this one change in the expression for Δx, the steady-state differential equations satisfied by $F_i(x)$, $0 \leq i \leq M$, are readily shown to be given by

$$(iA - C)K \frac{dF_i(x)}{dx} = [M - (i - 1)]\alpha F_{i-1}(x)$$

$$-[i\beta + (M - i)\alpha]F_i(x) + (i + 1)\beta F_{i+1}(x)$$

(3–99)

Equation (3–99) is to be compared with equation (3–15) in section 3.3. Equation (3–99) holds for all i, $0 \leq i \leq M$, with the proviso that $F_{-1}(x) = F_{M+1}(x) = 0$. Details of the derivation are left to the reader. (Note the change in notation from equation (3–15) as well: Equation (3–15) was based on the two-state voice model of Figure 3–3. The minisource two-state model of Figure 3–21c uses α in place of λ, and β in place of α in Figure 3–3).

We now simplify equation (3–99), somewhat, by factoring the parameter A out of the left-hand side and β out of the right-hand side. The resultant set of normalized equations to be solved for $F_i(x)$ is then given by

$$\frac{KA}{\beta}\left(i - \frac{C}{A}\right)\frac{dF_i(x)}{dx} = [M - (i - 1)]\frac{\alpha}{\beta} F_{i-1}(x)$$

$$-\left[i + (M - i)\frac{\alpha}{\beta}\right]F_i(x) + (i + 1)F_{i+1}(x)$$

(3–99a)

Defining the row vector $\boldsymbol{F}(x) = [F_0(x), F_1(x), \ldots, F_M(x)]$ as was done in section 3.3, equation (3–99a) may be written in matrix-vector form as

$$\frac{KA}{\beta}\frac{d\boldsymbol{F}(x)}{dx}D = \boldsymbol{F}(x)B$$

(3–100)

Here, D is the $(M+1) \times (M+1)$ diagonal matrix

$$D = \text{diag }(i - C/A) \qquad 0 \leq i \leq M$$

(3–101)

and B, the $(M+1) \times (M+1)$ matrix

$$
B = \begin{bmatrix}
-M\alpha/\beta & M\alpha/\beta & 0 & 0 \\
1 & -(M-1)\alpha/\beta - 1 & (M-1)\alpha/\beta & 0 \\
0 & 2 & -(M-2)\alpha/\beta - 2 & (M-1)\alpha/\beta \\
0 & 0 & 3 & -(M-3)\alpha/\beta - 3 & \cdots \\
\vdots & \vdots & \vdots & \vdots
\end{bmatrix}
\tag{3-102}
$$

Equations (3–100) to (3–102) are to be compared with equations (3–15b), (3–16), and (3–11), respectively. (Note that equation (3–102) is in a normalized form, while (3–11) is not). Except for the multiplicative constant KA/β, the two sets of equations are of the same form. Without this multiplicative constant, the solution to equation (3–100) is precisely that given by equation (3–17). It is left to the reader to show that the solution to equation (3–100) is of the same form: sums of exponentials involving eigenvalues. It is also left to the reader to show that the effect of the multiplicative parameter KA/β is to multiply the eigenvalues appearing in equation (3–17) by the reciprocal of the parameter, β/KA. The solution to equation (3–100) may thus be written, following equation (3–17), as

$$
F(x) = \sum_{i=0}^{M} a_i F_i e^{\beta z_i x / KA}
\tag{3-103}
$$

with z_i the ith eigenvalue and Φ_i the corresponding eigenvector satisfying the eigenvalue equation

$$
z_i \Phi_i D = \Phi_i B
\tag{3-104}
$$

All the results of section 3.3 now carry over to the solution here. The corresponding general results appearing in [ANIC 1982] apply as well, with the appropriate modification of the eigenvalues by multiplication by β/KA, as shown in equation (3–103). Specifically, for the case of an infinite buffer, the sum in equation (3–103) can only be taken over the nonpositive eigenvalues. The a_i's corresponding to positive eigenvalues must be zero. Since $F(\infty) = \pi$ [equation (3–98)], one of the eigenvalues must be zero, and we get, as in equation (3–17b),

$$
F(x) = p + \sum_{i : \mathrm{Re}[z_i < 0]} \alpha_i F_i e^{\beta z_i x / KA}
\tag{3-103a}
$$

Letting $F(x)$ be the (marginal) probability distribution function that the queue occupancy is less than or equal to x, we have, generalizing equation (3–37),

$$
F(x) = \sum_{j=0}^{M} F_j(x) = 1 + \sum_{i : \mathrm{Re}[z_i < 0]} \alpha_i \left[\sum_{j=0}^{M} \Phi_{ij} \right] e^{\beta z_i x / KA}
\tag{3-105}
$$

where we have assumed $\mathbf{\Phi}_i(x)$ to be written as

$$\mathbf{\Phi}_i(x) = [\Phi_{i0}, \Phi_{i1}, \ldots \Phi_{ij}, \ldots \Phi_{iM}] \tag{3-106}$$

Finally, the complementary distribution function or survivor function $G(x)$ (the probability the queue occupancy is greater than x) is given by

$$G(x) = 1 - F(x) = -\sum_{i:\mathrm{Re}[z_i < 0]} \alpha_i \left[\sum_{j=0}^{M} \Phi_{ij}\right] e^{\beta z_i x / KA} \tag{3-107}$$

The a_i coefficients are found in the manner described in section 3.3. Thus, recall for the fluid model that the overload states are those for which the queue is tending to fill. For these states we must have $F_i(0) = 0$; that is, the buffer cannot be empty. For the model under discussion here, the overload states are the ones for which $iA > C$, or $i > C/A$. There are $M - \lfloor C/A \rfloor$ such states, precisely the number of negative eigenvalues satisfying the eigenvalue equation (3–104), with the diagonal matrix D defined by equation (3–101) [ANIC 1982]. Setting $F_i(0) = 0$ for the $M - \lfloor C/A \rfloor$ overload states, we get the requisite number of equations needed to find the a_i's. This is exactly the same procedure followed in section 3.3.

It was pointed out in section 3.3 that the dominant negative eigenvalue, satisfying the eigenvalue equation (3–18), is shown in [ANIC 1982] to be given by equation (3–42). Comparing equation (3–18) with the corresponding eigenvalue equation (3–104) appearing in this section, we note that the capacity C in that section must be replaced by C/A here, while $\gamma \equiv \lambda/\alpha$ there is equivalent to α/β here. (Compare equation (3–11) in section 3.2 with equation (3–102) here). From equation (3–42), then, the magnitude r, of the equivalent dominant eigenvalue in the case under consideration here, must be given by

$$r = (1 - \rho)(1 + \alpha/\beta)/[1 - (C/MA)] \tag{3-108}$$

Here, the utilization ρ is just

$$\rho \equiv Mp\,A/C < 1 \tag{3-109}$$

$p = \alpha/(\alpha + \beta)$, for the multiplexed minisource model (Figure 3–21b), or

$$\rho = N\bar{\lambda}/C < 1 \tag{3-110}$$

for the N video sources multiplexed together (Figure 3–21a). Recall that for the specific example discussed in [MAGL 1988], $\bar{\lambda} = 0.52$ bit/pixel is the average bit rate of each of the N sources. From equation (3–107), approximating the survivor function $G(x)$ by the dominant (asymptotic) eigenvalue term only, as in equation (3–43), we get

$$G(x) \sim A_M \rho^M e^{-\beta r x / KA} \tag{3-111}$$

with r given by equation (3–108). A specific expression for the term A_M appears in [ANIC 1982].

Consider an example taken from [MAGL 1988]. Let $N = 1$ video source be approximated by $M = 20$ minisources. The average source bit rate is $\lambda = 0.52$ bit/pixel or the equivalent 3.9 Mbps in units of bits/sec, for 250,000 pixels/frame, and 30 frames/sec (that is, $K = 7.5 \times 10^6$ pixels/ sec). Let the transmission capacity be 4.875 Mbps or $C = 4.875/7.5 = 0.65$ bit/pixel. The utilization ρ is then $3.9/4.875 = 0.52/0.65 = 0.8$. This must be the equivalent utilization of the $M = 20$ minisource approximation. As a check, we showed previously that, for this example, $A = 0.13$ bit/pixel, $\alpha/\beta = 0.25$, and $p = \alpha/(\alpha + \beta) = 0.2$. Then $\rho = E(\lambda)/C = MpA/C = 0.8$, as required. From equation (3–108), then, $r = 0.333$. We also showed previously that $\beta = 3.12$/sec for this example. The survivor function is then approximated by its asymptotic value

$$G(x) \sim A_M (0.8)^{20} e^{-1.066 \times 10^{-6} x}$$

$$= A_M (0.012)\, e^{-1.066 \times 10^{-6} x}$$

from equation (3–111). This also provides an approximation to the probability of loss of a finite buffer if that probability is small, or the buffer large.

As was the case earlier, in section 3.3, the logarithm of the survivor function $G(x)$ should thus plot as a straight line as a function of buffer size x. Maglaris et al. [MAGL 1988] have chosen to plot the survivor function (their probability of loss) as a function of the queue size x measured in msec. To convert x in bits to sec, implies dividing by the transmission rate of 4.875 Mbps. Converting the result here to msec, we get

$$G(x) \sim A_M (0.012)e^{-0.0052x\,|\,ms}$$

where $x\,|\,ms$ means the buffer size is measured in msec. Maglaris et al. have compared the results of their fluid-flow analysis for the single video source case with simulation. The resultant curves are reproduced here as Figure 3–23. Note the straight-line characteristic for $x\,|\,ms > 100$ msec. The slope of the line can be seen to be approximately $-0.12/50 = -0.0024$. The slope of $\log_{10}G(x)$ versus $x\,|\,ms$ from the equation above is $-0.0052 \log_{10}e \doteq -0.0023$, validating this asymptotic result.

Another example taken from [MAGL 1988] appears in Figure 3–24. This is for the case of $N = 5$ video sources. The output transmission rate has been chosen at 5×4.875 Mbps = 24.375 Mbps. The utilization is again taken to be $\rho = 0.8$. From equations (3–108) and (3–111) the slope of the $\log_{10}$Prob(loss) curve versus x in bits, should be invariant with the number of sources if C is scaled with the number of sources, as is the case here. Converting to queue size $x\,|\,ms$, in msec, however, implies *increasing* the magnitude of the slope by N (and hence M). For $N = 5$, then, the slope should be $\doteq -0.0023 \times 5 = -0.012$.

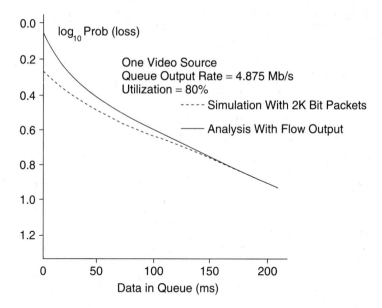

FIGURE 3–23 ■ Comparison of loss probabilities—single-source simulation and analysis (from [MAGL 1988], Figure 13. © 1988 IEEE).

From Figure 3–24, the slope is found to be approximately $-3/200 = -0.015$. This approximation is not too bad, considering that only one term (the asymptotic one) in the sum of exponentials has been used.

Note that the fluid-flow analysis in this case of multiplexed video sources provides a much better approximation to simulation than did the equivalent analysis for voice in section 3.3. In the case of voice, each source produces a periodic, continuous bit rate, when in talk spurt. The video sources considered here are examples of variable bit rate (VBR) sources, for which the fluid model is more appropriate. In addition, tl.e basic source rates are much higher, while the buffer sizes required are much larger, providing still further justification for the validity of the fluid-flow approximation.

Table 3–1, based on some of the curves appearing in [MAGL 1988], provides rough estimates of buffer sizes in Mbytes required to keep the loss probability (approximated by the survivor function) to 10^{-6} and 10^{-9}. The utilization $\rho = 0.8$ in all cases, and the sources, are assumed the same as those considered to this point. Dividing the buffer sizes shown by 50 provides an approximation to the buffer sizes in units of ATM cells. Note the extraordinarily large buffer sizes required to attain these very low probabilities of loss.

These large buffer sizes are necessary for the fluid approximation to be a valid one. How does one then obtain the full loss probability characteristic, exemplified by the simulation curves of Figures 3–23 and 3–24? The analysis in the next section, using a Markov-modulated Poisson process (MMPP) model

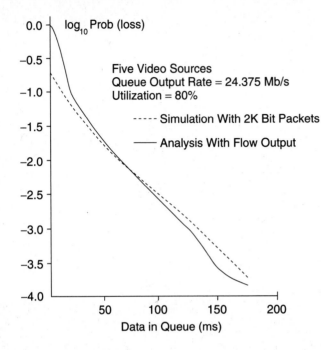

FIGURE 3–24 ■ Comparison of loss probabilities—five-source simulation and analysis (from [MAGL 1988], Figure 14. © 1988 IEEE).

to represent video, will cover the small buffer case. It is to be noted that the small and large buffer regimes for the loss probability characteristic appear in the characterization of various traffic sources of the VBR type. These sources may, in general, be characterized as doubly-stochastic sources: They are represented by multiple states, with transitions between states modeled as being governed by an underlying Markov chain. At each state, the traffic arrival characteristic is, in turn, stochastic (random) in nature. The MMPP is one example of such a process.

TABLE 3–1 ■ Approximate buffer sizes required, N video sources, ρ = 0.8

N	Buffer size			
	$P_L = 10^{-6}$		$P_L = 10^{-9}$	
	Mbytes	cells	Mbytes	cells
1	1.8	36,000		
2	1.8	36,000	2.5	40,000
4	1.6	32,000	2.5	40,000
10	1.5	30,000	1.8	36,000

(Based on [MAGL 1988], Figure 16)

The small buffer region to be discussed in the next section has been termed the "cell region"; the large buffer region is called the "burst region" [HUI 1988], [COST 1991]. We shall discuss these regions further in section 3.8.

3.7 ■ MMPP MODEL FOR VIDEO TRAFFIC: HISTOGRAM APPROXIMATION

It has already been noted a number of times that a variety of methods exist for characterizing variable bit rate video traffic. Two such models were discussed in the last two sections. We conclude this discussion of video traffic characterization by introducing a third model which has been found to be quite simple and useful in studying both video source multiplexing and video traffic control. This is a very natural model, which consists first of quantizing a single video stream and then approximating the video signal by its quantized version. As noted at the end of the last section, this model will also be found to be an example of one appropriate, in general, for analyzing the "cell region" of operation of the probability of loss—buffer size characteristic. We shall return to the cell/burst regions in section 3.8, after considering the third model for representing video in this section.

Given a single video stream then, and representing it by a quantized approximation, how many quantized levels are needed? It has been found experimentally, using a number of broadcast-quality (NTSC) video strips, as well as longer segments of a compressed version of the *Star Wars* movie, that eight quantization levels suffice to provide an accurate representation for calculating buffer occupancy when multiplexing a number of such sources at the access to an ATM network [SKEL 1993].

Given a number of such video sources, how should their outputs be transmitted to the network access multiplexer? It turns out that the way in which the video data is transmitted, frame-by-frame, has a significant impact on the multiplexer performance [DIXI 1991]. In particular, if the compressed data for each frame are buffered, converted to ATM cell format, and then transmitted at peak rate at the beginning of the next frame until exhausted, an undesirable correlation is introduced among the multiplexed signals. (Each signal is then converted to an on-off signal with period of one frame, the

[HUI 1988]   Hui, J. Y., "Resource Allocation for Broadband Networks," *IEEE JSAC, SAC-6*, (Dec. 1988): 1598–1608.

[COST 1991]   *Performance Evaluation and Design of Multiservice Networks,* J. W. Roberts, ed., Final report, Cost 224 project. Luxembourg: Commission of the European Communities, Oct. 1991.

[SKEL 1993]   Skelly, P. A., et al., "A Histogram-Based Model for Video Traffic Behavior in an ATM Multiplexer," *IEEE/ACM Trans. on Networking, 1,* 4 (Aug 1993): 446–459.

[DIXI 1991]   Dixit, S. S., and P. Skelly, "Video Traffic Smoothing and ATM Multiplexer Performance," *Proc. IEEE Globecom '91,* Phoenix, AZ, Dec. 1991.

"on" portion of the period being proportional to the amount of data in the frame). A scheme proposed to eliminate this correlation and provide good multiplexing performance is to transmit the buffered cells from each frame randomly and uniformly over the next frame interval. But this is precisely one way of defining a Poisson process if the frame-length interval is "long enough" [PAPO 1990]! This simple, intuitive expedient thus leads to our third video source model—that of the Markov-modulated Poisson process. (In discussing the cell/burst regions of loss probability performance in the next section, we shall describe a model appropriate for video in which buffered ATM cells are transmitted at uniform or deterministic spacings throughout a frame interval. This turns out to provide the best possible performance. We focus on the MMPP model here since it follows directly from our discussion of the MMPP in section 3.4. The histogram approximation discussed here has been generalized to include a variety of sources, including the one in which cells are deterministically transmitted in each frame interval [SHRO 1995]).

To summarize, we approximate a given video source by its quantized equivalent, consisting of one of eight levels of traffic, changing from frame to frame. The cells for a given frame, and hence quantized level, are transmitted as a Poisson stream to the ATM access multiplexer. We now assume, to complete the model, that transitions between levels, from frame to frame, are memoryless. This gives rise to a discrete-time eight-state Markov chain, with transitions taking place between states every frame interval—roughly 33 msec in length. This chain serves to modulate an underlying Poisson process, since each state is represented by a Poisson arrival process with arrival rate corresponding to the data in bits (or cells) to be transmitted at that state. Alternately, if we choose to study the process over many frame intervals and ignore the discreteness of the frame times, we may equally well approximate the process by a continuous-time Markov process. (Recall that we moved between discrete- and continuous-time processes in the video models discussed in the previous sections as well.)

We have thus arrived at a Markov-modulated Poisson process (MMPP) model for a VBR video source. An example of a continuous-time eight-state model is shown in Figure 3–25. Only some of the possible transitions are

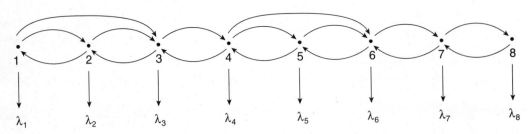

FIGURE 3–25 ■ Eight-state, continuous-time MMPP model for video source.

shown to avoid clutter. The λ_i's shown, represent the Poisson arrival rates corresponding to each of the states (quantized levels). The units of the λ_i's can be given in bits/frame or cells/frame, bits/sec or cells/sec, or even bits/pixel, as in previous sections. One can always convert from one set of units to another.

Given this model, how does one determine its parameters? There are a variety of ways of doing this [SKEL 1993]. One could calculate the video histogram (probability of falling into each of the bins centered at the quantized levels) as well as the autocovariance function for an actual sequence and then use these measured quantities to determine the transition probabilities. But then it turns out that there are too many transition probabilities to be calculated uniquely. Alternately, one can measure the transition probabilities from an actual sequence and use these to calculate the steady-state probabilities π_j, as well as the resultant autocovariance function. This was the method adopted in the work referenced [SKEL 1993].

Recall from equation (3–10) that the set of transition rates in the continuous-time model define the infinitesimal generating function M. Given M, we find the vector π by solving the matrix equation

$$\pi M = 0 \tag{3–112}$$

with the additional constraint

$$\sum_j \pi_j = 1$$

The equivalent equation for the discrete-time chain is readily shown to be given by

$$\pi P = \pi \tag{3–113}$$

with P the matrix of transition probabilities [KLEI 1976]. Letting f be the frame rate, in frames/sec, the two matrices M and P are then related by the simple expression

$$M = f(P - I) \tag{3–114}$$

with I the identity matrix. (Why does multiplying the transition probabilities by f convert them to the desired transition rates?)

An example appears in Figure 3–26 [SKEL 1993]. Plotted is the measured number of bits/frame over an interval 3000 frames long. The video sequence shown was quantized into eight evenly-spaced levels varying from 140,000 bits/frame to 350,000 bits/frame. The quantized version is shown overlaid on the original sequence. The transition probabilities between the states were then estimated from the quantized version. This provided the estimate of the matrix P, from which the generating matrix M was calculated as well. Equation (3–113) was then used to find the steady-state probability distribution π. The result appears in Figure 3–27a, where it is compared with

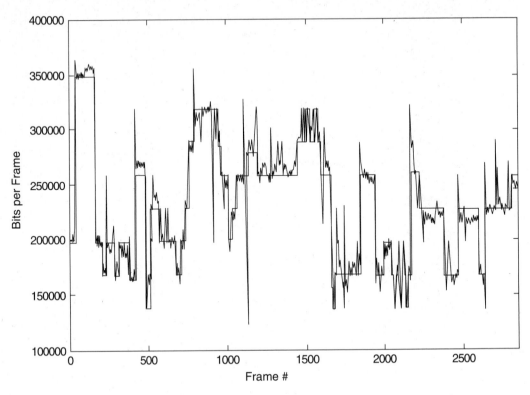

FIGURE 3–26 ■ *Star Wars* Sequence. Original and quantized version (from [SKEL 1993], Figure 4. © 1993 IEEE).

the measured histogram of the original quantized sequence. Note the closeness of the match. The one slight difference is that the model histogram has a somewhat higher average bit rate. This shows up in the comparison of calculated and measured autocorrelation functions, shown plotted in Figure 3–27b, where the calculated autocorrelation function lies above the measured one at larger time differences, although both drop off at about the same rate at lower values of time. Recall that the autocorrelation function, as contrasted to the autocovariance function discussed in previous sections, retains the expected average, or first moment. The autocorrelation function $R(\tau)$ was calculated using the transition probabilities as well as steady-state probabilities. In continuous-time form it is defined as

$$R(\tau) = E\big[\lambda(t)\lambda(t+\tau)\big]$$

$$= \sum_{i=1}^{8}\sum_{j=1}^{8} \lambda_i \lambda_j P\big[\lambda(t+\tau) = \lambda_j \mid \lambda(t) = \lambda_i\big]\, P\big[\lambda(t) = \lambda_i\big] \tag{3–115}$$

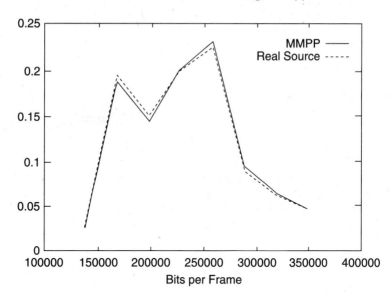

a.

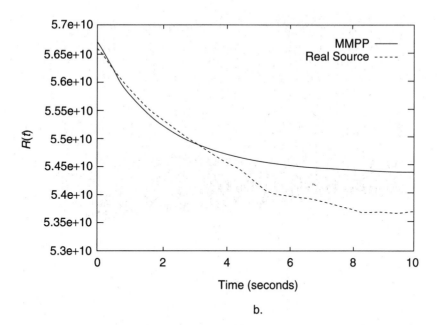

b.

FIGURE 3–27 ▪ a. A comparison of the model's steady state probability distribution compared with the histogram of the original sequence. b. A comparison of the model's autocorrelation function compared to that of the original model (from [SKEL 1993], Figure 9. © 1993 IEEE).

The probability $P[\lambda(t) = \lambda_i]$ is, of course, the steady-state probability π_i. (A cautionary note must be struck here. The match of calculated and measured autocorrelation functions referred to here is only over the range of 10 sec or 300 frames. The self-similarity or long-range dependence found in video signals that was mentioned earlier occurs over frames separated by thousands of frames [GARR 1994]. Although the measured autocorrelation function does decay to zero, as expected, at these time lags it is found to do so very slowly, showing the erratic behavior at all time scales characteristic of self-similar processes [GARR 1994]. The implications for design, and, in particular, for guaranteeing an appropriate QoS, particularly for very small cell loss probability, are not clear at this time. Despite this cautionary note, the studies carried out thus far ignoring the long-range dependence, appear to provide relatively good comparison between analysis and simulation, as will be seen in the material following.)

These results, and other examples like them, validate the representation of VBR video sequences by the eight-state MMPP model. Interestingly, however, when this model is applied to the design of the access buffer at the access to an ATM network, particularly when a number of such video sources are multiplexed, it turns out that the transition probabilities in the eight-state Markov chain play an insignificant role. The state probabilities π_i only are needed to carry out quite accurate calculations of the buffer occupancy distribution. This makes buffer occupancy studies relatively simple, particularly when multiple video sources are multiplexed together to carry out statistical multiplexing at the ATM access node. This gives rise to a simple video traffic control strategy.

A network user wishing to transmit a compressed (VBR) video source furnishes the network access controller the eight numbers corresponding to the histogram of the quantized version of the sequence to be transmitted. The access controller then determines whether or not network resources are available to handle this traffic request. A real-time histogram traffic policing control, to be described briefly at the end of the next chapter, has also been proposed to determine whether or not the video source, during transmission, is abiding by its admission contract [SKEL 1992].

There is an intuitive explanation as well as a rigorous mathematical proof, to explain why the video source histogram, alone, suffices to carry out accurate calculations of access buffer occupancy. (Note, incidentally, that this implies that the *time* variation of the video sequence, as reflected, for example, in its autocorrelation function, plays a relatively minor role in the determination of buffer occupancy statistics. It is the video histogram, the bits/frame distribution, that determines buffer occupancy).

[SKEL 1992]   Skelly, P., et al., "A Histogram-Based Model for Video Traffic Behavior in ATM Traffic Node with an Application to Congestion Control," *Proc. IEEE Infocom '92,* Florence, Italy, May 1992.

We focus first on the intuitive explanation. Note from Figure 3–26 that an average of about 250,000 bits are transmitted to the access buffer during every frame interval. This corresponds, in round numbers, to about 600 ATM cells per frame. If the buffer size per source is less than 100 cells, say, (this will be shown shortly to be adequate at normal values of utilization) this is a large enough statistical sample to have the buffer probability occupancy distribution come to equilibrium within a fraction of a frame interval. Hence the buffer occupancy distribution depends only on the number of cells arriving in each frame, not on the correlation of the numbers from cell to cell. Alternatively put, the frame-length interval of 33 msec is so long compared to the rate of cell arrivals that the access buffer occupancy distribution reaches steady-state each frame interval. The calculation of the buffer occupancy distribution $P(n)$, with n the number of cells in the buffer, is thus very simply carried out.

Let $P(n \,|\, \lambda = \lambda_i)$ be the conditional probability that the buffer occupancy is n, given the arrival rate is λ_i. Since the arrival-rate statistics are Poisson, based on our earlier discussion of transmitting each frame's cells in a random, uniformly-distributed fashion over the frame interval, this probability is fairly readily determined from elementary queueing theory. As an example, *if* the cells were exponentially-distributed in length with average length $1/\mu$, the buffer occupancy distribution would be that of a finite *M/M/1/K* queue. This is immediately written down as

$$P[n \,|\, \lambda = \lambda_i] = (1 - \rho_i)\rho_i{}^n/[1 - \rho_i{}^{K+1}] \qquad (3\text{–}116)$$

where the maximum buffer size is K, and $\rho_i \equiv \lambda_i/\mu$. In the case under discussion here, the cells are all of fixed length, and the link into the network is assumed to be transmitting cells out of the buffer at a fixed rate. The buffer occupancy distribution is that of a finite *M/D/1/K* queue. Although this distribution cannot be written down in closed form as readily as that of the *M/M/1/K* result of equation (3–116), it is easily approximated by using the r-stage Erlangian distribution E_r, with r large, to approximate the constant service time. The resultant queueing problem to be solved is the *M/E_r/1/K* queue, with r large. [KLEI 1975].

Given the conditional probability $P(n \,|\, \lambda = \lambda_i)$, the desired buffer occupancy distribution, $P(n)$, using this histogram approximation, is given by summing over all eight values of the video histogram, after appropriately weighing by the steady-state probability π_i of being at that state:

$$P(n) = \sum_{i=1}^{8} P(n \,|\, \lambda = \lambda_i)\pi_i \qquad (3\text{–}117)$$

An example of the application of this 8-bin (level) histogram approximation to the calculation of the buffer occupancy distribution for the *Star Wars* sequence of Figure 3–26 appears in Figure 3–28. This has been calculated for a

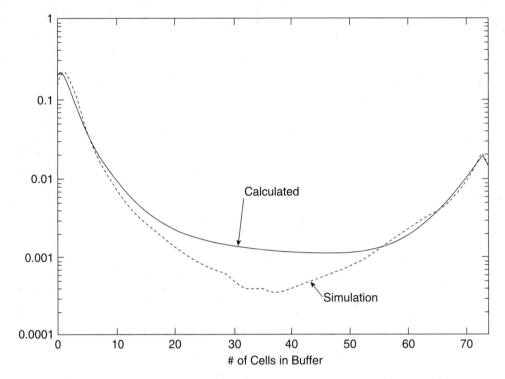

FIGURE 3–28 ■ Predicted and simulated buffer occupancy distributions for a buffer size of 74 cells and utilization $\rho = 0.8$ (from [SKEL 1993], Figure 4. © 1993 IEEE).

buffer size of 74 cells and a queue utilization of $\rho = 0.8$. Superimposed on this figure, as shown by dashed lines, is the measured distribution, obtained by simulation. Similar results for a different video sequence appear in Figure 3–29 for two values of utilization, $\rho = 0.5$ and 0.8. Note how closely the histogram approximation result tracks the distribution generated by simulation. (The utilization ρ is defined as the average arrival rate divided by the output transmission rate, in cells/sec, the same definition used in previous sections).

Given an individual video source's 8-bin histogram, one can obtain the equivalent histogram for any number of multiplexed sources by numerical convolution. An example appears in Figure 3–30. Part (a) of the figure compares the predicted histogram with the actual bit rate histogram of the composite stream. Note, by comparing with Figure 3–27a, how the convolved histogram approaches the Gaussian distribution more closely. This is, of course, to be expected because of the central limit theorem.

Figure 3–30b compares simulated and calculated buffer distributions for the seven multiplexed sources using a buffer size of 512 cells, with utilizations $\rho = 0.8$ and 0.5. Note by comparing with Figure 3–29 that the probability of high buffer occupancy has been reduced substantially because of the multi-

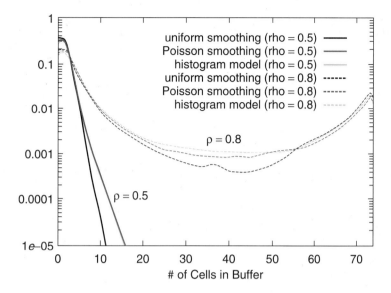

FIGURE 3–29 ■ Predicted and simulated buffer occupancy distributions for a buffer size of 74 cells and utilization ρ = 0.5 and ρ = 0.8 (from [SKEL 1993], Figure 3. © 1993 IEEE).

plexing. The cell loss probability is thus reduced correspondingly as shown by Figure 3–31. In the multiplexed case, the loss probability begins to become measurable (say > 10⁻⁴) only at utilizations exceeding 0.85. This is due to the smoothness introduced by the statistical multiplexing process and demonstrates the multiplexing gain achievable for these video sequences.

The convolved histogram, and the buffer occupancy distribution based on this, serve to distinguish the histogram model from the minisource model representation of video presented in the previous section. Recall that, there, M "on-off" (two-state) minisources were used to represent N video sources multiplexed together. First and second moment matching were then used to complete the representation. There is nothing particularly intuitive or natural about that representation. It is simply a convenient representation with calculations of buffer distribution then readily carried out. But insight into characteristics of the multiplexed stream is then lost, since there is no guarantee that the model "looks" in any realistic way (other than having the same first two moments) like the multiplexed stream. The histogram approximation described in this section works directly with an intuitively satisfying and relatively accurate model of each video signal. The multiplexed stream approximation thus retains the features of the actual multiplexed stream. Another difference between the two characterizations arises when dealing with heterogeneous sources multiplexed together. The multiple minisource representation cannot really capture the effects of distinctive differences in individual source characteristics. It only does this on the basis of first and second

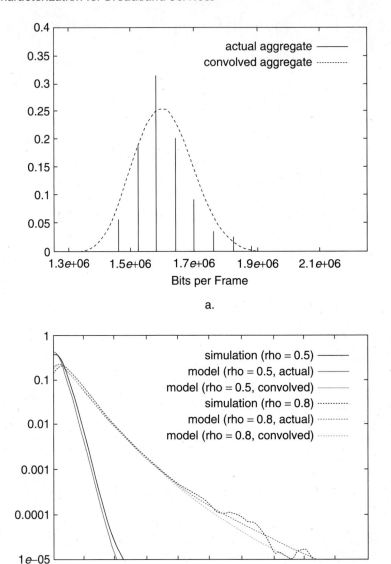

FIGURE 3–30 ■ a. Actual 5-rate histogram of seven multiplexed sources compared to the histogram derived by convolving the histograms of the individual sources. The result of the convolution is scaled for comparison. b. Buffer occupancy distributions, seven sources, buffer size 512, $\rho = 0.5$ and $\rho = 0.8$ (from [SKEL 1993], Figure 5. © 1993 IEEE).

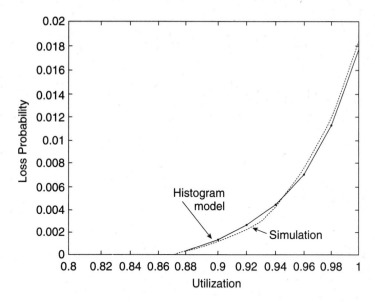

FIGURE 3–31 ■ Loss probability generated by the simulator (dashed line) and by the histogram model (solid line) as a function of utilization for seven sources using a buffer size of 512 (from [SKEL 1993], Figure 7. © 1993 IEEE).

moments. The histogram model, on the other hand, retains the characteristics of each source when the convolution is carried out.

There is a price to be paid for this "more natural" representation, however: An 8-bin histogram is clearly a much more complex set of numbers to be provided by the video source user than a set of first and second moments. Whether or not processing the 8-bin histogram and carrying out the corresponding traffic control function can be carried out readily at high ATM rates remains to be seen.

It was noted earlier that the histogram approximation can be validated rigorously in addition to intuition, as supported by the examples provided in the discussion just completed. The mathematical validation, which is also based on the fact that the frame length is much larger than the cell service time, relies on a concept called decomposition: in any system with widely-differing time scales or rates of change, subsystems with the same time scale may be aggregated together and solved independently of subsystems with substantially different time scales.

This concept has been applied rigorously by P. J. Courtois to systems such as the one under discussion in this section in which a Markov-modulated Poisson process drives a finite queue [COUR 1977]. These systems, called

[COUR 1977] Courtois, P. J., *Decomposability: Queueing and Computer System Applications,* Academic Press, 1977.

nearly completely decomposable (NCD) systems, are represented by matrix equations involving stochastic matrices such as those we discussed in section 3.4 (see equation (3–60) or (3–113) in this section). The stochastic matrices in NCD systems have the special property that they are decomposable into two sets of matrices, the elements of one of which are much smaller than the other. In particular, matrices whose off-diagonal terms are much smaller than those along the diagonals, have this property. This turns out to be the case here. These nearly completely decomposable systems turn out to have approximate solutions given by the matrix with the larger elements. The solution in the case under discussion here, an ATM multiplexer driven by variable bit rate video, turns out to be the histogram approximation. Error bounds on the validity of the approximation may be determined as well. Details appear in [SKEL 1993]. Suffice it to say that the error in the approximation depends on the ratio of the maximum transition rate in the video MMPP source model to the cell service time (the multiplexer capacity in cells/sec). This ratio is the order of 10^{-4}, demonstrating the validity of the approximation [SKEL 1993]. (As a check, note that the highest possible transition rate is the frame rate; that is, the source can at most move from state to state at the frame rate. Typically, however, because of the correlation, the transition from state to state will be the order of a magnitude less. For a frame rate of 30 frames/sec, a typical transition rate is then 3 state transitions/sec. For a single video source of the type under discussion here, the cell service rate is of the order of 20,000 cells/sec. The rate is of the order of 10^{-4}, as noted above.)

How do we now relate the video histogram model introduced in this section to the one using fluid analysis discussed in the previous section? We noted at the beginning of this section that the histogram model was appropriate for determining small buffer behavior, while the fluid model was appropriate for analyzing large buffer loss characteristics. Thus, they complement one another. Note, in particular, the difference in the buffer sizes encountered in these two sections. The examples shown in this section involved buffer sizes of 74 cells for the single video source and 512 cells for the case with seven sources multiplexed together. These compare with buffer sizes of thousands of cells obtained using the fluid model of the previous section!

But note also that the loss probabilities shown in Figure 3–31 in this section are of the order of 10^{-4} or greater for utilizations greater than 0.85 as already noted, while those calculated using the fluid approximation are 10^{-6} and less for a utilization of 0.8. It is thus clear that if it is desired to multiplex video streams at high utilization, yet obtain very low loss probabilities of the order of 10^{-6} or less, very large buffer sizes are needed. This also implies substantial queueing delay, depending of course on the actual ATM capacity. For real-time video transmission with some interactive component, as in video conferencing, significant transmission delay may be intolerable. In this case it is clear that the solution is to increase the transmission capacity used, thereby reducing the utilization.

In the next section we continue this analysis of the small and large buffer regions, using the terminology "cell" and "burst" regions, respectively, that has been introduced in the literature [HUI 1988], [COST 1991]. We will introduce a simple ad hoc technique that enables us to combine the curves obtained in the two regions quite simply, thereby obtaining a smooth, single loss probability curve that shows the variation with buffer size. The cell/burst region characterization is found to be applicable not just to video sources, but to any sources modeled as doubly-stochastic sources, as noted earlier.

3.8 ▪ DOUBLY-STOCHASTIC PROCESSES—CELL AND BURST REGIONS

As noted at the end of the previous section, as well as in a number of places earlier, the loss probability performance curve of a statistical multiplexer, obtained by plotting cell loss probability as a function of multiplexer buffer size, is found to break into two separate regions. The region of small buffer sizes has been termed the "cell region" [HUI 1988], [COST 1991]. In the previous section we implicitly discussed the small buffer, cell region for the video traffic case. The large buffer region was the one modeled, using fluid analysis to represent multiplexed video sources, in section 3.6.

We now discuss these two regions in more detail. Consider the basic queueing model of a statistical multiplexer and its resultant loss performance characteristic portrayed in Figure 3–32. For small buffer sizes, the cell loss probability is found to, at first, drop rapidly as the buffer size increases; at some point, depending on the utilization and traffic characteristic, the loss probability begins to decrease more slowly, albeit at an exponential rate, as the buffer size continues to increase. The first region of decrease is the one we have been calling cell region, the second, the burst region, as indicated in Figure 3–32b.

The simplest explanation for the initial rapid decrease in loss probability, as the buffer size increases, is the obvious one: for a given utilization (average source arrival rate divided by link capacity), the larger the buffer the smaller the probability the buffer will be full and hence lose cells. The $M/M/1$ queueing model, assuming Poisson arrivals and exponentially-distributed cell (or packet) lengths demonstrates this very clearly. Given a buffer size of K cells and a utilization ρ, the probability the buffer is full is given by

$$P(K) = (1-\rho)\rho^K / \left(1 - \rho^{K+1}\right) \qquad (3\text{--}118)$$

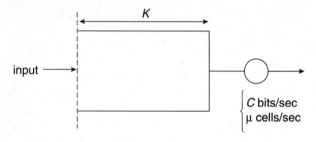

a. Statistical multiplexer queueing model.

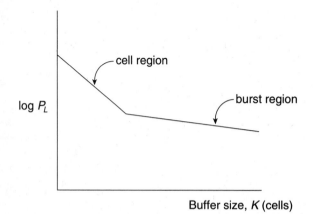

b. Loss performance, fixed utilization.

FIGURE 3–32 ■ Cell/burst regions, typical traffic input.

This is a special case of equation (3–116). For K large enough and $\rho < 1$, this probability decreases as ρ^K, hence linearly with K on a log scale.

To account for the two regions, however, that appear with more complex traffic types than the simple Poisson-exponential model, such as VBR video, one must resort to more realistic models of the type we have discussed thus far in this book. More specifically, we shall use a doubly-stochastic process to model the traffic arrivals. The MMPP of section 3.4 and the fluid model of section 3.6 are examples of such processes.

More generally, in such a process, the source is modeled as moving randomly between a set of states, each state characterized by an arrival process with some specified statistical behavior. The generalization of Figures 3–11 and 3–25 for the MMPP, or Figure 3–22 for the fluid-flow model, is given by allowing the arrival in each state to be some general random process rather than Poisson or constant flow as in those cases respectively.

In the cell region, movement between states is assumed to take a very long time; that is, the transition rates between states are small compared to the arrival rates at the various states. This implies that the correlation interval (related to the transition time between states) is long compared to the arrival rate process. The buffer is small enough that it may thus be assumed to reach steady state with the source in any state. Its occupancy distribution, and hence the loss probability, are thus obtained by focusing on individual states and ignoring the transitions between states. This is precisely the approach used in obtaining the video histogram model of the previous section.

Now let the buffer size continue to increase. Eventually a point is reached at which the buffer is large enough to absorb individual cell arrivals, and no loss at the individual cell level occurs. Losses are now due to bursts of cells arriving and overflowing the buffer. Continued increase of the buffer size results in relatively little decrease in the loss probability since the buffer is large enough to generally absorb bursts when they occur. The burst arrivals can be modeled as a fluid arrival process, since individual cells no longer play a role, and fluid analysis takes over in this region.

In this section we summarize an ad hoc technique developed by Shroff that captures the cell and burst region loss probabilities quite simply and accurately with minimal calculation required [SHRO 1995]. It uses a so-called Generalized Histogram Model to represent the doubly stochastic source in the cell region, extending Skelly's video histogram model described in the previous section. This model predicts that the loss probability will level off and remain constant with buffer size at some buffer threshold value. This is the point at which the burst region begins. From this point on, the fluid-flow representation of the doubly stochastic source is used to determine the loss probability characteristics in the burst region. Another approximation technique appearing in the literature models the special case of the superposition of two-state on-off sources such as those discussed earlier in this chapter by a suitably chosen two-state MMPP [BAIO 1991]. This two-state MMPP is found to generate both the cell and burst region quite accurately in this case. The ad hoc technique we describe in this section gives results comparable to their approximation in this special case [SHRO 1995].

To introduce the ad hoc technique for connecting the cell and burst regions, we focus first on a deterministic arrival process. In this case all cells arrive equally spaced. There are two reasons for starting with this process. The first is that we can obtain the loss probability very simply, as we shall see. The second is that study indicates that this type of arrival process results in the lowest possible buffer occupancy, and hence lowest loss probability, for a video source at an ATM multiplexer [SHRO 1995].

Recall that, in the last section, in introducing the histogram model for VBR video, we assumed the cells generated during each frame interval were transmitted out randomly and uniformly during the next frame interval. This

---

[BAIO 1991]   Baiocchi, A., et al., "Loss Performance Analysis of an ATM Multiplexer Loaded with High Speed On-Off Sources," *IEEE JSAC, 9,* 3 (April 1991): 388–393.

resulted in a good approximation to a Poisson source, and enabled us to model a given video source as a MMPP. If, instead, one transmits the cells generated during each frame uniformly spaced over the next frame interval, one obtains the deterministic arrival process noted above. In particular, if the video stream is quantized to a number of levels, as was assumed in the previous section, one gets as a model of the video signal, in this case, a Markov-modulated deterministic arrival process. But, as was the case in the previous section, one can readily show, because of the high correlation from frame-to-frame, that, with small buffer sizes, a buffer accepting such a deterministic stream comes to its steady-state distribution very quickly each frame interval. We can thus ignore the Markov state transitions and assume, for the analysis of this model, that each of the states—or levels of the histogram—lasts for a very long (read infinite) time. The analysis of this model, buttressed by simulation, shows the loss probability to be lower than that obtained for the MMPP model of the previous section [SHRO 1995]. There is, however, one potential problem with deterministic smoothing, frame-by-frame. It can result in periodic correlation among multiplexed sources, giving rise to periodic increases in buffer occupancy. This can be remedied by introducing some random jitter in the arriving streams.

The traffic model with which we choose to begin this discussion is one in which the signal is quantized into B levels or bins, generalizing the specific eight-level case of the previous section. Level i, $1 \le i \le B$, for which λ_i cells/sec are transmitted (λ_i cells/frame in the case of video), is represented by its probability of occupancy π_i, as in previous sections. This is portrayed schematically in Figure 3–33. Note that this picture is the same as would be drawn for the video histogram approximation of the last section, except that here we are assuming deterministic arrivals at each state, as indicated in the figure.

By first calculating the probability of loss for a given arrival rate (a given bin), and then weighting appropriately by the arrival rate and probability π_i of that bin, one can calculate the overall loss probability in a manner similar to what was done in determining the buffer occupancy distribution [equation (3–117)] in the previous section. The loss probability calculation for a deterministic arrival stream at an ATM queue is particularly simple. Figure 3–34 displays a deterministic stream of rate λ cells/sec arriving at a finite buffer K cells in size, which is in turn served by a deterministic server outputting μ cells/sec, uniformly spaced, when the queue is nonempty, as in the case of an ATM node. This of course represents a $D/D/1/K$ queue. To be general here, we take the units of λ and μ to be cells/sec. In doing calculations later we shall sometimes refer to λ in units of bits/sec, or bits/frame in the case of video. In those cases we have to be careful to reference λ to the capacity C, in the same units. Since the utilization $\rho = \lambda/\mu$ or λ/C, with consistent units used, is dimensionless, it does not matter which units we use for λ, pro-

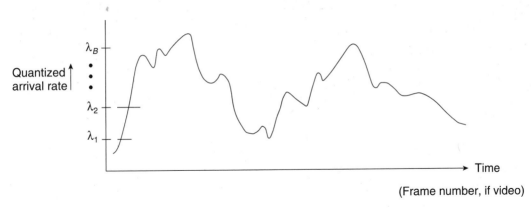

a. Quantization of signal.

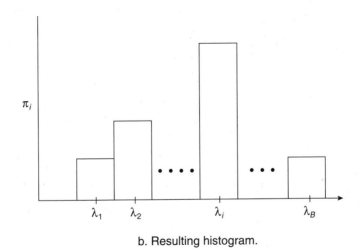

b. Resulting histogram.

FIGURE 3–33 ■ Histogram approximation, deterministic arrivals.

vided we *are* consistent. Note from the figure, that when the cell arrival spacing $1/\lambda$ is greater than the departing cell spacing $1/\mu$, no loss can occur: Each cell is immediately served on arrival. We thus have

$$P_L = 0: \quad 1/\lambda > 1/\mu, \quad \text{or} \quad \lambda < \mu \tag{3–119}$$

In this case the buffer is either empty, or serving (transmitting) a cell. There are no other possibilities. In particular, it is left for the reader to show that the probability p_0 the queue is empty, is simply

$$p_0 = 1 - \lambda/\mu = 1 - \rho \tag{3–120}$$

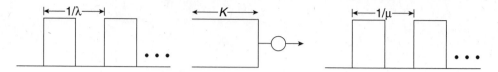

FIGURE 3–34 ■ Loss probability calculation, $D/D/1/K$ queue.

The probability a cell is being transmitted is

$$p_1 = \rho = \lambda/\mu \qquad (3\text{--}121)$$

[Hint: If there is no loss, the throughput must be λ (the arrival rate), which, in turn, is given by $\lambda = \mu(1 - p_0)$ for a single-server queue. Here, p_0 is the probability the queue is empty. Why? See section 5.4, later in this book. In particular, note equation (5–19) and the discussion following].

Now consider the other possibility $\lambda > \mu$, for which the spacing $1/\lambda$ of arriving cells is less than the spacing $1/\mu$ of departing cells. Clearly there will be cell loss in this case, while the buffer occupancy will hover close to full occupancy. To determine the loss probability, consider a very long interval T, starting with the buffer initially empty. In this interval, exactly λT cells will arrive. In this same interval, the first K cells will be buffered, and, from that point on, the number lost will be the difference between the number arriving and the number served. The loss probability is the ratio of the number lost to those arriving, in the limit, as $T \to \infty$. We thus have the loss probability in this case given by

$$\lambda > \mu: \qquad P_L = \lim_{T \to \infty} \frac{\lambda T - \mu T - K}{\lambda T}$$

$$= 1 - \frac{1}{\rho} \qquad \rho \equiv \lambda/\mu > 1 \qquad (3\text{--}122)$$

(This is actually a general expression applicable to other arrival processes as will be seen later in this section as well as in Chapter 4. See equation (4–51a) and the discussion leading to it, for example).

We use equation (3–119) and (3–122) to determine the loss probability of a Markov-modulated deterministic arrival stream for the case when transitions between states (histogram bins or levels) are very slow compared to arrivals when in a given state. Specifically, refer back to our B-bin histogram model. We consider the general arrival case first, then return to the deterministic case. Let P_{L_i} be the loss probability conditioned on being in bin i with arrival rate λ_i. The number of cells lost over a long interval T, while in this state, is $P_{L_i}\lambda_i T\pi_i$, with π_i, again, the (histogram) probability of being in this state. The total number of cells lost is obtained by summing over all B states (bins). The ratio of this number to the total number arriving is just the desired loss probability P_L. In particular, the reader is asked to verify that the loss probability is found to be given by

$$P_L = \frac{1}{E(\lambda)} \sum_{i=1}^{B} P_{L_i} \lambda_i \pi_i \qquad (3\text{--}123)$$

with

$$E(\lambda) = \sum_{i=1}^{B} \lambda_i \pi_i \qquad (3\text{--}124)$$

(Although the units of λ_i and $E(\lambda)$ are both taken as cells/sec here, we could equally-well have used bits/sec, or bits/frame. Note that the resultant expression for P_L is independent of the units chosen).

For the special case of deterministic arrivals (deterministic video smoothing as an example),

$$P_{L_i} = 0, \qquad \lambda_i < \mu$$

$$P_{L_i} = 1 - \frac{1}{\rho_i} \qquad \rho_i \equiv \frac{\lambda_i}{\mu} > 1 \qquad (3\text{--}125)$$

Loss just occurs, using this model, in the higher-arrival rate states for which the deterministic arrival rate is greater than the buffer service rate. Consider the JPEG-coded *Star Wars* video sequence of Figure 3–26 of the previous section as an example. Its (quantized) eight-bin histogram in units of bits/frame rather than cells/frame, appears in Figure 3–27a and an equivalent table of histogram entries is reproduced in Table 3–2. From either the figure or the table, we find $E(\lambda) \doteq 235,000$ bits/frame. Letting the link capacity C be written in the same units of bits/frame and taking, as an example, the utilization $\rho \equiv E(\lambda)/C = 0.7$, we have $C = 336,000$ bits/frame. (This corresponds to a transmission capacity of approximately 10 Mbps if a 30 frame/sec rate is used). Then the only histogram level contributing to the loss is the highest one, with $\lambda_8 = 350,000$ bits/frame. At this level, the probability of occurrence π_8 is $\doteq 0.04$. The utilization at this state is $\rho_8 = \lambda_8/C = 1.04$, with the conditional probability of loss P_{L_i} readily found, using equation (3–125), to be 0.04. We thus have, from equation (3–123), $P_L = 0.002$. If we decrease the transmission capacity to $C = 294,000$ bits/frame, or 8.8 Mbps at a 30 frame/sec rate, the overall utilization increases to $\rho = 0.8$. Two histogram levels, one at 320,000 bits per frame and the highest at 350,000 bits/frame, now result in cell loss. Repeating the calculation, again using equations (3–125) and (3–123), we now find $P_L = 0.016$. This clearly shows the dependence on transmission capacity.

Note that nowhere does the buffer size K enter into the calculations. The histogram approximation for the case of deterministic smoothing predicts a single probability of loss value, independent of buffer size. Both the cell and the burst region thus coalesce into one constant value according to this approximation. Simulation shows that the loss probability in the case of deter-

TABLE 3–2 ■ Histogram Entries, Figure 3–27a

λ_i (bits/frame)	π_i
140,000	0.025
170,000	0.19
200,000	0.145
230,000	0.21
260,000	0.24
290,000	0.09
320,000	0.06
350,000	0.04

ministic smoothing of real video traffic does, in fact, decrease slightly with buffer size, as predicted by the flow model in the burst region. Figure 3–35, taken from [SHRO 1995], shows the results of both analysis and simulation for a VBR video strip taken from another portion of the *Star Wars* sequence referred to in the previous section (see Figure 3–26). The calculations in the case of Figure 3–35 were carried out for ten levels of quantization and for the capacity C chosen to have an overall $\rho = 0.5$. Note how closely simulation and analysis track one another, with the simulation loss probability decreasing slightly with buffer size, as noted above.

Also shown in the same set of figures are comparable results for the same video sequence using random (Poisson) smoothing, just as described in the previous section. Note that the loss probability in this case is always higher than that of the deterministically-smoothed case, as noted previously, approaching the deterministic value for large buffer sizes. In this case, the determination of P_{L_i} (the loss probability at histogram level i) is carried out assuming Poisson arrivals and deterministic service time; that is, a finite $M/D/1/K$ queue. As noted in the discussion in the previous section, following equation (3–116), this calculation at each histogram level is most easily carried out using an r-stage Erlangian distribution, r large, to approximate the deterministic service time.

The reason why random arrivals provide a higher loss probability than do deterministic arrivals is fairly clear: Because of the variation in arrival times, some cells may arrive bunched up, resulting in buffer overflow for small buffer sizes, even when the histogram-level utilization $\rho_i < 1$. As the buffer size increases beyond a certain point, the buffer is large enough to absorb these arrival-time variations, and the random arrival loss probability approaches that of the deterministic case.

Note, however, that for large enough buffer sizes the assumption made that each histogram state reaches steady state is no longer valid. The histogram steady state model, neglecting state transitions, predicts the loss

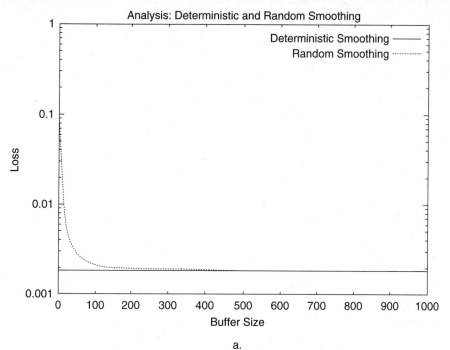

a.

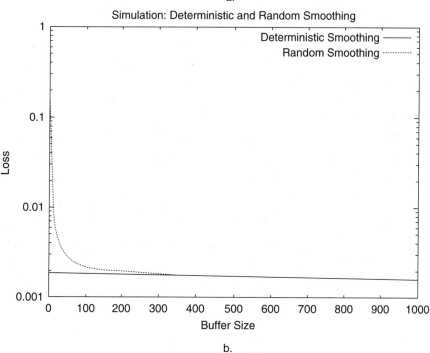

b.

FIGURE 3–35 ■ Cell and burst regions for deterministic and random smoothing obtained by a. analysis and b. simulation. Video signal, $\rho = 0.5$ (from [SHRO 1995], Figure 2–13).

probability will level off at a constant value, independent of buffer size, as already noted. In actuality, the state transitions must now be taken into account, leading to continued reduction in loss probability as the buffer size increases rather than leveling off. This represents the onset of the burst region. In this region, as already noted, loss probability calculations may be carried out quite accurately using fluid-flow analysis.

Recall from section 3.6 that fluid-flow analysis is conceptually quite simple and the calculation of the loss probability, as approximated by the survivor function $G(x)$, is relatively straightforward. In fact, as we showed in that section, for large buffer sizes the single eigenvalue simple exponential variation of loss probability with buffer size is quite accurate. The only problem is that of calculating the constant term in front of the exponential [see equation (3–111)]. This is where we invoke Shroff's ad hoc approximation combining the cell and burst region results [SHRO 1995]. The histogram approximation, as extended to arrival streams other than those of the Poisson type (MMPP) discussed in the previous section, and neglecting state transitions, is used to calculate the loss probability in the small buffer, cell region. At the point where the loss probability begins to level off with buffer size and the slope of the curve equals that of the fluid approximation single exponential result, that is, as given by the leading eigenvalue, we continue the curve using the fluid approximation result. This takes us into the burst region [SHRO 1995]. This approximation is diagrammed in Figure 3–36.

In particular, let $P_L(K)|_{cell}$ be the loss probability as a function of buffer size K in the cell region. Let $P_L(K)|_{burst}$ be the loss probability in the burst region. In that region, from fluid-flow analysis, we have, as an asymptotic approximation (see equation (3–43) as an example),

$$P_L(K)|_{burst} \sim Ae^{zK} \tag{3–126}$$

with z the leading (smallest negative) eigenvalue and A an undetermined constant. At some buffer size K_o, the slope of the logarithm of the loss probability in the cell region equals z, the slope in the burst region. Shroff's ad hoc technique matches the loss probabilities at this buffer value:

$$K = K_0: \qquad \frac{d}{dK} \log P_L(K)|_{cell} = z \tag{3–127}$$

From the point K_o on, we now use the fluid-flow approximation. Hence, in the burst region we write

$$P_L(K)|_{burst} = P_L(K_0)|_{cell}\, e^{z(K-K_o)} \tag{3–128}$$

Clearly, the undetermined constant A in equation (3–126) is given, using this ad hoc approximation technique, by

$$A = P_L(K_0)|_{cell}\, e^{-zK_o} \tag{3–129}$$

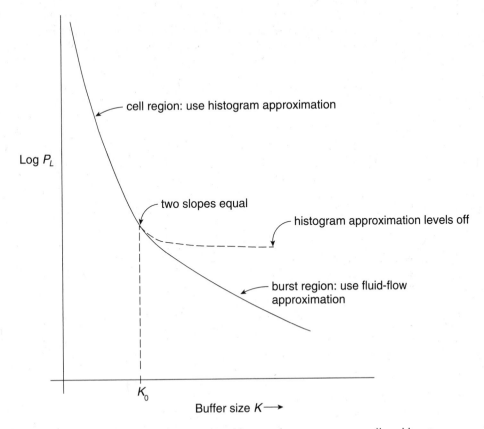

FIGURE 3–36 ▪ Determination of loss performance curve, cell and burst regions.

(Recall again, to avoid confusion, that the eigenvalue z is a *negative* real number).

We provide an example of the application of this approximation using $M/M/1/K$ analysis; that is, assuming exponentially-distributed cell (packet) lengths, to simplify the calculation of the cell region. Specifically, we again use the eight-bin (level) histogram approximation to the JPEG-coded *Star Wars* video sequence of Figure 3–26 that we used as an example in calculating the deterministic arrival case loss probability. Recall that the histogram for this case is tabulated in Table 3–2. The resultant loss probability, independent of buffer size K, was found to be $P_L = 0.016$ for a utilization of $\rho = 0.8$. We focus first on the cell region.

Each of the eight states in this case is now represented by an $M/M/1/K$ queue with the utilization appropriately chosen for that state. More specifically, say a frame of the quantized video sequence is at level i, $1 \leq i \leq 8$, outputting λ_i bits/frame. We assume these bits are formed into exponentially-

TABLE 3–3 ■ State Utilizations, $\rho = E(\lambda)/C = 0.8$, Table 3–2

λ_i (bits/frame)	$\rho_i = \lambda_i/C$ ($C = 294{,}000$ bits/frame)
140,000	0.476
170,000	0.578
200,000	0.680
230,000	0.782
260,000	0.884
290,000	0.986
320,000	1.088
350,000	1.190

distributed cells, which are in turn fed randomly into the multiplexer queue, approximating a Poisson arrival process. Conditioned on being at this level or state, with corresponding utilization ρ_i, the loss probability P_{L_i} is just the probability the buffer is full, and, from equation (3–116), is given by[4]

$$P_{L_i} = (1 - \rho_i)\rho_i^K/[1 - \rho_i^{K+1}] \qquad (3\text{--}130)$$

This is to be compared with the deterministic cell arrival, cell departure result of equation (3–125). Equation (3–130) is then used together with equation (3–123) to determine the cell loss probability P_L for a given buffer size K. Varying K and calculating the corresponding loss probability, we can trace out a complete loss probability vs. buffer size curve for this traffic model in the cell region.

As an example, take the overall utilization $\rho = E(\lambda)/C = 0.8$. Recall that for the histogram of Table 3–2 we had $E(\lambda) = 235{,}000$ bits/frame, so that for a utilization of $\rho = 0.8$, $C = 294{,}000$ bits/frame. The corresponding bin, or level, utilizations are then given by $\rho_i = \lambda_i/C$, $1 \leq i \leq 8$, and are tabulated in Table 3–3. (Note, as a check, that in the deterministic arrival, deterministic departure case, only the two highest states or levels contribute to the loss probability. Calculating the loss probability for these two states gives the value of $P_L = 0.016$ quoted earlier). These values of state utilization ρ_i, $1 \leq i \leq 8$, are used first in equation (3–130) and then in equation (3–123), together with the corresponding state probabilities from Table 3–2 to trace out the loss probability curve in the cell region. The resultant curve is plotted in Figure 3–37.

Note that as the buffer size K is increased indefinitely, the conditional loss probabilities P_{L_i}, for $\rho_i < 1$, go to zero from equation (3–130), as expected. For values of $\rho_i > 1$, however, it is readily shown from equation (3–130) that

---

[4]Strictly speaking, equation (3–130) represents the blocking probability of the $M/M/1/K$ queue. For Poisson arrivals, the loss and blocking probabilities are the same, however [SCHW 1987].

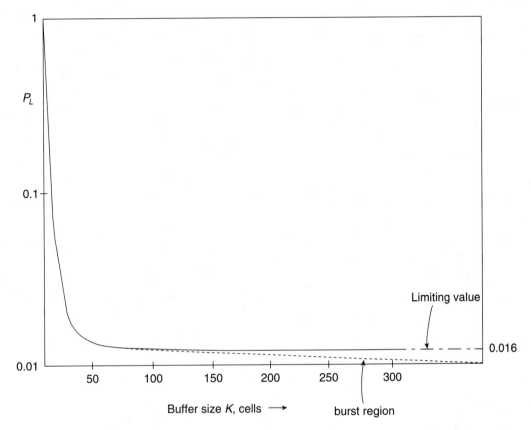

FIGURE 3–37 ▪ Loss probability curve, cell region, *M/M/*1*/K* model, data of Figure 3–27a, ρ = 0.8.

P_{L_i} approaches the limiting value $1 - 1/\rho_i$. This is precisely the value obtained for the deterministic arrival—deterministic service model discussed earlier and summarized by equation (3–125). From equation (3–123), then, the *M/M/*1*/K* model result thus approaches that of the deterministic case, as noted earlier. In particular, for this example, with ρ = 0.8, the limiting loss probability predicted by this model, as $K \to \infty$, is just $P_L = 0.016$, the value found earlier using the deterministic model for the same example. This limiting loss probability is so indicated in Figure 3–37.

That this asymptotic result, $P_{L_i} \to 1 - 1/\rho_i$, $\rho_i > 1$, is quite general, is readily shown using the following simple argument. Consider a single-server queue such as the one representing a statistical multiplexer feeding a single transmission link of the type we have been discussing. This was represented by Figure 3–32a, and is repeated, with the arrival rate λ and throughput γ explicitly shown, in Figure 3–38. (We focus on one state only and drop the

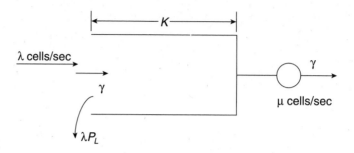

FIGURE 3–38 ■ Calculation of throughput.

subscript i for simplicity). We show in this figure the relation between arrival rate (load) λ and throughput γ.

$$\gamma = \lambda(1 - P_L) \tag{3–131}$$

But for a single-server queue, it is also well-known that the throughput is simply the capacity μ of the queue, times the probability the queue is non-empty:

$$\gamma = \mu(1 - p_0) \tag{3–132}$$

Here, p_0 is the probability the queue is empty. Equating equations (3–131) and (3–132), and solving for the loss probability P_L, we have

$$P_L = 1 - \frac{(1 - p_0)}{\rho} \tag{3–133}$$

For $\rho > 1$ and buffer size K increasing the probability p_0 the buffer is empty approaches zero. We thus have $P_L \to 1 - 1/\rho$, as predicted. [Alternately, for large enough ρ, the throughput levels off at $\gamma = \mu$. Then $P_L \to 1 - 1/\rho$, from equations (3–131) and (3–132)].

We return now to our example and show how we use fluid analysis to determine the loss probability for a Markov-modulated source in the burst region. We continue to represent the source by the same underlying eight-state, continuous-time Markov process as in the cell region. The only difference now is that, with the buffer size K large enough, groups of cells arriving together may be aggregated into a continuous stream of traffic representable by a fluid. State i, $1 \le i \le B$, is then represented not as a Poisson source, but as a constant-rate source of rate λ_i. The n-state Markov-modulated Poisson process (MMPP) source of Figure 3–11 here becomes the B-state Markov-modulated fluid source of Figure 3–39. Transitions between states are governed by the same rate parameters, μ_{ij}, as in the MMPP model, as shown in Figure 3–39, but now the time scale in the burst region is such as to specifically require them, rather than ignoring them, as in the cell region.

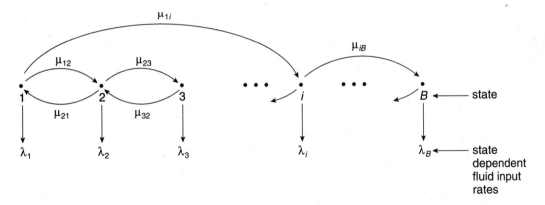

FIGURE 3–39 ▪ Markov-modulated fluid source model (fluid analog of MMPP model, Figure 3–11).

The underlying continuous-time Markov chain is again represented by its $B \times B$ infinitesimal generating matrix M, given, in general, by

$$
M = \begin{bmatrix}
\mu_{11} & \mu_{12} & \mu_{13} & \cdots & \mu_{1j} & \cdots & \mu_{1B} \\
\mu_{21} & \mu_{22} & \mu_{23} & \cdots & \mu_{2j} & \cdots & \mu_{2B} \\
\vdots & & & & & & \\
\mu_{i1} & \mu_{i2} & \mu_{i3} & \cdots & \mu_{ij} & \cdots & \mu_{iB} \\
\vdots & & & & & & \\
\mu_{B1} & \mu_{B2} & \mu_{B3} & \cdots & \mu_{Bj} & \cdots & \mu_{BB}
\end{bmatrix}
\tag{3–134}
$$

The diagonal rate parameter μ_{ii} is given by

$$
\mu_{ii} = -\sum_{\substack{j=1 \\ i \neq j}}^{B} \mu_{ij} \qquad 1 \leq i \leq B
\tag{3–135}
$$

The B stationary state probabilities, $\pi_i,\ 1 \leq i \leq B$, are again represented, in vector form, as the solution to the matrix equation

$$
\pi\, M = 0
\tag{3–136}
$$

How do we now invoke the fluid model? The procedure is conceptually quite simple and generalizes the fluid source model analysis of section 3.6. Since the buffer the source accesses is taken to be very large, we take the buffer or queue occupancy as a continuous random variable x. This is shown in Figure 3–40. We define a steady-state probability $F_i(x)$, as the probability *jointly* that the queue size is less than or equal to x, with the source in state i:

$$
F_i(x) \equiv P\ [\text{queue} \leq x,\ \text{state } i]
\tag{3–137}
$$

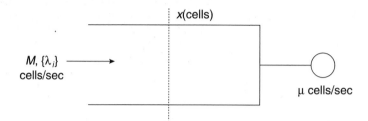

FIGURE 3–40 ■ Markov-modulated fluid source applied to a queue.

Note that this definition generalizes equation (3–97) in section 3.6, where state i specifically represented i mini sources on. As done first in section 3.3 and then again in section 3.6, we derive a set of first-order differential equations for $F_i(x)$, $1 \le i \le B$. It is left to the reader to show that, by following the same approach as in deriving equation (3–99) in section 3.6, one obtains the following differential equation for $F_i(x)$:

$$(\lambda_i - \mu)\frac{dF_i x}{dx} = \sum_{j=1}^{B} \mu_{ji} F_j(x) \qquad 1 \le i \le B \qquad (3\text{--}138)$$

The parameter μ is the link capacity in cells/sec, as shown in Figure 3–40. The units of λ_i and x are cells/sec and cells, respectively. Note that we must have $\lambda_i \ne \mu$, as was the case with the corresponding rates and capacities encountered previously in this chapter.

We can now write equation (3–138) in our familiar vector form,

$$\frac{dF(x)}{dx} D = F(x)M \qquad (3\text{--}139)$$

with

$$F(x) \equiv [F_1(x), F_2(x), \ldots F_B(x)] \qquad (3\text{--}140)$$

M, the $B \times B$ matrix of equation (3–134), and

$$D \equiv \text{diag}[\lambda_i - \mu] \qquad (3\text{--}141)$$

The solution to equation (3–139) is again given by the sum of B exponentials involving the B eigenvalues and eigenvectors satisfying the eigenvalue equation

$$z_i \Phi_j D = \Phi_j M \qquad 1 \le j \le B \qquad (3\text{--}142)$$

The eigenvalues can readily be found as the eigenvalues of the matrix MD^{-1}, or by defining a reduced matrix M', obtained by dividing the right-hand side of equation (3–138) through by $(\lambda_i - \mu)$. This was the procedure proposed in section 3.3. One then obtains the same form of matrix equation as shown in equation (3–15c) in that section:

$$\frac{d\boldsymbol{F}(x)}{dx} = \boldsymbol{F}(x)M' \qquad\qquad (3\text{--}143)$$

The matrix M' generalizes the one used previously in writing equation (3–15c).

Rather than proceed, as was done earlier, by setting up boundary conditions to find the complete solution $\boldsymbol{F}(x)$, in terms of the eigenvalues and eigenvectors, we proceed directly to the result of interest here. Letting z be the smallest negative, or dominant, eigenvalue, writing $F(x) = \sum_{j=1}^{B} F_j(x)$, and then letting $G(x) = 1 - F(x)$, the survivor function, we have, finally, as was found previously in equations (3–107) and (3–111),

$$G\,(x) \doteq Ae^{zx} \qquad\qquad (3\text{--}144)$$

We now let $G(x)$ (the survivor function) be an approximation to $P_L(K)$ (the desired loss probability in the burst region) with the buffer size K represented by the continuous variable x. We thus equate equations (3–144) and (3–126). The whole point of this analysis, then, is to find the dominant eigenvalue z, the smallest negative eigenvalue satisfying equation (3–142) or (3–143).

As an example of the utility of this analysis, we continue with the eight-level video signal example for which we obtained the loss probability cell region shown in Figure 3–37. Recall that this video sequence is represented by the quantized version of the 3000-frame video sequence of Figure 3–26. Measurements have been made of the transition rates appearing in the infinitesimal generating matrix M for this signal. The video frame rate was set at 24 frames/sec in this case [SKEL 1993]. They appear, reproduced, in Table 3–4. Note that the diagonal elements μ_{ij} have all been set equal to the negative sum of the elements in their respective rows, as required. Note also that most of the nonzero entries cluster around the diagonal, indicating that most transitions take place to adjacent states. The dominant (smallest negative) eigenvalue corresponding to the eigenvalue equations (3–142) or (3–143) for this case turns out to be given by $z = -0.95 \times 10^{-3}$. Details are left to the reader as an exercise. (Although the calculation of this eigenvalue is relatively straight-

---

TABLE 3–4 ▪ Generating Matrix M, Video Sequence, Figure 3–26

$$M = \begin{bmatrix}
-4.737 & 4.105 & 0.000 & 0.316 & 0.000 & 0.316 & 0.000 & 0.000 \\
0.643 & -1.714 & 0.771 & 0.043 & 0.129 & 0.043 & 0.086 & 0.000 \\
0.000 & 1.408 & -2.254 & 0.845 & 0.000 & 0.000 & 0.000 & 0.000 \\
0.000 & 0.082 & 0.740 & -1.562 & 0.616 & 0.082 & 0.000 & 0.041 \\
0.000 & 0.000 & 0.111 & 0.741 & -1.333 & 0.407 & 0.074 & 0.000 \\
0.000 & 0.000 & 0.000 & 0.095 & 1.518 & -3.130 & 1.423 & 0.095 \\
0.000 & 0.000 & 0.000 & 0.000 & 0.137 & 2.606 & -2.743 & 0.000 \\
0.000 & 0.000 & 0.000 & 0.000 & 0.189 & 0.000 & 0.189 & -0.378
\end{bmatrix}$$

(From [SKEL 1993])

forward, care has to be taken to ensure the units of the diagonal matrix D are in cells/sec. In getting this value for the eigenvalue, we have assumed each ATM cell contains 48 video octets. Note also that the histogram entries of Table 3–2 are in bits/frame).

The buffer size at which the slope of the cell region of Figure 3–37 equals the value of -0.95×10^{-3} is at about $K_0 = 75$ cells. This is then the point at which we enter the burst region, following Shroff's ad hoc approximation for this example. The beginning of the burst region is also indicated in Figure 3–37. In Figure 3–41 we portray the combined cell-burst region for this exam-

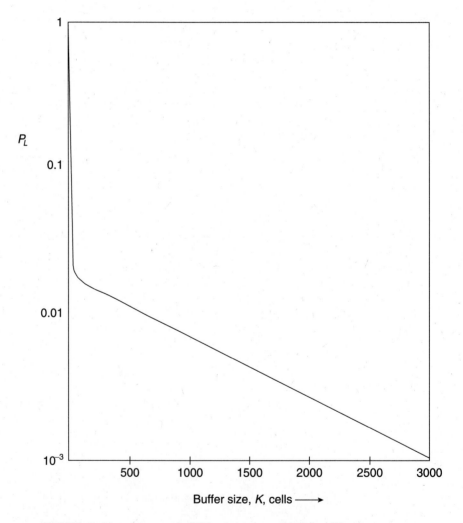

FIGURE 3–41 ■ Loss probability curve, combined cell/burst regions, $M/M/1/K$ model, data of Figure 3–27a, $\rho = 0.8$.

ple, with emphasis on the burst region. The equation for loss probability in the burst region is given by

$$P_L(K)\big|_{burst} \sim 0.017e^{-0.95 \times 10^{-3}\,(K-75)} \qquad\qquad (3\text{--}145)$$

A number of other examples using this ad hoc approximation appear in [SHRO 1995]. Two of these are reproduced here in Figures 3–42 and 3–43. Figure 3–42 shows the loss probability buffer size curve for a JPEG-coded video source with random (Poisson) smoothing. Analysis using the MMPP model shows relatively good agreement with simulation for various values of utilization ρ. Figure 3–43 shows the loss probability characteristic for a number of multiplexed on-off sources such as those used in modeling video sources in section 3.6. The example chosen appears in [BAIO 1991] and the simulation points shown are taken from their paper as well. The ad hoc approximation analysis result is indicated by "Hybrid Model". The analysis of Baiochi et al., using one equivalent on-off model to represent the multiplexed on-off sources, tracks the simulation results accurately as well. Also shown for comparison is the loss curve predicted by using an $M/D/1/K$ approximation. Note that this result fails completely to capture the loss curve, except at extremely low values of buffer size.

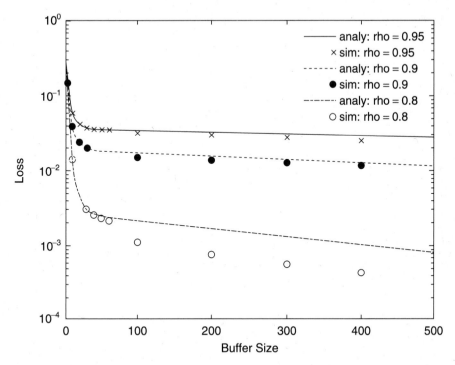

FIGURE 3–42 ▪ Loss versus buffer size for JPEG video source modeled as MMPP source (from [SHRO 1995], Figure 4–11).

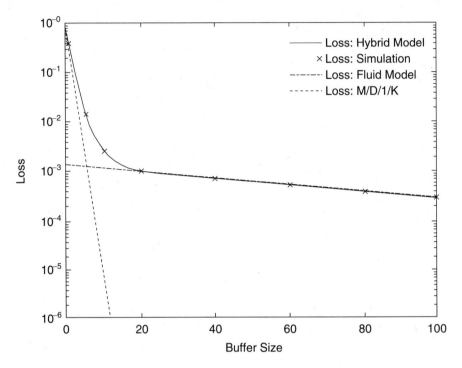

FIGURE 3–43 ■ Loss-buffer characteristic of multiplexed on-off sources (from [SHRO 1995], Figure 4–13).

3.9 ■ BURSTY TRAFFIC MODEL

In the previous sections in this chapter we have focused on a number of ways of characterizing voice and video. We complete our discussion of traffic characterization by introducing a simple two-state model for bursty traffic. Recall that a two-state model was used to characterize voice (Figure 3–3). It was used as well in our mini-source modeling of video traffic (Figure 3–21).

We have already hinted at such a two-state model for bursty traffic in section 3.1 (Figure 3–2c). We indicated there that a bursty source is one that is characterized by alternating periods of inactivity and activity. This is similar to the silent/talk spurt characterization of voice introduced in section 3.2. The basic difference is that in the case of bursty sources, the period of inactivity is much longer than the active period, during which the source transmits. Stated another way, a bursty source is generally taken to be one in which, after a period of quiescence, it transmits a burst of cells, then lapses back into inactivity, repeating this process in alternating fashion. A variety of models have been proposed for such a process. One of the most common is the "bulk arrival process," a Poisson arrival process in which a number of cells or packets are generated at each Poisson arrival time [KLEI 1975]. (In the queueing literature, reference is made to a burst, or group, of customers arriving at the same time). As previously noted, we shall use a somewhat different, two-state model. It appears to reflect the characteristics of the bursty traffic to be represented more accurately. However, it will be noted that the two-state model degenerates into the bulk arrival process if the time between arrivals is negligible.

Consider two specific examples of the bursty traffic type we are discussing. One is a set of images stored in an image library that are to be sequentially called on for display at a terminal or some other display system. Say that each image corresponds to 10^6 pixels (for example, 1000×1000-line resolution), a pixel requiring from 0.25 bit to 1 bit for transmission in compressed form. Various ways could be used to transmit each image. The simplest procedure, and the one we shall implicitly assume, is to transmit each image at a fixed, peak rate, until completely transmitted. Say $T1$ transmission, at 1.544 Mbps, is used in this example. Then images would then require from 0.16 to 0.65 sec to be transmitted in this example. Say they are destined to be viewed by a human. Say it takes from 5 to 15 sec to view each image and request the next in the sequence. The image transmission in time thus appears as shown in Figure 3–44. The rate of transmission, 1.544 Mbps, is represented in Figure 3–44 by the symbol R_p, for peak rate. There is an active transmission time, as noted earlier, alternating with a much longer inactive time during which, in this case, the human at the destination scans the transmitted image. (Note that propagation delay, usually in the order of msec, can be subsumed into the inactive time, as can the time required to process the image and bring it up on the screen). The alternating sequence of active and inactive times is of course precisely the picture we portrayed earlier in Figure 3–2c.

Another example is a set of files to be transmitted at irregular intervals from a database to a destination. This could again be a human, who will use and manipulate each file in turn, or it could be another database or some application geographically distant that requires the sequence of files during its

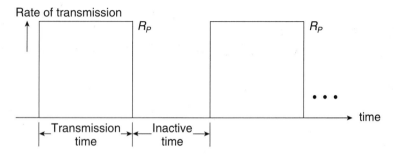

FIGURE 3–44 ■ Bursty image transmission.

run time. If the files range in length from 250,000 bits (31,250 bytes) to 1 Mbit (125,000 bytes), and are transmitted at a rate of R_p = 1.544 Mbps, the diagram of rate of transmission versus time would be identical to that of the image example. Changing the numbers in either case still results in a figure similar to that of Figure 3–44. It is clear that as long as the transmission time, although short compared to the inactive time, is non-negligible, the use of a bulk arrival process as a model for this type of bursty traffic may be questionable. Bulk arrival models are probably appropriate for cases where the active, transmission time is a very small fraction of the inactive time, or time between bulk transitions. At any rate, we choose instead to use a two-state Markov process, as used earlier for both voice and minisources, in the case of video, to represent bursty traffic such as that of Figure 3–44.

The specific Markov model for bursty traffic that we shall use in Chapter 4 appears in Figure 3–45. Note that it is identical to the model of Figure 3–21, used earlier to represent a minisource in our discussion of video modeling. The symbol R_p used here is equivalent to A, appearing in Figure 3–21. The units of R_p could be bits/sec, cells/sec, or any other comparable unit for digital transmission. As already noted a number of times, the Markov model used implies that both the "on" and "off" states (active and inactive respectively) are exponentially distributed. This is clearly not the case in the examples provided above. But, as always, one tries to pick as simple a model as possible, consistent with reality. No one, of course, knows how accurate this model is for image and file transfers over ATM networks since no studies have been carried out as yet. As will be seen in the next chapter, many investigators have used this model in studies of ATM admission and policing control.

Focusing on the model of Figure 3–45, we have already noted earlier in this chapter that the average on-, or transmission-, time is 1/β sec. The corresponding off-, or inactive time is 1/α sec. The probability a source is transmitting is $p = \alpha/(\alpha + \beta)$. The average rate of transmission is pR_p. In the image transfer example described above, the average transmission time would be about 1/β = 0.4 sec, while the average "off" time is about 1/α = 10 sec. The ratio of the two is then 0.04. The probability a source of this type is on is p = 0.4/10.4 = 0.038. The average rate of transmission is pR_p = 58.7 kbps, letting R_p again be 1.544 Mbps in this example.

Note that the bulk arrival process mentioned earlier is a special case of this two-state process. If 1/β (the average transmission time) is truly negligible in any particular example, the two-state process degenerates into the bulk-arrival Poisson process. In some cases this may just imply 1/β << 1/α, as

FIGURE 3–45 ▪ Two-state, on-off model for bursty traffic source.

in the example above. In others, this condition may not be sufficient. The distinction depends on the application. If one is interested in assessing performance with a human in the loop, the effect of varying the transmission time from $1/\beta = 0.4$ sec to $1/\beta = 2$ sec, say, is significant, and may impact design parameters even though the source inactive time $1/\alpha$ is 1 minute say, with α/β always a very small number. On the other hand, if $1/\beta$ is in the range of msec or μsec, while $1/\alpha$ is the order of seconds, a bulk arrival process may be a good model. In our study of the leaky-bucket policing mechanism in Chapter 4, with a human not involved, we shall find that $1/\beta$ does play a significant role and cannot be neglected.

▪ PROBLEMS

3–1 Refer to the multiplexed voice sources of Figure 3–4. Each is represented by the two-state model of Figure 3–3.

    a. Find the probability a voice source is active (in talk spurt). What is this probability for the average talk spurt length $1/\alpha = 1$ sec and the average silent interval $1/\lambda = 1.5$ sec?

    b. Show the utilization of the outgoing link of Figure 3–4 is given by equation (3–2a). Find the capacity C for $N = 10$ sources and the example of **a.** above if $\rho = 0.85$. What are J_o and J_u in this case?

    c. Verify that Figure 3–5 represents the composite (multiplexed) source model of the N sources in Figure 3–4. Sketch this figure for the example of **a.** and **b.** above. Indicate J_u and J_o.

    d. Derive equation (3–6) from birth-death analysis using equation (3–7) as a start. Show that equations (3–5) and (3–6) are the same.

    e. Using Figure 3–5, show the balance equations are given by equation (3–8). Show the set of equations (3–8a) are represented by the matrix equation (3–10), with M given by equation (3–11). Fill in some additional rows and columns of equation (3–11), including, specifically, the last two rows and columns.

    f. Find the matrix M for the ten-source example of parts **a.** and **b.**

3–2 This problem focuses on the fluid-source model of section 3.3.

    a. Explain, following the discussion in the book, how Figure 3–4 is converted to Figure 3–7.

    b. Derive equation (3–13), and, from this, equation (3–15).

    c. Show that equation (3–15) is represented by the matrix equation (3–15b) or its equivalent (3–15c).

    d. Write out some of the equations of equation (3–15a) for the ten-source case of problem **3–1a, b.**

    e. Some computational simplification results in equations (3–15) and

(3–15a) if α is factored out of both sides of the equations. Let the parameter γ be used to represent λ/α. Now define D and M.

3–3 Show equations (3–17) and (3–18) are the solutions to equation (3–15b).

3–4 Consider the special case of $N = 2$ voice sources, $1/\alpha = 1$ sec and $1/\lambda = 1.5$ sec.

    a. Find C, J_o, and J_u for the two cases $\rho = 0.75$ and $\rho = 0.85$. Indicate all three values on the $(N + 1)$-state diagram of Figure 3–5.

    b. Find and compare the eigenvalues of equation (3–18) (or the normalized equivalent of problem **3–2e**) for the two cases of **a.** above. Show that in both cases one eigenvalue is always zero.

    c. Find the eigenvectors for the two cases.

3–5 Extend problem **3–4** above to other, larger, cases with $N > 2$. Try different values of α, λ, and ρ.

3–6 In problem **3–5,** find the most significant eigenvalue in all cases. This is the negative eigenvalue with the smallest absolute value. Show this agrees with equation (3–42). (The general proof appears in [ANIC 1982], as pointed out in the text.)

3–7 In all cases of problem **3–5,** find the survivor function $G(x) = 1 - F(x)$.

3–8 Plot $G(x)$ in problem **3–7** for some of your examples and compare with the single exponential approximation equation (3–43).

3–9 Calculate and plot $P(l > i) = G\ (\alpha i/V)$, using equation (3–12), for the $N = 2$ example of problem **3–4.** Use $V = 170$ cells/sec. How large a buffer size is needed to have the buffer overflow probability equal 10^{-2} for each of the two values of ρ indicated in problem **3–4**? Repeat for an overflow probability of 10^{-3}. Repeat for the examples of problem **3–8.** Comment on the effect of statistical multiplexing. Comment on the effect of changes in the utilization ρ.

3–10 The discussion of voice-sample generation in this chapter focuses on 64-kbps voice: During each talk spurt interval the voice process is sampled every 125 μsec, that is, at a rate of 8000 samples per sec, with each sample coded into eight bits. Compression techniques allow voice to be transmitted at much lower rates. Find the ATM cell rate V, in cells/sec, for the following compressed voice rates: 32-kbps, 16-kbps, 13-kbps, and 8-kbps.

3–11 One hundred voice sources are multiplexed at an ATM access buffer. Each voice source has an average talk spurt length of 0.8 sec. Its average silent interval is 1.2 sec.

    a. What is the probability a voice source is in talk spurt?

    b. When in talk spurt, a source generates ATM cells at the rate of 100 cells/sec. Find the link capacity C_L, in cells/sec, if the link utilization ρ is to be set at 0.7.

    c. Determine the overload region for the 100 sources, based on **b.** above.

d. Fluid analysis is used to size the buffer. Approximate the survivor function by the asymptotic value $G(x) \sim e^{-rx}$, that is, taking $A_N \rho^N = 1$. What is r in this case if the unit of x is *cells*? Find x, in cells, if $G(x) = 10^{-5}$.

3–12 Show that the stationary state probabilities for the Markov-modulated Poisson process of Figure 3–11 are given by the solution of the matrix equation (3–46).

3–13 Show that Figure 3–15 is the two-dimensional state-space representation of the statistical multiplexor of Figure 3–14.

3–14 This problem focuses on the two-dimensional balance equations representing the two-dimensional state-space of Figure 3–15.

a. Show that the matrix-vector equation representing the first, $i = 0$, row of Figure 3–15, is given by equation (3–57), with the matrices B_0 and B_1 given by equations (3–58) and (3–59), respectively.

b. Verify that equation (3–60), with P given by equation (3–62), represents the entire set of balance equations of Figure 3–15. Specify A_0, A_1, and A_2.

3–15 Consider the special case in problem 3–14 of $N = 1$. All the A_i and B_i matrices are then 2×2. The matrix-geometric technique is used in an example in this case to solve for the two-dimensional state-probabilities, and, from these, for the buffer occupancy probabilities.

a. First verify for this 2×2 case that P is a stochastic matrix, with all of its rows summing to 1. (In the general case of equation (3–62), show that $B_0 + A_0$ is a stochastic matrix. What about $B_1 + A_1 + A_0$ and $A_2 + A_1 + A_0$?)

b. Consider the voice source example of section 3.3, with the average talk spurt length $1/\alpha = 1.25$ sec and the speech-activity factor $p = \lambda/(\lambda + \alpha) = 0.4$. Let the voice source generate $\beta = 170$ cells/sec, on the average. (Recall that the assumption here is that the cell-generation rate is Poisson). Take $\rho = 0.5$. What is then the link-service rate v? Follow the procedure outlined following equation (3–65c) to find R, $\boldsymbol{p}_0$, and then $\boldsymbol{p}_1$. [Recall that $\boldsymbol{p}_i$ in our case, is equivalent to $\boldsymbol{x}_i$ in the discussion of the matrix-geometric technique. Normalize $\boldsymbol{p}_0$ using equation (3–65c). Use either of the recursive techniques described in the text to find R. You may find convergence is quicker with one technique than the other.]

c. Given $\boldsymbol{p}_i$ as found above in **b.**, use equation (3–52) to find p_i, the marginal probability that the buffer occupancy (queue length) is i. If possible, find i such that Prob(buffer occupancy $> i$) = 0.01. This requires calculating the sum of p_k, $i + 1 \leq k \leq$ some large number. If you cannot do this computationally, find i for Prob(buffer occupancy $> i$) = 0.1. Compare with equation (3–41), the result found using the fluid approach. [But note that, strictly speaking, equation (3–41) should only be valid for very small probabilities. Why is this so?]

3–16 A traffic source may be modeled as a two-state MMPP. When in state one, it emits packets at a Poisson rate of 12,000 packets/sec. When in state two, the Poisson rate is 6,000 packets/sec. The transition rates between states are $\mu_{12} = 10$/sec and $\mu_{21} = 5$/sec. The packets are exponentially-distributed in length, each 100 μsec long, on the average. The source accesses an infinite buffer fed by a transmission link of average capacity C_L packets/sec.

a. What are C_L and the link utilization ρ?

b. Use the matrix-geometric approach to calculate the probability $p(n)$ that there are n packets in the buffer, for $n = 0, 1, 2$, and as many other values of n as you wish. For this purpose equations (3–53) to (3–58), in section 3.4, have to be modified to accommodate this two-state MMPP. Recall that those equations were found specifically for the case of multiplexed voice sources. New balance equations have to be written for this two-state MMPP.

3–17 This problem deals with the autoregressive representation of a compressed video sequence.

a. Show that for the autoregressive model equation (3–86) for the frame bit rate, the average bit rate is given by equation (3–87), while the autocovariance function has the exponential decay form of equation (3–88). *Hint:* To get equation (3–87), take expectations, term-by-term, of equation (3–86) and assume stationarity. To find σ_λ^2, first find $E(\lambda^2)$ (second moment of λ) using equation (3–86) and assume stationarity. To find $C(n)$, first find $C(1)$ using equations (3–85) and (3–86). Repeat for $C(2)$, etc.

b. Show the model parameters for the video strip of Figure 3–19 are given by $b = 0.11$ and $\eta = 0.58$.

3–18 Consider the N video sources of Figure 3–21.

a. Show their covariance functions add, as in equation (3–91).

b. Represent the sum by M minisources as in Figure 3–21. Use equations (3–95) and (3–96) to match the M minisource parameters α, β, A to the measured video source parameters for the example of Figure 3–19, obtaining the results shown following equation (3–96).

c. Verify that the Markov chain of Figure 3–22 represents the sum of the M minisources and that $\pi_I = \text{Prob}(i \text{ minisources on})$ is given by equation (3–98).

3–19 Fluid-flow analysis is used to study the buffering of the M minisources representing N multiplexed video sources, as in problem **3–18,** and as discussed in section 3.6. The analysis begins by defining the steady-state probability distribution function $F_i(x)$ that the buffer occupancy is less than or equal to x, with i minisources in the "on" state.

a. Following the discussion in section 3.6, show that $F_i(x)$ obeys the differential equation (3–99).

b. Show the set of differential equations for $F_i(x)$, $0 \leq i \leq M$, may be written in the matrix-vector form of equation (3–100), with the matrices D and B defined, respectively, by equations (3–101) and (3–102).

c. Show the solution for the vector $F(x)$ is given by equations (3–103) and (3–103a).

3–20 Consider the fluid-flow analysis of M summed minisources, as carried out in section 3.6, or as in problem **3–19** above. The analysis provides the solution to $F_i(x)$, the probability the buffer occupancy is less than or equal to x, with i of the minisources in the "on" state.

a. Show the probability $F(x)$ that the buffer occupancy is less than or equal to x is given by equation (3–105). From this expression, show the probability $G(x)$ that the buffer occupancy in Figure 3–21 is greater than x, is given by equation (3–107), using the minisource model.

b. Validate equation (3–111) as the asymptotic approximation to $G(x)$. Show ρ is given by equation (3–110) and that its minisource equivalent is equation (3–109). Show the parameter r must be given by equation (3–108).

c. The example worked out in the text applying the fluid model is for the case $N = 1$ and the video source example appearing in [MAGL 1988]. Take different values of N and let $M = 20N$. Pick $\rho = 0.8$ in all cases and find the capacity C, in bits/sec, for each case if each video source has the same characteristics as in [MAGL 1988]. Find and sketch $G(x)$ as a function of the buffer size x in bits. (A log scale would be appropriate.) Assume $A_M = 1$. (This may be quite inaccurate! If you are venturesome you can refer to the Anick et al. paper, [ANIC 1982], for a closed-form expression for A_M that involves the eigenvalues—there may, of course, be a lot of these!) With $A_M = 1$, what size buffer is required to have $G(x) = 10^{-4}$? Find the buffer size for each of your examples.

3–21 The multiple minisource model used by [MAGL 1988], and summarized in section 3.6, to represent multiplexed video sources is to be used to model five video sources multiplexed at an access buffer. Each source generates, on the average, 4.5 Mbits/sec. The standard deviation is $\sigma = 2$ Mbits/sec. The autocovariance time constant is 2.5 sec. The source output is converted to 45-octet cells before transmission to the buffer. The buffer in turn transmits into the network at a rate of 80,000 cells/sec.

Use 20 minisources to model each video source. Apply fluid analysis to obtain as the asymptotic survivor function $G(x) \sim A_N \, \rho^N \, e^{-kx}$.

    a. Find the constant k if x is measured in cells.

    b. Say a buffer size of $x = 3500$ cells is necessary to have $G(x) = 10^{-6}$. What buffer size, in cells, is required to have $G(x) = 10^{-4}$? Repeat for $G(x) = 10^{-9}$.

3-22 The fluid model used in sections 3.3 and 3.6 is to be extended to apply to an n-state Markov-modulated source. This source is similar to the MMPP source described by equations (3–45) to (3–48) and Figure 3–11, except that state i is represented by a constant-rate source, of rate λ_i, rather than by a Poisson source at that rate. A model of such a source with B states appears in Figure 3–39. This traffic source transmits cells to an access buffer which in turn outputs them onto a link at a rate of C cells/sec. This link rate is then equivalent to VC in the access buffer model of Figure 3–4 or to C, in bits/pixel, of the statistical multiplexor model of Figure 3–21. (The fluid-flow discussion in section 3.8, following equation (3–133), parallels the development in this problem, except for slightly different notation: B states in place of n, and link capacity μ instead of C). Let the buffer occupancy x be given directly in units of cells, rather than information units in the voice model analysis of section 3.3, or in bits, as in the minisource model of section 3.6. It would be helpful at this point if you drew a figure of a buffer showing input, output, and indicating x as the buffer state.

    a. Assume λ_i and C large enough that the buffer occupancy x may be approximated by a continuous random variable. Define $F_i(t,x) \equiv$ Prob[buffer $\leq x$, input in state i, time t]. Extend the analysis of equation (3–13) to this case. Show that under stationary conditions, that is, letting $t \to \infty$, with $F_i(x)$ thus replacing $F_i(t, x)$, one gets

$$(\lambda_i - C)\frac{d}{dx}F_i(x) = \sum_{j=1}^{n}\mu_{ji}F_j(x) \qquad 1 \leq i \leq n$$

Show that this set of equations is equivalent to equation (3–15) or (3–99) if one chooses the μ_{ji}'s and defines the parameters appropriately. Compare as well with equation (3–138).

    b. Show the equations in **a.** above may be written in the following matrix-vector form:

$$\frac{d}{dx}F(x)D = F(x)M$$

Here, M is the infinitesimal generating matrix given by equation (3–47), D is an $n \times n$ diagonal matrix with elements $(\lambda_i - C)$, $1 \leq i \leq n$, and $F(x)$ the row vector with the ith component $F_i(x)$. [Compare with equations (3–139) to (3–141) and (3–134).] From here on, the solution for $F(x)$ follows the same procedure as in equations (3–17) to (3–19).

  c. Show, for an infinite buffer, that $F(x)$ is given by equation (3–17b). Note that the sum in equation (3–17b) is taken over the overload states for which $\lambda_i > C$. Why can't $C = \lambda_i$ for some i?

  d. Write an expression for the utilization ρ in terms of λ_i, C, and π_i.

3–23 Refer to problem **3–16**. That problem is to be repeated using the fluid analysis approach of problem **3–22** above. For this purpose the packets (or cells) are all of fixed length 100 μsec. When in state one the source emits packets at the constant rate of 12,000 packets/sec. When in state two it emits them at the fixed rate of 6,000 packets/sec.

  a. What is the link capacity C defined in problem **3–22**?

  b. Find specific expressions for the matrices M and D.

  c. Find a specific expression for $G(x) \equiv$ (buffer occupancy $> x$). (Note— Don't guess at the form of $G(x)$. Derive it explicitly.)

  d. Find the buffer size x, in packets (cells), if the overflow probability is approximated by $G(x)$ and is to be 10^{-5}.

3–24 Consider the *Star Wars* video sequence of Figure 3–26. Its quantized histogram for eight quantization levels appears in Figure 3–27a, while its autocorrelation function appears in Figure 3–27b. The histogram entries are tabulated as well in Table 3–2.

  a. Show from Figure 3–27(a) that the sequence has, on the average, 235,000 bits per frame. Calculate the mean-square number of bits per frame (the second moment) as well, and, from this, show the standard deviation of the bits per frame is $\sigma_\lambda \approx 5.2 \times 10^4$ bits per frame.

  b. The autocorrelation function $R(\tau)$ is defined as $E[\lambda(t)\lambda(t + \tau)]$. For $\tau = 0$, $R(0) = E[\lambda^2]$, just the second moment. For large τ, $R(\tau) \to E^2(\lambda)$. Taking the difference, one gets the variance of λ, σ_λ^2. Calculate the variance from Figure 3–27b, and compare with the result of part a above.

3–25 The video histogram approximation of section 3.7 is to be studied using the $M/M/1/K$ queueing model of equation (3–116). This implies packets are exponentially distributed in length rather than being fixed-length cells as in the ATM, B-ISDN, case discussed in the text.

  a. A single Poisson source of average rate λ_i packets/sec is applied to a buffer, holding at most 74 packets. The packets average $1/\mu$ sec in length. The outgoing link capacity is then μ packets/sec. The buffer occupancy distribution is then given by equation (3–116). Calculate and plot this distribution for (1) $\rho_i = 0.5$, (2) $\rho_i = 0.8$. Compare with Figure 3–29.

  b. Repeat **a.** using the eight-state histogram of Figure 3–27a: Calculate the conditional buffer occupancy distribution for each state, given by equation (3–116), using the average traffic arrivals for each state obtained from Figure 3–27a. Alternately, the entries of Table 3–2 can be used. The average utilization ρ in this case is defined as the average, over all eight states; that is, it is given by $E(\lambda)/\mu$, with $E(\lambda)$ the average packet arrival rate, averaged over all eight states. Take the two cases $\rho = 0.5$ and 0.8 again. Apply equation (3–117) and compare the resultant buffer occupancy distribution with those shown in Figure 3–29.

c. For those readers with some advanced knowledge of queueing theory: Repeat **b.** above using the r-stage Erlangian distribution E_r, with r very large to approximate the fixed cell-length case. Solve the resultant $M/E_r/1/K$ queueing problem to obtain the conditional buffer occupancy distribution $P(n \mid \lambda = \lambda_l)$. Again apply equation (3–117) and compare your results with those of Figure 3–29.

3–26 This problem compares the approximate solution technique of section 3.7 with the matrix-geometric approach. To keep things simple, a two-state Markov process only is used. Specifically, let a two-state MMPP model a traffic source accessing an infinite buffer multiplexor. $\lambda_1 = 500$ cells/sec is the Poisson rate when in state one; $\lambda_2 = 1000$ cells/sec is the rate when in state two (see Figure 3–25). The average time in state two is $1/\beta = 0.5$ sec. The average time in state one is $1/\alpha = 1$ sec. Cells are exponentially distributed in length (this simplifies the analysis) with average length $1/\mu = 0.8$ msec (then $\mu = 1250$ cells/sec). The objective is to calculate the buffer occupancy probability $p(n)$, n the state of the buffer.

a. The approximate method, based on the discussion in section 3.7, gives

$$p(n) \cong p(n \mid \lambda_1)\pi_1 + p(n \mid \lambda_2)\pi_2$$

Here, π_i is the probability the MMPP is in state i, $i = 1$ or 2. This is of course a special case of equation (3–117). Calculate $p(n)$ for several values of n. (Would you expect the approximation to be accurate, given the discussion in section 3.7?)

b. Compare the result of **a.** with the exact solution obtained using the matrix-geometric approach. To do this you will have to draw the appropriate two-dimensional state diagram and set up the balance equations, as was done in section 3.4, equations (3–53) to (3–59), to find the matrices A_0, B_0, etc., for this case. (Recall that the analysis in section 3.4 was for the special case of multiplexed voice sources. See problem **3–16** for another example.)

c. Looking at the elements of the matrices appearing in **b.** above, show under what conditions the approximation of **a.** might arise. For the numbers given in this problem does it appear the approximation might be valid? Does this conclusion agree with the results of **b.**?

3–27 The matrix-geometric technique of section 3.4 is to be used to verify the histogram approximation technique of section 3.7. However, to simplify the analysis packet (cell) lengths are assumed to be exponentially distributed rather than of fixed length. Table 3–4 contains the measured transition rates μ_{ij} defining the matrix M for the *Star Wars* video sequence of Figure 3–26. Using these rates and the eight arrival rates shown in Table 3–2, redo the analysis of equations (3–53) to (3–59), setting up the two-dimensional balance equations appropriate to this case. Hence, come up with the matrix equation (3–60) for this case. Use this to calculate the buffer occupancy distribution for the two cases of problem **3–25b.** Compare with the result of problem **3–25b,** based on the histogram approximation (3–117).

3–28 The general expression for loss probability for a quantized traffic source in the cell loss region is given by equation (3–123).
 a. Derive this expression.
 b. Consider the *Star Wars* video sequence of Figure 3–26 as an example. Say it is quantized to eight levels, with the resultant histogram of Figure 3–27 or Table 3–2. Cells in each video frame are delivered to a buffer uniformly distributed over the frame. The output link transmission rate is chosen so that the link utilization is $\rho = 0.8$. Show the link capacity is 294,000 bits/frame. Show the loss probability is $P_L = 0.016$. Repeat for $\rho = 0.7$. Show the link capacity in this case is 336,000 bits per frame, with a loss probability of 0.002. What is the link capacity in each case, in cells/sec, if frames are generated 24 times per second, and cells contain 48 video octets each?

3–29 Repeat problem **3–28** above if cells are delivered randomly distributed over a frame. Consider buffer sizes ranging from $K = 10$ cells to 500 cells. Cells are exponentially-distributed in length with an average length of 48 video octets. Frames are generated 24 times per second. Plot P_L vs. K for the two cases of $\rho = 0.7$ and 0.8. Does the $\rho = 0.8$ curve agree with that of Figure 3–37? Compare the values at $K = 500$ cells with those obtained in problem **3–28.** What are the limiting values of P_L for these two cases as $K \rightarrow \infty$? Compare with the results of problem **3–28.** *Hint:* Use equation (3–116) here. Why?

3–30 Refer to the video conference histogram of Figure 3–18. Quantize this into twelve equally-spaced bit rates ranging from 1 to 15 Mbps and tabulate the probability of occurrence at each rate. (Because of the difficulty of determining probabilities accurately from the figure, this will have to be done as best as possible. Check that the sum of the probabilities is close to one.) Show the average bit rate is 5.4 Mbps, as indicated in the figure. The bits in each frame are combined into ATM cells containing 48 video octets each and are delivered to a buffer, uniformly distributed across each frame. Find the link output rate, in Mbps, if the link utilization is to be $\rho = 0.5$. Show that the loss probability at this utilization is $P_L = 0.004$. Repeat for $\rho = 0.8$. Show the loss probability is now 0.08.

3–31 Figure 3–41 portrays the complete loss probability-buffer size curve for the *Star Wars* JPEG-coded video sequence of Figure 3–26, for a utilization of 0.8, assuming the bits in each frame are assembled into packets that vary exponentially in length and that are then randomly sent to the buffer. The frame rate is 24 frames per second. The average cell length is 48 video octets. The cell region portion of the curve is obtained in problem **3–29,** following the method outlined in section 3.8. The cell region curve appears in Figure 3–37. The purpose of this problem is to determine the burst region part of the curve using the fluid-flow technique discussed in the same section and then match the two regions, obtaining the composite curve on combining them. It is thus necessary to obtain the dominant eigenvalue corresponding to the matrix-vector equation (3–139) with matrix M, in this case given by Table 3–4. Show this eigenvalue has the value -0.95×10^{-3}, as noted in the text. Use the technique described by equations (3–126) to (3–129) to determine the form of the curve in the burst region and show it is given by equation (3–145); that is, that the slopes of the curves in the two regions coincide at about $K_0 = 75$ cells. Sketch the composite loss probability, buffer size curve and compare with Figure 3–141. Repeat this problem for $\rho = 0.7$ and sketch the resultant loss probability, buffer size curve on the same axes as the $\rho = 0.8$ case. Compare the two results. For each case, determine the buffer size required to have a loss probability $P_L = 10^{-4}$. What buffer size would be required to have $P_L = 10^{-6}$? How do these numbers compare with those shown in Table 3–1 for one video source with the characteristics of Figure 3–19?

Chapter 4

Admission and Access Control in Broadband Networks

In the previous chapter we focused on models for characterizing traffic in broadband networks. As noted, this is critical in the design of such networks. It is expected that these networks, when deployed, will be carrying high-resolution images, higher-resolution video, multimedia traffic, and other types of "bandwidth-hungry" traffic, in addition to interactive data, computer traffic, and voice, that existing networks currently handle. This projected mix of traffic is much more difficult to characterize than current traffic, particularly if differing qualities of service (QoS) are required for each. It is clear that the common Poisson model for traffic may not always provide accurate design results. This point was made at the beginning of the last chapter. This fact motivated our discussion of other traffic models.

In this chapter we begin to apply some of these models to a fundamental question that arises with the design and deployment of any network: How much traffic can it handle if a prescribed quality of service for each traffic class is to be maintained while the network utilization, that is, traffic throughput (hence revenue), is to meet some minimum goal? Alternatively put, what resource requirements, in terms of link and buffer capacities, number of links, number of nodal switching points, etc, are imposed on a network design if it is to handle a specified broadband integrated traffic load? We clearly cannot hope to answer this question definitively here. What we will do in this chapter is to focus first on admission control in the context of B-ISDN: Given virtual paths set up in a network, how many virtual connections (that is, calls with specified QoS) can it handle? Given this number, does one admit a new call when a request to set one up arrives? Even here, we shall have to restrict our discussion sharply because of the complexity of the issue and the lack of specific results at this point: We shall discuss admission policies based solely on traffic occupancy at one point in the network, generally the access node. We shall not attempt to study admission control based on bandwidth available along an entire virtual path.

Given a decision to admit a call, the traffic generated by this call must be monitored to ensure it does not start congesting the network. We have already noted in the previous chapter that traffic can only be described statistically. This has always been the case, whether in the voice-based, circuit-switched telephone networks, or the more recent data networks. As a result, congestion may develop despite a good admission policy. (Malicious misuse of the network by some users must be guarded against as well). To prevent congestion from occurring, control at the access point (the user-network interface of UNI), as well as within the network, must be exerted. In the context of B-ISDN, this is sometimes referred to as a "policing function".

ATM documents refer to this policing function as *Usage Parameter Control* (UPC). Usage Parameter Control is used to ensure that users do not violate their traffic contracts, negotiated during admission control. These contracts include various conditions of operation such as peak and average rate of cell transmission, and maximum cell burst size, among others. It is the possible violation of these contracts that can result in network congestion.

A literal torrent of studies on both admission and access control has been carried out, worldwide, in the context of B-ISDN. Because of the complexity of the issues involved and the difficulty of both analysis and simulation, there is no universal agreement on methods of control. There probably never will be, because of the enormous number of networks expected to be deployed, as well as the variety of wideband applications expected for them. This chapter thus serves only as an introduction to this field. In the first section, we shall describe and analyze quantitatively some simple procedures proposed for handling call admission at the access to a network. The analysis will rely on the traffic model described in the last chapter; that of multiplexed on-off sources. Recall that this model, with appropriate adjustment of parameters, can be used to describe voice, compressed (VBR) video, and image traffic, as well as other bursty traffic. We will also apply some of our fluid-flow analysis to the study of this problem.

In section 4.2 we introduce the concept of access control by focusing on one particular strategy, the "leaky bucket" algorithm, that has received a great deal of attention in the literature. We evaluate the performance of this technique in a number of ways, concluding in section 4.3 with a fluid-flow analysis for the case of a single on-off (bursty) source.

4.1 ▪ ADMISSION CONTROL

The objective here is clearly very simple: given a call arriving, requiring a virtual connection with specified QoS (bandwidth, loss probability, delay, etc.), should it be admitted? The implementation of the control can be quite complex. In a real network control, messages would have to be sent along the complete virtual path that would have to provide this connection to ascertain whether the QoS objectives could be met without adversely affecting other calls already in progress. In general, this would imply checking not only the specific VP within which this VC would be established, but all other VP's sharing a part or all of the route to be used in the network, end-to-end.

A simple solution to this problem would be to allocate a specific bandwidth to each VP along its complete path, end-to-end, and then allocate that bandwidth to each VC using that VP on the basis of its *peak-rate* requirement. The path chosen and buffer allocations at each nodal switch along the path could then be used to guarantee the desired QoS. Such a solution to the problem has in fact been proposed [CCITT 1992d]. The control is indeed quite simple. Monitoring peak rate is also relatively simple: This rate is, by definition, the reciprocal of the minimum cell spacing for a given connection. The only problem is that peak-rate allocation precludes the use of statistical multiplexing, requiring possibly much wider bandwidth usage than might otherwise be the case.

Other, more complex, control algorithms can presumably provide statistical multiplexing, thus enabling network resources to be used more efficiently. But there is clearly a tradeoff: The greater the complexity of the algorithm the more costly and difficult its implementation becomes. The objective is thus to come up with reasonably simple control algorithms, capable of being implemented at B-ISDN rates, that provide the desired QoS for each connection, while at the same time allowing efficient use of the network. This is, in general, a difficult problem to solve. In this section we provide some proposed, simple, solutions, focusing exclusively at a single access point, rather than along the full VP.

As stated earlier, we will focus in this section on on-off models of traffic, since we have shown in Chapter 3 that these may be used to model voice, bursty sources, including images, and video, among other sources. Recall that an on-off traffic source requires at least three parameters to represent it: the peak rate R_p of cell transmission, in units of cells/sec (or bps, as the case may be), the average length of a burst $1/\beta$, in sec, and the average off-time $1/\alpha$. These are indicated in Figure 4–1a. We use the same notation adopted in the latter part of Chapter 3. Recall that for voice $\alpha/\beta \doteq 0.4$, and $R_p \doteq 170$ cells/sec, for 64-kbps signals and 48-byte cells. The peak rate parameter R_p is equivalent to the parameter V used in modeling voice in Chapter 3. Bursty traffic would have $1/\beta \ll 1/\alpha$, or $\alpha/\beta \ll 1$. A 2-Mbyte image transmitted from a source at a 50-Mbps rate would require 0.4 sec to be transmitted, ignoring ATM-cell overhead. In this case R_p is 50 Mbps, or roughly 120,000 cells/sec. The on-, or

---

[CCITT 1992d]   "Traffic and Congestion Control in B-ISDN, I. 371," Recommendation, CCITT Study Group XVIII; Contained in Temporary Document 62 (XVIII), CCITT, Geneva, June 1992.

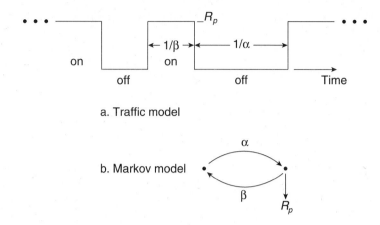

FIGURE 4–1 ■ Basic on-off traffic source.

burst-time $1/\beta$ is 0.4 sec. If the average time $1/\alpha$ between images is 10 sec, $\alpha/\beta = 0.04$. For the video minisource model discussed in section 3.6, $R_p = AK$, the minisource parameter used there, with K in units of pixels/sec.

These three parameters are examples of what are called "traffic descriptors," the parameters a user must provide the network, in addition to QoS requirements, to be used for both admission and access control. Peak rate control requires, of course, only one parameter, R_p. We say three is the *minimum* number of parameters required for this model because the statistics of the burst ("on") interval and the "off" interval might be of interest as well. In this section we implicitly assume the statistics of both intervals are exponential. Each source is thus represented by the two-state, continuous-time Markov chain of Figure 4–1b. Heterogeneous sources would each have different values for the three parameters. For homogeneous sources they would be the same. We are also implicitly assuming that during the burst period, cells are either transmitted continuously or periodically, as in the case of voice, at the peak rate R_p.

Using this basic on-off source model, we are now in a position to begin our discussion of admission control. Say that there are k traffic classes, each with its own traffic descriptors, to be multiplexed onto one network access link, of capacity C_L cells/sec. Initially, let each traffic class access its own buffer, as shown in Figure 4–2. It is clear from the pictorial representation of Figure 4–2 that the network throughput and traffic class quality of service are closely related to the way in which each buffer is served by the access link. Improved performance, in terms of increased throughput and/or better QoS parameters, should be obtained by dynamically scheduling classes for transmission, depending on class traffic statistics, buffer occupancies, and desired QoS. The type of scheduler used, in turn, impacts on the admission policy. The design of "optimum" and "near-optimum" schedulers, in the sense noted above, has been discussed in the literature and is an active area of re-

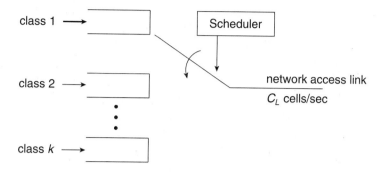

FIGURE 4–2 ■ Network access node with access scheduler.

search [HYMA 1992]. In our discussion in this section, we focus exclusively on the simplest scheduling strategy—FIFO. In this case all source buffers are combined to form one buffer holding cells from all the sources in FIFO order.

Whether more optimum scheduling or the simple FIFO strategy are used, it is clear that there must be a maximum number of connections or calls of each class for the given strategy that can be handled by the access link. This maximum number depends on the scheduling strategy, the access capacity C_L, the number of classes, and the QoS requirements for each. These maximum numbers, in turn, represent vertices in a k-dimensional region representing an admissible region for this system. The "optimum" strategy would then provide the "largest" region; the FIFO strategy the "smallest" one. Given the admissible region, in principle a call is admitted if the system, with the call present, still operates within the admissible region. A call is blocked if its acceptance would take the system outside of the admissible region.

Hypothetical two-dimensional ($k = 2$) regions appear in Figure 4–3. Some work has been done on joint scheduling—admission control for three classes of traffic [HYMA 1991], [HYMA 1992]. Simulation and analysis have been used to obtain the admissible regions for a variety of two-class admission control strategies, with or without scheduling. Selected examples appear in [FERR 1990], [DZIO 1990], [DECI 1990a]. The strategies that do not involve

[HYMA 1992]   Hyman, J., et al., "Joint Scheduling and Admission Control for ATS-Based Switching Nodes," *Proc. ACM SIGCOMM 92,* Baltimore, MD, Aug. 1992: 223–234.

[HYMA 1991]   Hyman, J., et al., "Real-Time Scheduling with Quality of Service Constraints," *IEEE JSAC, 9* (Sept. 1991): 1052–1063.

[FERR 1990]   Ferrari, D., and D. C. Verma, "A Scheme for Real-Time Channel Establishment in Wide-Area Networks," *IEEE JSAC, SAC-8* (April 1990): 368–379.

[DZIO 1990]   Dziong, Z., et al., "Admission Control and Routing in ATM Networks," *Computer Networks and ISDN Systems, 20* (1990): 189–196.

[DECI 1990a]   Decina, M., et al., "Bandwidth Assigment and Virtual Call Blocking in ATM Networks," *Proc. IEEE Infocom 90,* San Francisco, June 1990: 881–888.

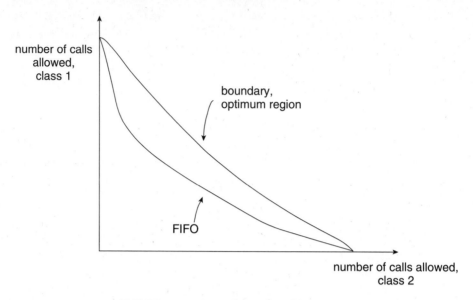

FIGURE 4–3 ■ Two-class admissible regions.

scheduling implicitly assume FIFO transmission, but with some bandwidth assignment rule defined for each class.

    This work on admissible regions for ATM admission control is motivated, in part, by earlier work on call admission strategies in the circuit-switched environment. In this earlier work, the objective was to develop admission-control policies for classes of traffic, each with possibly different bandwidth requirements, and each with different blocking probability and delay objectives [KRAI 1984], [GOPA 1983]. In the work described in this chapter, we focus on single-class admission control only. This means each user connection, with possibly different traffic descriptors, must receive the same grade of service. In ATM terms, this means we focus on a particular VP that is assumed to have already been set up that is designed to provide the given QoS. This VP is assigned the capacity C_L. The question now is to determine how many calls or virtual connections of each type can be handled. For homogeneous user connections, the question is to determine the total number of VCs that may be handled. Alternatively, for a given number of connections to be handled, one would like to know the capacity C_L required for a given performance objective.

[KRAI 1984]   Kraimeche, B., and M. Schwartz, "Circuit Access Control Strategies in Integrated Digital Networks," *Proc. IEEE Infocom 1984,* San Francisco, April 1984: 230–235.

[GOPA 1983]   Gopal, I. S., and T. E. Stern, "Optimal Call Blocking Policies in an Integrated Services Environment," *Proc. 17th Conf. on Info. Sciences and Systems,* Johns Hopkins University, Baltimore, MD, 1983.

One obvious way of admitting calls is to determine the maximum number whose aggregate *average* rate of transmission (bandwidth) does not exceed the capacity C_L. A little thought will indicate that this provides the maximum statistical multiplexing advantage or gain. In particular, for many very bursty sources ($\alpha/\beta \ll 1$) one would expect very high gain. This procedure clearly allows the absolute maximum number of calls to be admitted if FIFO transmission (scheduling) is used.

The problem with this technique is that it doesn't take statistical fluctuations into account, and may, in fact, result in a high cell loss probability. Designing on the basis of average bandwidth assignment is equivalent to a link utilization of 1. This is easily demonstrated for the on-off traffic source model of Figure 4–1. Consider the single FIFO access buffer feeding a link with capacity C_L, shown in Figure 4–4. For simplicity's sake, assume homogeneous sources. (The heterogeneous case provides the same results with details left to the reader). Figure 4–4 is thus precisely the statistical multiplexor model described in Chapter 3 (see Figure 3–21 for example). The difference now is that we are interested in finding the maximum number of sources N that may be multiplexed. Conversely, given N, what is the capacity C_L required?

For the source model of Figure 4–1 we have precisely the same model and same statistics described in Chapter 3. The probability a source is in the "on," or burst, state is $p = \alpha/(\alpha + \beta)$. Its average rate of transmission is thus pR_p. For N such sources, the average rate of transmission is NpR_p and the utilization is provided by our familiar expression.

$$\rho = NpR_p/C_L \tag{4–1}$$

Setting the average rate to the link capacity C_L, to determine the maximum number of sources that can be multiplexed, is obviously equivalent to having $\rho = 1$. It is left to the reader to demonstrate that a similar result is obtained when k classes, each with different traffic descriptors, are maximally multiplexed on the basis of *average* bandwidth occupancy. In that case, however, tradeoffs are possible among the maximum number of calls allowed per user class. Specifically, the maximum utilization of 1 is again attained when

$$\sum_{i=1}^{k} n_i p_i R_{pi} = C_L \tag{4–2}$$

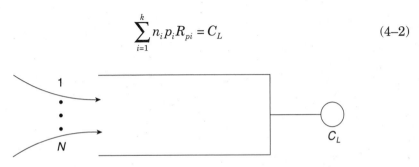

FIGURE 4–4 ▪ Statistical multiplexing of homogeneous sources.

Different choices of n_i are possible in this case.

We focus on the homogeneous case for the time being. The "best" multiplexing strategy in terms of utilization, or multiplexing gain, is the average bandwidth assignment method just described. This provides the maximum number of calls N allowed for C_L given, but it may be unacceptable in terms of cell loss. It thus provides an upper bound on the number of calls that can be accepted or, conversely, provides a lower bound on the capacity C_L required to handle a given number of calls. The peak assignment strategy, which guarantees no cells lost (that is, the best cell loss performance) provides the lower bound on the number of calls that can be accepted, given a link capacity C_L. In this case $NR_p = C_L$. As $p \to 1$ (that is, the sources become less and less bursty) all admission control schemes merge. A source that is always "on" must be given its full bandwidth requirement R_p at all times. This is essentially circuit switching, and statistical multiplexing provides no gain.

A graphical representation of these comments is provided in Figure 4–5. It shows the $C_L - N$ tradeoff as well as the one-dimensional admissible region with C_L given and the QoS specified. (We shall focus on cell loss probability or related parameters). As the QoS parameters become more strict, the control assignment curve approaches the peak assignment curve; as they are relaxed, the assignment curve approaches the average assignment line. The admissible region widens correspondingly.

The objective is to find the admissible region: Given a set of sources with traffic descriptors specified, what is the maximum number of calls N that can

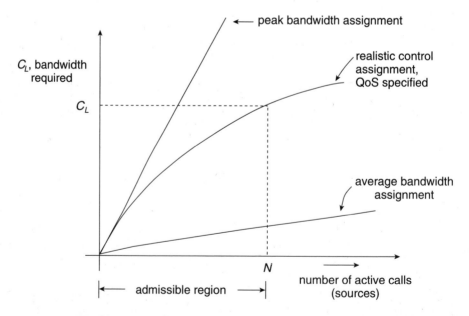

FIGURE 4–5 ■ Admission control, homogeneous on-off sources.

be admitted for a given QoS? If the number connected is less than N, any new call can be admitted without affecting the quality of service adversely. We shall approach this problem in the equivalent, alternative, manner already indicated. For a given QoS and given traffic descriptors, we find the capacity C_L required to handle N calls. This is then inverted to find N, given C_L. We proceed intuitively and heuristically at first, then more systematically later. To simplify the notation, define $m \equiv pN$ as the mean (average) number of sources "on." The mean bit rate inputted by these m connections is, as already noted, mR_p. From the discussion above, as well as from consideration of Figure 4–5, it is apparent that $C_L \geq mR_p$. A simple first guess at an acceptable value for the capacity C_L is to have it differ from the mean value mR_p by some multiple of the standard deviation σR_p. We thus write, as our first possible value of C_L,

$$C_L = (m + K\sigma)R_p \qquad (4\text{--}3)$$

with K a constant to be determined, which varies with the quality of service specified. This constant should *increase* as the QoS is more strictly defined, and should *decrease,* approaching 0, as the QoS is made more lax. We now propose two simple procedures for finding K. They are related, as we shall see, and give results which are nearly the same.

Note first, however, that the capacity allocation specified by equation (4–3) is not restricted to multiplexed on-off sources. This could represent any multiplexed VBR sources as well, with mR_p and σR_p the mean and standard deviation, respectively, of the multiplexed bit rates. But focusing here on the on-off burst model of Figure 4–1, we again write $m = Np$ and note that $\sigma^2 = Np(1 - p) = m(1 - p)$. To simplify the analysis and notation again, we rewrite equation (4–3) in the equivalent normalized form,

$$C = m + K\sigma = Np + K\sqrt{Np(1-p)} \qquad (4\text{--}3a)$$

with $C = C_L/R_p$ just the capacity parameter $C \leq N$ introduced in Chapter 3 (see Figure 3–4, for example).

Recall from our discussion of multiplexed on-off sources in Chapter 3 that they may be represented by an $(N + 1)$-state birth-death process, with the familiar state diagram reproduced in Figure 4–6. We focus particularly on the overload state J_o, the underload state $J_u = J_o - 1$, and the capacity parameter C set between them.

Recall from Chapter 3 that $J_o = \lceil C \rceil$ and $J_u = \lfloor C \rfloor$. All states $i \geq J_o$ represent the overload region in which the buffer of Figure 4–4 tends to fill; $i \leq J_u$ corresponds to the underload region, in which the buffer tends to empty. The average number of sources "on," m, lies somewhere in the underload region, either from equation (4–3a), or from noting that $\rho = NpR_p/C_L = m/C < 1$.

We now propose the following heuristic method for obtaining the constant K in equation (4–3a) and, from this, one admission control procedure for on-off sources. Let the desired QoS be the cell loss probability P_L. This is the

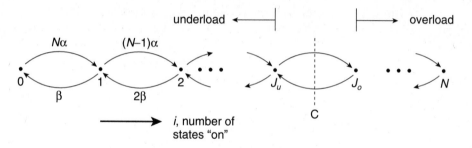

FIGURE 4–6 ■ State diagram, N on-off sources.

QoS measure we shall use consistently in our discussion of admission control. (Maximum buffer delay will be introduced as an additional measure later). A conservative estimate of loss probability proposed in the literature is the ratio of the cell input rate when the $(N + 1)$-state system of Figure 4–6 is in the overload region to the average input rate [COST 1991]. From Figure 4–6, this is the number

$$P_L = \sum_{i=J_o}^{N} (i - C)\pi_i / m \tag{4-4}$$

with π_i the probability the system is in state i (Chapter 3). This is a conservative estimate since it assumes that any input rate above the capacity will result in cell loss. It ignores the buffer completely. Given P_L, and the one traffic descriptor p that a source is "on" in this case, we can find the desired relation between the capacity C and the number of calls N connected.

A related measure of loss suggested in the literature is simply the probability of being in the overload region, that is, the probability the input rate exceeds the capacity C [GUER 1991]. Calling this measure ε, we have

$$\varepsilon = \sum_{i=J_o}^{N} \pi_i \tag{4-5}$$

We shall see that for very small P_L and ε, as would be desired in practice, either measure provides very nearly the same $C - N$ relation; that is, the same value of K.

To attain small P_L and/or ε, requires a relatively large number of sources to be multiplexed. We thus assume $N \gg 1$. We also take $p \ll 1$; that is, we as-

[COST 1991]   *Performance Evaluation and Design of Multiservice Networks*, J. W. Roberts, ed., Final report, Cost 224 project. Luxembourg: Commission of the European Communities, Oct. 1991.

[GUER 1991]   Guerin, R. et al., "Equivalent Capacity and Its Application to Bandwidth Allocation in High-Speed Networks," *IEEE JSAC, 9*, 7 (Sept. 1991): 968–981.

sume the sources to be quite bursty. These assumptions enable us to find the constant K quite readily. Once we do this we can simply conjecture, as a heuristic, that the admissible region, or the equivalent capacity C, with N given, obeys equation (4–3a). With N large and p small, it is well known that the binomial distribution solution for π_i,

$$\pi_i = \binom{N}{i} p^i (1-p)^{N-i} \tag{4–6}$$

is approximated quite closely by the normal distribution with the same mean value $m = Np$ and variance $\sigma^2 = Np(1-p)$. This approximate distribution is sketched in Figure 4–7. The overload region corresponds to the tail of the distribution, as indicated. The sums of equations (4–4) and (4–5) must then be approximated by integrals of the Gaussian distribution over the same region. This is, in fact, another reason for requiring $N \gg 1$. It should be apparent that the tail of the Gaussian distribution should be a poorer approximation to the tail of the binomial distribution than the main body of the distribution centered about the mean m, necessitating N large.

Converting sums to integrals implies converting the integer random variable i to the equivalent continuous r.v. x, as shown in Figure 4–7. The two

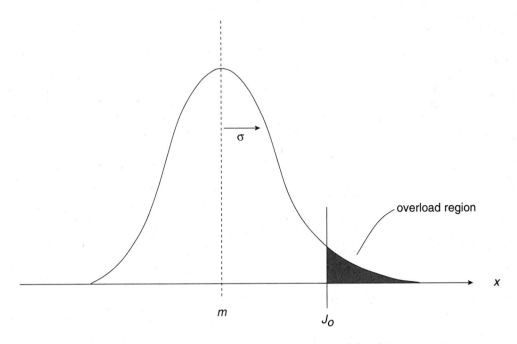

FIGURE 4–7 ▪ Gaussian approximation to binomial distribution: $m = Np$; $\sigma^2 = m(1-p)$.

probabilities P_L and ε, given by equations (4–4) and (4–5), are then approximated respectively by

$$P_L \doteq \frac{1}{m} \int_{J_o}^{\infty} \frac{e^{-(x-m)^2/2\sigma^2}(x-C)}{\sqrt{2\pi\sigma^2}} \, dx \qquad (4\text{–}4a)$$

and

$$\varepsilon \doteq \int_{J_o}^{\infty} \frac{e^{-(x-m)^2/2\sigma^2}}{\sqrt{2\pi\sigma^2}} \, dx \qquad (4\text{–}7)$$

Note that because of the continuous distribution involved, we can just take $J_o = C$, and shall do so in the calculations following. Note also that although we have obtained equations (4–4a) and (4–7) by approximating the binomial distribution by the Gaussian distribution, the distribution of multiplexed variable bit rate (VBR) traffic sources, such as multiplexed video sources, tends to the Gaussian directly (see Chapter 3). The analysis to follow applies to these sources directly, with m and σ^2 appropriately defined.

Equation (4–4a) may be rewritten in an equivalent form by writing $(x - C) = (x - m) - (C - m)$, and replacing equation (4–4a) by the sum of two integrals. This then gives us

$$P_L \doteq \frac{1}{m} \left[\int_C^{\infty} \frac{(x - m)e^{-(x-m)^2/2\sigma^2} \, dx}{\sqrt{2\pi\sigma^2}} - (C - m)\varepsilon \right]$$

$$= \frac{\sigma}{m} \frac{e^{-(C-m)^2/2\sigma^2}}{\sqrt{2\pi}} - \frac{(C - m)\varepsilon}{m} \qquad (4\text{–}8)$$

after replacing J_o by C, integrating the first integral directly, and noting that the second integral is just the definition of ε.

We now have to evaluate ε, as defined by the integral of equation (4–7). This is a standard problem. Two equivalent solutions are possible. One, which we use, replaces the integral by an asymptotic series. The second invokes a Chernoff bound [HUI 1988]. The asymptotic series, appropriate for small tail probabilities, is found in the following way. Consider the integral on the left-hand side of equation (4–9), following, which is equivalent to the expression for ε. Multiply numerator and denominator by y. (This can only be done for $x > 0$. We shall, in fact, require x to be greater than 3).

$$\int_x^{\infty} e^{-y^2} \, dy = \int_x^{\infty} \frac{ye^{-y^2} \, dy}{y} \qquad (4\text{–}9)$$

[HUI 1988]   Hui, J. Y., "Resource Allocation for Broadband Networks," *IEEE JSAC*, SAC-6 (Dec. 1988): 1598–1608.

Integrating the right-hand side of equation (4–9) by parts, one obtains

$$\int_x^\infty e^{-y^2} dy = \frac{e^{-x^2}}{2x} - \int_x^\infty \frac{e^{-y^2} dy}{2y^2}$$

(4–9a)

Integrating the second integral by parts in the same manner, (this can be done as often as desired), one obtains

$$\int_x^\infty e^{-y^2} dy = \frac{e^{-x^2}}{2x} - \frac{e^{-x^2}}{4x^3} + \frac{3}{4} \int_x^\infty \frac{e^{-y^2}}{y^4} dy$$

(4–9b)

This suffices for our purposes. Continuing in the same manner results in an asymptotic series in the sense that convergence is guaranteed only for large x. Comparing the second term with the first, note that it is small compared to the first term (less than 5% of the first term say) if $x > 3$. Extending this approach to more terms shows that the successive terms get progressively smaller and negligible.

It is a simple exercise to now show that the first term in equation (4–9b) is sufficient to provide a good approximation for ε if $(C - m) > 3\sqrt{2}\ \sigma$, with ε then given by

$$\varepsilon \doteq \frac{\sigma\, e^{-(C-m)^2/2\sigma^2}}{\sqrt{2\pi}\ (C-m)} \qquad \frac{(C-m)}{\sqrt{2}\ \sigma} > 3$$

(4–10)

Similarly, the loss probability P_L, defined by equation (4–8), is readily shown, after some algebra, to be given by

$$P_L \doteq \frac{\sigma^3 e^{-(C-m)^2/2\sigma^2}}{\sqrt{2\pi}\ m(C-m)^2}$$

$$= \frac{(1-p)\sigma\, e^{-(C-m)^2/2\sigma^2}}{\sqrt{2\pi}\ (C-m)^2} = \frac{(1-p)}{(C-m)}\ \varepsilon < \varepsilon \qquad \frac{(C-m)}{\sqrt{2}\ \sigma} > 3$$

(4–11)

if one replaces σ^2 by $m(1 - p)$. Note that P_L and ε differ by the factor $(C - m)/(1 - p)$. For P_L and ε very small, however, as is true for $(C - m) > 3\sqrt{2}\ \sigma$, the exponent in equations (4–10) and (4–11) dominates, and these differences do not affect the results very much. (Generally speaking, however, the ε approach is more conservative than the P_L approach resulting in a larger capacity requirement if used.)

Specifically, consider equation (4–10) for ε. Taking natural logs, one finds

$$\ln\ (\sqrt{2\pi}\ \varepsilon) = \ln\left(\frac{\sigma}{C-m}\right) - \frac{(C-m)^2}{2\sigma^2}$$

Neglecting the first term on the right-hand side in comparison with the second term, (this corresponds to focusing principally on the dominant exponential in equation (4–10)), one can solve easily for the capacity C to obtain a desired value of ε. This is given simply by

$$C \doteq m + \sigma\sqrt{-\ln (2\pi) - 2 \ln \varepsilon} \qquad (4\text{--}12)$$

Note that this is precisely in the form of equation (4–3a), just what we had started out to show! We thus have

$$C = m + K\sigma \qquad (4\text{--}3a)$$

with the constant K now given by

$$K = \sqrt{-\ln (2\pi) - 2 \ln \varepsilon} \qquad (4\text{--}13)$$

As an example, if we take $\varepsilon = 10^{-5}$, we find

$$C = m + 4.6\,\sigma \qquad \varepsilon = 10^{-5} \qquad (4\text{--}14)$$

Inserting the value for m for the N multiplexed on-off sources, we get

$$C = Np + 4.6\sqrt{Np\,(1-p)} \qquad \varepsilon = 10^{-5} \qquad (4\text{--}14a)$$

For other values of ε, the constant K can be adjusted accordingly. Note also that equation (4–11) for P_L, which is dominated by the same exponent, would give about the same result.

Consider an example now. Let $p = 0.02$. (This represents a very bursty source which is "off" 98% of the time, "on" only 2% of the time.) Then, from equation (4–14a), we have

$$C = 0.02N + 0.64\sqrt{N} \qquad \varepsilon = 10^{-5}, \quad p = 0.02 \qquad (4\text{--}14b)$$

This is shown plotted, versus the number of sources N, in Figure 4–8. Note the curve has precisely the shape expected, as sketched previously (in unnormalized form) in Figure 4–5. For larger values of ε (or P_L), the constant K in equation (4–13) would decrease, moving the equation for C closer to the average bandwidth assignment curve shown in Figure 4–5. For smaller ε (or P_L) the curve would move closer to the peak assignment curve of Figure 4–5, just as expected. More interestingly, Decina and Toniatti have reported on simulation results to find the equivalent bandwidth of N bursty sources required to attain a cell loss probability of 10^{-5} [DECI 1990b]. Their Figure 3 plots the results for $p = 0.02$, a cell burst size (our $1/\beta$) of 100 cells, and a buffer size of 50 cells, as the number of sources N increases. Their simulation curve is tracked almost exactly by equation (4–14b)! Figure 4–8 shows their simulation points superimposed on the analytical curve obtained using equation (4–14b). Our simple expression for the capacity C (or $C_L = CR_p$), originally motivated by in-

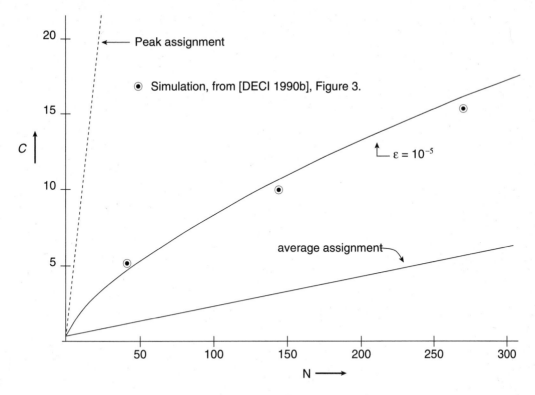

FIGURE 4–8 ■ Admission control, N homogeneous sources, $p = 0.02$.

tuition [equation (4–3)], and then found analytically by use of the Gaussian approximation to the distribution of N on-off sources (Figure 4–7), is thus verified by simulation. We now show that this expression agrees closely with other results appearing in the literature.

The simple normalized capacity expression of equation (4–12) defines the capacity required at an access buffer to handle a traffic source whose average normalized bit rate is m, with a standard deviation about m of σ. (Recall that normalization is with respect to the peak bit rate R_p, so that the actual link rate is $C_L = CR_p$). This is often called the "equivalent" or "effective" capacity of the source. For N multiplexed homogeneous on-off sources, we have $m = Np$ and $\sigma^2 = Np\,(1 - p)$, with $p = \alpha/(\alpha + \beta)$ the probability a source is in the "on" state. We can invert this expression easily in this case to obtain a specific value for N, the number of such on-off connections allowed, given the actual link capacity C_L (or its normalized form $C = C_L/R_p$) and the QoS para-

[DECI 1990b]   Decina, M., and T. Toniatti, "On Bandwidth Allocation to Bursty Virtual Connections in ATM Networks," *Proc. IEEE ICC 90,* Atlanta, GA, April 1990.

meter ε. Specifically, introducing the constant K defined by equation (4–13), we have,

$$C = Np + K\sqrt{Np(1-p)} \qquad (4\text{–}15)$$

This is solved quite easily for N, resulting in the equation

$$N = \frac{C}{p} - \frac{1}{p}\left[\sqrt{4\alpha(C+\alpha)} - 2\alpha\right] \qquad (4\text{–}16)$$

where the parameter α is defined as

$$\alpha \doteq K^2(1-p)/4$$

to simplify the appearance of the expression. Equation (4–16) defines the admissible region in this case: It is the specific expression for N shown generally in Figure 4–5. It represents, for example, the value of N in the curve of Figure 4–8 with C specified and $\varepsilon = 10^{-5}$. An admission control using this relation would thus admit a new call if fewer than N calls were connected.

In addition to providing a specific expression for the admissible region in this case of multiplexed homogeneous on-off sources, equation (4–16) allows us to focus specifically on the advantage to be obtained by statistically multiplexing these sources. Refer back again to Figure 4–4. This shows schematically that the N sources, once admission has been allowed, are combined statistically at the access buffer, with cells from each transmitted in FIFO order over the outgoing access link. One can use the analysis leading to equation (4–16) to define a statistical multiplexing gain to be accrued by combining and smoothing the source cell arrivals at the buffer.

This gain G_ε, which in our case is specified by the allowable probability QoS parameter ε and more generally by the tolerable probability of loss P_L, is the increase in connections allowed over the case in which peak bit rate allocation was to be used. If peak bit rate admission control were used, the number of calls allowed into the system would be

$$C_L/R_p = C$$

This would of course result in no cell loss; that is, P_L(or ε) = 0. In terms of our multiplexing model of Figure 4–6, this says that the number of connections allowed is such as to keep the system always in the underload region. Multiplexing gain is obtained by allowing the number N to increase beyond C, thereby incurring a cell loss penalty. The multiplexing gain G_ε is thus defined as

$$G_\varepsilon \equiv N/C \qquad (4\text{–}17)$$

with the QoS parameter implicitly contained in the value of C.

The maximum possible value of gain is easily found. This is obtained when admission control is based on *average* bandwidth assignment, that is, when the number of calls allowed in is determined from $mR_p = C_L$, or $m = C$. Since $m = Np$ for the on-off source model, the maximum multiplexing gain G is given by

$$G = N/C = 1/p \qquad (4\text{--}18)$$

This has a nice intuitive feel: for highly-bursty traffic, with $p \ll 1$, $G = 1/p$ can be quite large. As the probability p that a source is in the "on" (transmitting) state increases, the gain possible by multiplexing such sources decreases. Sources that are "on" all the time, with $p = 1$, cannot be statistically multiplexed, peak rate control must be used, and the gain $G = 1$.

The problem is that the maximum gain cannot be attained. This corresponds to average rate admission control, which we have already seen is not acceptable. This is apparent as well from equation (4–18), which shows that to attain this gain the system must be operated at a utilization of one:

$$\rho \equiv NpR_p/C_L = Np/C = 1 \qquad (4\text{--}19)$$

The actual gain G_ε possible, for a given normalized capacity C, the burstiness parameter p, and an allowable loss probability ε, is obtained directly from equation (4–16). Writing the parameter α out to show the specific dependence on p, and dividing N in equation (4–16) by C to obtain the gain as defined by equation (4–17), we obtain

$$G_\varepsilon = \frac{1}{p} - \frac{1}{p} \left\{ \sqrt{\frac{K^2(1-p)}{C}\left[1 + \frac{K^2(1-p)}{4C}\right]} - \frac{K^2(1-p)}{2C} \right\} \qquad (4\text{--}20)$$

The parameter K depends on the loss probability ε, as given by equation (4–13). Note, as expected, that as either the capacity C increases or K decreases, a greater gain is possible.

Figure 4–9 is a plot of equation (4–20) for $\varepsilon = 10^{-5}$ (in this case $K = 4.6$, as already noted), for $C = 10$ and 100. The curves plotted agree with those appearing in [COST 1991], Figure 3–2–2, p. 38. Also shown is the "ideal" gain curve $G = 1/p$.

These curves have been plotted on a log-log scale to show that over most of the range of p they are very nearly linear. This implies that $G_\varepsilon p = $ constant. But note from the definition from equation (4–17) of the multiplexing gain that $G_\varepsilon p = Np/C$ is the utilization p. We thus have

$$G_\varepsilon p = \rho = \text{constant} \qquad \rho < 1 \qquad (4\text{--}21)$$

This observation has been previously made in [COST 1991] and, in fact, is shown by curves plotted there of ρ versus p for a loss probability of 10^{-9}. For the curves of Figure 4–9, with $\varepsilon = 10^{-5}$, we find that $G_\varepsilon p = \rho \doteq 0.64$ for $C = 100$

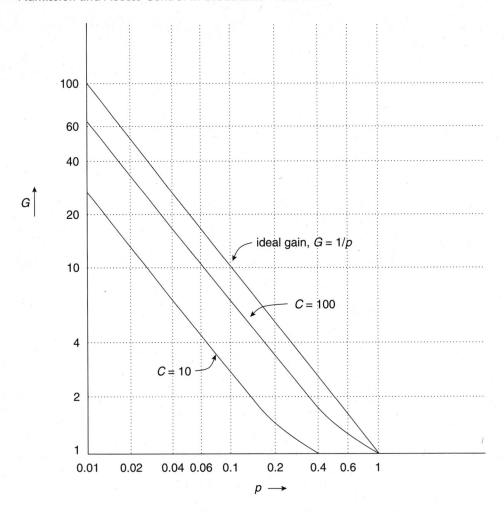

FIGURE 4–9 ■ Multiplexing gain, on-off sources, $\varepsilon = 10^{-5}$.

and $\rho \doteq 0.27$ for $C = 10$. A higher gain is possible if the allowable capacity C is increased, with correspondingly more sources allowed to be connected, and the utilization thus increasing.

In the material preceding, we have focused on a simple formulation of the admission control problem, relying both on an intuitive, heuristic approach as exemplified by equation (4–3), and a more rigorous analytical approach appropriate to many multiplexed bursty on-off sources, as well as "Gaussian-type" VBR sources, as exemplified by equations (4–10) and (4–11). The problem with this approach is that it ignores the multiplexing buffer completely, and relies on conservative bounds on the cell loss probability, captured, in the case of multiplexed on-off sources, by the probability the composite traffic stream will exhibit overload behavior. To include the effect of the access buffer and resultant cell loss probability on admission control, as well as the buffer delay (another significant QoS parameter), is an inherently difficult problem. It turns out, however, that the fluid-flow analysis of the previous chapter can be used for this purpose, in quite a straightforward, relatively simple manner. We summarize one method proposed, following the work of [GUER 1991]. This again assumes multiple on-off sources are multiplexed, with heterogeneous sources included quite naturally. To simplify the analysis, one has to again adopt conservative estimates of cell loss probability, leading to conservative estimates of the "equivalent," or "effective", capacity required. To redress this problem somewhat, Guérin et al. [1991] propose choosing, as the equivalent capacity (hence implicitly adopting an admission control strategy), the smaller of either of two capacities: the capacity obtained by using the fluid-flow analysis and the capacity calculated from equation (4–15).

The equivalent capacity using fluid-flow analysis follows directly from section 3.6. We focus on homogeneous sources first. Refer, in particular, to Figure 3–21, parts (b) and (c), which shows M on-off minisources statistically multiplexed at an access buffer. If we compare these parts of Figure 3–21 with Figures 4–1 and 4–4 in this chapter, we note that they represent the same multiplexing model if M, there, is replaced by N, here, KA bits/sec ($K = 7.5 \times 10^6$ pixels/sec) is replaced by R_p, the peak on-off source rate, and KC bits/sec is replaced by the link capacity C_L. But recall from section 3.6 that the survivor function $G(x)$ for the M-minisource model, the probability the buffer occupancy exceeds x bits, was given by equation (3–111). Introducing the changes in notation indicated above, we immediately have as the probability the buffer occupancy in Figure 4–4 exceeds x bits, the asymptotic approximation

$$G(x) \sim A_N \rho^N e^{-\beta r\, x/R_p} \qquad (4\text{–}22)$$

with the parameter r given by

$$r = (1-\rho)\left(1+\frac{\alpha}{\beta}\right)/(1-C_L/NR_p) \qquad (4\text{–}23)$$

and

$$\rho = NpR_p/C_L < 1 \qquad (4\text{–}24)$$

Note that the capacity C_L appears explicitly in the expression for $G(x)$ in the exponent r and in the term ρ^N, as well as implicitly in the parameter A_N. Letting $G(x)$ be an approximation to the probability of loss P_L (the approximation mentioned first in Chapter 3), and letting all the parameters in equation (4–22) be specified, except for the capacity C_L, one can, in principle, solve equation (4–22) for C_L. This then results in the link (actually virtual path) capacity required to obtain a specified quality of service P_L. Note that the buffer size x must be specified as well. One can choose the maximum buffer size on the basis of some hardware or processing constraint or on the basis of maximum delay. This latter constraint requires some iteration, since the delay depends both on the buffer size and the capacity C_L. Given x, one can find C_L, check to see that the maximum delay constraint is not violated, and if it is, repeat the process with a smaller value of x. Clearly the larger the value of x, the smaller the loss probability or, with P_L fixed, the smaller the capacity required.

The solution for C_L with loss probability $G(x)$, x, and the traffic parameters specified, requires iteration of equation (4–22). A simple, closed-form expression for the capacity C_L required can, however, be obtained from equation (4–22) if one focuses on the dominant exponent only. Specifically, set the function $A_N \rho^N = 1$. This is expected to be a relatively good approximation when the utilization ρ is relatively close to 1, in which case $A_N > 1$ and $\rho^N < 1$ compensate for one another to some extent. When ρ becomes smaller, however, ρ^N decreases rapidly for large N. This means that the capacity found by using only the exponent in equation (4–22) in this case is larger than it should be; that is, the capacity obtained is a conservative estimate. These observations are borne out by calculations summarized in [GUER 1991], as will be noted later.

Using the exponent in equation (4–22) only, one then has as the proposed approximation for the loss probability

$$P_L \doteq e^{-\beta r\, x/R_p} \qquad (4\text{–}25)$$

From this expression one finds immediately that

$$\beta\, rx/R_p = -\ln P_L \qquad (4\text{–}26)$$

Using equations (4–23) and (4–24) in equation (4–26), one obtains a quadratic equation for C_L. The solution is easily shown to be given by

$$C_L/R_p N = \frac{1-k}{2} + \sqrt{\left(\frac{1-k}{2}\right)^2 + kp} \qquad (4\text{–}27)$$

with the parameter k defined as

$$k \equiv \beta x/R_p(1-p)\ln(1/P_L) \qquad (4\text{–}28)$$

As a check, let $p \to 1$ with β fixed. Then $k \to \infty$. This implies the "off" interval $1/\alpha$ goes to zero. From equation (4–27), one readily shows that $C_L/R_p N \to 1$. This is as to be expected: With all N sources "on" all the time, the capacity required to handle them is NR_p, that is, the peak assignment, independent of loss probability P_L.

Consider an example [GUER 1991]. Let $P_L = 10^{-5}$, take as the buffer size $x = 3$ Mbits, $R_p = 4$ Mbps, and $1/\beta = 100$ msec. (The average number of bits generated by each source during an average burst interval is $R_p/\beta = 400$ kbits. Note that this is much less than the buffer size x.) For these numbers, we have $k = 0.65/(1-p)$. Equation (4–27) now predicts that the equivalent capacity per source C_L/N is independent of the number of homogeneous sources N. Its specific value depends on the probability p a source is in the "on" state.

How valid is this result? Guérin et al have tested this conclusion out for this specific example, among others. Their results for this example appear reproduced in Figures 4–10 and 4–11. Figure 4–10 is for the case of $N = 1$ on-off source only. For this case $A_N\rho^N = \rho = pR_p/C_L$ (see equation (3–38) in Chapter 3). One would expect the effect of ignoring the term $A_N\rho^N$ in equation (4–22) to obtain the exponential approximation of equation (4–25) to P_L to be negligible for $P_L \ll 1$, as is the case here. This is borne out by Figure 4–10, which compares the "flow approximation" capacity obtained using equation (4–27) (derived from equation (4–25)) to the "exact value" that is calculated using the full fluid-flow

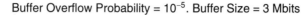

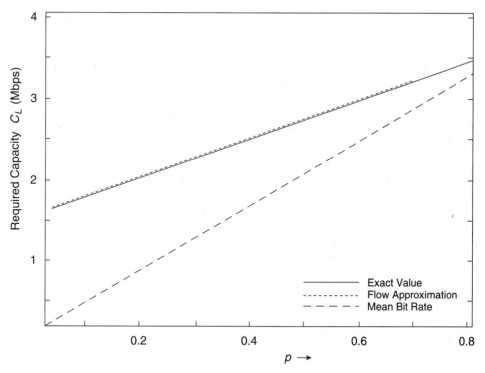

FIGURE 4–10 ■ Equivalent capacity for a single source with 4 Mbs peak rate and 100 ms mean burst period (from [Guer 1991], Figure 3. © 1991 IEEE).

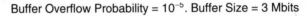

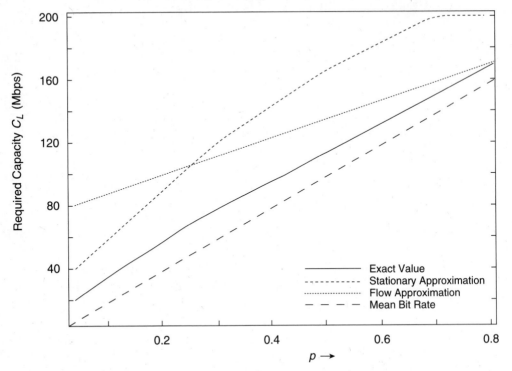

FIGURE 4–11 ■ Equivalent capacity for 50 sources, each with 4 Mbs peak rate and 100 ms mean burst period (from [Guer 1991], Figure 5. © 1991 IEEE).

analysis, to which equation (4–22) is the asymptotic approximation. The capacity is plotted as a function of p, as indicated. Note that for this single source case, equation (4–27) provides an excellent approximation. Figure 4–11 shows the equivalent capacity C_L required for $N = 50$ such on-off sources. Note that here, equation (4–27) only provides relatively good results for $p \geq 0.6$. The capacity found using equation (4–27) is much too conservative for p below that value. This corresponds to $\rho \geq 0.83$ for that case. This agrees with our earlier statement that assuming $A_{N\rho}N = 1$ in going from equation (4–22) to (4–25) should result in values of capacity that are too conservative for ρ^N small.

Figure 4–12, also taken from [Guer 1991], shows the results for another example, this time for $N = 5$ sources, each with a 40 Mbps peak rate. Here, equation (4–27) provides results intermediary between those of Figures 4–10 and 4–11. Note that here equation (4–27) (the "flow approximation" curve) provides a relatively good approximation to the full fluid-flow analysis for $p \geq 0.4$, or $\rho \geq 0.67$. This is as expected.

Guérin et al have proposed as a "good" approximate measure of equivalent capacity C_L the minimum of C_L, as calculated from equation (4–27), and

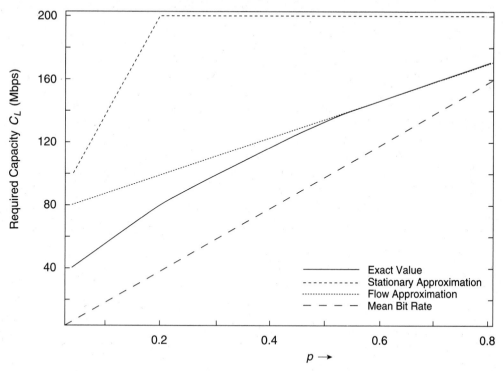

Buffer Overflow Probability = 10^{-5}. Buffer Size = 3 Mbits

FIGURE 4–12 ▪ Equivalent capacity for five sources, each with 50 Mbs peak rate and 100 ms mean burst period (from [GUER 1991], Figure 4. © 1991 IEEE).

the value obtained using our earlier simple measure of equivalent capacity [equation (4–12)]. They call this earlier value the "stationary approximation," and it is so labeled in the curves of Figures 4–11 and 4–12. It is clearly an inappropriate approximation for the $N = 5$ source case of Figure 4–12. This is as to be expected since we assumed $N \gg 1$ in obtaining equation (4–12). In Figure 4–11, for $N = 50$ sources, however, it does provide a better approximation than the flow approximation of equation (4–27) for $p \leq 0.25$. Using either approximation, whichever is smaller, thus does provide a closer fit to the capacity obtained using the complete fluid-flow analysis over the complete range of variation of p.

Specifically, letting

$$C_{LS} = mR_p + \sigma R_p \sqrt{-\ln(2\pi) - 2\ln \varepsilon}$$

from equation (4–12), and labeling C_{LF} the fluid approximation value of equivalent capacity from equation (4–27), [GUER 1991] propose as a measure of equivalent capacity

$$C_L = \min[C_{LS}, C_{LF}] \qquad (4\text{--}29)$$

The discussion thus far has focused on the loss probability P_L as a measure of quality of service. As noted earlier, however, the choice of buffer size x implicitly provides a bound on the maximum wait time in the buffer. Consider the example just discussed in which x was chosen as 3 Mbits. For the single-source case of Figure 4–10, with C_L varying from 1.4 Mbps with $p = 0$ to the peak value of 4 Mbps with $p = 1$, the maximum buffer delay (wait time) ranges from 2.1 to 0.75 sec. This number might be considered excessive in some applications, particularly since this is only one buffer in a number that might be encountered as the traffic moves through a network. But note also that with $p \ll 1$, the source "off" time $1/\alpha$ is very long, so that 2 sec, in the case of some image transmission applications, for example, might not be considered too long.

But more importantly, for broadband networking one would presumably use much higher bit rates with statistical multiplexing invoked. The results of Figures 4–11 and 4–12 are then more significant. Note that in these cases, the capacities range from 20–200 Mbps, with the corresponding maximum buffer delays ranging from 15–150 msec. These numbers appear much more tolerable for bursty source applications such as images and file transfers with the mean burst intervals of 100 msec and 10 msec chosen for Figures 4–11 and 4–12, respectively.

All of the discussion to this point has focused on equivalent or effective capacity and admission control for multiplexed homogeneous sources. We conclude this section with some brief extensions to the case of multiplexed heterogeneous sources. First note that our simple expression equation (4–12), for the equivalent capacity of multiplexed sources, lends itself quite readily to heterogeneous sources of various types, since it only involves two moments: the mean bit rate and standard deviation. The basic assumption is that the central limit theorem applies, that is, that the histogram of the bit rates of the traffic sources summed (multiplexed) approaches a normal distribution. If so, one simply adds mean bit rates and variances of the bit rate distributions to obtain m and σ^2 directly.

The second, fluid approximation to the equivalent capacity can be readily extended to heterogeneous bursty (on-off) sources as well. To show this, we first rewrite equation (4–27) in an equivalent form. Replacing the on-state probability p in that expression by $\alpha/(\alpha + \beta)$, one readily shows that the equivalent capacity C_L can be written in the following form:

$$C_L/N = \frac{R_p}{2} - \frac{(\alpha + \beta)x}{2\ln(1/P_L)} + \sqrt{\left(\frac{R_p}{2} - \frac{(\alpha + \beta)x}{2\ln(1/P_L)}\right)^2 + \frac{\alpha R_p x}{\ln(1/P_L)}} \qquad (4\text{--}27a)$$

Now consider N heterogeneous on-off sources multiplexed together, each with different peak bit rates, mean "on" (burst) times, and mean "off" intervals. For the ith source, $1 \leq i \leq N$, these are R_p^i, $1/\beta_i$, and $1/\alpha_i$, respectively. We shall show in chapter 6 that the equivalent, or effective, capacity C_L required for the multiplexed sources accessing a single buffer is given by

$$C_L = \sum_{i=1}^{N} \left[\frac{R_p^i}{2} - \frac{(\alpha_i + \beta_i)x}{2\ln(1/P_L)} + \sqrt{[\frac{R_p^i}{2} - \frac{(\alpha_i + \beta_i)x}{2\ln(1/P_L)}]^2 + \frac{\alpha_i R_p^i x}{\ln(1/P_L)}} \right] \qquad (4\text{--}30)$$

The assumption here is that each source requires the same QoS parameter P_L. This is consistent with the FIFO service discipline we have been assuming throughout. Capacities defined in this manner thus add.

The concept of equivalent or effective capacity can be generalized to a variety of source models, including those such as the Markov-modulated models used to describe voice and video signals, as discussed at length in Chapter 3. We shall return to a detailed discussion of effective capacity in Chapter 6, after developing the analytical tools required to present this concept properly. We note here that, in general, the effective capacity is found to provide a conservative estimate of the bandwidth requirements of various sources. This is in agreement with the conclusions of [GUER 1991]. Yet it is a useful tool in many situations because of its additive property, as shown by equation (4–30). Given any set of multiplexed sources, one calculates the capacity of each source, and simply adds the capacities, assuming each source requires the same QoS. Details appear in Chapter 6, where we present both the benefits and deficiencies of this technique.

4.2 ▪ ACCESS CONTROL—LEAKY BUCKET TECHNIQUE

In the previous section we discussed admission control in the context of B-ISDN. The objective there was to determine whether or not a call requiring a virtual connection (VC) with specified QoS should be admitted to a network. A comprehensive admission control admits the call if it is found that the quality of service of existing connections on the source-destination path is not affected. The difficulty of evaluating performance end-to-end along a complete virtual path (VP), forced us to focus on a more restricted class of admission controls, those exerting control at the access point only. (More generally, the results obtained apply within the network at nodal switching points if the traffic characteristics of both the new connection and those already in existence may be assumed known and statistically independent of one another.)

Assuming a call has been admitted and the connection established, it is necessary to monitor and control the traffic actually generated by the call to ensure it conforms to the traffic descriptors originally specified. This is required because of the statistical nature of the traffic generation process. It is also required because of the possibility of malicious behavior on the part of some users. This procedure of controlling the traffic during the period of a connection is variously referred to as Usage Parameter Control (UPC), access control, credit management, or traffic "policing". Users found violating their connection "agreement" (the traffic descriptors specified during the admission phase) may have arriving cells dropped to avoid network congestion or adverse impact on the QoS of the traffic of other users. Proposals have also been made to "tag" cells of user traffic violating the agreement. These cells are then allowed into the network, to be dropped later should congestion be encountered.

Alternatively, entering traffic may be "shaped" or smoothed to reduce any adverse impact on the network. There are two possibilities here: to first buffer the traffic and then read cells out at a smoothed, more regular rate; or, as another possible policy, to control the flow of traffic at the source to prevent it from congesting the network. We describe the first method briefly in this section. The second method has, in the past, been somewhat controversial, since investigators feel that at the high bit rates proposed for ISDN, B-ISDN flow control cannot be exerted effectively. A source located some distance away from the control would not be able to react quickly enough to flow control signals, and might continue to overrun or congest the network.

Despite these concerns, the ATM Forum has proposed a feedback control mechanism be adopted for the control of available bit rate (ABR) traffic. This mechanism, which controls the rate of transmission of cells at the source along a given virtual circuit, has been found by simulation to potentially provide appropriate congestion control over wide-area networks. We discuss this mechanism in Chapter 7.

In Chapter 7 we also describe briefly another traffic case in which flow control *is* feasible. This is the case of multiplexed video and bursty, nonreal-time, sources. Recall from our discussion of video traffic in Chapter 3 that we noted that compressed (VBR) video may retain frame-to-frame correlation for the order of 10–20 frames. This implies being able to predict video traffic intensity over more than one frame interval, or 30 msec. This interval is long enough to allow flow control signalling back to the source of the bursty traffic. (Round-trip propagation delay across the United States is 40–50 msec, which is just in the range of video correlation time). As noted above, we defer discussion of possible flow control procedures to a later chapter. In this section we focus on "open loop" access control. Each connection requires its own access controller and possibly a traffic shaper before being multiplexed with other connections for entry into the network. The general picture appears as shown in Figure 4–13. In the material following, we at first discuss access control without shaping, then include it through the use of an access control buffer.

A variety of techniques have been proposed and compared for access control of ATM networks [RATH 1991]. We focus here on the one most commonly discussed in the literature, the "leaky bucket" policing mechanism. The Usage Parameter Control technique proposed by the ATM Forum, called the Generic

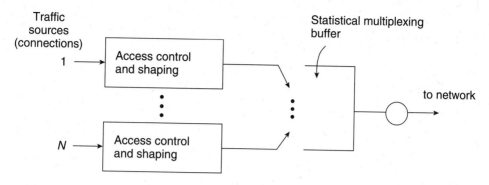

FIGURE 4–13 ▪ Access control in B-ISDN networks.

Cell Rate Algorithm, has a number of equivalent representations, one of which is the leaky bucket technique. By generalizing some of the features of this technique, including making it adaptive or dynamic, one can come up with a number of related control procedures as well. The leaky bucket control method, in its basic form, is quite simple and would appear to be particularly appropriate for bursty sources of the on-off type that we encountered both in the previous section and in Chapter 3. It does two things—it restricts the average cell throughput into the network to a specified maximum value, and allows bursts of cells up to some maximum number. (Depending on the burst length allowed, the peak rate may thus be quite higher than the average rate). It was first proposed as a possible traffic control procedure by Jonathan Turner [TURN 1986].

The algorithm is very simple and may be described and/or implemented in several equivalent ways. One method proposed involves incrementing a counter C by 1, periodically every D sec, until a maximum value of M is reached. The counter is decremented by 1 for every cell transmitted. Transmission is interrupted and cells are dropped whenever the counter reaches 0. (Alternatively, in the "violation tagging" mode noted above, cells are "tagged"; that is, a bit is set, when the counter is at 0. We discuss the cell dropping mode only in the material following). The average rate of transmission is then limited to a maximum of $r = 1/D$ cells/sec. The counter setting M allows a maximum burst of M cells to be transmitted. There are thus two parameters to adjust in this algorithm. Because cells may be occasionally dropped, (the counter is 0 when a cell arrives), the average throughput is less than its maximum possible value r. Increasing the burst size M allowed reduces this effect, but slows down the system response to congestion.

[RATH 1991]   Rathgeb, E. P., "Modeling and Performance Comparison of Policing Mechanisms for ATM Networks," *IEEE JSAC, 9,* 3 (April 1991): 325–334.

[TURN 1986]   Turner, J. S., "New Directions in Communications (or Which Way in the Information Age?)," *IEEE Commun. Mag., 24,* 10 (Oct. 1986): 8–15.

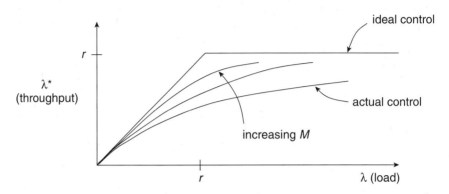

FIGURE 4–14 ■ Throughput-load curve, leaky bucket algorithm.

An ideal control curve would have the throughput, in cells/sec, equal the traffic load until that load reached r. As the load continued to increase beyond r, the throughput would stay at r. This curve is shown sketched diagrammatically in Figure 4–14. The load is represented by the symbol λ, the throughput by the symbol λ^*.

A second representation of the algorithm has the counter decremented periodically until it reaches 0. It is incremented by 1 whenever a cell is transmitted, until a maximum value of M is reached, at which time no cells can be transmitted. (This again ignores violation tagging). A third representation involves the use of a "token pool" buffer as shown in Figure 4–15. A cell must have a token waiting to be transmitted. Tokens are generated once per D sec, as shown, and wait in the buffer, until the buffer fills. At this time no further tokens are generated. It is left for the reader to show that all three representations are identical. As indicated in Figure 4–15, the average throughput λ^* differs from the load λ because of possible cell loss. The parameter P_L in Figure 4–15 represents, as it did in the previous section, the cell loss probability. Variations of this basic algorithm include, in addition to the possibility of violation tagging already mentioned, adding a cell smoothing buffer, adapting both the token arrival rate r (the counter increment rate) and the maximum token buffer (counter) size M to the traffic load and/or congestion conditions in the network, as well as other possibilities. A simple modification of the algorithm to handle variable-length packets instead of fixed-size cells has been proposed as well [BALA 1990]. In this procedure a given block of octets within a packet requires a token. Longer packets thus require more tokens to be transmitted.

We shall focus first on the basic algorithm, showing how one obtains the $\lambda^* - \lambda$ (throughput-load) curve analytically. We do this first through a very

[BALA 1990]   Bala, K., et al., "Congestion Control for High-Speed Packet-Switched Networks," *IEEE Infocom '90,* San Francisco, (June 1990): 520–526.

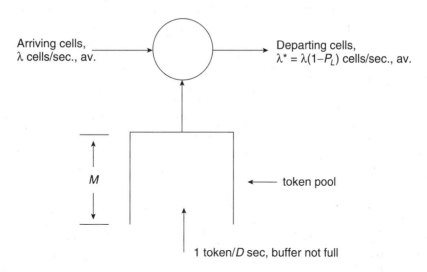

Arriving cells,
λ cells/sec., av.

Departing cells,
$\lambda^* = \lambda(1 - P_L)$ cells/sec., av.

M

← token pool

1 token/D sec, buffer not full

FIGURE 4–15 ■ Leaky bucket algorithm.

simple approximate technique, appropriate only for Poisson cell arrivals. This serves to reinforce the leaky bucket concept and provides simple, first-order results. We then provide a more detailed discrete-time analysis of the leaky bucket algorithm using a simplified version of an approach proposed in the literature. Finally, in the next section, we generalize the algorithm to include a data shaping buffer and show how the fluid-flow analysis of Chapter 3 can be used to provide useful performance results for on-off, bursty traffic in this case.

The simple approximate analysis of the leaky bucket procedure is based on the closed queueing network model shown in Figure 4–16. A little thought will indicate that this model captures the essence of the leaky bucket procedure diagrammed in Figure 4–15. Cells are assumed generated at a Poisson rate λ, as indicated by the upper server. But these will only be generated if the upper queue has at least one "occupant" or token. That queue increases at an average rate $r = D^{-1}$, as shown. (Note that this rate is also assumed Poisson with this model, rather than the desired periodic incrementing of the counter in the leaky bucket algorithm). The closed network has M tokens circulating in it, as shown. At most M cells can thus be served in succession. If all M circulating tokens are in the lower queue, the upper queue is empty, and cell service is blocked. This two-queue model of the leaky bucket algorithm and the analysis based on it are due to Wong and Kramer [WONG 1988].

[WONG 1988]   Wong, L-N, and M. Kramer, "A Performance Analysis of a 'Leaky Bucket' Access Control Scheme for Broadband MANs," unpublished paper, Nynex Science and Technology, August 1988.

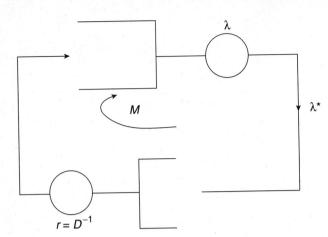

FIGURE 4–16 ■ Closed queueing network model, leaky bucket, $M/M/1$ approximation.

The throughput λ^* of this system is now written simply as

$$\lambda^* = \lambda(1 - p_0)$$
$$= \lambda(1 - P_L)$$

(4–31)

where $p_0 = P_L$ is the probability the upper queue is empty or, from Figure 4–16, the probability the lower queue is full. But either queue behaves as a finite $M/M/1$ queue, of maximum occupancy M, under the Poisson assumptions made above. In particular, from finite $M/M/1$ analysis, the probability the lower queue is full is

$$P_L = \rho^M(1 - \rho)/[1 - \rho^{M+1}]$$

(4–32)

with $\rho \equiv \lambda/r = \lambda D$.

Inserting equation (4–32) in (4–31), and simplifying, we have

$$\lambda^* = \lambda\left[\frac{1-\rho^M}{1-\rho^{M+1}}\right]$$

(4–33)

This may also be written in normalized form as

$$\lambda^*/r = \lambda^* D = \rho\left[\frac{1-\rho^M}{1-\rho^{M+1}}\right]$$

(4–33a)

Equation (4–33a) has been plotted in Figure 4–17. Note that it has the expected form sketched previously in Figure 4–14. As M increases, the throughput-load characteristic approaches the ideal characteristic in which the throughput λ^* equals the load λ for $\lambda \leq r$, and saturates at the maximum value of r for $\lambda >> r$.

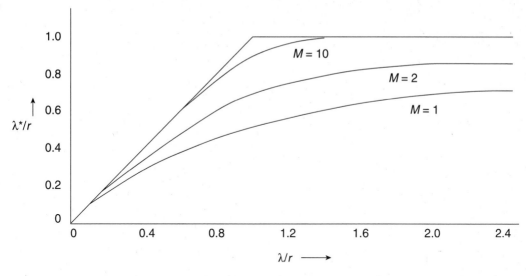

FIGURE 4–17 ▪ Throughput-load characteristic, model of Figure 4–16.

A number of more sophisticated analyses of the leaky bucket algorithm have appeared in the literature [SIDI 1989], [BERG 1990], [HEYM 1992], [BUTT 1991]. They differ in the way in which they model the leaky bucket technique and in the types of traffic and traffic models they can handle. Interestingly, the curve for $M = 10$ in Figure 4–17 tracks the equivalent curve in [BERG 1990] reasonably well [BERG 1990, Figure 3]. The critical design parameter may not be average throughput shown in Figure 4–17, however, but the loss probability P_L. For small values of P_L, the approximate solution may not be accurate enough and the more sophisticated analyses may be required. This point is pursued later, at the end of the next section.

We now proceed with two more sophisticated, albeit relatively simple, analyses of the leaky bucket algorithm. The first is a Markov chain discrete-time analysis due to Sidi et al. [SIDI 1989]. The second, described in the next section, uses the fluid-flow approximation generalized to finite buffers and ap-

[SIDI 1989]   Sidi, M., et al., "Congestion Control Through Input Rate Regulation," *Proc. IEEE Globecom 89,* Dallas, TX, Nov. 1989: 1764–1768.

[BERG 1990]   Berger, A. W., "Performance Analysis of a Rate Control Throttle Where Tokens and Jobs Queue," *Proc. IEEE Infocom 90,* San Francisco (June 1990): 30–38.

[HEYM 1992]   Heyman, D. F., "A Performance Model of the Credit Manager Algorithm," *Computer Networks and ISDN Systems, 24* (1992): 81–91.

[BUTT 1991]   Butto, M., et al., "Effectiveness of the 'Leaky Bucket' Policing Mechanism in ATM Networks," *IEEE JSAC, 9,* 3 (April 1991): 335–342.

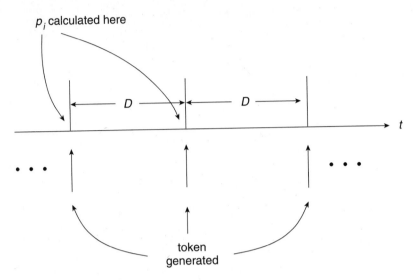

FIGURE 4–18 ■ Discrete-time calculation, leaky bucket algorithm.

propriate to bursty on-off sources or Markov-modulated models of traffic [ELWA 1991].

The Markov chain discrete-time analysis proceeds as follows. Let i be the number of tokens in the token buffer pool of Figure 4–15. We shall calculate the steady-state data throughput λ^* by first calculating the steady-state probability p_i that i tokens are in the pool just *before* a token is generated. Recall that tokens are generated periodically every D sec. Token generation times are thus spaced D sec. apart, as shown in Figure 4–18. Let α_j be the probability j cells (packets) arrive in any D sec interval. Arrivals are assumed independent from interval to interval. (The Markov chain model arises from this assumption). As an example, if the arrivals are Poisson with average rate λ,

$$a_j = (\lambda D)^j e^{-\lambda D}/j! \qquad j = 0,1,2,\ldots \qquad (4\text{–}34)$$

If the arrival process is Bernoulli, with probability $a_1 = p$ that one cell arrives in a D sec interval, we have

$$a_1 = p \qquad a_0 = 1 - p \qquad (4\text{–}35)$$

Other models can be invoked as well. But note that the on-off traffic models discussed previously are not captured easily with this analysis.

[ELWA 1991]   Elwalid, A. I., and D. Mitra, "Stochastic Fluid Models in the Analysis of Access Regulation in High Speed Networks." *Proc. IEEE Globecom 91*, Phoenix, Dec. 1991: 1626–1632. (A more detailed version appears in *Communication Systems*, Special issue of *Queueing Systems*, D. Mitra and I. Mitrani (eds.), *9* (1991). Switz.: J. C. Baltzer A. G., Basel, 29–63.)

In the steady state one expects the probability p_i that there are i tokens in the token buffer just before a token arrival (Figure 4–18) to be the same in any D sec interval. We can thus equate the probability p_i at the end of one interval to the sum of the probabilities of the various states the token buffer could have been in, exactly one interval earlier. This gives rise to a set of discrete-time balance equations. As an example, consider the state $i = M$; that is, the state for which the token buffer is full. For the buffer to be in this state just before a possible token arrival, there can only have been two possibilities one interval earlier: the buffer was in state $(M-1)$, a token was added and *no* cells arrived during the entire interval, *or* the buffer was in state M, no token was added and again *no* arrivals took place. We must thus have as the discrete-time probability balance equation for this case,

$$p_M = (p_{M-1} + p_M)a_0 \tag{4–36}$$

Consider state $M-1$ now. Repeating the same kind of argument, it is left for the reader to show that the balance equiation is now given by

$$p_{M-1} = p_{M-2}a_0 + p_{M-1}a_1 + p_M a_1 \tag{4–37}$$

More generally, allowing any number j of data cells to arrive in an interval, with its corresponding probability of arrival a_j, the probability p_i the system is in state i just before a token arrival is given by the set of balance equations

$$p_i = \sum_{j=1}^{M} p_{j-1}a_{j-1} + p_M a_{M-i} \qquad 1 \le i \le M \tag{4–38}$$

and

$$p_0 = \sum_{j=0}^{M-1} p_j \,\bar{a}_j + p_M \,\bar{a}_{M-1} \tag{4–39}$$

Here

$$\bar{a}_j \equiv 1 - \sum_{k=0}^{j} a_k = \sum_{k=j+1}^{\infty} a_k \tag{4–40}$$

It is again left for the reader to verify these equations.

One can now solve these equations recursively for p_i, and from this, as we shall show shortly, one obtains the desired data throughput as a function (implicitly) of D, M, and, of course, the traffic arrival statistics a_j. The recursive technique proceeds as follows:

Choose some value of $p_M < 1$. Then from equation (4–36), we have

$$p_{M-1} = p_M(1 - a_0)/a_0 \tag{4–41}$$

From equation (4–37), one then finds

$$p_{M-2} = \{[p_{M-1}(1 - a_1)] - p_M a_1\}/a_0 \qquad (4\text{--}42)$$

Proceeding in this manner, we have, recursively,

$$p_i = \left[p_{i+1} - \sum_{j=1}^{M-1-i} p_{i+j} a_j - p_M a_{M-1-i} \right]/a_0, \qquad 0 \leq i \leq M - 2 \qquad (4\text{--}43)$$

But recall that the value of p_M was arbitrarily chosen. We now collect all the p_i's generated and calculate the sum

$$S = \sum_{i=0}^{M} p_i \qquad (4\text{--}44)$$

Dividing all the p_i's through by S to obtain the desired probability normalization, we have, finally,

$$p_i = p_i/S \qquad 0 \leq i \leq M \qquad (4\text{--}45)$$

Given p_i, the probability the token buffer of Figure 4–15 is in state i, how does one now determine the data throughput from this? Recall that to be transmitted, each cell (packet), on arrival, must find a token waiting; otherwise it is dropped. Say the token buffer is in state M. Then at most, M cells can be transmitted. (No token can be added since the token buffer state has been defined just prior to a possible token arrival. This arrival is blocked if the buffer is full). Exactly M cells will be transmitted if M or more cells arrive in the interval D sec long. If fewer arrive they will all be transmitted. Consider a token buffer state $k \leq (M - 1)$ now. Then the number of cells that can be transmitted in one token generation interval varies from 1, with arrival probability a_1, to at most $(k + 1)$, since an additional token will be added during that interval. (The buffer is no longer full). Putting this all together, we get as the throughput $\lambda^* D$, the average number of cells transmitted in a D sec interval,

$$\lambda^* D = p_M \left[\sum_{i=0}^{M} i a_i + M \sum_{i=M+1}^{\infty} a_i \right]$$

$$+ \sum_{k=0}^{M-1} p_k \left[\sum_{i=1}^{k+1} i a_i + (k + 1) \sum_{i=k+2}^{\infty} a_i \right] \qquad (4\text{--}46)$$

This is comparable to the normalized load λ^*/r given by equation (4–33a) for the earlier approximate analysis.

Consider some examples. Take $M = 1$ first. One token at a time only is allowed in the token buffer. Hence individual data cells only may be transmitted. If more than one arrives in the interval D, one will be transmitted and the others dropped. From equations (4–38) to (4–40), or (4–41) to (4–45), we find that

$$p_0 = 1 - a_0 \qquad p_1 = a_0 \qquad M = 1 \qquad (4\text{–}47)$$

From equation (4–46) we find the throughput to be given by

$$\lambda^* D = (1 - a_0)(p_0 + p_1) = 1 - a_0 \qquad M = 1 \qquad (4\text{–}48)$$

For the case of Poisson arrivals [equation (4–34)], one then has

$$\lambda^* D = 1 - e^{-\lambda D} = 1 - e^{-\rho} \qquad M = 1 \qquad (4\text{–}48a)$$

with $\rho \equiv \lambda D$.

This is sketched, as a function of the normalized load $\rho = \lambda D = \lambda/r$, in Figure 4–19. Also shown for comparison is the comparable curve found using the approximate analysis, as previously plotted in Figure 4–17. Note that the earlier curve provides a conservative estimate of the throughput. This is found to be true in general.

The second simple example is that for $M = 2$. One finds here, using the equations derived above, that

$$\begin{aligned} p_0 &= (1 - a_1 - a_0)/(1 - a_1) \quad p_1 = a_0(1 - a_0)/(1 - a_1) \\ p_2 &= a_0^2/(1 - a_1) \qquad M = 2 \end{aligned} \qquad (4\text{–}49)$$

Using these values of the token buffer probabilities to calculate the normalized throughput from equation (4–46), it is easy to show that

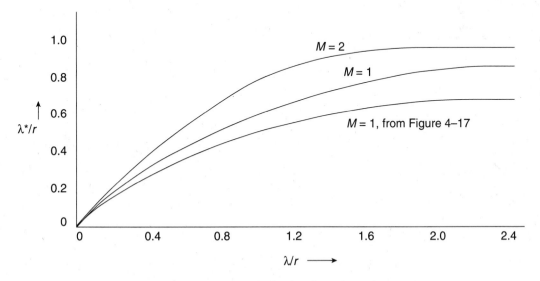

FIGURE 4–19 ■ Leaky bucket throughput characteristic.

$$\lambda * D = \lambda */r = 1 - \frac{a_0^2}{(1-a_1)} \qquad M = 2 \qquad (4\text{–}50)$$

Taking Poisson arrivals again as an example,

$$\lambda */r = 1 - \frac{e^{-2\rho}}{(1-\rho e^{-\rho})} \qquad \rho \equiv \lambda D \qquad M = 2 \qquad (4\text{–}50\text{a})$$

The curve for this case is also plotted in Figure 4–19. By comparison with Figure 4–17, one can again see that the approximate analysis provides a conservative estimate of throughput here.

Although we have focused on the average throughput in the analysis above, since that is one useful measure of performance controlled by the leaky bucket technique, the loss probability is of particular interest. Recall that this was the measure of QoS on which we focused in the previous section on admission control. Ideally, as noted in discussing the form of the throughput-load curve sketched in Figure 4–14, one would like a control to track the load exactly until the maximum average throughput r is reached, and then saturate at that value. This implies zero loss probability for $\lambda \leq r$, and then the value, from equation (4–31), required to have $\lambda* = r$ beyond that point. Specifically, the ideal $P_L - \lambda$ curve would have the form

$$P_L = 0 \qquad \lambda/r \leq 1$$
$$P_L = 1 - 1/(\lambda/r) \qquad \lambda/r \geq 1 \qquad (4\text{–}51)$$

In normalized form, letting $\rho \equiv \lambda/r$, we can also write

$$P_L = 1 - \frac{1}{\rho} \qquad \rho \geq 1 \qquad (4\text{–}51\text{a})$$

How well does the leaky bucket mechanism perform compared to this ideal characteristic? The performance using the approximate model of Figure 4–16 is readily obtained from equation (4–32), the explicit expression for the loss probability for this model. Note first, as expected, that for large token pool size M, the loss probability is small for $\rho < 1$. At $\rho = 1$, the reader can readily ascertain that

$$P_L = \frac{1}{(M+1)} \qquad \rho = 1$$

while for $\rho \gg 1$,

$$P_L \to 1 - \frac{1}{\rho} \qquad \rho \gg 1$$

as desired for the ideal characteristic. By increasing the token pool size M, then, one can approach the ideal characteristic more and more, but again at the cost of slower response time of the control. This is expected of course, since we noted the same behavior with the throughput characteristic.

The loss probability performance using the discrete-time model of [SIDI 1989] can also be obtained quite readily from the throughput equation of (4–46). Using this together with equation (4–31), one can calculate the loss probability directly as

$$P_L = 1 - \frac{\lambda^*D}{\lambda D} = 1 - \frac{\lambda^*D}{\rho} \tag{4–51b}$$

with ρ again defined as λD. Sidi et al have carried out this calculation for the case of Poisson arrivals [equation (4–34)] and their results are reproduced, for $\lambda D \equiv \rho < 1$, in Figure 4–20. Note that the control behaves as expected. The larger the token pool size M, the closer the control comes to the ideal control just described. But, as already noted, larger values of M result in correspondingly longer times required to detect violations of the control, however [BUTT 1991], [RATH 1991]. There is thus a tradeoff between rapidity of response and the ability to detect violations.

One approach proposed to overcome this problem is to introduce a "smoothing" buffer as part of the leaky bucket mechanism. This extended form of the leaky bucket procedure is shown schematically in Figure 4–21.

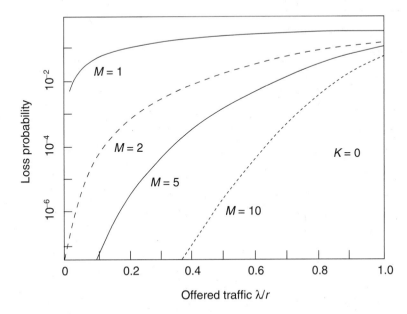

FIGURE 4–20 ▪ Loss probability, leaky bucket (from [SIDI 1989], Figure 4. © 1989 IEEE).

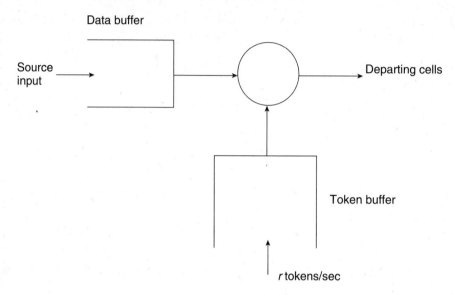

FIGURE 4–21 ■ Leaky bucket access control with data "shaping" buffer.

Bursts of data cells are queued with this scheme instead of being dropped if tokens are not immediately available. The traffic leaving the leaky bucket controller is thus "smoothed" before accessing the network. As will be shown in the analysis in the section following, the loss probability now turns out to depend on the *sum* of the buffers. This has been noted a number of times in the literature [SIDI 1989], [BERG 1990], [ELWA 1991]. One can use a smaller token buffer and increase the data buffer size correspondingly to attain the same loss probability performance. The price paid, however, is additional delay introduced in the data path.

4.3 ■ LEAKY BUCKET WITH DATA BUFFERING–FLUID ANALYSIS

We concluded the last section by noting the leaky bucket can be extended by adding a data buffer. This serves to buffer and smooth out bursts of cells arriving, enabling the control to be exerted more quickly with a smaller value of token buffer (or maximum counter value) required. The price paid of course is some delay introduced in buffering incoming cells.

We now quantify these remarks by carrying out an analysis of the extended leaky bucket mechanism of Figure 4–21. We use a fluid model approach for this purpose, repeating, and extending, the analysis of section 3.8.

Figure 4–22 portrays a fluid analysis version of the extended leaky bucket mechanism of Figure 4–21. The traffic source is, most generally, represented by an N-state Markov-modulated fluid source such as that introduced

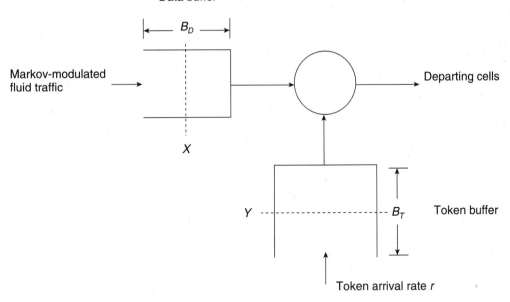

FIGURE 4–22 ■ Fluid-flow analysis, leaky bucket of Figure 4–21.

in section 3.8. The traffic model, equivalent to that presented in Figure 3–39, is shown schematically in Figure 4–23. We repeat some of the analysis of section 3.8 for completeness here. Transitions between states are governed by an underlying Markov chain, only a few of which are shown in Figure 4–23. This chain is again represented by an $N \times N$ infinitesimal generating matrix M, defined (as it was previously in Chapter 3 by equation (3–47)) by

$$
M = \begin{bmatrix}
\mu_{11} & \mu_{12} & \cdots & \mu_{1j} & \cdots & \mu_{1N} \\
\mu_{21} & \mu_{22} & \cdots & \mu_{2j} & \cdots & \mu_{2N} \\
\vdots & \vdots & \cdots & \vdots & \cdots & \vdots \\
\mu_{i1} & \mu_{i2} & \cdots & \mu_{ij} & \cdots & \mu_{iN} \\
\vdots & \vdots & \cdots & \vdots & \cdots & \vdots \\
\mu_{N1} & \mu_{N2} & \cdots & \mu_{Nj} & \cdots & \mu_{NN}
\end{bmatrix}
\tag{4–52}
$$

(Compare with the $B \times B$ matrix of equation (3–134) as well.) The diagonal rate parameter μ_{ii} is again given as

$$
\mu_{ii} = -\sum_{\substack{j=1 \\ j \neq i}}^{N} \mu_{ij} \qquad 1 \leq i \leq N
\tag{4–53}
$$

Row sums are thus all zero. The steady-state probability π_i that the Markov chain is in state i is then again given by solving the matrix equation

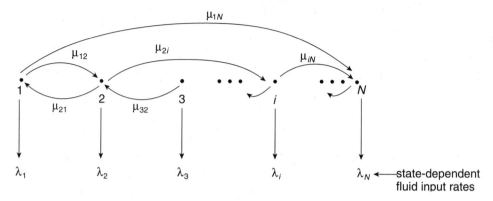

FIGURE 4–23 ■ Markov-modulated fluid source model (fluid analog of MMPP, Figure 3–11).

$$\boldsymbol{\pi}\, M = 0 \qquad\qquad (4\text{--}54)$$

with

$$\boldsymbol{\pi} \equiv [\pi_1, \pi_2, \ldots \, \pi_i, \ldots, \pi_N] \qquad\qquad (4\text{--}55)$$

the row vector of the N steady-state probabilities. (A separate normalization condition $\sum_{i=1}^{N} \pi_i = 1$ is needed to ensure the π_i's represent probabilities).

As in Figure 3–39, the input traffic rates shown in Figure 4–23 are constant flows, as appropriate to a stochastic fluid source. As a special case, the one on which we shall focus later, let the traffic source be modeled as the simple on-off source of Figure 4–1. This is reproduced here as Figure 4–24. Then, for this case,

$$M = \begin{bmatrix} -\alpha & \alpha \\ \beta & -\beta \end{bmatrix} \qquad\qquad (4\text{--}56)$$

and

$$\boldsymbol{\pi} = \begin{bmatrix} \dfrac{\beta}{\alpha+\beta}, & \dfrac{\alpha}{\alpha+\beta} \end{bmatrix} \qquad\qquad (4\text{--}57)$$

In this model $\lambda_1 = 0$, $\lambda_2 = R_p$. We use the same notation used previously in Figure 4–1 to preserve continuity.

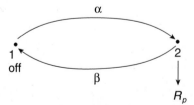

FIGURE 4–24 ■ Simple on-off fluid source.

Returning to Figure 4–22 (the model of the leaky bucket algorithm augmented with a finite data smoothing buffer), note that we have changed the notation somewhat from that used previously. The maximum token pool is now given as B_T tokens rather than the symbol M used previously. The finite data buffers shown can accommodate, at most, B_D data cells. The objective is now to find the steady-state occupancy statistics of the two buffers, X and Y for the data and token buffers respectively, from which performance measures of interest can be found.

It turns out, as noted earlier, that the performance of the extended leaky bucket algorithm depends only on the *sum* of the buffer sizes shown, $B = B_T + B_D$. (Note again that the token buffer is only a model representation. The data buffer, on the other hand, is a real buffer.) This is due to the fact that the two random variables X and Y are related to one another. In fact, as shown below, one doesn't find the statistics of X and Y separately, but, rather, jointly, by defining an equivalent "virtual" queue representation from which the statistics of either one can be found [ELWA 1991]. To demonstrate this, note two facts from the leaky bucket technique:

1. The data buffer can be occupied only if the token queue is empty; otherwise the data cells would be transmitted, one per token. Hence we must have

$$Y = 0, \qquad X > 0 \qquad\qquad (4\text{–}58)$$

2. Conversely, the token buffer can be occupied only if the data buffer is empty. If data cells were queued, they would each capture a token and be transmitted. Hence we also have

$$X = 0, \qquad Y > 0 \qquad\qquad (4\text{–}59)$$

Conditions of equations (4–58) and (4–59) are both encapsulated in the single condition

$$XY = 0 \qquad\qquad (4\text{–}60)$$

Following the approach of Elwalid and Mitra [ELWA 1991], we now define the following single "virtual buffer" random variable

$$W \equiv X - Y + B_T \qquad\qquad (4\text{–}61)$$

Note that because of the conditions on the random variables X and Y,

$$0 \leq X \leq B_D, \qquad 0 \leq Y \leq B_T, \qquad XY = 0$$

W has the following properties:

1. $$0 \leq W \leq B_T + B_D = B \qquad\qquad (4\text{–}62)$$

2. In the range $0 \leq W \leq B_T$,

$$X = 0, \qquad W = B_T - Y \qquad\qquad (4\text{–}63)$$

3. In the range $B_T \le W \le B = B_T + B_D$,

$$Y = 0, \qquad W = X + B_T \qquad (4\text{-}64)$$

Since X and Y appear at disjoint ranges of W, one need only find the statistics of W. From these, one can find the statistics of X and Y, using equations (4–64) and (4–63) respectively. The range of W and its relation to Y are diagrammed in Figure 4–25.

Because of the stochastic fluid process assumed driving the data buffer (Figure 4–22), X and Y, and hence W, are all continuous r.v.'s. To find the statistics of W, and from these, those of X and Y, if desired, we proceed as previously in our fluid-flow analysis. We dispense here with the initial incremental time analysis used to find the equivalent probability distribution in Chapter 3 (see equation (3–13) for example), and proceed directly to the steady-state analysis as was done in section 3.8. Thus define the joint probability

$$F_i(x) \equiv \text{Prob. } [W \le x, S = i] \qquad (4\text{-}65)$$

with $S = i$ the state of the input source Markov chain, $1 \le i \le N$. Note from the definition of W that this implies

$$F_i(B) = \pi_i \qquad (4\text{-}66)$$

Proceeding as was done in Chapter 3, one then shows that the desired solution for $F_i(x)$, $1 \le i \le N$, is given by the solutions to our familiar set of linear differential equations now specialized to this problem,

$$(\lambda_i - r)\frac{dF_i(x)}{dx} = \sum_{j=1}^{N} \mu_{ji} F_j(x) \qquad 1 \le i \le N \qquad (4\text{-}67)$$

Here μ_{ij} is the transition rate between states i and j of the underlying N-state Markov chain (Figure 4–23), λ_i is the input fluid rate at state i, and

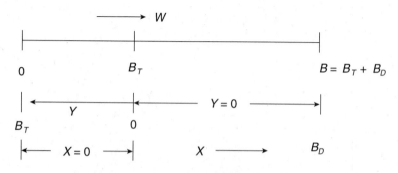

FIGURE 4–25 ■ "Virtual buffer" variable W.

$\mu_{ii} = -\sum_{j=1, j\neq 1}^{N} \mu_{ij}$. This is to be compared with equation (3–138). Details are left to the reader.

More compactly, in vector form, we have our familiar equation

$$\frac{d\boldsymbol{F}(x)}{dx} D = \boldsymbol{F}(x)M \tag{4–68}$$

with

$$\boldsymbol{F}(x) \equiv [F_1(x), F_2(x), \ldots, F_N(X)] \tag{4–69}$$

M the $N \times N$ matrix of equation (4–52), and

$$D \equiv \text{diag. } [\lambda_i - r] \tag{4–70}$$

(Compare with equation (3–139) to equation (3–141). Note that the token arrival rate r, the counter increment (or decrement) rate in the leaky bucket procedure, takes the place of the capacity C_L or μ in our earlier work using fluid analysis. As noted much earlier in Chapter 3, we clearly must have $\lambda_i \neq r$, all i. The solution to equation (4–68) is again given by sums of exponentials:

$$\boldsymbol{F}(x) = \sum_{j=1}^{N} a_j \Phi_j e^{z_j x} \tag{4–71}$$

with (z_j, Φ_j) the (eigenvalue, eigenvector) pair satisfying the eigenvalue equation

$$z_j \Phi_j D = \Phi_j M \qquad 1 \leq j \leq N \tag{4–72}$$

The a_j's, $1 \leq j \leq N$, are again constants to be determined by invoking N boundary conditions.

Note a basic difference beween this solution and that found earlier using the fluid source process: Here the "buffer" occupancy r.v. W is *bounded* $(0 \leq W \leq B = B_T + B_D)$, whereas previously we had always assumed the buffer was infinite. The variable x (the continuous-valued state of W), is thus finite as well. Hence we must retain *all* the eigenvalues, positive as well as negative, in the solution of equation (4–71). This is where the analysis here deviates from that of section 3.8. As previously, one eigenvector is known. Since $\pi M = 0$, one eigenvalue of equation (4–72) must again be zero. Calling this eigenvalue z_1, its associated eigenvector $\Phi_1 = \pi$. Hence equation (4–71) can be simplified to

$$\boldsymbol{F}(x) = a_1 \pi + \sum_{j=2}^{N} a_j \Phi_j e^{z_j x} \tag{4–71a}$$

We now need N boundary conditions to find the unknown constants a_j, $1 \leq j \leq N$. (Why is a_1 not equal to 1, as in our earlier fluid analysis?)

To establish these, we note that, just as in our discussion of statistical multiplexing in Chapter 3, as well as our admission control analysis earlier, some of the Markov chain states must be underload or "emptying" states; the others must be overload or "filling" states. (What is "filling" or "emptying" here?) Specifically, with r taking the place of our link capacity C_L in the previous discussions, there must exist some Markov states i for which

$$\lambda_i - r < 0: \text{emptying states;}$$

and some i for which

$$\lambda_i - r > 0: \text{filling states.}$$

(Why must this be so? What would happen if $r < \lambda_i$, all i; or $r > \lambda_i$, all i?) Hence all N states of the Markov chain modulating the source arrival rate can be divided into two disjoint sets,

$$S_F \equiv \{i\varepsilon N | \lambda_i - r > 0\}: \text{filling states}$$

and

$$S_E \equiv \{i\varepsilon N | \lambda_i - r < 0\}: \text{emptying states}$$

We have said nothing about the relative size of the λ_i's in Figure 4–23 thus far. Without loss of generality, assume that the Markov chain states are chosen such that the λ_i's monotonically increase with the state number. Hence we have

$$\lambda_1 < \lambda_2 < \lambda_3 < \ldots \lambda_l < \lambda_{l+1} < \ldots \lambda_N \tag{4–73}$$

Let λ_l correspond to the largest source rate such that the system is in the emptying range. Then we must have $(\lambda_l - r) < 0$, $(\lambda_{l+1} - r) > 0$ and $\lambda_l < r < \lambda_{l+1}$. State l is thus equivalent to L_u in our earlier work, while $(l + 1)$ is equivalent to L_o.

Consider the l emptying states now, $i\varepsilon S_E$. Since the data arrival rate is less than the token arrival rate in these states, $\lambda_i < r$, the tokens are tending to collect. The data queue of Figure 4–22 is tending to empty ($X \rightarrow 0$) and the token queue is tending to fill ($Y \rightarrow B_T$). Hence

$$W = X - Y + B_T \rightarrow 0$$

For these states then, the probability the "virtual queue" is full tends to zero, or we have

$$\text{Prob. } [W = B, S = i] = \text{Prob. } [X = B_D, S = i] = 0 \qquad i\varepsilon S_E \tag{4–74}$$

But note that

$$\text{Prob. } [W = B, S = i] = P[W \le B, S = i] - P[W \le B^-, S = i]$$

From equation (4–74) we thus have

$$P[W \le B^-, S = i] = P[W \le B, S = i] = \pi_i$$

In our probability distribution function notation, then,

$$F_i(B^-) = \pi_i \qquad i \varepsilon S_E \qquad (4\text{--}75)$$

This provides l of the N boundary conditions.

Consider the remaining $(N - l)$ filling states, $i \varepsilon S_F$. For these states, with $\lambda_i > r$, the token buffer of Figure 4–22 tends to empty ($Y \to 0$), the data buffer tends to fill ($X \to B_D$), and

$$W = X - Y + B_T \to B_D + B_T = B$$

For these states, then, the probability that the virtual queue is empty must be zero. We thus have

$$P[W \le 0^+, S = i] = F_i(0^+) = 0 \qquad i \varepsilon S_F \qquad (4\text{--}76)$$

Since $S_E \cup S_F = N$, equations (4–75) and (4–76) provide the necessary boundary conditions from which to find the N unknown constants a_i, $1 \le i \le N$, of equation (4–71a). The N equations to be solved for the N unknown a_i's may be written out in scalar form as follows:

1. $i \varepsilon S_E$:

$$F_i(B^-) = \pi_i = a_1 \, \pi_i + \sum_{j=2}^{N} a_j \Phi_{ji} e^{z_j B^-} \qquad (4\text{--}77)$$

2. $i \varepsilon S_F$:

$$F_i(0^+) = 0 = a_1 \, \pi_i + \sum_{j=2}^{N} a_j \Phi_{ji} \qquad (4\text{--}78)$$

(To get these equations, the jth eigenvector Φ_j has been defined as $\Phi_j \equiv [\Phi_{j1}, \Phi_{j2}, \ldots \Phi_{ji}, \ldots \Phi_{jN}]$).

We now apply this analysis to the simplest example, the basic on-off source of Figure 4–24. This could be representative of a voice source or an image source, depending on the choice of parameters. But note that this is precisely the example used in section 3.3 in our first discussion of the fluid source model. For this example there is of course only one eigenvalue z to be found. Using the results of the earlier analysis (as a check, see equations (4–23) and (4–24) in the admission control analysis of section 4.1), we have immediately for this case

$$z = -\frac{(\alpha + \beta)}{(R_p - r)}(1 - \rho) \qquad (4\text{--}79)$$

where now

$$\rho \equiv \frac{R_p}{r}\left(\frac{\alpha}{a + \beta}\right) = \frac{R_p p}{r} \qquad (4\text{--}80)$$

$p \equiv \alpha/(\alpha + \beta)$.

(Compare with equations (3–25a), (3–108) and (3–111), and (4–22) to (4–24)). Recall again that the token parameter r here corresponds to C_L in section 4.1. Note that the *average* load pR_p here corresponds to the average load λ (the Poisson arrival rate), on which attention was focused in the previous section. The parameter $\rho \equiv pR_p/r$ defined here then corresponds to the normalized load λ/r appearing in the previous two models. Recall that we used the symbol ρ to represent the normalized load in those models as well.

The single eigenvector $\boldsymbol{\Phi} = [\Phi_1, \Phi_2]$ appearing in equation (4–78) for this on-off traffic model was found as well in section 3.3. See equation (3–30) for that result. In terms of the notation used here, we have

$$\Phi_1/\Phi_2 = (R_p - r)/r = \left(\frac{R_p}{r} - 1\right) \tag{4–81}$$

Letting $\Phi_2 = 1$ arbitrarily (we could just as well have set $\Phi_2 = r$, $\Phi_1 = (\lambda - r)$), we get, for this example,

$$\boldsymbol{F}(x) = a_1\boldsymbol{\pi} + a_2\left[\left(\frac{R_p}{r} - 1\right), 1\right]e^{zx} \tag{4–82}$$

The two unknown constants a_1 and a_2 are found using the boundary conditions of equations (4–77) and (4–78). In this simple example, with $N = 2$ states only, state one with $\lambda_1 = 0$ is the emptying state and state two with $\lambda_2 = R_p$ is the filling state. We must thus have $0 < r < R_p$ for the fluid analysis to provide a stationary solution in this case. This implies that the single eigenvalue z of equation (4–79) will be negative if the parameter ρ defined by equation (4–80) is less than 1. This corresponds to the region $\lambda < r$ in Figures 4–14, 4–17, and 4–19, since the λ there is the average (Poisson) arrival rate, comparable to ρ here, as noted above.

From equation (4–77) we have, using equation (4–82),

$$F_1(B^-) = \pi_1 = a_1\pi_1 + a_2\left(\frac{R_p}{r} - 1\right)e^{zB^-} \tag{4–83}$$

with $\pi_1 = (1 - p) = \beta/(\alpha + \beta)$.

Similarly, from equations (4–78) and (4–82) we have

$$F_2(0^+) = 0 = a_1\pi_2 + a_2 \tag{4–84}$$

Here $\pi_2 = p = \alpha/(\alpha + \beta)$.

Note that the parameter $B = B_T + B_D$, the *sum* of the two buffer sizes, enters naturally here, as noted earlier. It is this parameter that will play a role in determining the throughput and loss probability performance of the extended leaky bucket procedure. Solving equations (4–83) and (4–84) simultaneously for a_1 and a_2, we get

$$a_1 = 1/\left[1 - \frac{\alpha}{\beta}\left(\frac{R_p}{r} - 1\right)e^{zB}\right] \tag{4-85}$$

and

$$a_2 = -\pi_2 a_1 = -a_1\, a/(a + \beta) \tag{4-86}$$

(Note that we have dropped the $-$ from B^- since it is no longer needed here.) Using equations (4–85) and (4–86) in equation (4–82), and following the notation of [ELWA 1991], we finally get for the two probability distribution functions in this case of a single on-off source,

$$F_1(x) = \pi_1 \Delta(x)/\Delta(B) \tag{4-87}$$

and

$$F_2(x) = \pi_2(1 - e^{zx})/\Delta(B) \tag{4-88}$$

with

$$\Delta(x) \equiv 1 - \frac{\alpha}{\beta}\left(\frac{R_p}{r} - 1\right)e^{zx} \tag{4-89}$$

$\pi_1 = \beta/(\alpha + \beta)$, $\pi_2 = 1 - \pi_1 = \alpha/(\alpha + \beta)$, and z given by equation (4–79).

All the performance parameters of interest can be obtained from $F_1(x)$ and $F_2(x)$. We shall obtain these after first developing performance parameters for the general N-state Markov chain model.

Consider the average throughput λ^*, in cells/sec, first. This can be calculated in a number of equivalent ways. One way is to say that this is the average load, less the cell loss when the data buffer is full. This may be written as

$$\lambda^* = \sum_{i=1}^{N} \lambda_i \pi_i - \sum_{i=1}^{N} (\lambda_i - r)P[X = B_D, S = i] \tag{4-90}$$

The first term on the right-hand side is of course the average load, averaged over all N states. The second term is the average cell loss, also averaged over the N states. But note that the $(N - l)$ filling (overload) states only will be included in the sum since we have already seen that in the emptying (underload) states the data buffer cannot be full and cells cannot be lost [see equation (4–74)]. The probability $P[X = B_D, S = i]$ that the data buffer is full with the system in overload state i, is readily calculated as

$$P[X = B_D, S = i] = P[W = B, S = i]$$

$$= P[W \leq B, S = i] - P[W \leq B^-, S = i] \tag{4-91}$$

$$= \pi_i - F_i\,(B^-)$$

This is similar to the analysis following equation (4–74) above.

We thus have, from equation (4–90),

$$\lambda^* = \sum_{i=1}^{N} \lambda_i \pi_i - \sum_{i=1}^{N} (\lambda_i - r) \ [\pi_i = F_i(B^-)] \qquad (4\text{–}90a)$$

This can be rewritten in somewhat different form by expanding the second sum and noting that the first sum then cancels:

$$\lambda^* = r + \sum_{i=1}^{N} F_i(B^-)(\lambda_i - r) \qquad (4\text{–}90b)$$

An alternate approach is to focus on average token throughput. Since every cell requires a token for transmission, the average token throughput must equal the average cell throughput. We thus have, immediately,

$$\lambda^* = r - \sum_{i=1}^{N} (r - \lambda_i)F_i(0) \qquad (4\text{–}90c)$$

The second term here represents a mean token "loss" due to a full token buffer, since

$$P[Y = B_T, \ S = i] = P[W = 0, \ S = i]$$

(See equation (4–63) or Figure 4–25.) This implies, comparing equations (4–90b) and (4–90c), that

$$\sum_{i=1}^{N} (\lambda_i - r)F_i(B^-) = \sum_{i=1}^{N} (\lambda_i - r)F_i(0) \qquad (4\text{–}92)$$

More generally, Mitra has shown [MITR 1988] that the following identity holds:

$$\sum_{i=1}^{N} F_r(x)(\lambda_i - r) = \text{constant}, \quad \text{all } X \qquad (4\text{–}93)$$

Consider the on-off source of Figure 4–24 as an example. Recall again that $\lambda_1 = 0$, $\lambda_2 = R_p$, $\rho \equiv R_p p / r$, $p = \alpha/(\alpha + \beta)$ in this case. Then it is readily shown, using equations (4–87) and (4–88) in either (4–90b) or (4–90c), that the normalized throughput for this example is given by

[MITR 1988]   Mitra, D., "Stochastic Theory of a Fluid Model of Producers and Consumers Coupled by a Buffer," *Adv. Appl. Prob., 20* (1988): 646–676.

$$\lambda^*/r = 1 - (1-\rho)/\Delta(B) \qquad (4\text{-}94)$$

The term $\Delta(B)$ is again found from equation (4–89). It is also left as an exercise for the reader to demonstrate identity (4–93) in this case.

The cell loss probability P_L is easily obtained in this case from equation (4–94), using equation (4–31):

$$P_L = 1 - \lambda^*/\sum_{i=1}^{N} \lambda_i \pi_i = 1 - \frac{\lambda^*/r}{\rho} \qquad \rho \equiv \frac{R_p p}{r} \qquad (4\text{-}95)$$

Note that this is identical to equation (4–51b), as it should be. As already noted, pR_p in the on-off case and more generally $\sum_{i=1}^{N} \lambda_i \pi_i$ for the N-state Markov chain modulating traffic model, correspond to the average Poisson arrival traffic rate λ in the models discussed previously.

How can we use these results for the on-off case for design purposes? Consider the range $\rho = pR_p/r < 1$ first. We must also ensure that $R_p > r$; that is, that there exists a filling or overload region of operation. Calculations can thus only be carried out for $\rho > p$. Recall that this is the range of operation in which we would like the loss probability to be very small. From equations (4–94) and (4–95), using equation (4–89) to evaluate $\Delta(B)$, we then get

$$P_L \doteq \left(\frac{1}{\rho} - 1\right)\left[1 - \Delta(B)\right] = \left(\frac{1}{\rho} - 1\right)\frac{\alpha}{\beta}\left(\frac{R_p}{r} - 1\right)e^{zB} << 1 \qquad (4\text{-}96)$$

Since $z < 0$ in this range [See equation (4–79)], the loss probability decreases exponentially with $B = B_T + B_D$. We take two examples now.

Example 1 [ELWA 1991]:
This is a voice-like source. Let $1/\beta = 1$ sec, $1/\alpha = 1.86$ sec, p = 0.35. Take $\rho = 0.7$. Then $R_p/r = 2$. From equation (4–96) it is then readily found that

$$\log_{10} P_L = -0.38\left(\frac{B}{R_p}\right) - 0.636 \qquad \rho = 0.7 \qquad (4\text{-}97)$$

For voice we have $R_p = 170$ cells/sec when in talk spurt (see Chapter 3). Table 4–1 shows the values of B required for various values of P_L. Note that doubling the value of B changes P_L by two magnitudes in this case. As the value of ρ is increased, approaching $\rho = 1$, correspondingly larger values of B are required.

Example 2: A very bursty image source [BUTT 1991].
Let the average burst interval $1/\beta = 0.5$ sec, while the average "off" time is $1/\alpha = 11$ sec. Then $p = \alpha/(\alpha + \beta) = 0.0435$. Let the image transfer rate during the burst interval be $R_p = 5200$ cells/sec. (Note that this is then 30 times the rate required for a voice source). An average image thus consists of

TABLE 4–1 ■ Leaky Bucket Control, Voice-like Source, 170 cells/sec, average talk spurt = 1 sec, average silent interval = 1.86 sec, $\rho = 0.7$, $r = 85$

P_L	B (cells)
10^{-9}	3550
10^{-7}	2700
10^{-5}	1850
10^{-3}	1000

2600 cells, or 114,400 octets (915,200 bits), if 44 octets of payload appear in each cell, as proposed for the class 3/4 ATM Adaptation Layer. (The actual ATM transfer rate is 2.2 Mbps, using 53-octet ATM cells).

Let us (naively, it will appear) choose $\rho = 0.7$ as the nominal operating point. Since $\rho = pR_p/r$, this implies the token (or counter) increment rate is $r = R_p/16.1 = 323$ tokens/sec. This appears to be a reasonable number. Using equation (4–96), we then calculate the "buffer" size B required for a given value of cell loss probability P_L. For images, this number is usually much smaller than the value allowed for voice. Say, specifically, that we require $P_L = 10^{-9}$ at the nominal operating point. For the number chosen here we then find $B \doteq 152,000$ cells! This is clearly an exceptionally large number, even if B can be split between the data buffer of size B_D and the token pool of size B_T. The problem is that with bursty traffic, with a relatively high peak rate when transmitting, one needs a much larger token (or counter) increment rate. This requires increasing r considerably, or, equivalently, reducing the operating value of ρ.

[BUTT 1991] have developed some design rules for choosing the two leaky bucket parameters r and B. They consider a number of control scenarios involving two types of traffic—voice and the bursty, image-like source, we have been discussing. It turns out the proper choice of the two parameters depends on what the leaky bucket technique is designed to control and how tight a control is required. If, for example, it is the peak data transfer rate R_p that is to be controlled, then it turns out the token increment rate r should be close to R_p. This implies operating at a value of $\rho \sim p \ll 1$, *not* the relatively high value of $\rho = 0.7$ chosen above. Increasing the rate r brings the value of B required down considerably.

The design rule they propose for this case of packet rate control is the following: Choose the loss probability P_L required at the normal operating point. As an example, let it be $P_L = 10^{-9}$. Choose a fractional increase in the data transfer rate beyond which the system should not go. The loss probability should thus increase considerably beyond that point. (Note that this approach is similar in philosophy to the comment made in the previous section that an ideal control is one that has zero loss up to a particular operating point and then clamps the data rate to a maximum average value beyond that point.) Consider, as an example, the following design rule [BUTT 1991]:

1. $P_L = 10^{-9}$ at the normal operating values of α_0, β_0, and R_{p0}.
2. $P_L \geq 0.07$ for $R_{pi} \geq 1.2\,R_{p0}$, α_0, β_0 unchanged.

(Note the tightness of control here: a 20% increase in the peak rate R_p results in more than eight magnitudes of increase in the loss probability P_L!) Using equation (4–96), we get two equations to be solved for the desired design values of r and B.

In particular, for the example under consideration here, we find

$$r \doteq 0.99\,R_{p0} = 5150 \text{ tokens/sec}$$

and

$$B \doteq 0.077\,R_{p0} = 400 \text{ cells}$$

The operating point turns out to be $\rho \doteq p$, as noted above. Note, in particular, the drastic decrease in the value of B required.

The discerning reader may have been wondering why the buffer sizes obtained here differ so much from the values used in the previous section (see Figures 4–17, 4–19, and 4–20, with the maximum value of M chosen as 10). There are two reasons: 1. The traffic source models are clearly different; 2. The controls were, implicitly, not as tight as the one chosen here. Consider, for example, Figure 4–20, taken from [SIDI 1989]. Note that the control becomes tighter as the token pool size M (comparable to B here) increases. This is of course as to be expected and agrees with the throughput-load curves of Figures 4–17 and 4–19. But note from Figure 4–20 that with $M = 10$, the loss probability increases by three orders of magnitude as the load increases by 50%. Although this is a relatively tight control, it is not as stringent as the one proposed above with P_L increasing by eight orders of magnitude for a 20% increase in the load.

To show the impact of tightening the control in a very simple manner, consider the first, very approximate leaky bucket model described in the previous section. Just as we showed that we should choose $r \sim R_p$ for bursty on-off sources, pick $r \sim \lambda$ as the desired operating point for the Poisson model. In particular, let $\rho = \lambda/r = 0.9$. Say we again want $P_L = 10^{-9}$ at this load. Then, from equation (4–32) we readily find that $M = 184$ is the token buffer size required. A 10% increase in load to $\rho = 1$ then increases the loss probability to $P_L = 1/(M + 1) \doteq 0.005$ in this case, a $10^5 - 10^6$ increase in loss probability. Another 10% increase, to $\rho = 1.1$, increases P_L to $P_L \doteq 1 - 1/\rho \sim 0.1$, just the 10^8 increase in loss probability required in the on-off example. So note that one gets comparable results with these two very different models.

Say a still tighter control is desired with the Poisson approximate model. Let $\rho = \lambda/r = 0.99$ as the normal operating point, with $P_L = 10^{-9}$ desired at this point. Then, from equation (4–32), we find $M = 1600$. If the load now increases 1%, to $\rho = 1$, P_L increases to $P_L = 1/(M + 1) \sim 6 \times 10^{-4}$. If it increases 20% to $\rho = 1.2$, the loss probability increases to $P_L \doteq 1 - 1/\rho = 0.17$, again an increase of 10^8. So it appears that the tightness of control required is principally responsible for the size of the buffer required.

The discussion above related to peak rate control. Similar design rules for the leaky bucket algorithm can be adopted for the control of other parameters [BUTT 1991]. Consider, for example, the control of the average on-time interval $1/\beta$ of a bursty on-off source, or, equivalently, the average number of cells transmitted by the source at a fixed peak rate R_p. The design rule might then be to limit any increase in $1/\beta$ to some tolerable value. For increases beyond this value, the loss probability P_L should again increase substantially.

Consider the following example of this control approach. Let a bursty on-off source have an average nominal transmission interval (on-time) of $1/\beta_0 = 1$ sec, while it is nominally off for $1/\alpha_0 = 10$ sec. During the on-time, it transmits at a peak rate of $R_p = 10,000$ cells/sec. (This corresponds to a 4.24 Mbps transmission rate if 53-octet cells are used. The actual data transmitted in the 1-sec, average, on-time interval, using a figure of 44 octets of data per cell, is 3.52 Mbits.) Say it is desired to have $P_L = 10^{-6}$ for these normal source characteristics, but to have P_L increase to at least 10^{-4} (two orders of magnitude) if the average on-time increases to 1.5 sec. (a 50% increase). Then it is left to the reader to show that the appropriate values of r and B are $r = 5700$ tokens/sec and $B = 60,000$ cells, respectively.

We have thus far described the performance of the leaky bucket technique with a shaping or smoothing data buffer (Figure 4–21), independently of the size of the data buffer. All the results, thus far, have been shown to depend on the *total* "buffer" size $B = B_T + B_D$. Recall that B_T is not really a buffer but the token pool size in the token model (Figure 4–21), or the maximum counter size in the leaky bucket counter implementation. Given the proper choice of B and r discussed above, how does one now decide on the distribution between the actual data buffer B_D and the token pool (or maximum counter value) B_T? This is where the "smoothing" or "shaping" introduced by the data buffer, as noted earlier, comes into play.

Consider the extreme case in which there is no token buffer (or, equivalently, no counter) for the leaky bucket. All buffering is then done by the data buffer. As a burst of up to B cells arrives at the leaky bucket controller, it is stored in the data buffer, to be read out at the fixed rate of r cells/sec. The "burstiness" of the source has then been "absorbed" by the leaky bucket data buffer, and the output process is much more regular. In essence, the introduction of the data buffer has reduced the variation in time of the input (traffic) process. This is measured by the coefficient of variation c_v^2, defined to be the ratio of the variance to the first moment (mean) squared. A deterministic process has $c_v^2 = 0$, c_v^2 for a Poisson process is 1, and a bursty on-off process has $c_v^2 = \sigma^2/m^2 = p(1 - p)/p^2 = (1 - p)/p$, with p again defined as the probability the source is in its on-state.

Elwalid and Mitra [ELWA 1991] have calculated the first and second moments of the leaky bucket output process, from which the output coefficient of variation is readily obtained. The first moment for the on-off bursty source considered in detail in this section is of course the average throughput λ^* as shown to be given earlier by equation (4–94). This depends on the *total* buffer size $B = B_T + B_D$, as noted a number of times. The second moment is found, however, to depend on *both* B_D and B_T. In particular, with $B = B_T + B_D$ kept fixed, the output coefficient of variation is found to *decrease* with increasing data buffer size B_D. Similar results are obtained for more complex sources modeled as three-state Markov chains [ELWA 1991, detailed version]. These results validate the intuitive comment made above that introducing a data buffer "smooths" the output process, reducing its variation.

Consider Example 1, the voice-like source model mentioned briefly earlier. Recall that this had the following parameters: $R_p = 170$ cells/sec, $1/\beta = 1$ sec, $1/\alpha = 1.86$ sec, $p = 0.35$, $\rho = 0.7$, and hence $r = 85$ tokens/sec. For this example, the input coefficient of variation $c_v^2 = (1-p)/p = 1.86$. Elwalid and Mitra have plotted the output coefficient of variation as a function of the token pool size B_T (hence B_D as well) for $P_L = 2.26 \times 10^{-5}$ and $B = 1700$ cells.[1] For $B_T = 0$ (that is, $B_D = 1700$ cells), the output coefficient of variation is reduced from 1.86 to 0.4. The trade-off, however, is that the data traffic experiences delay. Specifically, for $B_D = 1700$ cells and a peak rate of 170 cells/sec, the maximum delay becomes 10 sec. The average delay, as calculated by Elwalid and Mitra, is 2.17 sec [ELWA 1991]. This is clearly intolerable for real-time voice with maximum end-to-end delays, source to destination, limited to 100 msec. But for certain nonreal-time data traffic with these characteristics, such delays might be acceptable.

Both the maximum and average delay decrease, of course, as B_T increases (B_D decreases), with B fixed. But the output coefficient of variation increases rapidly as well. In the example calculated by Elwalid and Mitra, B_T can be no more than 10% of B if the output c_v^2 is to be kept relatively low. For $B_T = 170$ tokens and $B_D = 1700 - 170 \doteq 1500$ cells, the output coefficient of variation is about 1 (still considerably less than its maximum value of 1.86), while the average delay reduces by about a factor of two to 1 sec [ELWA 1991].

This chapter has focused on the leaky bucket algorithm as a method of carrying out Usage Parameter Control or policing of traffic sources admitted to an ATM network. This is the technique most commonly discussed in the lit-

---

[1]Note that Elwalid and Mitra use the "unit of information" formulation discussed in Chapter 3. The unit of information is the number of cells transmitted in an average on-interval. For $R_p = 170$ cells/sec and $1/\beta = 1$ sec, this is just 170 cells. Their buffer sizes are all shown normalized to the unit of information. Hence $B = 10$ in this example, using their notation.

erature and is the basis of the Generic Cell Rate Algorithm proposed by the ATM Forum, as already noted. But it is clear from our discussion that not all source types lend themselves to leaky bucket control. This mechanism has two control parameters only, and although adaptive versions incorporating additional adjustable parameters have been proposed in the literature, the control of more complex traffic types may require completely different approaches to the policing or access control function. In particular, Skelly has proposed a so-called Worst-case Histogram Control method for policing VBR video traffic to ensure it conforms to its agreed-on traffic descriptors [SKEL 1992]. This method applies the video histogram representation of section 3.7 to the access control problem in this case.

In particular, the proposal here is to supply the network admission controller with the video histogram parameters. (Recall from section 3.7 that eight such numbers were found to provide a good representation of the video signal.) In the case of stored video, such as might be available on tape, the numbers can be measured beforehand and be made available to the network during the admission control procedure. In the case of video being produced in real time, these parameters could be measured at the beginning of the filming. The control procedure than consists of continuously monitoring these parameters as the video signal is generated and transmitted into the network. A window of measurement has to be chosen, both for the admission procedure and for the subsequent control phase. Measurements are made offline of these parameters as the window is scanned across a segment of the signal and the worst-case parameter measurements are selected and compared with the agreed-on parameters. (The phrase "worst-case" here implies the largest parameters or those with the highest bit rates.)

A relatively long window provides more accurate control, but suffers from a longer delay in detecting violations of the agreed-on traffic descriptors. A short window provides more rapid detection of violations, but tends to approach peak-rate control as the window gets smaller.

Two methods of dealing with violations can be used, as noted earlier. Cells can be dropped if a violation is detected, or cells can be tagged for future dropping further into the network wherever congestion might be detected. Simulation of this technique has shown that cell dropping is more effective than cell tagging in detecting violations, and that the technique can do so successfully in a multiplexed environment without harming conforming sources [SKEL 1992].

▪ PROBLEMS

4–1 a. Verify that the two probabilities P_L and ε given by equations (4–4) and (4–5), respectively, may be approximated by equations (4–4a) and (4–7).

b. Show that P_L and ε are related by equation (4–8).

c. Derive equation (4–10) for ε, using the approach suggested in equations (4–9) to (4–9b). From this, show the normalized capacity C is given by equation (4–12). For $\varepsilon = 10^{-5}$ show C is given by equations (4–14) and (4–14a).

d. Repeat **c.** using P_L in place of ε, and find the capacity expressions equivalent to equations (4–12), (4–14), and (4–14a). (Here $P_L = 10^{-5}$). How do the two sets of expressions compare?

e. Consider the case of N multiplexed on-off sources. Take $p = 0.02$ and $R_p = 4$ Mbps. Plot $C_L = CR_p$ vs. N for the three separate cases $\varepsilon = 10^{-4}, 10^{-5}, 10^{-6}$. For each case, include curves for peak and average capacity assignments superimposed on the same figure.

f. Consider the case $\varepsilon = 10^{-5}$, $p = 0.02$, $R_p = 4$ Mbps, $C_L = 200$ Mbps. What is the maximum number of sources allowed (This is the admission policy.) How does this change if $C_L = 100$ Mbps?

4–2 Consider the multiplexing gain defined by equation (4–20). Plot this vs. p on a log-log scale for ε (or P_L) $= 10^{-7}$ and $C = 10, 100$, and compare with Figure 4–9. Calculate $\rho = G_e p$ and plot vs. p as well.

4–3 a. Using the fluid-analysis loss-probability approximation of equation (4–25), show the equivalent capacity is given by equation (4–27).

b. A particular image source generates traffic at a peak rate of $R_p = 5200$ cells/sec (What is the rate in Mbps?) Its average burst interval is $1/\beta = 0.5$ sec (What is the average image size, in octets? Don't forget to take off the 5 octets of header per cell.) $N = 100$ such sources are multiplexed. Calculate and plot the capacity C_L, in cells/sec, required as the average "off" interval $1/\alpha$ is varied from a very large to a very small value. The buffer size chosen is $x = 3900$ cells. $P_L = 10^{-6}$ is required. Find the maximum buffer delay as well. Repeat for different values of x and P_L of your own choosing.

4–4 Calculate the equivalent capacity for the examples of problem **4–3b.** above using the simple estimate of equation (4–12). Superimpose on the same plots as those of problem **4–3b.** and plot the smaller of the two, as proposed by [GUER 1991], equation (4–29). Discuss your results.

4–5 N bursty on-off sources are to be multiplexed together at an ATM access port. Each source has exponentially-distributed on- and off-times, with average values of 1 sec and 10 sec, respectively. When "on," a source transmits at its peak rate of 5 Mbps. The outgoing link capacity of the multiplexer is 100 Mbps.

a. Find the number of sources that may be accommodated if (1) peak-rate allocation is used; (2) average rate allocation is used. What is the probability of loss with peak-rate allocation?

b. Find the number of sources that may be multiplexed if the probability of loss is $P_L = 10^{-6}$. P_L is approximated by the average time the multiplexer is in the overload region.

   c. Repeat **b.** if approximate fluid-flow analysis is used, with the probability of loss defined as $P_L = P[\text{buffer occupancy} > x]$, x chosen such that the maximum buffer delay is 100 msec. Compare all four values of N in **a., b., c.**

   d. Repeat **a., b., c.,** if the average off-time is reduced to 5 sec. Compare with the previous case of 10 sec.

4–6 Three different representations of the leaky-bucket algorithm, two using counter implementations, the third using the concept of a token pool, are described in section 4.2. Show all are equivalent.

4–7 This problem focuses on the analysis of the leaky bucket access control carried out by [SIDI 1989], as summarized in section 4.2.

   a. Using steady-state balance arguments, as described in the text, show the steady-state probability p_i that there are i tokens in the token buffer of Figure 4–15 is given by equations (4–38) to (4–40).

   b. From **a**. above, validate the recursion relations of equations (4–41) to (4–43).

   c. $M = 5$ is the maximum burst size. The arrivals are Poisson [equation (4–34)]. Find p_i, $i = 1$ to 5, for a number of values of $\lambda D \equiv \lambda/r$, $0 < \lambda D < 2.5$. *Note:* You'll have to use a normalization technique such as the one proposed in equations (4–44) and (4–45).

   d. Show the normalized throughput $\lambda^* D$ (or $\lambda*/r$), the average number of cells getting through the leaky bucket regulator in a D-sec interval, is given by equation (4–46).

   e. Plot the normalized throughput-load curve, $\lambda^* D$ vs. λD (or $\lambda*/r$ vs. λ/r), for $M = 5$, using the results of **c.** above. Superimpose the curve obtained using the much simpler approximation of equations (4–31) to (4–33a) and compare.

   f. Using equation (4–51b) and the results of **e.** above, plot the loss probability P_L as a function of λ/r for the same example and over the same range of normalized load. Compare with Figure 4–20. (But note that that figure only has λ/r up to 1).

4–8 Starting with the "virtual buffer" r.v. W, as defined by equation (4–61), show that the joint probability $F_j(x)$, as defined by equation (4–65), satisfies the differential equation (4–67). Compare with the differential equation obtained in problem **3–22a**. Show the solution to equation (4–67) is given by equation (4–71a). Why is a_1 not equal to 1 in this case? Carry out your own analysis to show that the equations providing the N unknown boundary conditions appearing in equation (4–71a) are given by equations (4–77) and (4–78).

4–9 This problem focuses on the leaky bucket fluid-flow analysis for the on-off (bursty source) model:

a. Show that for this model the joint probability vector $F(x)$ is given by equation (4–82), with the eigenvalue given by equation (4–79).

b. Show that the two constants a_1 and a_2 in equation (4–82) are given by equations (4–85) and (4–86). Show that the two components of $F(x)$ in this case are given by equations (4–87) and (4–88).

c. Determine the normalization throughput $\lambda*/r$ for this case and show it is given by equation (4–94). Calculate the loss probability P_L and verify it is given by equation (4–95). Show that for very small values, P_L is approximated by equation (4–96).

4–10 Consider an on-off source with the following characteristics: the average on-time $1/\beta = 0.35$ sec. The average off-time $1/\alpha = 0.65$ sec. The peak rate of transmission $R_p = 100$ cells/sec. (What traffic source has these characteristics?)

a. Find the leaky bucket token increment rate r for $\rho \equiv pR_p/r = 0.5, 0.7, 0.9$.

b. Calculate and plot P_L vs. B for each of the three values of ρ above. Take $0.1 \geq P_L \geq 10^{-9}$. Use a log scale in plotting P_L.

c. Take $\rho = 0.5$ as the access control operating point. B is chosen to have $P_L = 10^{-5}$ at that point. Calculate P_L if R_p increases to 120 cells/sec, and then to 140 cells/sec. Repeat if $\rho = 0.7$ is chosen as the operating point. Which point provides tighter control? What are the tradeoffs with respect to B and r?

4–11 A human user interacts through a network with an image source file. Each image averages 800,000 bits (100,000 octets) in size. The image source, during admission control, is allocated 2 Mb/s transmission rate in transmitting images across the UNI to the network access buffer. The time between images requested by the human user is estimated to average 10 sec. An exponential on-off model is assumed to be valid.

a. A leaky bucket policing mechanism is to be designed to have $P_L = 10^{-9}$ for the traffic descriptors noted above, but to increase to 0.1 if the transmission rate increases to 2.4 Mb/s. Find r and B to satisfy these conditions.

b. With r and B as chosen above, determine the sensitivity of P_L to changes, first, in image length; second, to changes in average off time. Are there better operating points for these parameters?

4–12 a. Starting with equation (4–90) as the leaky-bucket throughput, show one obtains equation (4–90b).

b. Demonstrate why equation (4–90c) also represents the throughput. This implies identity (4–93) must hold. Show that equation (4–94) is the throughput in the on-off source case. Demonstrate that equation (4–93) does in fact hold in the on-off source case.

c. Show that the leaky bucket loss probability in the range of small values, for the on-off source case, is approximated by equation (4–96).

4–13 Each on-off source in problem **4–5** is connected to a leaky-bucket access controller before being multiplexed at the access port. Each leaky bucket has a data buffer holding at most B_D cells. Fluid-flow analysis is to be used to design the leaky-bucket control, that is, to choose the token (counter) increment rate r and $B = B_D + B_T$.

a. It is desired to have $P_L = 10^{-6}$ for the normal source characteristics as described in problem **4–5 a–c**. Work with cells/sec so that the normal peak source rate (on-state) is 10,000 cells/sec, assuming a cell size of 500 bits for simplicity. Find r and B so that $P_L \geq 0.02$ if the source cell rate in the on-state increases by more than 10%.

b. Repeat **a.** if the average on-time interval is to be controlled: find r and B so that $P_L \geq 10^{-4}$ if the average on-time increases to 1.5 sec.

4–14 The fluid-flow leaky bucket analysis in the text is specialized to the case of on-off sources. Choose a more complex Markov chain to model the source and derive equations for the throughput and cell loss probability. *Note:* An example of a three-state model appears in problem **4–15** following.

4–15 A leaky bucket mechanism controls access to a network. The source to be controlled is modeled as a three-state Markov process: $\mu_{12} = \mu_{23} = 5$/sec.; $\mu_{21} = \mu_{32} = 10$/sec. All other transition rates are zero. The source generation rates in each of the three states is given by 100,000 cells/sec when in state one, 200,000 cells/sec when in state two, and 300,000 cells/sec when in state three. The token generation rate is $r = 250,000$ tokens/sec. There is no data buffer.

a. Find the steady state probability that the source is in each of its three states. Find the average load in cells/sec emitted by the source.

b. Find and plot the throughput λ^* of the leaky bucket controller for various values of the token pool size B_T. The particular choices of B_T are part of the problem to be solved: They should cover small, moderate, and large values of B_T, that is, at least three values of B_T. Use fluid-flow analysis.

c. Find and plot the cell loss probability P_L for the same values of B_T as in **a.**

Chapter 5

ATM Switches

5.1 ■ INTRODUCTION

In the previous chapter we focused on admission and access control in the B-ISDN, ATM environment. Recall that admission control determines whether or not a new call (connection) can be guaranteed its required quality of service (QoS) once admitted to the network, without adversely impacting already existing connections. The admission determination would, in an operating network, presumably be made end-to-end, from the originating UNI (user-network interface) to the destination UNI, following the virtual path chosen to carry the new connection. The admission determination relies on a set of traffic descriptors such as peak and average bit rates, as well as average on- and off-times for bursty traffic, among other parameters.

Access control, on the other hand, is used to ensure that each connection abides by its traffic descriptors. The specific example discussed in detail in the previous chapter was the leaky bucket control mechanism. Access and admission controls are shown exerted at the network boundary in Figure 5–1.

Once in the network, each ATM cell moves along the virtual connection associated with the virtual path established end-to-end. The routing function required to move the cells along their respective virtual paths is carried out at the network nodes shown in Figure 5–1. These nodes are called packet switches in the packet-switching world [SCHW 1987]; they are more specifically called ATM switches in the B-ISDN environment described in this book. The prime purpose of the ATM switch, or any switch, whether a packet or a circuit switch, is to switch incoming cells (packets more generally) arriving on a particular input link to the output link associated with the appropriate virtual path (route). This generic function is portrayed schematically in Figure

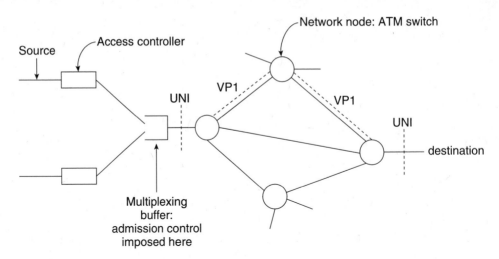

FIGURE 5–1 ■ Rudimentary ATM network.

5–2. In the example of Figure 5–2, cells following VP1 are shown arriving on link 1 and being switched to output link N. Although we shall refer most often to $N \times N$ switches in this book (those with equal numbers of input and output links), one could, more generally, have $N \times M$ switches with the number of input and output links different.

What are the various ways of carrying out this switching function? Three basic techniques have been proposed. One uses a "shared memory" approach: let time at both input and output of the switch be slotted into intervals, each being one cell time long. Cells arriving on each input link are aligned in time (using a small elastic buffer on each link for this purpose), and are then switched into a common memory within the switch at each cell interval. A central controller selects cells destined for each output, using possibly a VP lookup table, and then switches them onto the appropriate output link. One of the first such switches proposed was the Prelude switch

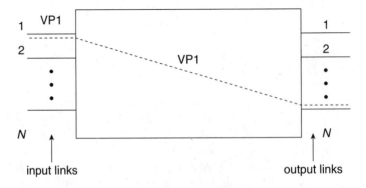

FIGURE 5–2 ■ ATM switch.

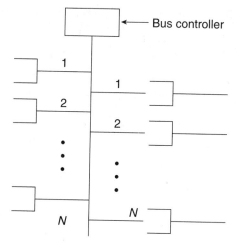

FIGURE 5–3 ■ Shared medium ATM switch: bus example.

[THOM 1984], [COUD 1987], [DEVA 1988]. More recent examples of ATM switch prototypes built using the shared memory approach include those described in [KOZA 1991] and [ENG 1995]. This type of switching is very similar to the older technique of time-division switching using time-slot interchangers used extensively in digital circuit switches for telephone applications [SCHW 1987, Chapter 10].

The second generic approach to carrying out the switching function uses a shared medium concept. A common high-speed bus, as shown in Figure 5–3, provides a simple example. Note that a central controller, or arbitration unit, is required to ensure that only one cell at a time appears on the bus in this example. One cell at a time would be selected from each input, in round-robin fashion, to be launched onto the bus. Each output link, using the VC-VP i.d. in the header, would then accept cells destined for it. A number of small ATM switches developed for the private LAN-interconnect market use the shared

[THOM 1984]   Thomas, A., et al., "Asynchronous Time Division Techniques: An Experimental Packet Network Integrating Video Communication," *Proc. ISS 84,* paper 32C2; Florence, Italy, May 1984.

[COUD 1987]   Coudreuse, J. P., and M. Servel, "Prelude: An Asynchronous Time-Division Switched Network," *Proc. IEEE ICC 87,* Seattle, WA, June 1987: 769–773.

[DEVA 1988]   Devault, M., et al., "The Prelude ATD Experiment: Assessments and Future Prospects," *IEEE JSAC, 6,* 9 (Dec. 1988): 1528–1537.

[KOZA 1991]   Kozaki, T., et al., "32 × 32 Shared Buffer Type ATM Switch VLSIs for B-ISDN," *Proc. IEEE ICC 91,* June 1991: 711–715.

[ENG 1995]   Eng, K. Y., and M. K. Karol, "State of the Art in Gigabit ATM Switching," *Proc. 1st IEEE International Workshop on Broadband Switching Systems,* Poznan, Poland, April 1995: 3–20.

bus architecture. These include the Fore Systems AXS-100 switch [FORE 1992], the GTE SPAnet switch, the Cascade B-STDX 9000, and the Wellfleet switch. An early IBM experimental switching system, the PARIS system, used a shared-medium architecture [GOPA 1987], as does the plaNET system, a later IBM switching system [CIDO 1993].

Finally, the third general type of ATM switch uses space division switching. Examples include a simple crossbar, the "Knockout" switch, multistage crossbars, and multistage Banyan architectures. We shall have more to say about this type of switch later, including reference to a number of specific examples. For the moment we focus on the simple crossbar, diagrammed in Figure 5–4. The inputs and outputs are connected to a set of switching points called crosspoints, as shown in Figure 5–4.

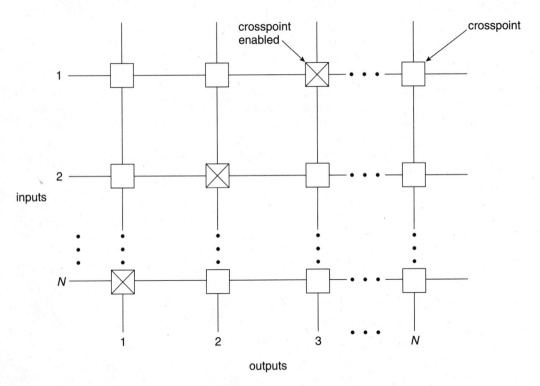

FIGURE 5–4 ■ $N \times N$ crossbar.

[FORE 1992] *ForeRunner™ ASX-100 ATM Switch Architecture Manual*, Release 2.1. Pittsburgh, PA: Fore Systems, Inc., 1992.

[CIDO 1993] Cidon, I., et al., "The plaNET/ORBIT High-Speed Network," *J. High Speed Networks, 2,* 3 (Sept. 1993): 1–38.

[GOPA 1987] Gopal, I. S., et al., "Paris: An Approach to Integrated Private Networks," *Proc. IEEE ICC 87,* Seattle, WA, June 1987: 764–773.

One crosspoint in any one row and column can be set at any one time. Input 1 in Figure 5–4, for example, is shown connected to output 3. Similarly, input 2 and output 2 are connected; input N and output 1 are shown connected. Connections are made each cell time by a central controller.

The crossbar switch is the oldest type of switch and has served as the basic switching structure or fabric for many years in the circuit-switched world (SCHW 1987, Chapter 10]. Note the distinction imposed by the type of switch application. In the circuit-switched, telephone case, switch connections are held for the length of a call. In the ATM, cell-based case, switch connections would presumably change every cell time.

How does one choose among the different types of switch architectures? Cost clearly plays a critical role, as does the ability to sustain the cell switching rates required. The type of control (distributed or centralized), the ability to move the architecture down to the chip level (which is related to the number of internal switching elements in a space-division switch, for example), the delay through the switch, and the throughput capability all play a role in determining the type of switch architecture to be used.

Comparative properties of the various switching techniques will be discussed as we proceed through the chapter. We shall then summarize these comparisons at the end of the chapter, after having considered them in some detail throughout the chapter.

Consider the cell switching rate required as an example. Let the input line rate be L cells/sec. For a 155-Mbps line rate and 53-octet cells, L is 366,000 cells/sec; that is, the input line operates on each cell for 2.7 μsec. Consider the shared-memory switch first. Since a shared-memory switch must read cells in from all lines, in one cell time, and then read them out, distributing them out over the N output lines, the fabric must switch at a rate of $2LN$ cells/sec. For an 8×8 switch and a line rate of 366,000 cells/sec, this means moving 5.9×10^6 cells/sec. (The aggregate throughput is then 2.9×10^6 cells/sec, or 1.24 Gbps). Now consider an 8×8 switch with a 2.5 Gbps line rate. The aggregate switch throughput is then 20 Gbps. Since the cell interval is approximately 170 nsec at the 2.5 Gbs rate, cells from all eight lines must be read in and then read out in just over 10 nsec. 10-nsec RAM chips are commercially available, so a shared-memory switch of this aggregate throughput is feasible. Higher aggregate throughputs would require a different approach, using multiple stages of a space division switch, such as those to be discussed later in this chapter [ENG 1995].

The switching burden on the shared-medium switch (a bus, for example) is one-half that of the shared-memory system. All N input lines must be scanned every cell interval. The medium (the bus) must thus handle LN cells/sec. For the same two examples used above, the results are thus 2.9×10^6 cells/sec handled for 1.24 Gbps throughput for the 155-Mbps system; 47×10^6 cells/sec switched for 20 Gbps throughput for the 2.5-Gbps system. The shared-memory and shared-medium systems must clearly "run out of steam" at some maximum switching rate. There is thus a limit on the number of input lines N, or, given, N, the input line rate L that can be supported. This still allows practical, albeit relatively small, switches to be designed and developed. As already noted, ATM switches developed for the private LAN market use both shared-memory and shared-medium fabric designs. Larger switches, designed for the public networking market, for example, must, however, use multiple stages of switching, as incorporated in space-division switches, to overcome the practical cell switching speed limitation.

Space-division switches have no specific limitation on the number of input lines (or ports) that may be supported, because of constraints on switching rate. They *can* switch at the input line speed L. The price paid, however, as we shall see, is a potential tradeoff between throughput and complexity or cost: The throughput is reduced if the switching rate is not speeded up, unless parallel paths through the switch are provided, or added switching structures are added to reduce potential congestion and ensuing cell loss.

The focus above, quite briefly, was on switching speed. Now consider the switch size and cost. This is related in some way to the number of input and output lines, N, to be handled. In the circuit-switching world, it was customary for many years to rate switches on the number of elementary crosspoint switches required. An $N \times N$ crossbar switch clearly requires N^2 such crosspoints (see Figure 5–4). The cost of these space switches depended principally on the crosspoints, and led to the introduction of multistage space switches, with a corresponding reduction in the number of crosspoints [SCHW 1987, Chapter 10]. This is no longer as much the case, particularly with the introduction of time-slot interchangers. In the ATM switch world, however, multistage switch fabrics tend to use 2×2 basic switches, and the cost does depend, to some extent, on the number of these elementary switches required. We shall see that for the multistage, Banyan-type architecture, the number of 2×2 switches is $O(N \log_2 N)$. This is a substantial reduction over N^2, as required for the crossbar. The price paid, however, is a considerable reduction in the throughput possible with a concurrent increase in delay through the switch, unless the overall switch can be run at higher switching rates. This will also be discussed in detail later in this chapter.

It is clear then that there are a number of cost and performance issues to be discussed. Some of these will be discussed in detail in the sections following, with a summary appearing at the end of this chapter, as already noted.

We begin by discussing switch buffering in the next section, with emphasis on its relation to throughput.

5.2 ■ OUTPUT VERSUS INPUT QUEUEING

Why focus on queueing? Since multiple cells from a number of input lines may be destined for the same output, with only one in each cell interval able to be accepted, queueing is required. There are three possibilities: buffer (queue)

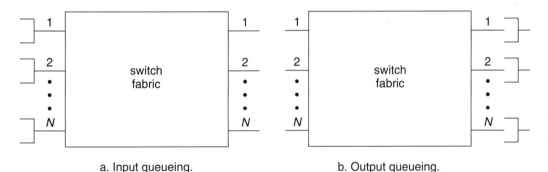

a. Input queueing.   b. Output queueing.

FIGURE 5–5 ■ Input and output queueing, ATM switch.

cells at the input to the switch; buffer internally; buffer at the output. Input and output queueing are shown schematically in Figure 5–5. The shared-memory system uses internal buffering, with buffers shared by all the output lines. The multistage Banyan switch, to be discussed in a later section, uses internal buffering with buffers dedicated to each internal elementary switch.

In section 5.4 we show that output queueing is preferable to input queueing (if possible to be used), since input queueing results in throughput degradation. This is demonstrated with the simple example of Figure 5–6. This represents a 2×2 switch, with each input capable of being connected to either of the two outputs. Say that each cell at the head of the two input queues is destined for output 2, as shown. Only one at a time can be selected so the other is blocked. In Figure 5–6, say the bottom cell is selected. Then the upper one is blocked. But queued behind the head cell in the upper line is one destined for output line 1. This too is blocked, even though output 1 is available, because the one in front of it, at the head of the queue, cannot move. This results in a reduction in throughput. (The maximum throughput of a 2×2 switch with input queueing, will be shown later to be 75% of the maximum throughput of one cell per output line each cell interval, using a simple Bernoulli traffic model). This phenomenon is referred to as head-of-the line, or HOL, blocking. For large input-queued switches, with $N \gg 1$, the maximum throughput will be shown to be limited to 59% of the maximum

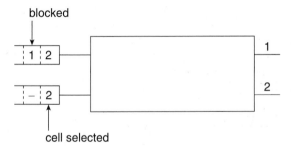

FIGURE 5–6 ■ Head-of-line blocking, 2×2 switch.

possible of one cell per output line per cell interval, as a result of HOL blocking.

This simple argument showing how HOL blocking arises, assumes the switch fabric switches at the line rate of L cells/sec. If the fabric speed is increased, more cells can be moved (switched) to any one output in a given cell interval, reducing HOL blocking. With more than one cell switched to a given output in any one cell interval, buffers are required at the output lines, leading to output queueing, as shown in Figure 5–5b. Running an $N \times N$ switching fabric with HOL blocking at N times the line speed will eliminate the blocking (in the simple 2×2 example of Figure 5–6, running the switch at $2\times$ line speed allows the blocked cell destined for output line 1 to reach that output, effectively eliminating HOL blocking). The shared-memory and shared-medium configurations discussed in section 5.1 require switching fabric speedup and thus gain in throughput, using output queueing. The "Knockout" switch, to be discussed in a later section, uses output queueing without an explicit speedup of the switch fabric.

Before studying input- and output-queueing in detail, it is useful to return to the nonbuffered $N \times N$ crossbar of Figure 5–4. We can quantify the effect of no queueing very simply in this case. This also enables us to introduce the cell arrival model to be used throughout this chapter. Note that if more than one of the N inputs has a cell destined for the same output, all except one will have to drop the cells. This results in the throughput reduction already mentioned.

In particular, we model this effect by saying that in any one cell interval, a given input line either has a cell present to be switched, with probability p, or no cell is available, with probability $(1 - p)$. Cells in different time slots are assumed to be independently generated with the same probability p. The traffic at each input line is thus modeled as a Bernoulli process. This appears at first glance to be questionable, given our strong emphasis in earlier chapters on B-ISDN traffic characterization. But note that, generally speaking, we have been implicitly assuming the traffic appearing at any ATM switch input line is a multiplexed stream from many independent traffic sources. This is apparent from the picture of Figure 5–1. This assumes, then, that no one source dominates, and that cells are well-mixed on leaving the multiplexer at the entrance to a network, or on arriving at a network node (ATM switch) once within the network.

This may not, of course, be the case if relatively high bit rate sources, such as high-definition video, dominate a given input line. This model may fail as well, in the case of ATM LANs, with the traffic on any one switch input coming from one source. The models used in this chapter, and conclusions drawn from them, must thus be used with caution.

These caveats aside, we return to the nonbuffered $N \times N$ crossbar of Figure 5–4. Assume that the traffic at each input link is not only Bernoulli, but independent and homogeneous (uniform) from link to link. There is thus the same probability p across the links that a cell is present in any time slot. Each cell is in turn assumed to be equally-likely to be switched to any output link. Focus on one (typical) output in a given time slot. The probability a given input line has a cell destined for this output is then p/N. The probability this output will receive one cell in the given time interval is the probability that *at least* one cell is destined for this output and is given by

$$1-\left(1-\frac{p}{N}\right)^{N}$$

(Recall again that with no buffering, at most one cell can be accepted at a given output in a given time slot. Any others are dropped). Letting the cell interval, or time slot, be T sec long, the throughput γ_o in cells/sec at a given output, is just

$$\gamma_o =\left[1-\left(1-\frac{p}{N}\right)^{N}\right]\frac{1}{T} \qquad (5\text{–}1)$$

The switch throughput γ_s is then just

$$\gamma_s = N\gamma_o =\left[1-\left(1-\frac{p}{N}\right)^{N}\right]\frac{N}{T} \qquad (5\text{–}2)$$

The maximum possible switch throughput is obtained when a cell is always available in any time slot. This corresponds to setting $p = 1$. Note that for a 2×2 crossbar, equation (5–1) gives $\gamma_o = 0.75\ 1/T$ in this case, as stated earlier. For very large crossbars, however, with $N \gg 1$, equation (5–1) becomes

$$\gamma_o =\left(1-e^{-p}\right)\frac{1}{T} \qquad (5\text{–}3)$$

(Note that this is just the Poisson arrival result, with p the Poisson parameter). In particular, the maximum possible crossbar throughput per output line, with $p = 1$, is

$$\gamma_o|_{\max} =\left(1-e^{-1}\right)\frac{1}{T}= 0.632\frac{1}{T} \qquad (5\text{–}4)$$

The maximum throughput is thus reduced by a factor of $e^{-1} = 0.368$ because no buffers are available. (Note that for $N = 4$, the maximum throughput is 0.684; for $N = 8$, it is 0.656, rapidly approaching the case of $N \gg 1$.) Input buffers would not help in this case, however, since, as will be shown later, HOL blocking results in a maximum throughput of 0.59 $1/T$ for large N, less than the result of equation (5–4). Output buffers, resulting in the desired maximum throughput of $1/T$ cells/sec, would only work if the crossbar fabric switching rate were increased. (We leave it to the reader to explain this.)

5.3 ■ MATHEMATICAL INTERLUDE: MOMENT-GENERATING FUNCTIONS, WITH APPLICATION TO ATM (DETERMINISTIC SERVICE) QUEUES

To proceed further in our comparative discussion of input and output queueing it is necessary to interrupt the discussion at this point, and introduce some basic material on moment-generating functions and their application to queueing. Readers knowledgeable in this area can skip directly to section 5.4.

To motivate this material, consider the ATM statistical multiplexer discussed in Chapters 3 and 4. A queueing model similar to that of Figure 4–4 appears here as Figure 5–7. We assume that the buffer is infinite in size, and we want to study the statistics of buffer occupancy. If the arrival statistics are Poisson, the resultant system is the familiar $M/D/1$ queue. Other arrival statistics yield other types of FIFO queueing structures with deterministic departures. We are familiar with the first-order statistics of the $M/D/1$ queue (the average number of customers in the queue); the use of moment-generating functions enables us to determine the general statistics of this queue.

Specifically, let n be the queue occupancy, in cells, as indicated in Figure 5–7. It is desired to find the steady-state (stationary) probability $p(n)$ that the queue is in state n. The simple "trick" to be used here is to write down a discrete-time equation that governs the buffer occupancy and, from this, obtain the desired statistics. This approach can be used to solve, quite readily, for the statistics of the $M/G/1$ queue, as well as other queueing structures of interest [KLEI 1975]. The same approach will be used, in the next section, to handle output queueing at an ATM switch. We shall see shortly that the use of moment-generating functions provides a solution to the queue-governing equation.

Consider a sequence of time intervals spaced one cell-time interval, or $1/C_L$ sec, apart, as shown in Figure 5–8. Let n_k represent the buffer contents

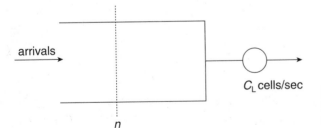

arrivals →

C_L cells/sec

n

FIGURE 5–7 ■ Queue, ATM statistical multiplexer (deterministic service).

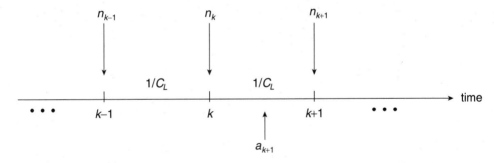

FIGURE 5–8 ▪ Discrete-time intervals and buffer state occupancy.

at time k and n_{k+1}, the corresponding value for the buffer contents at time $k+1$, as shown in Figure 5–8. Let a_{k+1} represent the (random) number of arrivals to the buffer in the interval $(k, k+1)$. The equation governing the evolution of n_k is then readily shown to be given by

$$
\begin{aligned}
n_{k+1} &= (n_k - 1) + a_{k+1} & n_k &\geq 1 \\
&= a_{k+1} & n_k &= 0
\end{aligned}
\tag{5-5}
$$

It is left to the reader to show that this equation may also be written in the more compact form

$$
n_{k+1} = (n_k - 1)^+ + a_{k+1}
\tag{5-6}
$$

where the function r^+ is defined as

$$
\begin{aligned}
r^+ &= r & r &\geq 0 \\
&= 0 & &\text{otherwise}
\end{aligned}
\tag{5-7}
$$

This equation governing the evolution of the queue could be used in simulations to determine the queue occupancy as a function of time. Assume, however, that the arrival statistics are independent of time and that the queueing system is a stable one. The queue occupancy statistics should thus approach stationary values $p(n)$. Using equation (5–5) or (5–6) we are in a position to determine these. Thus, let $k \to \infty$, with $a_{k+1} = a$, a random variable independent of time. Equation (5–5) or (5–6) can then be used to find $p(n)$, using a moment-generating approach.

We define the moment-generating function $G_n(z)$ of the random variable n as the expectation $E(z^n)$ of z^n:

$$
G_n(z) \equiv E(z^n) = \sum_{n=0}^{\infty} p(n)z^n
\tag{5-8}
$$

Alternately put, $G_n(z)$ is the z-transform of $p(n)$. It is called the moment-generating function because the mean (first moment) of n is obtained by calculating the derivative of $G_n(z)$ and setting $z = 1$:

$$E(n) = \frac{dG_n(z)}{dz}\bigg|_{z=1} = \sum_{n=0}^{\infty} np(n) \qquad (5\text{--}9)$$

Similarly, differentiating $G_n(z)$ a second time, and setting $z = 1$ provides a measure of the second moment:

$$\frac{d^2 G_n(z)}{dz}\bigg|_{z=1} = E(n^2) - E(n) \qquad (5\text{--}10)$$

Higher moments may be found in a similar manner by successively differentiating $G_n(z)$, often a simpler task than the corresponding sum required to find the moment from knowledge of $p(n)$. It is clear as well, from its defining equation (5–8), that the moment-generating function has the following properties:

$$G(1) = 1 \qquad (5\text{--}11)$$

and

$$G(0) = p(0) \qquad (5\text{--}12)$$

Details are left to the reader.

As examples, it is also left for the reader to show that the discrete probability distributions following have the moment-generating functions indicated, while the means and variances shown can be obtained by differentiating $G_n(z)$:

1. Poisson distribution.

$$p_n = \lambda^n e^{-\lambda}/n! \qquad n = 0, 1, 2, \ldots$$

$$G_n(z) = e^{-\lambda(1-z)} \qquad E(n) = \sigma_n^2 = \lambda$$

2. Geometric distribution.

$$p_n = pq^{n-1} \qquad q = 1 - p, \qquad n = 1, 2, \ldots$$

$$G_n(z) = \frac{pz}{1 - qz} \qquad E(n) = \frac{1}{p} \qquad \sigma_n^2 = q/p^2$$

3. Bernoulli distribution.

$$n = 0 \text{ or } 1 \text{ only}$$

$$p_0 = q \qquad\qquad p_1 = 1 - q \ = p$$

$$G_n(z) = q + pz \qquad E(n) = p \qquad \sigma_n^2 = qp$$

4. Binomial distribution.

$$p_n = \binom{N}{n} p^n q^{N-n} \qquad\qquad q = 1 - p \qquad\qquad 0 \leq n \leq N$$

$$G_n(z) = (q + pz)^N \qquad\qquad E(n) = Np \qquad \sigma_n^2 = Npq$$

We will be using one other property of the moment-generating function that is important to note. Consider N independent random variables $n_1, n_2,$ $\ldots n_N$. Let y be their sum:

$$y = \sum_{j=1}^{N} n_j \tag{5-13}$$

Then

$$G_y(z) = E\left(z^y\right) = \prod_{j=1}^{n} E\left(z^{n_j}\right) = \prod_{j=1}^{n} G_{n_j}(z) \tag{5-14}$$

The sum of independent random variables has as its moment-generating function the product of the moment-generating functions. As a special case, let the statistics of each of the random variables be the same. Then, from equation (5–14), we have $G_y(z) = [G_n(z)]^N$. As an example, consider the binomial distribution. Recall that the random variable n, in this case, may be written as the sum of N independent Bernoulli random variables. Then $G_n(z) = (q + pz)^N$ directly, checking the binomial distribution entry in the set of examples preceding.

We now return to equation (5–6), governing the evolution of the buffer contents of an ATM multiplexer. Note that since the buffer occupancy n and the random variable a representing the arrival statistics are independent, the right-hand side of equation (5–6) represents the sum of two independent random variables. Letting $x \equiv (n - 1)^+$, we then have, in the steady-state ($k \to \infty$),

$$G_n(z) = G_x(z)G_a(z) \tag{5-15}$$

with $G_a(z)$ the moment-generating function (mgf) of the random variable a, and $G_x(z)$ the moment-generating function of the variable x.

Now consider $G_x(z)$. Since x is related to n, we can rewrite $G_x(z)$ in terms of $G_n(x)$. To do this, note that, by definition, we have from equation (5–7),

$$x = 0 \qquad\qquad n = 0$$
$$x = n - 1 \qquad\qquad n \geq 1$$

Then

$$G_x(z) = \sum_{x=0}^{\infty} p_x z^x = p(0) + p(1) + p(2)z + p(3)z^2 + \dots \qquad (5\text{–}16)$$

introducing $p(n)$ in place of p_x. Comparing equation (5–16) with equation (5–8), which defines $G_n(x)$, we have

$$G_x(z) = p(0) + \frac{G_n(z) - p(0)}{z} \qquad (5\text{–}17)$$

with $p(0)$ the probability the buffer is empty. Introducing equation (5–17) in equation (5–15) and solving for $G_n(z)$, we have, immediately, the desired solution for $G_n(z)$ in terms of the arrival distribution mgf $G_a(z)$:

$$G_n(z) = p(0)\, (z - 1)G_a(z)/[z - G_a(z)] \qquad (5\text{–}18)$$

Using moment-generating functions, buffer occupancy statistics can be found in terms of the arrival statistics, precisely the problem we set out to solve.

We are not completely finished, however. From equation (5–18), $G_n(z)$ depends also on $p(0)$, the (unknown) probability the buffer is empty. However, this is easily shown to be $(1 - \rho)$, with ρ being the utilization of the outgoing link of capacity C_L cells/sec. To demonstrate this, we use the property of equation (5–11) of any mgf that $G_n(1) = 1$. But $G_a(1) = 1$ as well, making equation (5–18) indeterminate. To resolve this indeterminancy, we simply invoke L'Hôpital's rule, differentiating the numerator and denominator of equation (5–18) separately, before setting $z = 1$. It is then left to the reader to show that

$$p(0) = 1 - G'_a(1) = 1 - E(a) \qquad (5\text{–}19)$$

using the property of equation (5–9) of the moment-generating function. But recall that the random variable a represents the number of arrivals in the cell service time $1/C_L$ sec (see Figure 5–8). Hence $E(a)$ is the average number of arrivals in the service-time interval $1/C_L$, just the definition of the utilization ρ.[1] We thus have $p(0) = 1 - \rho$, and

---

[1] Recall that ρ can be defined either as the average arrival rate (load) divided by the service rate, or the arrival rate multiplied by the average service time. Here the average arrival rate λ, in cells/sec, is just $C_L E(a)$. Using either definition, then, $\rho = E(a)$.

$$G_n(z) = (1 - \rho)(z - 1)G_a(z)/[z - G_a(z)] \qquad (5\text{–}18a)$$

Consider the following examples. (These will be used in studying output queueing in ATM switches in the next section.)

1. Bernoulli arrivals.

$$G_n(z) = (1 - \rho)(z - 1)(q + pz)/[z(1 - p) - q] = (q + pz) \qquad (5\text{–}20)$$

For this simple arrival process the queue statistics and the arrival statistics are identical! But this is as to be expected: Only one arrival at a time can take place during a cell arrival interval. Hence this cell is immediately served. There is thus no queue, and no buffer required!

2. Binomial arrivals.

$$G_n(z) = (1 - \rho)(z - 1)(q + pz)^n /[z - (q + pz)^n] \qquad (5\text{–}21)$$

3. Poisson arrivals.

$$G_n(z) = (1 - \rho)(z - 1)e^{-\rho(1-z)}/[z - e^{-\rho(1-z)}]$$
$$= (1 - \rho)(z - 1)/[z\, e^{\rho(1-z)} - 1] \qquad (5\text{–}22)$$

Here ρ represents the Poisson parameter. (Why is this so?)

Focus, in particular, on the Poisson arrival case. For this case we have precisely the *M/D/1* queue. (Explain this). Expanding $G_n(z)$ in an infinite series in powers of z^n, we can find the corresponding probabilities $p(n)$ of queue occupancy, using the definition of equation (5–8) of the moment-generating function. Specifically, recall the Taylor series expansion

$$G_n(z) = \sum_{n=0}^{\infty} G_n^{(n)}(0)z^n / n! \qquad (5\text{–}23)$$

with

$$G_n^{(n)}(0) \equiv \frac{d^n G_n(z)}{dz^n}\bigg|_{z=0}$$

Then we have, immediately,

$$p(n) = \frac{1}{n!}\frac{d^n G_n(z)}{dz^n}\bigg|_{z=0} \qquad (5\text{–}24)$$

As examples, it is left to the reader to show that for the *M/D/1* queue,

$$p(1) = (1 - \rho)(e^\rho - 1) \qquad (5\text{–}25)$$

and

$$p(2) = (1 - \rho) \, e^{\rho}[e^{\rho} - (1 + \rho)] \tag{5-26}$$

As a check, from equation (5–22) we also have

$$E(n) = \frac{dG_n(z)}{dz}\bigg|_{z=1} = \left(\frac{\rho}{1-\rho}\right)\left[1 - \frac{\rho}{2}\right] \tag{5-27}$$

This is, of course, the well-known expression for the average occupancy of the $M/D/1$ queue (see the Appendix).

As an extension of these results applying the moment-generating function approach to determining the statistics of discrete-time (ATM-type) queues, focus now on the statistics of the buffer, *not including* any cell in service. Let q represent the number of cells in the buffer, as shown in Figure 5–9. Then, clearly, q must be given by

$$\begin{aligned} q &= n - 1 && n \geq 1 \\ &= 0 && n = 0 \end{aligned} \tag{5-28}$$

with n again representing the number in queue, including any in service. The moment-generationg function $G_q(z)$ of q is then given by

$$G_q(z) = E(z^q) = \sum_{q=0}^{\infty} p_q z^q \tag{5-29}$$

with p_q the probability that q cells are buffered. From equation (5–28) this must be given by

$$G_q(z) = p(n = 0) + p(n = 1) + \sum_{n=2}^{\infty} p(n)z^{n-1} \tag{5-30}$$

with $p(n = 0) \equiv p(0)$ and $p(n = 1) \equiv p(1)$, in terms of our earlier notation. Rewriting in terms of $G_n(z)$ we find that

$$G_q(z) = \frac{1}{z}[G_n(z) - p(0)(1 - z)] \tag{5-31}$$

with $p(0) = 1 - \rho$, as found previously. Using equation (5–18) or (5–18a) in equation (5–31), we get, finally, for the mgf of the buffered cells,

$$G_q(z) = (1 - \rho)(z - 1)/[z - G_a(z)] \tag{5-32}$$

As an example, let the arrival statistics again be Poisson, with parameter ρ. As previously, $G_a(z) = e^{-\rho(1-z)}$. Then, from equation (5–32), one can show quite easily that

$$E(q) = \frac{dG_q(z)}{dz}\bigg|_{q=1} = \frac{\rho^2}{2(1-\rho)} \tag{5-33}$$

As a check,

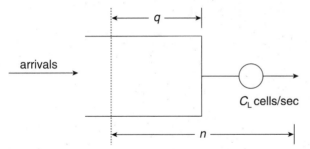

FIGURE 5–9 ■ Queue of Figure 5–7, focus on buffered cells.

$$E(n) - E(q) = \rho = 1 - p(0) \qquad (5\text{–}34)$$

This is of course a well-known result: the average number in service is $1 \cdot \text{prob}\,(n \geq 1) = 1 - p_0$. This, in fact, provides the justification for the general result $p(0) = 1 - \rho$ for a *single server,* work-conserving queue.

To complete this section, we write the equation governing the evolution of q_k, the number of cells buffered in the deterministic service queue of Figure 5–9 as a function of time. It is left to the reader to show that q_k evolves according to the following equation:[2]

$$q_{k+1} = \max\,(0,\, q_k + a_{k+1} - 1) \qquad (5\text{–}35)$$

The symbol a_{k+1} again represents the number of arrivals in the interval $(k, k+1)$, as in Figure 5–8. Equation (5–35) is comparable to equations (5–5) and (5–6), which expressed the evolution in time of the total queue contents, including any in service. Letting $k \to \infty$, as previously, equation (5–35) must represent the evolution of the steady-state (stationary) random value q whose mgf is given by equation (5–32). Thus, just as equation (5–18) represents the steady-state mgf solution to the governing equations (5–5) or (5–6) for the total number in the deterministic service queue of Figure 5–9, equation (5–32) provides the steady-state mgf solution for the random variable q, representing the number of cells *not* in service, in the queue of Figure 5–9. We use these results in studying output queueing in the next section.

5.4 ■ OUTPUT AND INPUT QUEUEING IN ATM SWITCHES

We now return to the discussion of output vs. input queueing for ATM switches begun in section 5.2. First, we will carry out an analysis of output queueing, using the moment-generating function results of the previous section. We show that for switches for which output queueing can be incorporated, there is no blocking, and that the statistical description of the output

---

[2]Hint: What are the possible values of q_{k+1} in the two cases $a_{k+1} = 0$ and $a_{k+1} \geq 1$? Why can't equation (5–35) be written in the form of equation (5–6)?

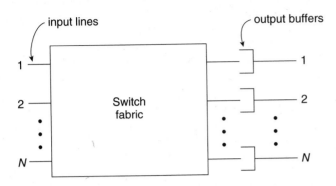

FIGURE 5–10 ■ Output queueing.

queues is captured by the statistics of the random variable q, the buffered cells in the queueing model of Figure 5–9. This is to be contrasted with input queueing, for which, as already noted in section 5.2, there is a limit on throughput due to HOL blocking. In carrying out the analysis in this section, we follow the work of Karol, Hluchyj, and coworkers [KARO 1987a]; [HLUC 1988].

Consider an ATM switch incorporating output queueing, as shown in Figure 5–10. We use the same uniform, Bernoulli traffic model introduced in section 5.2: A cell appears at each input line with probability p, each cell interval. There is a corresponding probability $(1 - p)$ no cell arrives. Let each cell, on arrival, be equally-likely to be destined to any output line. There is thus, a probability p/N in each cell interval that a given input line has a cell ready to be transferred to a given output line. We assume that all cells arriving at the input in a given cell interval are transferred to the appropriate output line within one cell time. (This, as was pointed out in section 5.2, is a requirement for output queueing to be applicable. This is discussed further, later, in terms of switch fabric architectures that obey this critical assumption).

Now focus on one (typical) output queue. With the traffic model defined above, it is clear that the (random) number of cells A transferred to this queue within one cell interval from all inputs obeys a binomial distribution:

$$P(A = j) = \binom{N}{j}(p/N)^j(1 - p/N)^{N-j} \qquad j = 0, 1, \dots, N \qquad (5\text{–}36)$$

(Note, as an aside, that as $N \to \infty$, $P(A = j)$ approaches a Poisson distribution with parameter p. This observation will be pursued later.) The ATM switch output lines each run at the same rate L cells/sec as the input lines. As a cell

[KARO 1987a]   Karol, M. J., et al., "Input vs. Output Queueing on a Space-Division Packet Switch," *IEEE Trans. on Commun., COM-35,* 12 (Dec. 1987): 1347–1356.

[HLUC 1988]   Hluchyj, M. G., and M. J. Karol, "Queueing in High-Performance Packet Switching," *IEEE JSAC, 6,* 9 (Dec. 1988): 1587–1597.

arrives on a given output, it is immediately clocked out over the output line if the buffer is empty; otherwise it is queued, while the first cell in the queue is transferred out.

Now let Q_m represent the number of cells in a given output queue at the end of cell time slot m. This is shown in Figure 5–11. We use notation different from that used previously in section 5.3 (see Figures 5–7 to 5–9) to emphasize the fact that here we are focusing on an output queue of the ATM switch of Figure 5–10, while in section 5.3 we were discussing the example of the ATM statistical multiplexer of Figure 5–7. As further shown in Figure 5–11, we use the symbol A_m to represent the (random) number of arrivals at this typical switch output queue during slot time m. The statistics of A_m, in our model, are given precisely by the binomial distribution of equation (5–36); that is, the assumption, based on the Bernoulli model, is that arrivals at a given output queue are independent from time slot to time slot, the statistics in each time slot obeying the binomial distribution of equation (5–36).

But now note the connection between Q_m, the number in a given output queue at the end of time slot m, and the number of arrivals A_m to that queue during time slot m. If there are no arrivals ($A_m = 0$), with probability $(1 - p/N)^N$ from equation (5–36), $Q_m = Q_{m-1} - 1$ if $Q_{m-1} \geq 1$; $Q_m = 0$ if $Q_{m-1} = 0$. For one or more arrivals, $A_m \geq 1$, $Q_m = Q_{m-1} + A_m - 1$. In closed form,

$$Q_m = \max (0, Q_{m-1} + A_m - 1) \tag{5–37}$$

Note that this is *identical* to equation (5–35), obtained previously as the equation governing the statistics of the number of cells waiting in the statistical multiplexer queue of Figure 5–9, the example discussed in the previous section. Each output queue of the ATM switch of Figure 5–10 thus behaves statistically like the waiting room (nonservice) or buffered portion of the statistical multiplexer of Figure 5–9. More specifically, if we let $G_A(z)$ and $G_Q(z)$ represent the moment-generating functions, respectively, of the random variables A and Q (we can drop the subscript m because of the stationarity of the statistics), the two must be related by

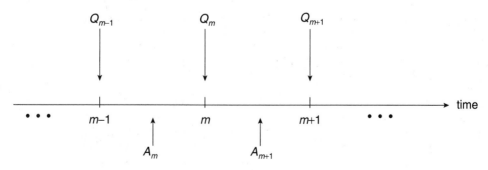

FIGURE 5–11 ■ Output queue occupancy.

$$G_Q(z) = (1 - \rho)(z - 1)/[z - G_A(z)] \qquad (5\text{--}38)$$

This is apparent from equation (5–32), the mgf solution to equation (5–35), governing the evolution of the number of cells q in the buffered portion of the queue of Figure 5–9, as discussed previously in section 5.3. Our example of the statistical multiplexer of section 5.3, used to motivate the introduction of moment-generating functions, thus leads directly to the solution of the statistics of the output queues of the ATM switch of Figure 5–10.

In particular, since the random variable A has the binomial distribution of equation (5–36), we have, immediately,

$$G_A(z) = (1 - p/N + zp/N)^N \qquad (5\text{--}39)$$

In addition, as discussed in the example of the previous section, the utilization ρ for the discrete-time process under discussion is given by

$$\rho = E(A) = N(p/N) = p \qquad (5\text{--}40)$$

that is, the utilization is just the average number of arrivals $E(A)$ at an output queue in one cell time interval, and this turns out to be the Bernoulli parameter p in this case. As a check, it is left for the reader to show, using equations (5–39) and (5–9), that $E(A) = G_A'(1) = p$.

Using equations (5–39) and (5–40) in equation (5–38), one can find any desired statistics of the output queues of Figure 5–10. Specifically, the average queue occupancy $E(Q)$ is just $G_Q'(1)$, again using the property of equation (5–9) of the moment-generating function. It is left to the reader to show that this is given by

$$E(Q) = \frac{N - 1}{N} p^2/2(1 - p) \qquad (5\text{--}41)$$

This average queue occupancy is to be compared with equation (5–33), the average number of cells *waiting* for service in an $M/D/1$ queue. Note that for large N, $N \gg 1$, the two results approach one another, with the Bernoulli parameter p here playing the role of ρ in the previous case. This is as to be expected, since the limit of the binomial distribution of equation (5–36), as $N \to \infty$, is just the Poisson distribution with parameter p. In particular, from equation (5–41), there is no throughput limitation with output queueing: all values of p, $0 \leq p < 1$, are allowable, and no cells are blocked. As the probability p of a cell appearing at any of the N inputs to the switch increases, however, approaching the limiting value of 1, the wait time at an output queue increases, following the familiar $1/(1 - p)$ form. This is as to be expected, since only one cell at a time can be transmitted out over an output line, in any one time interval. Since the average number of cell arrivals to an output queue is p and approaches 1, as $p \to 1$, the number of cells waiting for transmission must increase rapidly as p (the utilization) approaches 1. Figure 5–12 is a plot of $E(Q)$ vs. p for two cases, $N = 10$ and $N \to \infty$ (the Poisson arrival case). Note

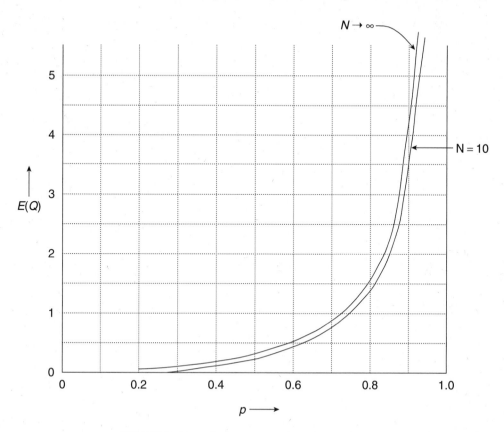

FIGURE 5–12 ▪ Average queue length, output queue.

from equation (5–41) that for $N = 10$, the average queue length is already 90% of the length for the $N \rightarrow \infty$, Poisson arrival, case.

We show next that, unlike the case of output queueing, for which cell blocking does not occur and for which the throughput can approach its maximum possible value of 1 cell transmitted per output port (line) each cell length time slot, input queueing permits only a limiting maximum throughput of $(2 - \sqrt{2}) = 0.586$ cell transmitted per output port for $N \gg 1$. This is due to head-of-the line (HOL) blocking, as noted earlier in section 5.2.

Since input queueing limits the throughput, why not always use output queueing? Shared-medium switches, such as those incorporating a bus (Figure 5–3), do utilize output queueing since the bus speed is such as to allow all N input links to move waiting cells to the output. The crossbar of Figure 5–4, on the other hand, is normally designed to connect only one input to a given output each time slot. It thus cannot make use of output queueing unless its connection speed is increased commensurately. Multistage, space-division switches, to be discussed in the next section, generally suffer a throughput penalty as well, unless their switching speed is increased substantially. A clever switch fabric design, the AT&T Bell Laboratories "Knockout" switch, does incorporate output queueing without requiring the switching speed to be increased. This switch architecture will be described briefly after a quantitative analysis of input queueing.

In demonstrating the limiting throughput performance of input queueing, we follow the approach of [KARO 1987a]. We focus our attention on one (typical) output line, say the ith output (Figure 5–13), as was done above in studying the performance of output queueing. Let all input lines be saturated with a probability $p = 1$ that a cell is available each time slot on each input line. (This was the same limiting case chosen earlier in section 5.2 in calculating the throughput of the nonbuffered crossbar.) With input queueing used, at most one of the input lines can be selected to deliver a cell to output line i. With our uniform traffic model, all N input lines are equally-likely to have a cell ready to be switched to output line i.

Now let time be slotted into units a cell length long, as was done previously. Let F_{m-1} represent the total number of cells transmitted through the switch, summing over all output lines, in time slot $(m - 1)$ (see Figure 5–14). Then, clearly, $F_{m-1} \leq N$. F_{m-1} input queues must each have transmitted a cell, one to each of F_{m-1} output lines, freeing up F_{m-1} spaces at the heads of the input queues. Since $p = 1$, by assumption, each free head of a queue must be filled by a cell during the next interval. Let A_m^i represent the number of these cells moving to the head of the freed-up input queues in time slot m, that are destined for output line i. By continuity, we must have

$$F_{m-1} = \sum_{i=1}^{N} A_m^i \tag{5–42}$$

In addition, because of our assumption that a cell is equally-likely to be destined to any output, the probability that k of the F_{m-1} cells moving to the head

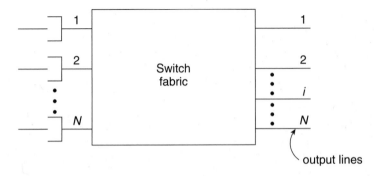

FIGURE 5–13 ▪ Input queueing

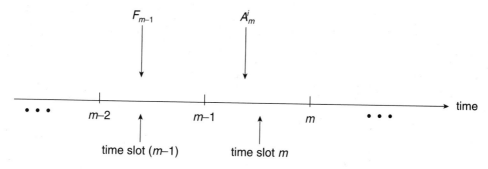

FIGURE 5–14 ▪ Time slot model, input queueing.

of input queues are destined for output i must be given by the binomial probability.

$$P\left(A_m^i = k\right) = \binom{F_{m-1}}{k}(1/N)^k\left(1 - \frac{1}{N}\right)^{F_{m-1}-k} \tag{5–43}$$

(Recall again that $p = 1$ here and that cells are equally-likely to be destined for any one of the output lines).

At most one cell in time slot m can be transmitted to output i. Any others destined for output i must be held at the head of their respective input queues. Let B_m^i represent the number of cells at the heads of input queues that are destined for output i, that are *not* selected for transmission in time slot m. A little thought will indicate that the following equation governs the evolution of B_m^i with time:

$$B_m^i = \max\left[0,\ B_{m-1}^i + A_m^i - 1\right] \tag{5–44}$$

Note that this equation is exactly of the form of equations (5–37) and (5–35), obtained previously in studying output queueing and the number of calls buffered in an ATM statistical multiplexer, respectively! Equation (5–44) may thus be visualized as representing the operation of a "virtual queue," even though no such queue exists.

In particular, as the size of the ATM switch increases, with the number N of input and input lines getting very large, the statistics of A_m^i approach Poisson under stationary conditions ($m \to \infty$) [KARO 1987a]. The random variable B_m^i represented by equation (5–44) takes on the statistics of the cells buffered in a "virtual" $M/D/1$ queue. In the limit $m \to \infty$, we have $B_m^i \to B^i$, independent of m. The mean of B^i must then be given by

$$E(B^i) = \rho_0^2/2(1 - \rho_0) \tag{5–45}$$

with the utilization ρ_0 as yet some undetermined value. (Compare with equation (5–33), the average number waiting for service in an $M/D/1$ queue).

To find ρ_0, we return to the parameter F_{m-1} defined earlier as the total number of cells transmitted across the switch in time slot $(m-1)$. Since a total of N cells are available for transmission in each time slot with $p = 1$, while B_{m-1}^i represents the number destined for output i that are *not* selected for transmission across the switch, we must have, by continuity of throughput,

$$F_{m-1} = N - \sum_{i=1}^{N} B_{m-1}^i \tag{5-46}$$

In the stationary case, with $m \to \infty$, $F_{m-1} \to F$, and $B_{m-1}^i \to B^i$, as already noted. Then $E(F)$ is the mean number of cells moving through the switch each time slot and $E(F)/N$ must represent the utilization of an output line. As a check, from equation (5–42), $E(A^i) = E(F)/N$, $A_m^i \to A^i$ as $m \to \infty$, the statistics of A^i being the same for any output line. [This agrees with $E(A^i)$ calculated using equation (5–43)]. But note from the same argument used in obtaining equation (5–40) that $E(A^i)$ is the utilization of an output line. This must in fact be the utilization ρ_0 introduced in equation (5–45). We thus have

$$E(A^i) = E(F)/N = \rho_0 \tag{5-47}$$

From equation (5–46), then, taking expectations and letting $m \to \infty$, so that stationarity applies,

$$E(F) = N\rho_0 = N[1 - E(B^i)] \tag{5-48}$$

From this equation, we have

$$E(B^i) = 1 - \rho_0 \tag{5-49}$$

Comparing with $E(B^i)$ in equation (5–45), the utilization ρ_0 must satisfy the following equation:

$$(1 - \rho_0) = \rho_0^2/2\,(1 - \rho_0) \tag{5-50}$$

Solving for ρ_0, we find

$$\rho_0 = 2 - \sqrt{2} = 0.586 \tag{5-51}$$

This is the "magic" number for the maximum utilization of the input-queued ATM switch that we have alluded to a number of times in this chapter. It represents the limiting throughput in cell/output port per cell interval for a very large, fully loaded switch ($N \to \infty$). Recall from equation (5–1), as well as the discussion surrounding Figure 5–6 in section 5.2, that a 2×2 switch has a limiting throughput (utilization) of 0.75 per output port due to HOL blocking. For $N = 4$, the maximum throughput achievable with input queueing is 0.655; for $N = 8$ it drops to 0.618. For $N > 10$ the maximum achievable throughput is already close to that of equation (5–51), obtained for $N \to \infty$ [KARO 1987a, Table 1 and Figure 6].

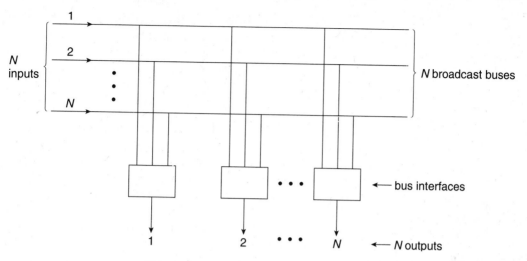

FIGURE 5–15 ■ Basic architecture, Knockout switch.

It was noted earlier that for many switch architectures, notably those incorporating multistage space switches, output queueing cannot be used unless switch speedup is utilized. One interesting example of an architecture that does not use output queueing, and hence attains an output line utilization close to the maximum value possible, is the "Knockout" switch. This switch architecture was proposed by a group at AT&T Bell Laboratories [KARO 1987b], [YEH 1987]. It uses N broadcast buses, each running at the line speed L, to reach the N outputs. A simple block diagram appears in Figure 5–15. Each cell transmitted onto its broadcast bus in each cell length time slot, carries the desired output port address. Each bus interface unit listens on all N buses, as noted. A bus interface recognizes its output port address and then takes the cell off the bus. This architecture, thus, achieves full output queueing capability—up to N cells transmitted through the switch to any one output port in a cell interval—without the accompanying switch speedup. (It of course accomplishes this by using N buses in parallel.)

The word "knockout" used in naming this switch architecture refers to the fact that it is not really necessary to buffer up to N cells at each output. Because it is generally highly unlikely that all N inputs will have a cell destined for a given output each cell interval, the number of cells accepted at each output port each time slot can be limited to a relatively small fixed number L, independent of N, the size of the switch. Analysis shows that this num-

[KARO 1987b] Karol, M. J., and M. G. Hluchyj, "The Knockout Packet Switch: Principles and Performance," *Proc. 12th Conf. on Local Computer Nets,* Minneapolis, MN, Oct. 1987: 16–22.

[YEH 1987]   Yeh, Y. S., et al., "The Knockout Switch: A Simple, Modular Architecture for High-Performance Packet Switching," *IEEE JSAC, SAC-5* (Oct. 1987): 1274–1283.

ber can be as small as 8–10 with negligible impact on cell loss probability. Special hardware must be provided, however, to limit the number of cells accepted at each output port each cell slot interval.

The word "knockout" comes from the concentration process, termed a "knockout competition," from which, at most, $L \leq N$ cells are retained and queued at each output port each cell time slot. This process is carried out at the bus interface in Figure 5–15. Figure 5–16 provides a simplified block diagram of the bus interface (KARO 1987b, Figure 4]. The concentrator shown carries out a pairwise knockout competition, as required, each time slot, guaranteeing uniform treatment of cells from different inputs; the shifter maintains the necessary FIFO order; the L cell buffers into which the shifter feeds hold cells in FIFO order. With this knockout architecture, the switch hardware complexity grows only linearly with N as the switch size increases, other than as N^2 which would be the case if up to N cells were accepted each time slot.

That the number L of cells accepted at each output port each cell interval can be limited to 8–10 with very small probability of cell loss can be demonstrated as follows [KARO 1987b]. We assume the same traffic model used throughout this chapter; that is, each of the N inputs has a Bernoulli

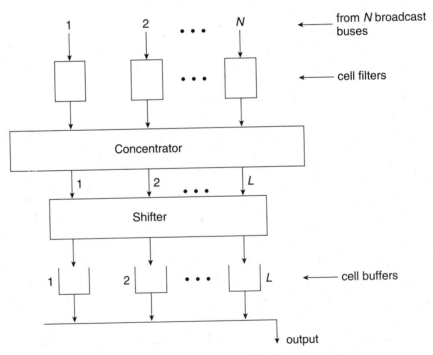

FIGURE 5–16 ▪ Bus interface at one output port, Figure 5–15, Knockout switch (from [KARO 1987b], Figure 4. © 1987 IEEE).

probability p that a cell appears in any one cell time slot, independent from slot to slot. We again assume the input traffic is uniformly distributed among the N outputs. Letting A represent the number to be transferred to an output queue, the probability that $A = j$ cells will be transferred in any one time slot is given by the binomial distribution of equation (5–36). Repeating that expression here, we have

$$P(A = j) = \binom{N}{j}(p/N)^j(1 - p/N)^{N-j} \qquad j = 0, 1, \ldots, N \qquad (5\text{–}36)$$

Consider many consecutive time slots S ($S \to \infty$). Then the cumulative number of cells destined for one output port must be $SE(A) = Sp$, recalling from equation (5–40) [or, directly, from equation (5–36)], that $E(A) = p$. For a lossless switch this would be the number delivered by the output port, agreeing with flow conservation.

In the case of the Knockout switch, however, at most $L \leq N$ cells can be accepted in one time slot. The number discarded over the S-cell interval must then be given by

$$S \bullet \sum_{k=L+1}^{N}(k - L)P(A = k)$$

The fraction discarded, the same as the *loss probability* P_L, if S is very large, as assumed here, must be the ratio of the number discarded to the number received at an output port, and is just

$$P_L = \frac{1}{p}\sum_{k=L+1}^{N}(k - L)P(A = k) \qquad (5\text{–}52)$$

(Note, incidentally, that this is precisely in the same form as the loss probability of equation (4–4) in Chapter 4, introduced in our study of admission control in that chapter.)

Equation (5–52) provides the desired loss probability resulting from the knockout process and can be calculated using equation (5–36) for any switch. The calculations are simplified considerably, however, for large N, the desired case. For N very large, the binomial probability of equation (5–36) approaches the Poisson probability.

$$P(A = j) = e^{-p}p^j/j! \qquad N \gg 1 \qquad (5\text{–}53)$$

The corresponding knockout loss probability is given by

$$P_L = \frac{1}{p}\sum_{k=L+1}^{N}(k - L)e^{-p}p^k/k! \qquad N \gg 1 \qquad (5\text{–}54)$$

It is left to the reader to show that equation (5–54) can be rewritten in the following form, more easily amenable to calculation:

$$P_L = \frac{p^L e^{-p}}{L!} + \left(1 - \frac{L}{p}\right)\left[1 - \sum_{k=0}^{L} \frac{p^k e^{-p}}{k!}\right] \qquad (5\text{–}54a)$$

In particular, for $p = 1$, the maximum throughput case,

$$P_L = \frac{e^{-1}}{L!} - (L-1)\left[1 - \sum_{k=0}^{L} e^{-1}/k!\right] \qquad (5\text{–}55)$$

For L large enough, the first term of the expression, $e^{-1}/L!$, provides a relatively tight bound to the loss probability. For $L = 8$, for example, this first term is 9.1×10^{-6}, while the actual value is $P_L = 1.3 \times 10^{-6}$. For $L = 9$, $P_L \sim 10^{-6}$, using the first term only; while for $L = 10$, the knockout process introduces a cell loss probability ranging from 10^{-8} to 10^{-10}. Letting $L = 11$ reduces P_L by yet another order of magnitude. This rapid reduction in loss probability with relatively modest values of L motivates the introduction of the knockout principle.

5.5 ▪ MULTISTAGE SPACE SWITCHES: SELF-ROUTING SWITCHES

Up to this point in discussing ATM switches, we have focused principally on the relative differences between input and output queueing in such switches. Except for some brief references to shared-medium (bus) and shared-memory switches, plus some discussion of the crossbar and Knockout switches, we have had little to say about actual switch architectures or fabrics. In this section we discuss multistage switch fabrics, with particular reference to Banyan-type architectures that have an interesting self-routing (decentralized) property.

To motivate the use of multistage fabrics, we refer back first to the square, $N \times N$, crossbar of Figure 5–4. This has N^2 elementary switches, called crosspoints, as already noted. In the early days of circuit-switched telephony, the cost of the space switches used was driven to a great extent by the crosspoint count. It was therefore important to reduce the number of crosspoints required for large ($N >> 1$) switches. Multistage switching fabrics were introduced to help with this problem [SCHW 1987, Chapter 10]. Consider, for example, the three-stage equivalent to the single-stage crossbar of Figure 5–4. This is obtained by first generalizing the square crossbar to the $n \times k$ switch of Figure 5–17a. Now let the N inputs be connected to N/n such switches, as shown in Figure 5–17b. (The "black boxes" shown in Figure 5–17b each represent a switch, as shown in Figure 5–17a). The $n \times k$ switches form the first stage of the three-stage switch. The k outputs of each $n \times k$ switch are in turn connected to k square crossbar switches, of size $N/n \times N/n$, as shown in Figure 5–17b. These $N/n \times N/n$ switches form stage two of the overall space switch, as shown. These k switches are then connected to the third and final stage of the overall switch, comprised of N/n $k \times n$ switches, as shown in Figure 5–17b. A five-stage space switch could similarly be found by further decomposing each of the middle (stage two) $N/n \times N/n$ swtiches into its own three-stage switch.

The crosspoint count C of the three-stage switch of Figure 5–17 is obviously given by

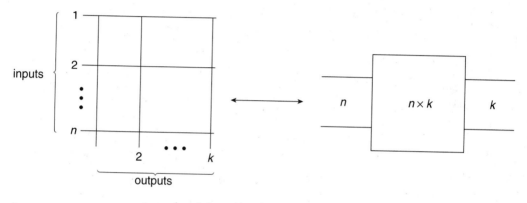

a. $n \times k$ switch and its simplified representation.

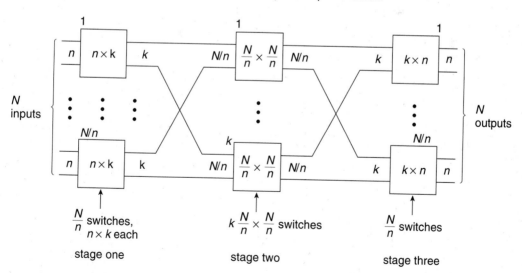

b. Three-stage switch using representation of a.

FIGURE 5–17 ■ Three-stage space switch.

$$C = 2 \, (kn)(N/n) + k \, (N/n)^2 = k \, (2N + N^2/n^2) \qquad (5\text{--}56)$$

By proper choice of n and k this number can be made substantially less than N^2, the crosspoint count of the original crossbar.

There is one basic problem with the switch of Figure 5–17. It is a potentially *blocking* switch in the sense that not all connections from the N inputs to the N outputs can be made if k, the number of possible paths between stages one and two, as well as stages two and three, is too small. Clos at Bell Laboratories demonstrated, many years ago, that the three-stage switch was always guaranteed to be nonblocking, that is, a free path between any input to any output could always be found, if the condition $k \geq 2n - 1$ were satisfied [CLOS 1953]. This is a worst case, sufficient condition for no blocking.

This is readily demonstrated for the switch of Figure 5–17. A connection is desired between a given input port and a given output port. Say that the other $(n - 1)$ input ports of the corresponding stage-one switch are occupied, while the other $(n - 1)$ output ports of the stage-three switch to which the connection is to be made are also occupied. This implies that $(n - 1)$ of the k outputs of the stage-one switch and $(n - 1)$ of the k inputs of the stage-three switch in question are also occupied. In the worst case, the busy $(n - 1)$ stage-one outputs and the busy $(n - 1)$ stage-three inputs use different stage-two switches. Since there are k stage-two switches to begin with, a new connection can only be made if $k - [(n - 1) + (n - 1)]$, the remaining number of free stage-two switches, is at least equal to one. We thus have, as the Clos, worst case condition for nonblocking, that is, a free connection between input and output can always be made,

$$k \geq 2 \, n - 1 \qquad (5\text{--}57)$$

Let $k = (2 \, n - 1)$, the minimum value of k for guaranteed nonblocking. Then, from equation (5–56),

$$C\big|_{\text{nonblocking}} = (2n - 1)(2N + N^2/n^2) \qquad (5\text{--}58)$$

This function exhibits a minimum with respect to n. For a large-sized switch, with $N \gg 1$, this minimum occurs approximately at

$$n_{\text{opt}} \doteq \sqrt{N/2} \qquad N \gg 1 \qquad (5\text{--}59)$$

for which case the minimum number of crosspoints is

$$C_{\text{min}} \doteq 4\sqrt{2} \; N^{3/2} \qquad N \gg 1 \qquad (5\text{--}60)$$

[CLOS 1953]   Clos, C., "A Study of Nonblocking Switching Networks," *BSTJ, 32,* 2 (March 1953): 406–424.

Consider an example. Let $N = 1024$. The crosspoint complexity of an $N \times N$ crossbar is then about 10^6. For this value of N, $n_{opt} \doteq 23$, and $C_{min} \doteq 185,000$, a significant reduction. But $n = 23$ is not a valid solution, since N/n must be an integer. Instead, let $n = 16$ with $N/n = 64$. Choose $k = 2n = 32$, to provide simple yet practical switch numbers. Then $C = 198,608$; not too much different from the minimum possible and still a factor of 5 less than the single-stage result.

In practice, large telephone circuit switches will often disregard the non-blocking condition and use smaller values of k than required, providing the probability of blocking through the switch is quite small [SCHW 1987]. Such switches are called *essentially nonblocking* switches. It is, in fact, possible to have a nonblocking three-stage switch with $k = n$ [HUI 1990]. But such a switch requires the ability to rearrange all connections each time a new connection is to be made, from input to output. Switches with the rearrangeability property have not been used in practice because of the complexity involved in rearranging connections. The concept of rearrangeable multistate switches does lead, however, to one important class of multistage ATM switches, the self-routing Banyan type, with $\log_2 N$ stages—each stage containing $N/2$ 2×2 switches. These switches do exhibit potential blocking, however, as we shall see, and require additional switching components to either reduce or eliminate the blocking.

The Banyan class of multistage switch follows naturally from a consideration of rearrangeable multistage switches. We ask, specifically, what type of rearrangeable nonblocking multistage switch exhibits a minimum crosspoint property? This question was considered by Benes of Bell Laboratories who came up with a class of rearrangeable nonblocking, multistage switch architectures that come close to providing the minimum number of crosspoints [BENE 1964). Consider the general input-output connection problem, first introduced in section 5.1 when discussing the problem of routing ATM cells across a switch fabric from a given input link to a prescribed output link (Figure 5–2). The basic task is to design a switch fabric that accomplishes this task with some nice properties such as minimum complexity (number of crosspoints in one measure proposed), simplicity of control, etc. This switch fabric design problem arises not just in the design of ATM switches. It arose much earlier in the design of telephone circuit switches, as noted above; it arises in the computer engineering world, in the design of interconnection networks for connecting parallel processors to multiple memory modules [PATE 1981].

[HUI 1990]   Hui, J. Y., *Switching and Traffic Theory for Integrated Broadband Networks*, Boston: Kluwer Academic Publishers, 1990.

[BENE 1964]   Benes, V. E., "Optimal Rearrangeable Multistage Connecting Networks," *BSTJ*, *43* (July 1964): 1641–1656.

[PATE 1981]   Patel, J. H., "Performance of Processor-Memory Interconnections for Multiprocessors," *IEEE Trans. Computers, C-30*, 10 (Oct. 1981): 771–780.

FIGURE 5–18 ■ General input-output connection problem.

Consider the general problem of interconnection, as exemplified by Figure 5–18. This figure is, of course, similar to Figure 5–2, but generalized to any type of interconnection, not just to ATM VP's. Given such an N-input, N-output system, there are clearly $N!$ possible connections, or permutations of N inputs with N outputs, that can be made. A crossbar realizes these with N^2 crosspoints. A three-stage Clos network requires $O(N^{3/2})$ crosspoints, as noted above. Say now that C crosspoints are to be used to attain the $N!$ connections. What is the minimum number of crosspoints that is required? Each crosspoint allows two possible connections to be made. We must then have, to attain all possible permutations,

$$2^C \geq N! \tag{5–61}$$

But by Stirling's approximation, we have

$$N! \doteq \sqrt{2n}N^{N+\frac{1}{2}}e^{-N} \tag{5–62}$$

Using this approximation in equation (5–61), and taking logarithms to the base 2, we find, after some simplification,

$$C \geq N\log_2 N - 1.44N + \frac{1}{2}\log_2 N + 1.33 \tag{5–63}$$

The right-hand side of equation (5–63) must thus represent the minimum number of crosspoints necessary. It is $O(N\log_2 N)$. The Benes network crosspoint count approaches this number.

To develop the Benes network, and, from this, the Banyan class of networks, we move from a consideration of crosspoints to a consideration of basic 2×2 switches. An example of such an elementary switch (a special case of the crossbar), appears in Figure 5–19. This switch has two possible connection states as shown: the bar state and the cross state. Say we want to implement a switch architecture with this type of switch. Let $S(N)$ be the minimum number of such 2×2 switches required. Then we again have, in the same manner that equation (5–61) was written,

$$2^{S(N)} = N!$$

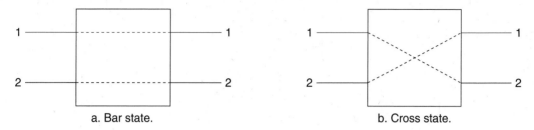

a. Bar state.   b. Cross state.

FIGURE 5–19 ■ 2 × 2 switch configurations.

or, proceeding as was done to find the minimum number of crosspoints,

$$S(N) = N \log_2 N - 1.44N + \frac{1}{2}\log_2 N \tag{5–64}$$

(We drop the inconsequential constant 1.33).

Equation (5–64) thus establishes the minimum number of 2×2 switches required, in theory, to attain all possible $N!$ permutations of N inputs with N outputs. (Note that if the 2×2 switches were themselves implemented using crosspoint technology, $4S(N)$ crosspoints would, in theory, be required using this approach since a 2×2 crossbar requires 4 crosspoints).

Now consider the Benes class of *rearrangeable,* nonblocking, switching networks. This class is made up of 2×2 switches, with N a multiple of 2, and is obtained by recursively decomposing a single-stage $N \times N$ crossbar into multiple stages until 2×2 switches only remain. The initial $N \times N$ switch and the three-stage switch obtained after the first iteration appear in Figures 5–20a and b respectively. In this recursion $N/2$ 2×2 switches are each pulled out at the input and at the output, as shown. Two $N/2 \times N/2$ switches remain in the center stage. The 2×2 switches are each connected to one of the two $N/2 \times N/2$ switches, in order, the topmost 2×2 switch to the topmost part of each of the two center switches, etc. This procedure is then repeated with each of the $N/2 \times N/2$ switches, leaving four $N/4 \times N/4$ switches in the center stage. This recursion is repeated until 2×2 switches only remain. An $N = 8$ Benes switch is shown, as an example, in Figure 5–21.

It is left to the reader to show that the Benes network has $(2 \log_2 N - 1)$ stages, with $N/2$ 2×2 switches per stage. The total number of 2×2 switches required to implement this class of multistage switches is

$$S_{\text{Benes}} = N \log_2 N - \frac{N}{2} \tag{5–65}$$

As a check, the $N = 8$ case requires five stages and has twenty 2×2 switches, as shown in the example of Figure 5–21. Note by comparison with equation (5–64), that

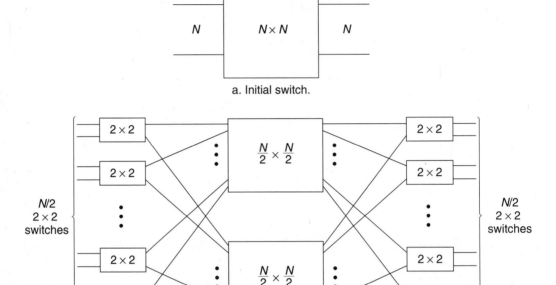

a. Initial switch.

b. Switch after first iteration.

FIGURE 5–20 ■ Recursion to obtain N-input Benes switch.

$$S_{\text{Benes}} > S(N) \qquad (5\text{–}66)$$

as expected. However, it is readily shown that the fractional difference approaches $0.94/\log_2 N$ for large N. For $N = 64$, for example, the number of 2×2 switches required to implement the Benes class is within 20% of the minimum number possible. For $N = 1024$, this difference has decreased to 11%.

Now consider the Banyan class of multistage, self-routing networks. This class, in its basic form, requires $\log_2 N$ stages of 2×2 switches to connect N inputs to N outputs. $N/2$ 2×2 switches are needed in each stage. There are thus a total of $N/2 \log_2 N$ 2×2 switches required. This is smaller than the number of 2×2 switches required for the Benes network [equation (5–65)], and, in fact, even smaller than $S(N)$, as given by equation (5–64). This class has internal blocking, however, as will be shown shortly, and requires additional switch stages and/or other modifications to overcome this problem.

The Banyan class of self-routing switches consists of a number of topologically equivalent switching networks. A simple example for $N = 8$ inputs and outputs appears in Figure 5–22. This is sometimes also referred to as a SW-Banyan or a delta-2 network. Note that this switch has $\log_2 N = 3$ stages, with $N/2 = 4$ 2×2 switches at each stage. It thus has a total of twelve 2×2

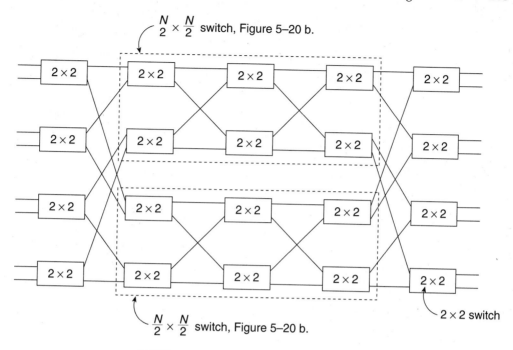

FIGURE 5–21 ■ Benes switch, $N = 8$ inputs/outputs.

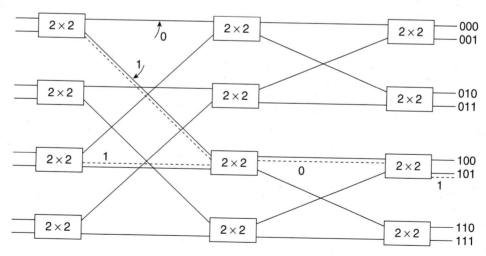

FIGURE 5–22 ■ $N = 8$ Banyan self-routing switch.

switches, as contrasted with the twenty 2×2 switches required for the $N = 8$ Benes network of Figure 5–21.

The self-routing property of the Banyan switch is demonstrated using this three-stage example. Let an incoming cell carry an added $\log_2 N$-bit header, representing the binary address of the destination (output) line of the switch to which the cell is to be directed. This header would be appended to the normal 53-byte ATM cell (or any other input if other than ATM cells are to be switched) by a hard-wired router, one for each input line (not shown in Figure 5–22). Each of the $\log_2 N$ bits is then used, in turn, to establish a switching decision in consecutive stages, from the first to the last, of the $\log_2 N$-stage network. Cells arriving on different input lines are assumed to be clocked through the $\log_2 N$-stage network in unison, the normal clocking time corresponding to a cell-length interval. (This time could be speeded up of course, eventually approaching the time required to have the switch operate in output-queued mode).

The switching decision for a cell arriving at a 2×2 elementary switch in a given stage is made as follows: a 0 entry in the $\log_2 N$-bit header corresponding to that stage's position directs the 2×2 switch to transfer the cell to its upper output link; a 1 directs the switch to transfer the cell to the lower output link. This is denoted in Figure 5–22 by the 0 and 1 accompanied by arrows.

Consider a cell directed to output line 011(3) of Figure 5–22 as an example. It would then carry the 3-bit header 011. This means the cell is to be routed up by the first-stage 2×2 switch, and then routed down by each of the two 2×2 switches through which it passes in successive stages. This is guaranteed to have the cell end up at output port 011 (number 3), independent of the port at which it enters the switch. The reader is urged to try this out, using 011 at any of the eight input ports.

Another example, for output port 5 (101), appears in Figure 5–22. Here two different cells (one entering the switch at input port 0 or 1, the other at input ports 4 or 5 (input ports are numbered 0–7), each carry the routing label 101. The first stage 2×2 switch routes down; the second up; the third down. Both cells end up at output port 101, as shown by the dashed lines representing the two paths through the switching network. This example also demonstrates the potential for internal contention and hence blocking in this switch. Both cell paths meet at the output of the same 2×2 switch in stage two. One cell would have to be blocked if a cell on each of the two paths were to require switching to the same output at the same time. Potential congestion, in fact, exists at each 2×2 switch in the entire switching network. It occurs not only if cells have the same destination; the potential for blocking occurs at any place paths meet. Such potential for internal collisions, or "hot spots" within the overall switch, exists anytime there are communities of interests, that is, switching points through which multiple cells may be routed.

Various methods have been proposed to reduce or eliminate potential internal blocking. One simple procedure is to provide internal buffering with one cell at a time transferred; another is to precede the Banyan switch by another multistage Banyan (called a distribution network) that alternately directs cells at each stage up or down, independently of destination address. Cells thus end up essentially uniformly distributed over all input ports of the actual routing Banyan. This helps to reduce hot spots. Another method proposed is to speed the fabric switching speed up: As noted above, it has been assumed thus far for normal operation that each cell is switched across each stage in one cell time. If the switch speedup is high enough (a factor of 4 or more has been found sufficient in practice), the case of output buffering is approached, as already noted, and internal blocking eliminated. A fourth technique, to be discussed in more detail later, uses a *sorting network* preceding the Banyan. This network sorts by destination address and effectively eliminates internal contention within the Banyan, except for cells with the same destination address.

Internal buffering, also to be discussed in more detail later, results in added (random) delay plus reduced throughput. The use of a distribution network can reduce the potential for "hot spots" due to communities of interest as noted above, but doubles the size of the switch. The sorting network also results in a larger switch. Despite these drawbacks, the Banyan architecture has found favor among some switch designs because of the self-routing property and also because the regularity in architecture, using simple, cascaded 2×2 switches, allows VLSI implementations to be relatively easily designed. The SynOptics LattisCell switch is of the buffered Banyan type. It runs at a speedup of two times the line speed to reduce blocking. Thus, a 2.5 Gbps-throughput, 16×16, switch with each input port (line) running at 155 Mbps, requires a switching rate of 5 Gbps, or 12×10^6 ATM cells/sec switched.

Figure 5–23 provides examples of two other $N = 8$ Banyan switching networks that are topologically equivalent to the one of Figure 5–22. Note that the only difference is in internal switch connections. The example of Figure 5–23a is called an Omega, or shuffle exchange network. The one of Figure 5–23b is called a baseline network. It is left for the reader to show that each network has the self-routing property of the switch of Figure 5–22, with internal blocking and "hot spots" possible as well. An item of note is the fact that the Benes network of Figure 5–21 is made up of two baseline networks, back-to-back: the first three stages of Figure 5–21 correspond to the baseline network of Figure 5–23b; the last three stages correspond to an inverse baseline network.

An ATM switch using the Banyan self-routing architecture for its switching fabric would, as noted earlier, require a high-speed hardware-based routing element preceding each input port. This routing element would conceptually contain a hardware table lookup, with each ATM VC-VP id mapped

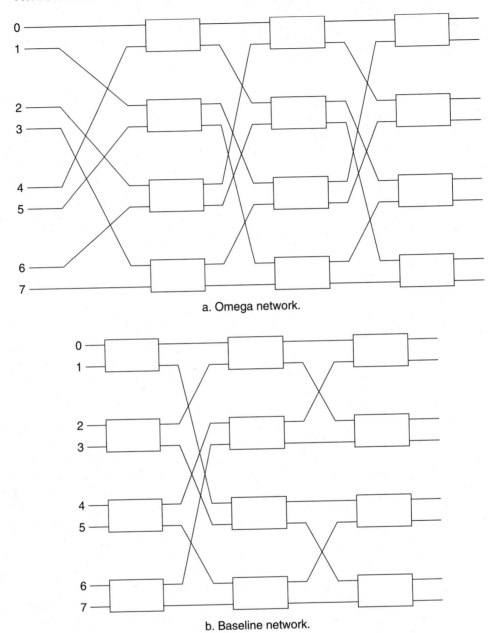

a. Omega network.

b. Baseline network.

FIGURE 5–23 ■ Other examples of $N = 8$ Banyan, self-routing, networks.

into an appropriate switch output port number. The element would append the $\log_2 N$-bit output port number to each ATM cell header, to be used in directing the cell through the switch. Without speedup, each cell would advance one stage of the switch each cell time. The minimum time required to traverse the switch thus increases with switch size. As we shall see later, the switch throughput decreases with switch size as well.

If internal buffering is to be used to control internal switch congestion, as noted above, control signals from downstream to upstream must be included to notify cells when they are able to move ahead, to the next stage. Note that a cell can only move ahead if the buffer at the next stage is ready to accept it. This will be true if the buffer is empty, or, if occupied, if the cell occupying it can itself move ahead. Figure 5–24 shows a 4×4 network incorporating single internal input buffers. Output buffers at each stage could be utilized instead, and may be shown to provide throughput improvement if more than one cell may be buffered [SZYM 1989]. To provide time for the control signals to propagate upstream, a two-part control cycle may be used each cell interval. During the first part of the cycle, 2×2 switches at each stage, starting with the last stage in the switch, signal the 2×2 switches to which they are connected in the adjacent upstream stage whether their buffers will be empty or not. In the second part of the cycle, a 2×2 switch using this information either forwards a waiting cell or continues to buffer it if no room will be available downstream. (If two buffered cells at the same switch must be transferred to the same output line, a random choice is made of the one accepted. The other is then held.) Note that this control signal process propagates to the Banyan network input, resulting in a decision at that point whether to accept a new cell at each input or not.

Internally buffered Banyans show a throughput reduction with size, as already noted. A Batcher bitonic sorting network may be used, preceding the Batcher routing network, to eliminate internal conflicts [HUI 1990], [TOBA 1990]. The Batcher network produces, at its output, cells sorted by the Banyan output port address. Two or more cells with the same output address will collide, however, so that all but one must be trapped at the output of the sorting network and recirculated back to the input of the Batcher network.

The Batcher bitonic sorter uses a cascaded series of 2×2 Banyan-type switching networks with shuffle interconnections to sort, first, by two, then by four, by eight, by sixteen, until all N inputs appear sorted by address at its output. An example for $N = 8$ inputs appears in Figure 5–25 [TOBA 1990]. The arrows at each 2×2 switch indicate the output to which the larger value

[SZYM 1989]   Szymanski, T. H., and S. Z. Shaikh, "Markov Chain Analysis of Packet-Switched Banyans with Arbitrary Switch Sizes, Queue Sizes, Link Multiplicities, and Speedups," *Proc. Infocom 89*, Ottawa, April 1989: 960–971.

[TOBA 1990]   Tobagi, F. A., "Fast Packet Switch Architectures for Broadband Integrated Services Digital Networks," *Proc. IEEE, 78,* 1 (Jan 1990): 133–167.

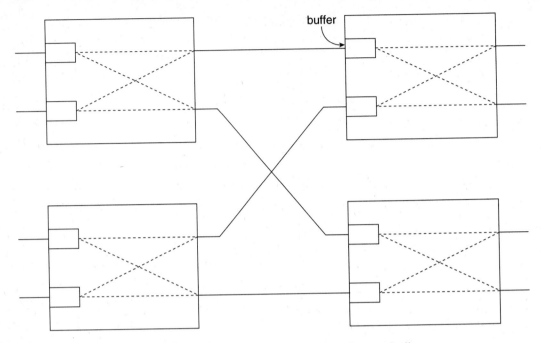

FIGURE 5–24 ■ 4 × 4 Banyan, single input buffers.

at the input is switched. An example is shown, indicating how randomly distributed addresses at the input emerge sorted by address at the output. In this example only six of the eight possible inputs are shown occupied. The two input lines for which cells are not present are denoted by dashes. The numbers at the inputs of the elementary 2 × 2 switches in successive stages of the sorter indicate how these six input cells are switched successively, stage by stage, through the sorter. Switches with no cell appearing at an input automatically direct the cell at the other input in the direction of the lower value. Note that by the time the six cells reach the output, they arrive sorted by destination, with the highest-numbered output lines empty, as they should be.

With cells now sorted by address, it is important to ensure that there be no internal collisions in the Banyan switch following. This is accomplished by connecting the bitonic sorter outputs appropriately to the Banyan inputs. Figure 5–26 shows how this is done for the $N = 8$ example. It is left to the reader to show that the six cells at the output of the bitonic sorter of Figure 5–25 do, in fact, reach their respective destination links at the Banyan network output without experiencing any internal collisions.

The example of Figures 5–25 and 5–26 shows how cells with *different* destination addresses arrive at the appropriate output lines while suffering no internal collisions. Cells with the *same* destination addresses would emerge at adjacent ports at the output of the sorter. These would then collide in the Banyan network following, unless provision were made to allow only

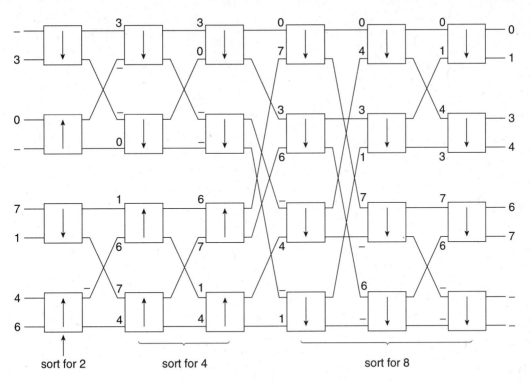

FIGURE 5–25 ■ Batcher bitonic sorting network, $N = 8$.

one of these cells to proceed. (In practice, the Batcher sorting network can be followed by multiple Banyan networks in parallel, allowing more than one cell/destination to proceed. This strategy has been adopted in the Bellcore "Sunshine" switch to be described shortly).

The number of stages M required in a Batcher bitonic sorting network is readily shown to be given by

$$M = \sum_{i=1}^{\log_2 N} i = \frac{1}{2}\log_2 N[\log_2 N + 1] \qquad (5\text{--}67)$$

This is clear from the $N = 8$ example of Figure 5–25. The number of 2×2 switches, as a measure of complexity, is $NM/2 = o\,[N(\log_2 N)^2] > o\,(N \log_2 N)$. The use of the sorter, although eliminating contention so long as two cells do not appear addressed to the same destination, thus increases the switching network complexity significantly. (But note again that the Batcher-Banyan network combination is internally nonblocking, providing no more than one cell at a time is directed to a given destination.) As an example, if $N = 8$, as in Figure 5–25, the number of sorting stages is $M = 6$ and the number of 2×2 switches required is 24. If $N = 16$, the numbers increase to 10 and 80, respec-

Bitonic sorter outputs

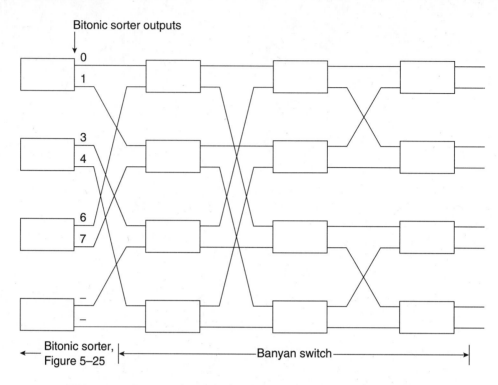

FIGURE 5–26 ■ Combination, bitonic sorter, and Banyan switch, $N = 8$.

tively; for $N = 1024$, $M = 55$ stages, and the number of switches required increases to 28,160!

Consider the Batcher-Banyan combination now, as shown schematically in Figure 5–27. The total number of 2×2 switches required for an $N \times N$ system is given by the sum of the switch counts of the Batcher and Banyan networks:

$$S_{B-B} = \frac{N}{4} \log_2 N [3 + \log_2 N] \qquad (5\text{–}68)$$

This number is tabulated in Table 5–1, where it is compared with the crosspoint count of the crossbar and an optimum multistage network requiring $S(N) = o(N \log_2 N)$ 2×2 switches. (Purists might argue that the Batcher-Banyan and the optimum switch numbers should be multiplied by four, to convert the numbers to "crosspoints" for comparison with the crossbar. The counterargument, however, is that the basic, repetitive, element for the Batcher-Banyan architecture is the 2×2 switch, while for the crossbar it is the crosspoint. Table 5–1 is just illustrative, however. More detailed considerations of switch complexity focus on the number of crosspoints, the number of

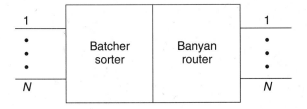

FIGURE 5–27 ■ $N \times N$ Batcher-Banyan network to eliminate internal blocking.

VLSI components, and pin-limited chip counts, among other considerations [SHAI 1990a], [ZEGU 1993], [COPP 1992].)

A block diagram of the Sunshine Batcher-Banyan ATM switch developed at Bellcore appears in Figure 5–28 [GIAC 1990]. Note the specific features of this switch. It uses K parallel Banyan routing networks to provide multiple paths for cells destined for any output port. This is similar to the technique used in the Knockout switch to reduce input queueing, and is equivalent to K-fold switch fabric speedup. (The Knockout switch uses a full N-fold speedup to provide output queueing, but then drops all but K of N possible cells destined for each output.) Recall that the Batcher bitonic sorter produces, at its output, cells sorted according to the output port (destination) address. With K Banyans connected in parallel, up to K cells with common output addresses may be routed, by the Banyans, to the appropriate output. Up to T additional cells with the same output address are trapped and recirculated back to the input of the Batcher sorter for another pass through the overall switch. The

TABLE 5–1 ■ ATM Space Switch Complexity

N	N^2	S_{BB}, Batcher-Banyan	Optimum, $o(N\log_2 N)$
	(crossbar crosspoints)	(2×2 switches)	(2×2 switches)
8	64	36	24
16	256	112	64
32	1,024	320	160
64	4,096	864	384
128	16,384	2,240	826

[SHAI 1990a]   Shaikh, S. Z., et al., "A Comparison of the Shufflenet and Banyan Topologies for Broadband Packet Switches," *Proc. Infocom 90,* San Francisco, June 1990: 1260–1267.

[ZEGU 1993]   Zegura, E. W., "Architectures for ATM Switching Systems," *IEEE Commun. Mag., 31,* 2 (Feb. 1993): 28–37.

[COPP 1992]   Coppo, P., et al., "Optimal Cost/Performance Design of ATM Switches," *Proc. Infocom 92,* Florence, Italy, May 1992: 446–458.

[GIAC 1990]   Giacopelli, J. N., et al., "Sunshine: A High-Performance Self-Routing Broadband Packet Switch Architecture," *Proc. XIII Internatl Switching Symposium,* ISS 90, Stockholm, May 1990.

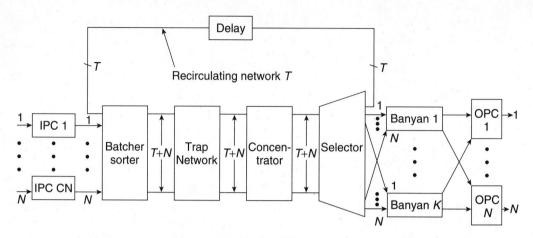

FIGURE 5–28 ■ Sunshine ATM Switch (from [GIAC 1990], Figure 1. Copyright © 1990, Bellcore. Reprinted with permission).

size of the Batcher sorter must thus be agumented by T, making it a $(T + N)$ sorter, to accommodate the recirculated cells.

The input port controllers (IPC) shown in Figure 5–28 are the devices that map the VC/VP ids of incoming cells to the appropriate switch output port addresses. They then insert the address field, the $\log_2 N$ destination address bits necessary for routing through the switch, into each cell header, followed by a priority field. The priority field contains two subfields: one carries quality of service (QoS) bits, the other indicates internal switch priority. This latter subfield indicates the number of time slots a cell has recirculated, priority increasing with recirculation time. Recirculated cells from a given source can thus be routed in order of initial arrival at the ATM switch. The trap network identifies the cells required to be recirculated; the concentrator and selector networks group them together and direct them to the recirculating network.

The use of multiple ($K > 1$) Banyans in parallel is necessary to keep the throughput high and cell loss probability low. If one Banyan is used, with no recirculation for example, ($K = 1$, $T = 0$), the maximum throughput for a large switch ($N \gg 1$) approaches the input buffer limit of 0.586. The Batcher-Banyan combination, with no internal buffering required, eliminates internal congestion, as already noted, but congestion is now moved to the input queues, with HOL blocking now developing. A large improvement in throughput results with the use of multiple Banyans, however. Thus, for example, if $N = 128$ and $K = 3$, so that three Banyans are used in parallel, recirculating at most 10% of the cells ($T/N = 0.1$) results in a cell loss probability of 10^{-6} at full load [GIAC 1990]. Increasing K to 4 reduces the loss probability to much less than 10^{-9} for the same size switch. The price paid, of course, is the additional switch complexity. (With $T/N = 0.1$ the Batcher sorter size is not affected very much, but multiple Banyans are now needed.)

We began this section on multistage space switches by discussing the three-stage Clos switching network designed originally to reduce the crosspoint count of telephone circuit switches. We then moved on to switching networks based on multiple stages of 2×2 networks, starting with the Benes rearrangeably nonblocking switch and concluding with Banyan routing switches, which require $o(\log_2 N)$ stages for an $N \times N$ switch. We pointed out that Banyan switching networks have the nice property of allowing self-routing of cells, but lead to internal blocking unless preceded by Batcher bitonic sorters. It is of interest to calculate the delay and throughput performance of the basic Banyan switch, showing that its throughput decreases with switch size. This we shall do in the next section. Before concluding this section by summarizing and categorizing the comparative properties of various switch architectures, however, we return to the simple three-stage Clos-type switch to show that it too can be modified to serve as an effective ATM switch. The 16×16 Newbridge switch is of the three-stage Clos type, incorporating output buffering at each stage.

A number of larger three-stage ATM space switches have been proposed, and prototypes built, by various research organizations and switch manufacturers. We focus here on one such switch proposed by researchers at AT&T Bell Laboratories because of its basic simplicity and because it can be designed in modular form, using small-size switches interconnected to form relatively large switches [ENG 1992]. Its architects include the group that developed the original Knockout switch, and it uses a generalized knockout concept to obtain, in principle, very small cell loss probability.

The basic idea is that of grouping the N outputs in an $N \times N$ switch into K groups, with n outputs in each. A maximum of m cells only are then allowed to access the n outputs each cell time slot. The switch architecture then takes the form of Figure 5–29. The interconnect fabric shown in Figure 5–29 will be discussed later. (The switch proposed can handle variable-size packets. We focus on the fixed-size ATM cell case for simplicity). This generalizes the knockout principle discussed in the previous section, where it was found that a maximum of 8–10 cells could be directed to each output port, independent of the switch size N, with loss probability $< 10^{-6}$. Analysis of the architecture of Figure 5–29 indicates that if $n > 10$, say, m/n need only be 2–3 to attain the same performance. This illustrates the law of large numbers in which larger groups outperform smaller units.

The analysis is quite simple, extending the approach used in the previous section in calculating the performance of the basic Knockout switch [ENG

[ENG 1992]   Eng, K. Y., et al., "A Growable Packet (ATM) Switch Architecture: Design Principles and Applications," *IEEE Trans. on Commun.*, 40, 2 (Feb. 1992): 423–430.

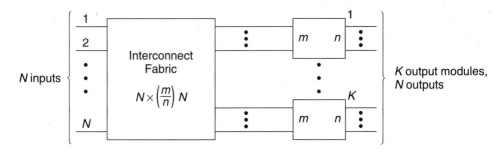

FIGURE 5–29 ▪ Growable switch architecture (from [ENG 1992], Figure 3. © 1992 IEEE).

1992]. Thus, assume a uniform Bernoulli model again, with p the probability that a cell appears at each input port each slot time. Assuming uniform traffic, with cells equally likely to be destined for each of the N output ports, the probability a cell at an input is destined for one of the K output modules is np/N. The probability of cell loss is then proportional to the probability that the number of cells arriving at an output model exceeds m. Comparing with equations (5–52) and (5–36) in section 5.4, we have the loss probability given by

$$P_L = \frac{1}{np} \sum_{k=m+1}^{N} (k-m)\binom{N}{k}\left(\frac{np}{N}\right)^k\left(1-\frac{np}{N}\right)^{N-k} \tag{5–69}$$

For large N ($N \to \infty$), the binomial probability term in equation (5–69) approaches the usual Poisson form. Simplifying the resultant expression, one then gets

$$P_L = \frac{(np)^m e^{-np}}{m!} - \left[\frac{m}{np}-1\right]\left[1-\sum_{k=0}^{m}(np)^k\frac{e^{-np}}{k!}\right] \qquad N \gg 1 \tag{5–70}$$

This is to be compared with equation (5–54a) obtained previously. Eng et al. have calculated this expression and show that, with $n = 16$ and $m = 33$, $P_L < 10^{-6}$ for $p = 0.9$ (90% load). (As a check, the leading term in equation (5–70) is 8×10^{-6}.) Thus, $m/n \sim 2$ provides $P_L < 10^{-6}$ for $n = 16$. Increasing m to 40 ($m/n = 2.5$) drops P_L to less than 10^{-10}. The loss probability is clearly sensitive to small increases in m.

    Returning now to Figure 5–29, how is the interconnect fabric shown to be designed? Recall that its function is to direct up to, at most, m cells to the appropriate output model. That output module, designed as a packet switch, in turn directs the cells to the particular output link among n possible desired. A variety of techniques could be used for the interconnect fabric, including the knockout architecture, the Batcher-Banyan architecture in somewhat modified form, and others discussed in this chapter. A particularly simple and growable approach involves the use of a two-stage interconnection fabric, the entire switch then taking on the form of the three-stage Clos network discussed previously and drawn schematically in Figure 5–17b. The resultant three-stage network appears in Figure 5–30 [ENG 1992]. Recall that the Clos network is strictly nonblocking if $m \geq 2n-1$ and rearrangeably nonblocking if $m \geq n$. Since we had noted earlier that $m \sim 2n-3n$ to provide the appropriate knockout performance in the general growable switch architecture of Figure 5–29, the three-stage switch of Figure 5–29 is nonblocking. Eng et al. discuss methods for providing fast path assignment through this switch [ENG 1992].

In more recent work, the AT&T group has replaced the $m \times n$ output modules of Figure 5–30 by 8×8 shared-memory ATM switches. The concentration is then carried out by $N \times 8$ concentrators in the stage preceding, as part of the interconnect fabric of Figure 5–30. A specific implementation has each input/output link running at 2.5 Gbps, for an aggregate throughput of 20 Gbps for each 8×8 switch. A 160-Gbps 64×64 prototype switch has been built and tested, using specifically-designed chips incorporating the 64×8 concentrators [ENG 1995].

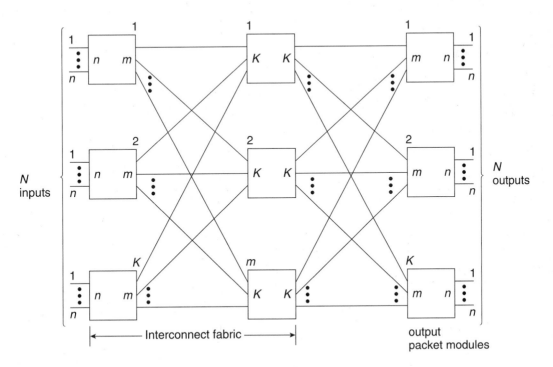

FIGURE 5–30 ■ Clos-type growable switch architecture (from [ENG 1992], Figure 4. © 1992 IEEE).

5.5.1 ■ Summary, ATM Switch Architectures

We have covered a variety of ATM switch architectures. It is useful at this point to summarize some of the salient features of each with some attempt made to compare them. This has been done in Table 5–2. We have grouped the different types of switches into three basic categories: shared memory, shared medium, and space-division switches. This last category has been further split into a number of types—single-stage crossbar, multistage Banyan, and multistage Batcher-Banyan. Not included in the table, to keep it as simple as possible, is the multistage non-Banyan type of switching architecture, exemplified by the growable switch architecture just described. The reader is urged to complete the table with this type of architecture.

For each category and type, we have included such comparative information as switch fabric speed, estimate of basic switching elements needed, maximum throughput (in units of cell/cycle per output line), type of cell control through the network, and whether input or output queueing is used, where applicable. We have also provided examples of the different architectures mentioned earlier in this section. A more comprehensive listing might include some estimate of switching network cost (other than the number of switching elements required) and details of the control function (our discussion in this chapter has been quite rudimentary), among other items.

TABLE 5–2 ■ $N \times N$ ATM Switch Summary

Type	Fabric Speed	No. Switch Elements	Normalized max. Throughput	Input/Output Routing Control	Examples
Shared memory	$2N \times$ line rate	—	1 (output queueing)	central	Prelude, AT&T
Shared Medium	$N \times$ line rate	—	1 (output queueing)	central	Paris, Fore
Space-division switch					
1. Crossbar	Line rate	N^2	0.632 (no queueing)	central	
	Line rate	N^2	0.586 (input queueing)	central	
	$N \times$ line rate	N^2	1 (output queueing)	central	
	Line rate, N buses		1 (output queueing)	decentralized	Knockout
2. Multistage Banyan	Line rate	$o(N\log_2 N)$	0.75–0.32 (single input buffer)	self	
3. Batcher-Banyan	Line rate	$o[KN(\log_2 N)^2]$	1 (K Banyans; $K > 1$)	self	Sunshine

Tobagi has classifed ATM cell-based packet switches into the same three basic categories in his paper [TOBA 1990]. Ahmadi and Denzel classify them in a somewhat similar fashion [AHMA 1989]. Decina and his co-authors have provided a table, somewhat different than that of Table 5–2, aligned along a variety of features, that shows examples of proposed switch architectures and which of the different features they incorporate [DECI 1990c]. These references and others provided in this chapter cover ATM switches in much more detail, and provide many other examples of architectures, both proposed and deployed.

Note that in Table 5–2, in the normalized throughput column, we show the multistage Banyan as having a maximum throughput ranging from 0.75 to 0.32 cell/cycle per output line. The value of 0.75 is the number we have already obtained for a single 2×2 switch. In the next section, dedicated to carrying out the performance analysis of multistage 2×2 Banyans, with a single input buffer at each input to the elementary 2×2 switches at each stage, we show that the maximum throughput obtainable, at a maximum input load of $p = 1$, approaches 0.32 for N very large (many stages) based on simulation results. The approximate model we adopt for analysis predicts a maximum throughput of 0.45 for $N \gg 1$. (For normal loading of $p = 0.5$ or 0.6, analysis and simulation do agree more closely.) This result is the one implied in our statement earlier in this section that the multistage Banyan does provide a throughput penalty as the size N of the switch increases. The delay through the switch goes up as well as the number of stages $n = \log_2 N$ increases, as would be expected.

5.6 ■ PERFORMANCE ANALYSIS, BANYAN SWITCH ARCHITECTURE

It was noted in the last section that multistage Banyan switching networks have received a great deal of attention in the ATM switch literature because of their self-routing property, as well as the fact that they require $o(N\log_2 N)$ elementary switches for implementation. VLSI implementation is enhanced as well because of their regular, repetitive structure. On the other hand, it was noted in passing that their throughput performance is relatively poor, decreasing as the size N of the switch increases, while the delay through the switch increases at least as $\log_2 N$, the number of switching stages required.

In this section we carry out a simplified analysis of the basic Banyan network, obtaining approximate expressions for the throughput and delay, to quantify the comments made above. The basic Banyan (the one discussed in

---

[AHMA 1982] Ahmadi, H., and W. E. Denzel, "A Survey of Modern High-Performance Switching Techniques," *IEEE JSAC, 7,* 7 (Sept. 1989): 1091–1102.

[DECI 1990c] Decina, M., et al., "Shuffleout Switching for ATM Interconnection Nets," *7th Specialist Seminar,* Morristown, NJ, Oct. 1990.

the previous section), uses 2×2 elementary switches in each stage. Extensions proposed in the literature include Banyans with $k \times k$ basic switches or nodes ($k \geq 2$) extending the usual 2×2 switch structures, as well as dilated Banyans, those in which each link is replaced by d parallel links ($d > 1$). It can be shown that Banyans with larger nodes ($k > 2$) outperform Banyans with smaller nodes, while Banyans with multiple links result in reduced blocking [SZYM 1989]. Replicated or parallel Banyans also improve the throughput, as noted in the previous section in discussing the Sunshine switch architecture. The choice of which Banyan architecture to use depends, as noted in passing in the previous section, on VLSI cost implementation, as well as pin count and other hardware limitations [ZEGU 1993], [SHAI 1990a], [COPP 1992], [SZYM 1989].

The Banyan network to be analyzed in this section is an internally buffered one, based on 2×2 switches or nodes, with a single buffer at each of the two switch inputs to help resolve potential collisions. We show in passing how the analysis may be extended to include $k \times k$ basic switches. We also note, later, the effect of using a single buffer at each of the elementary switch outputs, rather than at the inputs. We follow, in simplified form, the approach used in [SZYM 1989]. That paper extends the analysis to include arbitrary buffer sizes, dilated switches, and switch speedup. We adopt the Bernoulli input traffic model used throughout this chapter and use the uniform traffic model incorporated in our earlier analysis as well. Extension of this analysis to multiple classes of traffic appears in [SHAI 1989] and [SHAI 1990b].

Recall that, with the traffic model adopted here, there is a probability p each cell time that a cell appears at each of the N inputs to the Banyan network. Each cell is equally likely to be directed to each of the N output lines. Even with this simple traffic model the analysis rapidly becomes complex, since it involves the solution of an exponentially growing Markov chain as N increases. Instead we resort to an approximate analysis, based on earlier work by Jenq [JENQ 1983]. This makes use of an "independence" assumption: We assume the statistics of all buffers within the Banyan network are independent of one another. This is clearly not the case, since, as noted in describing the Banyan switch operation in the previous section, each elementary switch signals to the ones connected to it in the stage before, whether it will be able to accept a cell or not. This process begins with the switches in the last stage and propagates upstream to the first stage, input switches, once every

[SHAI 1989]   Shaikh, S. Z., et al., "Performance Analysis and Design of Banyan Network-Based Broadband Packet Switches for Integrated Traffic," *IEEE Globecom 89,* Dallas, TX, Nov. 1989.

[SHAI 1990b]   Shaikh, S. Z., et al., "Analysis, Control and Design of Crossbar and Banyan-Based Broadband Packet Switches for Integrated Traffic," *Proc. IEEE ICC 90,* Atlanta, GA, April 1990.

[JENQ 1983]   Jenq, Y. C., "Performance Analysis of a Packet Switch Based on a Single-Buffered Banyan Network," *IEEE JSAC, SAC-1,* 6 (Dec. 1983): 1014–1021.

cell time. There is thus dependence between all switches in the network. We do capture with this model however, the movement of cells, or lack thereof, between adjacent network stages, depending on the state of the adjacent downstream buffers.

Specifically, consider a typical 2×2 elementary switch at stage s, $1 \le s \le n$, $n = \log_2 N$. Each of its two inputs has a buffer capable of holding one cell, each input in turn connected to a 2×2 switch at stage $s-1$. (Stage $s = n + 1$ then represents the output of the Banyan switch.) Since traffic is assumed homogeneous and uniformly destined to each output in this model, the actual interconnection diagram between stages plays no role in the analysis. Any set of switches at stages s and $s-1$ will have the same statistical characteristics. This typical set of switches appears diagrammed in Figure 5–31.

At each cell time interval, called a "cycle", the decision is made as to whether or not a cell buffered in stage $s-1$ can move to a buffer in stage s. This is based on the information it receives from stage s during the first half of that cycle, as described in the previous section. We take the cycle time (cell interval) to be one unit long. Time t then corresponds to the cycle $(t, t + 1)$. (We are thus implicitly assuming no cycle speedup, which would approach the output queueing case.) More specifically, with the homogeneous and uniform traffic model assumed, it is clear that a cell buffered at stage $s-1$ is equally-likely to want to move to either one of the two possible switches to which it is

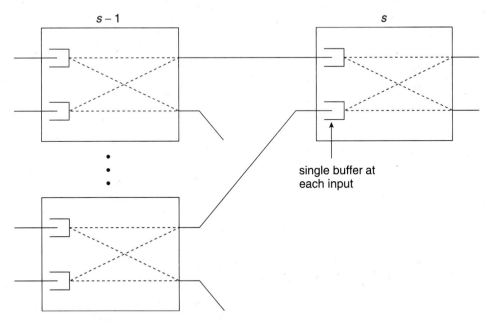

FIGURE 5–31 ■ Model for analysis of Banyan network, stage s, $1 \le s \le \log_2 N$.

connected in stage s. It will move if the buffer in stage s to which it is directed is empty *or* will become empty (that is, the cell in that buffer will move forward to stage $s + 1$) during the cycle.

To set up the equations describing the operation of the two-stage subsystem of Figure 5–31 we make the following definitions:

$u_{s,t}$ ≡ Prob. (stage s buffer is *not* empty at time t)

$r_{s,t}$ ≡ Prob. (cell is offered to stage s buffer, time t)

$m_{s,t}$ ≡ Prob. (cell in stage s buffer will move forward during cycle t, given buffer is not empty)

$\text{block}_{s,t} = 1 - m_{s,t}$ ≡ Prob. (cell in stage s buffer is not able to move forward during t, given buffer is not empty)

$e_{s,t}$ ≡ Prob. (stage s buffer is initially empty or will empty during cycle t; that is, will be able to receive a cell during t).

Then it is left for the reader to show that the following equations describe the dynamics of the Banyan switching network given the independence and homogeneous assumptions made, using Figure 5–31 as the specific model connecting switches at stage $(s - 1)$ to a typical switch at stage s:

$$r_{s,t} = 1 - [1 - u_{s-1,t}/2]^2 \qquad 2 \leq s \leq n + 1 \qquad (5\text{–}71)$$

(Note again that $n + 1$ refers to *departure* from the switch.)

$$m_{s,t}\, u_{s,t} = r_{s+1,t}\, e_{s+1,t} \qquad 1 \leq s \leq n \qquad (5\text{–}72)$$

(As a hint, note that the left-hand side of this equation is the probability a cell will move forward during cycle t. The right-hand side represents the probability the buffer at the next stage will receive a cell during cycle t. By flow continuity, the two must be equal.)

$$e_{s,t} = (1 - u_{s,t}) + u_{s,t} m_{s,t} \qquad 1 \leq s \leq n \qquad (5\text{–}73)$$

(Recall from the definition of $e_{s,t}$ that it is the probability the buffer is initially empty, $1 - u_{s,t}$, or empties during t.)

$$u_{s,t+1} = (1 - e_{s,t}) + e_{s,t} r_{s,t}$$
$$= 1 - e_{s,t}(1 - r_{s,t}) \qquad 1 \leq s \leq n \qquad (5\text{–}74)$$

As boundary conditions we also have

$$r_{1,t} = p \leq 1 \qquad (5\text{–}75)$$

because of the Bernoulli traffic assumption, and

$$e_{n+1,\,t} = 1 \qquad (5\text{–}76)$$

with cells certain to be removed from the switch at its output.

Equation (5–71) may be readily extended to the $k \times k$ node case, with the elementary switch at stage s incorporating k inputs and outputs. For this case, again assuming traffic equally-likely to be destined to any output port, equation (5–71) may be rewritten as

$$r_{s,t} = 1 - [1 - u_{s-1,t}/k]^k \qquad 2 \le s \le n+1 \qquad (5\text{–}71a)$$

The other equations remain the same. In the material following, we focus on the $k = 2$, 2×2 switch, case, however.

Now consider the steady-state case, with $t \to \infty$. All the equations must converge to an equivalent set appropriate to *any* cycle. These are simply the same set of equations with the parameter t suppressed. In particular, the steady-state throughput γ, in cell/cycle per link, must be given by

$$\gamma = u_s\, m_s \qquad (5\text{–}77)$$

and this must be the same constant value at each stage in the network. The total throughput of the Banyan network is then $N\gamma$ cells/cycle. Clearly we must have $\gamma \le p$. (Why is this so?)

Equations (5–71) to (5–74) may now be solved either one of two ways. We may retain the time dependence, initialize the system of equations at time $t = 0$, and then proceed to iterate with time, approaching the steady-state solution for large t. Alternately, we show below that the steady-state equations may by themselves be solved quite readily. We show first how the time-varying approach is handled, then focus on the steady-state case directly.

Consider the time-varying equations (5–71) to (5–74). They may be solved iteratively in both time and by stage. Specifically, initialize the system at $t = 0$ with all buffers empty. Then $u_{s,o} = 0$, $1 \le s \le n$. From equation (5–71), then, $r_{s,o} = 0$, all $s \ge 2$. From equation (5–73), $e_{s,o} = 1$, $1 \le s \le n$.

Now using equation (5–74), it is easy to show that at time $t = 1$, increasing the time by one cell unit interval (one cycle), $u_{1,1} = r_{1,0} = p$, while $u_{s,1} = r_{s,0} = 0$, $s \ge 2$. From equation (5–71), $r_{2,1} = p - p^2/4$, while $r_{s,1} = 0$, $s > 2$. Parameters $m_{s,1}$ and $e_{s,1}$ can then be found as well. The procedure is repeated for successive time intervals $t = 2, 3$, etc., until steady state (no noticeable changes in the parameters) is reached.

For the steady-state case, $t \to \infty$, the iterative procedure can be carried out more expeditiously. It is left for the reader to show that the steady-state equivalents to equations (5–71) to (5–76) plus the throughput equation (5–77) may be rewritten as the one equation

$$u_s = 1 + \gamma - \frac{\gamma}{u_{s-1}\left(1 - \dfrac{u_{s-1}}{4}\right)} \qquad 2 \le s \le n \qquad (5\text{–}78)$$

with

$$u_n = 2\left(1 - \sqrt{1-\gamma}\right) \qquad (5\text{–}79)$$

In addition, from the definitions of u_s and r_s, we must have

$$u_1 = r_1 = p \qquad (5\text{--}80)$$

The procedure to be followed to solve for the desired steady-state parameters is now fairly apparent:

1. Choose some throughput value $\gamma < 1$.
2. From equation (5–79) find u_n, and then from equation (5–78), find u_{n-1}. Keep iterating equation (5–78) for decreasing values of s until $u_1 = p$ is reached, or until at any iteration u_s falls outside the range $0 \le u_s \le 1$. In this case stop, go back to step 1, reduce γ and repeat the procedure. One thus finds the value of input load p to obtain a given throughput γ. Repeating this, one gets a set of values of the throughput γ vs. p.

The iterative process can be simplified somewhat by solving equation (5–78) directly for u_{s-1} in terms of u_s:

$$u_{s-1} = 2\left[1 - \sqrt{\frac{1-u_s}{\gamma + 1 - u_s}}\right] \qquad 2 \le s \le n \qquad (5\text{--}81)$$

The iterative analysis just described, whether iterating in time and space, or stage by stage, assuming steady-state conditions have set in, provides an approximation to the Banyan network throughput performance. The same analysis also leads to the approximate time-delay performance as well. This is done by first calculating the average delay at stage s, and then summing the delay over all $n = \log_2 N$ stages. This delay will be given in units of cycles or cell-time intervals, since we have been taking the cycle time to be unity for simplicity.

It turns out that the average delay at stage s is just $1/m_s$, m_s the probability a cell in the stage-s buffer will move forward. To demonstrate this, note that the probability a cell will not move forward is $(1 - m_s)$. The probability a cell requires two cycles to move forward must then be $(1 - m_s)m_s$. The probability that three cycles are required at stage s is $(1 - m_s)^2 m_s$, and the probability that k cycles are required is $(1 - m_s)^{k-1} m_s$. (This, thus, gives rise to a geometric distribution). The average delay T_s at stage s, in units of cycles (cell times if there is no network speedup), is then simply

$$T_s = \sum_{k=1}^{\infty} k m_s (1 - m_s)^{k-1} = 1/m_s \qquad (5\text{--}82)$$

as noted above. (This assumes that a cell may take as many cycles as needed to move ahead. In practice, of course, provision must be made to terminate the number of cycles.) The average delay through the n-stage switching network, $n = \log_2 N$, is then

$$\overline{T} = \sum_{s=1}^{n} 1/m_s \qquad (5\text{--}83)$$

To calculate m_s, the probability a cell at stage will move forward in a cycle, and from this T_s, the average time a cell will remain at stage s, one uses equation (5–77). Given the throughput γ and u_s, the probability a stage s buffer is *not* empty during a cycle, both corresponding to a given load parameter p using the iterative process described earlier, one calculates m_s, the average stage-s delay $1/m_s$ and then, summing over all $n = \log_2 N$ stages, the average network delay $\overline{T}$. (Note again that all delays are in units of cycle time. With no speedup, as stated above, this unit of time is just the cell interval.)

Figures 5–32 to 5–35 show the results of the analysis (the dotted curves) using the steady-state equations discussed above. These have been taken from [SZYM 1989], Figure 4. Superimposed are sets of simulation curves, taken from the same paper. The curves include not only single-buffer curves, corresponding to the analysis just described, but curves for larger input buffer sizes at each stage as well. These are designated by the parameter qs. Figure 5–32 shows a plot of throughput γ as a function of the number of stages

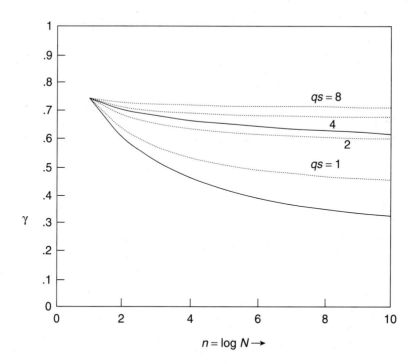

FIGURE 5–32 ■ Throughput, full-load, n-stage Banyan. qs = input queue size. Analysis (dotted curves) and simulation (solid curves) (from [SZYM 1989], Figure 4(a). © 1989 IEEE).

$n = \log_2 N$ for full input load, $p = 1$. Note that the throughput starts at a maximum value of 0.75 for a single 2×2 stage, as expected from our earlier discussion, and as is apparent from the basic equation (5–71). It then decreases as the Banyan size increases, indicating the chance of greater internal blocking as the network gets larger. In particular, analysis indicates that the throughput is leveling off at a value of 0.45 cell/cycle per output link. Simulation indicates that the performance is substantially poorer, however, being equal to $\gamma = 0.32$ cell/cycle per output link for a 10-stage, $N = 1024$, Banyan. For relatively large Banyans, then, the approximate analysis provides optimistic maximum throughput results.

Larger input buffers will reduce cell loss and improve the throughput characteristic. This is shown in Figure 5–32 for buffer sizes of $qs = 2$, 4, and 8. Just doubling the input queue size results in a substantial improvement in throughput. The equations required to obtain the analytical performance results for larger input buffers are extensions of the equations described in this section and appear in the work by [SZYM 1989].

Time-delay calculations turn out to be more accurate using the approximate analysis described in this section, as indicated by the curves of Figure 5–33 for the case of full load ($p = 1$). The curves shown there are normalized delay curves, representing average delay per stage, or $\overline{T}/n$, again in units of

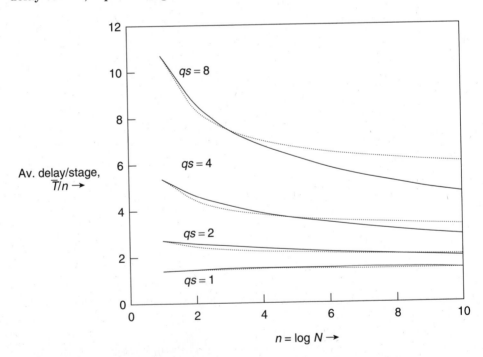

FIGURE 5–33 ■ Average delay, full load n-stage Banyan. $qs =$ input queue size. Analysis (dotted curves) and simulation (solid curves) (from [SZYM 1989], Figure 4(b). © 1989 IEEE).

cycle, or cell time. In particular, note that the single buffer result, $qs = 1$, using the analysis of this section, shows an average delay of somewhat more than one cycle time for a single 2×2 Banyan, increasing to somewhat under $2n$ in cycle times for an $n = 10$-stage ($N = 1024$) Banyan. The curves for $qs = 2,4,8$ input buffers at each stage have also been calculated using an extension of the analysis of this section [SZYM 1989]. These curves demonstrate the usual tradeoff: One can increase throughput by increasing input buffer size, as shown in Figure 5–32, but the delay goes up correspondingly. This is, of course, as to be expected.

Figures 5–34 and 5–35 show how throughput and delay, respectively, vary with the load parameter p, for a 6-stage, $N = 64$, Banyan network. Note that the analytical curves are fairly accurate, compared with simulation, for a load up to $p = 0.5$ for one input buffer ($qs = 1$). One wouldn't expect to run these switches at maximum load. The approximate analysis is therefore useful in evaluating the performance of these multistage networks. The average delay curves show a relatively small increase with load up to a load factor of 0.5, and then increasingly larger values of delay, leveling off at a substantially larger delay value for a maximum load of $p = 1$. This is consistent with typical queueing analysis with finite buffers.

Analysis of the equivalent output buffer case for an n-stage Banyan has been carried out by Szymanski and Shaikh [SZYM 1989]. The results indicate

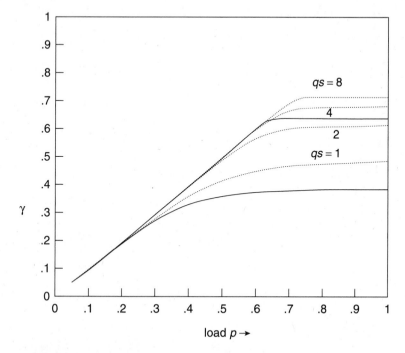

FIGURE 5–34 ■ Throughput-load curve, 6-stage Banyan, input buffers (from [SZYM 1989], Figure 4(c). © 1989 IEEE).

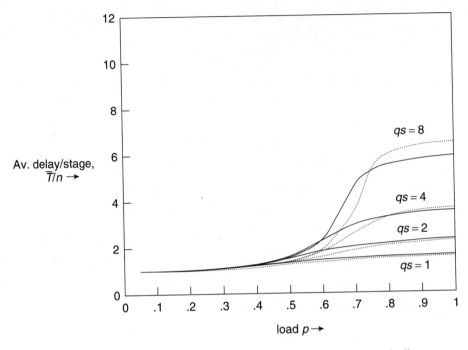

FIGURE 5–35 ■ Average delay-load curve, 6-stage Banyan, input buffers (from [SZYM 1989], Figure 4(d). © 1989 IEEE).

that there is some improvement in network performance over the input buffer case, because of a reduction of HOL blocking at each individual switch within the network. These authors have extended their analysis as well to dilated, multiple link, switches within a Banyan.

■ PROBLEMS

5–1 This problem is a tutorial on moment-generating functions.
  a. Refer to equation (5–8), the definition of the mgf. Check equations (5–9) to (5–12). Then calculate the mgf and, from this, the expected values and variances for the four probability distributions shown following equation (5–12).
  b. Prove the following additional properties of the mgf:

$$\sum_{n=1}^{\infty} p(n-1)z^n = zG_n(z)$$

$$\sum_{n=0}^{\infty} p(n+1)z^n = \left[G_n(z) - p(0)\right]/z$$

(These relations are used to solve difference equations as will be seen in the next problem).

5–2 Consider an infinite $M/M/1$ queue with average arrival rate λ and service time μ. The steady-state balance equation is readily shown to be given by

$$(\lambda + \mu)p(n) = \lambda p(n - 1) + \mu p(n + 1) \qquad n \geq 1$$

$$\lambda p(0) = \mu p(1)$$

(See equations (A–8) and (A–9) in the Appendix.)
One can solve for $p(n)$, the probability that there are n packets (customers) in the queue using the mgf as follows. (In this case it is much easier to solve for $p(n)$ directly. This is just a drill, but in other cases the mgf method is the preferred approach.)

Multiply each of the terms in the balance equation by z^n and sum over all values of n from 1 to ∞. Show, using problem **5–1b.** that one then obtains the following algebraic equation for $G_n(z)$:

$$(\lambda + \mu)[G_n(z) - p(0)] = \lambda z G_n(z) + \mu\{z^{-1}[G_n(z) - p(0)] - p(1)\}$$

Solve for $G_n(z)$, using the balance equation above relating $p(1)$ to $p(0)$ to eliminate $p(1)$. Show the solution is given by

$$G_n(z) = p(0)/(1 - \rho z) \qquad \rho \equiv \lambda/\mu$$

(A factor $z - 1$ common to left and right-hand sides has been cancelled in getting this result. This factor appears commonly in problems involving the application of mgfs to queueing systems.)

To find the remaining constant $p(0)$, one uses the relation $G_n(1) = 1$. (Why this relation?) Then $p(0) = 1 - \rho$. Show then that $E(n) = \rho/(1 - \rho)$. Expand $G_n(z)$ in an infinite series in z, assuming $\rho z < 1$. Show the coefficient in front of z^n is $(1 - \rho)\rho^n$. From the definition of $G_n(z)$ this must be $p(n)$. Are these results those you would expect for the $M/M/1$ queue?

5–3 Refer to the material in section 5.3 on the evolution of the buffer contents n_k of the ATM multiplexer. The equation governing n_k is given by equation (5–6). In the steady-state, time interval $k \to \infty$, one obtains equation (5–15) as the equation for the mgf of the buffer contents (state) n. Show, following the material in the text, that $G_n(z)$ is given, first, by equation (5–18), and then, finally, by equation (5–18a). Fill in all the missing material in the analysis.

5–4 a. Using equation (5–18a), the equation for the mgf of the buffer contents of the ATM multiplexer, find the mgf for the following arrival processes: Bernoulli, binomial, and Poisson. You should obtain equations (5–20) to (5–22).

b. Focus on the Poisson arrival case. Why is $G_n(z)$ in this case the mgf of the $M/D/1$ queue? Find $p(n)$ for a few values of n, including

$n = 0,1$, and 2, verifying equations (5–25) and (5–26). Calculate $E(n)$, and show equation (5–27) results.

5–5 a. Consider q_k, the number of cells waiting for service at time k in the ATM multiplexer. This is given by equation (5–28). Show the equation of evolution is given by equation (5–35). Can you write this alternately in terms of the r^+ function defined by equation (5–7)?

    b. Show that in the steady state the mgf of q is given by equation (5–32).

    c. As an example, consider a binomal arrival process with parameter p/N. (This turns out to be the arrival process for output queueing.) Then

$$G_\alpha(z) = \left(1 - \frac{p}{N} + \frac{zp}{N}\right)^N$$

Show

$$E(q) = \frac{N-1}{N} \frac{p^2}{2(1-p)}$$

    d. Repeat **c.** for a Poisson arrival process with parameter p. Show

$$E(q) = \frac{p^2}{2(1-p)}$$

Then $E(q)_{\text{binomial}} = (N-1)/N \; E(q)_{\text{poisson}}$. Show that this agrees with the result obtained for the binomial arrival process in the limit of $N \to \infty$.

5–6 Refer to the discussion in section 5.4 on output queueing. Show that the equation governing the evolution in time of the number of cells at an output queue is given by equation (5–37). Assuming a uniform Bernoulli model with parameter p as the arrival statistic at each input link to the $N \times N$ switch, show that the average queue occupancy is given by equation (5–41). [This implies justifying and using equations (5–38) to (5–41).] Note how this derivation is very similar to the analysis of the number of cells in queue in the statistical multiplexor of problem **5–5** above.

5–7 This problem relates to input queueing in $N \times N$ ATM switches. Consider first a 2×2 switch such as shown in Figure 5–6. A cell arriving at either input is equally-likely to be destined for output ports 1 or 2. In each time slot (cell interval) there is a probability p a cell arrives at each input. Show the *maximum* throughput on each output port is 0.75 cell per cell interval. Now consider a very large switch, with $N \to \infty$.

Filling in the details of the analysis in section 5.4, show the maximum throughput per output port is 0.586 cell per cell interval.

5–8 Provide justification for equation (5–44), the equation governing the number of cells at the heads of input queues destined for output port i that are not selected for transmission in time slot m. (Show equation (5–44) is the equation governing the evolution of B_m^i.)

5–9 Refer to the discussion in section 5.4 on the Knockout switch, a proposed ATM switch architecture that incorporates output queueing. Show the knockout loss probability for large N is given by equation (5–54). Show this may be rewritten as equation (5–54a). Plot P_L vs. p for $p = 0.6$, 0.9, and 1, and discuss the resultant curves. For what values of L will the loss probability be $<10^{-6}$ with $p = 0.9$? Repeat for $P_L = 10^{-9}$, $p = 0.9$.

5–10 Refer to the three-stage space switch of Figure 5–17. Demonstrate that, in the worst case, with $n - 1$ input ports at an input (stage 1) switch and $n - 1$ output ports at an output (stage 3) switch occupied, a connection can still be made from the remaining input port at the input switch to the remaining port at the output switch if $k \geq 2n - 1$. (This is the Clos worst-case nonblocking condition.) Show the minimum number of crosspoints is given by equation (5–60), with the corresponding value of n given by equation (5–59). Choose some values of overall switch size (number of input/output ports) N, and compare the crosspoint complexity of the optimum three-stage switch with the corresponding crossbar.

5–11 a. Refer to the discussion of Benes 2×2 space-switching networks in section 5.5. This class of rearrangeable, nonblocking switches is obtained by recursive decomposition starting with an $N \times N$ single-stage switch. Start with Figure 5–20, and carry the decomposition out recursively, as shown there, for $N = 8$, and show Figure 5–21 results. Repeat for $N = 16$ and sketch the resultant switch. How many stages of 2×2 switches are there in this case? How many 2×2 switches are there? Show that for any N there are $2 \log_2 N - 1$ stages, with $N/2$ 2×2 switches in each stage. The total number of 2×2 switches is then given by equation (5–65).

b. Show the minimum number of 2×2 switches required to realize an $N \times N$ configuration is given by equation (5–64). Compare with the number of such switches in the Benes class of part **a.** above for a number of values of N. Verify the statement made in the text that the Benes number approaches the minimum number possible for large N.

5–12 a. Construct an $N = 16$ Banyan (see [TOBA 1989], Figure 39, for a reference). Using several output links, demonstrate, by example, the self-routing property of this switch; that is, show cells at different inputs all arrive at the proper destination.

b. Show, by example, that the Omega and Baseline networks of Figure 5–23 have the self-routing property.

c. Show, by example, that cell conflicts may arise within each of the switching networks of Figures 5–22 and 5–23.

5–13 a. Refer to the bitonic sorter plus Banyan example of Figures 5–25 and 5–26. Demonstrate that cells with *different* destination addresses experience no conflict in moving to their respective destinations.

b. Provide an example of cells with different destinations appearing at the same time at each of the input ports of the bitonic sorter of Figure 5–25. Trace them through to the outputs of the Banyan switch following and show they all arrive at the proper outputs (destinations) with no conflicts arising.

c. Repeat **b.** with two or more cells from different inputs addressed to the same destination.

5–14 Show the number of 2×2 switches in the Batcher-Banyan combination is given by equation (5–68). Compare this number, for various values of N, with the number required for a single crossbar as well as the minimum number of 2×2 switches (see equation (5–64) or problem **5–11** above). Check your results with those of Table 5–1.

5–15 Refer to Figure 5–31, the model for two typical stages in a Banyan network used for an approximate performance analysis of the network. Definitions of terms used in the approximate analysis appear in section 5.6, just above equation (5–71).

a. Show equations (5–71) through (5–76) describe the dynamics of the Banyan, under the assumptions made.

b. Take the steady-state case, $t \to \infty$. Show the equations of operation may be written as the one equation (5–78), with (5–79) and (5–80) used as auxiliary conditions.

c. Show equation (5–78) can alternately be written as equation (5–81).

d. Why is $u_s m_s$ a constant at steady state, and why must it represent the throughput γ? Why is $\gamma \leq p$?

5–16 a. Consider a three-stage Banyan network ($n = 3$). What is N in this case? Carry out the approximate analysis using the results of problem **5–15** above to find the throughput γ vs. load p curve for this case.

b. Calculate the overall delay for this switch, in units of cell times. *Hint:* Use equations (5–82) and (5–83), first finding the parameter m_s in terms of γ as indicated in the text.

c. Compare the throughput and delay curves of **a.** and **b.** above with the results shown in Figures 5–32 and 5–33.

Chapter 6

End-to-End Traffic Bounds
and Effective Capacity

Previous chapters have focused on broadband network queueing and statistical multiplexing at a single node, usually the UNI, in a network. The admission control strategies and policing mechanisms we have discussed have all involved control at one node or switch in a network as well. Yet it is apparent that establishing and maintaining appropriate QoS performance for any multimedia connection must involve the traffic characteristics along a complete path, end-to-end, in an ATM network. (Recall that virtual paths, VPs, with VCs embedded in them, are defined from one end of an ATM connection to the other.) End-to-end traffic analysis has always been complex and difficult to carry out. In the case of circuit-switched telephone networks and packet-switched data networks, recourse has usually been made to independence assumptions, with analysis at individual nodes made independently and combined to form end-to-end QoS measures such as blocking probability or delay, as the case may be [SCHW 1987].

In the case of B-ISDN, with multiple traffic types and multiple performance QoS measures such as probability of cell loss, delay, and delay jitter, among others, it is not clear that performance at one node can be used to estimate performance along a complete path, end-to-end. Hence investigators have been developing techniques for studying end-to-end network performance. We focus in this chapter on work done to develop end-to-end delay bounds. We also reference some work on approximation techniques for studying end-to-end performance in an ATM fixed-cell size environment based on, and extending, the video histogram model described briefly in section 3.7.

Both worst-case deterministic and stochastic bounds have been developed for end-to-end network performance. We stress deterministic bounds here because of their relative simplicity. Interestingly, however, we shall see later on that the work on stochastic bounds leads directly to a measure of the "effective" or "equivalent" capacity of a traffic stream, generalizing our earlier discussion of this concept in section 4.1.

6.1 ■ DETERMINISTIC BOUNDS

Much work has been done on developing determnistic end-to-end delay bounds. Much work is still yet to be done, since the bounds we shall discuss are found, using simulation, to be quite loose. We discuss only a few of the more recent contributions in this area.

We begin with a discussion of the work by S. J. Golestani [GOLE 1990] of Bellcore. He has proposed a technique called *stop-and-go queueing* for processing cells (packets) at a given node along a path from source to destination that guarantees bounded delay, end-to-end, with zero cell loss. There are two problems as we shall see, with this technique: 1) The delay can be quite sizable; 2) The technique is not work conserving, that is, cells may not be served even though an output link is idle. Link capacity can thus be wasted. A different technique proposed by A. Parekh and R. Gallager, that we shall describe later, is work conserving, is thus more efficient (can provide higher throughput), and results in a lower, although still quite loose, bounded delay. Stop-and-go-queueing was originally described for a single class (type) of packet, but with multiple end-to-end connections within a network [GOLE 1990], [GOLE 1991a]. It was then extended to the case of multiple described for a single class (type) of packet, but with multiple end-to-end connections packet classes [GOLE 1991b]. We focus on the single packet class case only, for simplicity.

The basic idea of stop-and-go queueing is as follows: Packets are transmitted over a link within fixed-length frames T sec-long, contiguous to, and following one another. These frames have the same length T throughput the network. (In the multiclass extension, a given class k, $1 \leq k \leq K$, has its own frame length T_k.) A frame must be long enough to accommodate at least one packet. An example appears in Figure 6–1.

Consider a node n in a network with outgoing link l to the next node, along a path in the network. Feeding this node are links from previous nodes in the network. An example appears in Figure 6–2, with two links labeled l' and l'' connecting previous nodes to n. A typical T-sec. outgoing frame on link

[GOLE 1990]   Golestani, S. J., "Congestion-Free Transmission of Real-Time Traffic in Packet Networks," *Proc. IEEE Infocom 90*, San Francisco, June 1990.

[GOLE 1991a]   Golestani, S. J., "Congestion-Free Communication in High-Speed Packet Networks," *IEEE Trans. on Commun.*, *39*, 12 (Dec. 1991): 1802–1812.

[GOLE 1991b]   Golestani, S. J., "A Framing Strategy for Congestion Management," *IEEE JSAC*, *9*, 7 (Sept. 1991): 1064–1077.

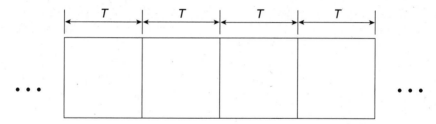

FIGURE 6–1 ▪ Stop-and-go frames along a link.

l is labeled F; typical frames on incoming links l' and l'' are labeled F' and F'', respectively. Say link l has capacity C_l bps. Consider an end-to-end connection k that uses this link. It requires a packet transmission rate r_k bps, end-to-end. Then, summing over all connections using link l, we must have

$$\Sigma r_k \leq C_l$$

With frame length T chosen, the maximum number of connection-k bits that can be included in a frame is $r_k T$ bits. For ATM connections, with all packets ATM cells 424 bits (53 octets) long, the maximum number of admissible cells within a frame for connection k is $r_k T/424$. As an example, let $T = 5$ msec, and $r_k = 1$ Mbps. Then the maximum number of connection-k cells occupying a frame is $\lfloor 5000/424 \rfloor = 11$ cells. As r_k increases, with T fixed, the number of cells in a frame clearly increases. The choice of T will be considered later. (But note now that the delay bound will be shown to be proportional to T. Hence it is desirable to keep T as small as possible, with a minimum value large enough to accommodate at least one cell of a connection.)

We now describe stop-and-go-queueing using Figure 6–2 as an example. The three sets of frames F, F', F'', in Figure 6–2 bear no specific time relation

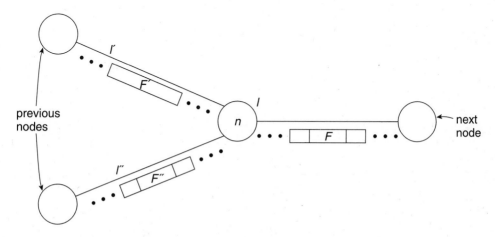

FIGURE 6–2 ▪ Example of stop-and-go queueing.

to one another except that all frames are T sec long. Each of the two incoming frames F' and F'' of Figure 6–2 is thus generally offset by some time $< T$ with respect to frame F. This is shown in Figure 6–3.

Stop-and-go queueing rules may then be stated as follows:

1. Packets (cells) in incoming frames F' and F'' are stored (queued) at node n, and cannot be transmitted (served) until the beginning of the outgoing frame F following completion of frames F' and F'' respectively. Such packets are called *eligible* packets.
2. A link should not stay idle while there is any eligible packet in the queue.

Note in the example of Figures 6–2 and 6–3 that packet P_1 in frame F' can be served in frame F since its frame ends before F begins. Packet P_2 in the frame following F'' cannot be served in F since its frame ends during transmission of F. Note however, that packet P_2 arrives at node n and is queued there before packet P_1 arrives, yet is served after packet P_1. FIFO order over a given link is, thus, not necessarily maintained. Over any given path, end-to-end, FIFO order is, however, maintained; that is, packets from a particular connection following the same path, are served in order of arrival. Note also that this scheme is not work conserving, despite rule 2, since a packet must wait until it becomes eligible even if a current frame is not occupied. Thus, in Figure 6–3, if frames F' and F'' were both empty (P_1 not present), outgoing frame F would remain empty despite P_2 having arrived before the beginning of F, since it does not become eligible until the end of F.

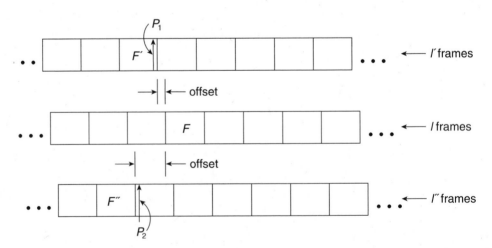

FIGURE 6–3 ■ Frames of Figure 6–2.

There are three results of these rules:

1. Once a packet is marked eligible, it is guaranteed to receive service within T sec; that is, the maximum offset is T sec.

2. There will be no bunching of packets within a connection; that is, they maintain their original smoothness property, despite the merging of multiple connections. (Note that the same number of packets per connection is served at each node.)

3. At most 3 $C_l T$ bits of buffer space is needed to have zero buffer overflow. (This is left for the reader to show.) Hence, another attribute of stop-and-go queueing, in addition to bounded delay, is a guarantee of no cell loss end-to-end, providing each buffer at each node is sized appropriately.

Given this brief summary of stop-and-go queueing, one can now determine its end-to-end delay performance over a given network path, leading to the delay bounds mentioned earlier. Consider a particular connection k which covers m links (hops) end-to-end over the network. This connection is portrayed schematically in Figure 6–4. Assume the propagation plus processing delay over link l on that end-to-end path is a fixed value τ_l. Frames for connection k arriving at node l are labeled F_{l-1}^a. Those departing node l, over link l, are labeled F_l^d. (Access frames are labeled F_0^a, as shown in Figure 6–4.)

Because of stop-and-go queueing, the maximum time between arrival of a typical frame F_{l-1}^a at node l and departure of frame F_l^d is

$$T + \theta_{l-1,l}^k$$

with $0 \leq \theta_{l-1,l}^k \leq T$ the offset between frames shown in Figure 6–3.

The total offset θ^k, end-to-end along the m-hop path, is thus

$$0 \leq \theta^k = \sum_{l=1}^{m} \theta_{l-1,l}^k \leq mT$$

The total fixed delay τ^k, for connection k, due to propagation delay and nodal processing, is $\tau^k = \sum_{l=1}^{m} \tau_l$. (Note that the hop count m depends on the particu-

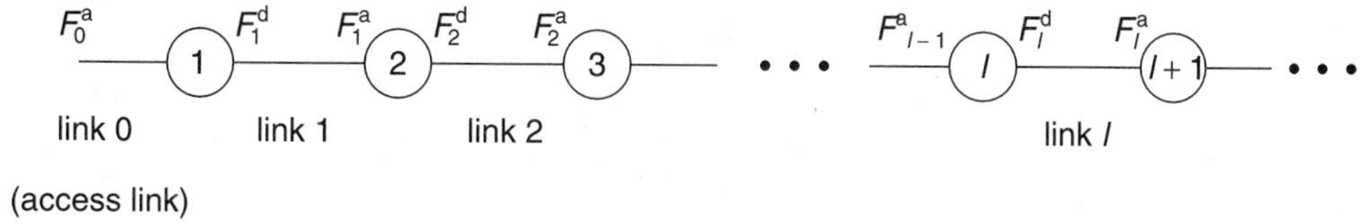

FIGURE 6–4 ■ Typical path for a given connection.

lar path or route selected.) The total delay end-to-end, for any packet, given by adding up the delay terms noted above, is thus

$$D_p = \tau^k + mT + \theta^k + d_p \qquad (6\text{--}1)$$

The term d_p has been added to account for delay jitter, the displacement of the packet in time, due to the difference in time between the initial frame F_0^a arriving at the access link and the final frame F_m^a arriving at the destination node. This added delay term is bounded by plus or minus the frame length T:

$$-T < d_p < T$$

This term depends on the particular packet arrival time. All the other delay terms are independent of particular packets.

Note, from equation (6–1), that the use of stop-and-go queueing has introduced an effective queueing delay, because of the frame structure, given by the term $mT + \theta^k$. Calling this term Q^k, it is clear that it is bounded as follows:

$$mT \leq Q^k \leq 2mT \qquad (6\text{--}2)$$

Hence the total delay, end-to-end, is bounded as well by

$$(m-1)\,T + \tau^k \leq D_p \leq (2m+1)\,T + \tau^k \qquad (6\text{--}3)$$

There is thus a guranteed upper bound on time delay at packets, end-to-end, using stop-and-go queueing; but it could potentially be quite sizable, depending on the frame length T and path length m. The effective queueing delay Q^k introduced by stop-and-go queueing is the price paid for the guaranteed maximum delay the scheme potentially offers.

Since the delay bound depends on the frame size T, one would like to keep T as small as possible. But recall from our discussion earlier that T must be large enough to allow at least one connection-k packet to be transmitted. The minimum value of T, and hence minimum guaranteed bound on end-to-end delay, can pose a problem, however, for real-time traffic, as indicated by an example.

Say ATM voice cells are to be transmitted using stop-and-go queueing. For 64-kbps voice calls, the minimum size of T required to accommodate one ATM voice cell is readily found to be 6.6 msec. This is a sizable length frame, since voice can then be delayed up to 13.2 msec per link. In particular, let the end-to-end path be 3000 km, with propagation delay given by 5 μsec/km. Neglecting processing delay, $\tau^k = 15$ msec. But real-time voice has some stringent requirements on end-to-end delay. If, for example, we require $D_p \leq 50$ msec as a typical maximum delay, the path can accommodate $m = 2$ or 3 hops at most. (If the allowable delay bound is increased to 100 msec, the number of hops allowed is of course doubled.) But this calculation is for the case of one ATM voice per frame. One would like to allow a large number of cells to be transmitted per frame. This requires a corresponding increase in frame size T, exacerbating the problem.

Now consider a nonreal-time traffic application such as file or image transfer. Say it is desired to transmit files at a 1 Mbps rate. Again assuming the files are transmitted as ATM cells, the minimum frame size is $T = 0.4$ msec. If T is chosen as 5 msec, ten cells can be accommodated per frame. The end-to-end delay for a 5-hop, 3000-km path, is then bounded by

$$35 \text{ msec} \leq D_p < 70 \text{ msec}$$

These numbers appear quite reasonable for nondelay-critical traffic. As the transmission rate increases to much larger values commensurate with ATM capability, the value of T becomes much smaller, and the stop-and-go queueing delay becomes correspondingly smaller. Propagation delay then becomes the dominant delay factor. The main problem then with the use of stop-and-go queueing is the mix of real-time voice traffic with nonreal-time data traffic that might be desired over ATM networks. For this reason we now discuss other techniques providing tighter and smaller guaranteed delay bounds. (Note, however, as will be discussed briefly later, that some simulation experiments indicate that normal statistical multiplexing may provide much lower delays in practice than a stop-and-go queueing system or other bounded-delay procedures proposed in the literature.)

Another approach to bounding the delay of a traffic stream end-to-end involves the use of a *regulator*, initially controlling the flow of a particular traffic type into a network. The concept here is that, given the regulation of the rate into a network, one should be able to quantify the characteristics of the traffic as the traffic moves through the network. The leaky bucket, discussed at length in section 4.2, is an example of such a regulator.

This approach was introduced by R. L. Cruz who was able to quantify the effect of various network elements on regulated traffic as it moves through a network [CRUZ 1991]. Examples he studied included delay elements, adders, work-conserving elements such as queues or multiplexers, and FIFO queues in particular. Cruz's approach was then adopted by a number of other investigators in proposing various scheduling and traffic service algorithms and finding bounds end-to-end for these. We focus here on the work of Parekh and Gallagher who, using Cruz's concept of regulated traffic and applying it to so-called *generalized processor sharing* of traffic at a node in a network, were able to show that this scheduling technique provides tighter end-to-end delay bounds than the stop-and-go technique just discussed [PARE

[CRUZ 1991]   Cruz, R. L., "A Calculus for Network Delay, Part I: Elements in Isolation," *IEEE Trans. on Info. Theory, 37*, 1 (Jan. 1991): 114–131; "Part II: Network Analysis." Same journal, same issue: 132–141.

[PARE 1993]   Parekh, A. K., and R. G. Gallager, "A Generalized Processor-Sharing Approach to Flow Control in Integrated Services Networks: The Single-Node Case," *IEEE/ACM Trans. on Networking, 1*, 3 (June 1993). Also, same title, "The Multiple-Node Case." *IEEE Infocom 93*, San Francisco (March 1993): 521–530.

1993]. Both techniques have, however, been found, through simulation, to provide relatively loose bounds, as already noted, and as will be discussed later.

Cruz's approach consists of defining a regulated traffic source in the following way: Say the source outputs $A(0,t)$ units of traffic, cells for example, in an interval of time $(0,t)$ that is, from some initial time to time t. Then this source is assumed to be regulated in the sense that

$$A\,(0,t) \le \sigma + \rho t \qquad (6\text{–}4)$$

The parameter σ, called the burstiness parameter, represents the maximum amount (units) of traffic that can arrive in a burst. The parameter ρ is an upper bound on the long-term average rate of flow of the traffic. Thus, over a long interval of time, t large, we have

$$\lim_{t\to\infty}\frac{A(0,t)}{t} \le \rho \qquad (6\text{–}5)$$

But note that the leaky bucket provides exactly this type of regulated traffic at its output. Consider the example of a leaky bucket regulator depicted in Figure 6–5. This is exactly the same representation as presented previously in Figures 4–15 and 4–22 of Chapter 4, except that here we use ρ to represent the token arrival rate, and σ to represent the maximum token pool (buffer) size. Then the output rate λ^* of this regulator is clearly bounded by the token arrival rate ρ, as demonstrated previously in Chapter 4.

In particular, starting at time $t = 0$ with a full token buffer of σ tokens, the maximum traffic delivered by time t is bounded by $\sigma + \rho t$, precisely the assumption of equation (6–4). The leaky bucket thus provides an example of Cruz's regulator.

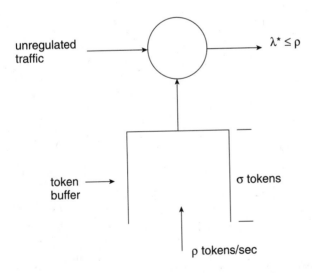

FIGURE 6–5 ▪ Example of a leaky bucket regulator.

a. $A_{in} \sim (\sigma, \rho)$  $A_{out} \sim (\sigma + \rho\bar{D}, \rho)$

b.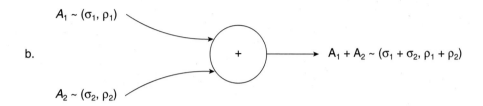

c. $A \sim (\sigma, \rho)$  C

d.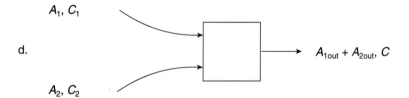

FIGURE 6–6 ▪ Examples of idealized network elements a pure delay element b adder c work-conserving element, output capacity C d work-conserving multiplexer.

Cruz, in his work, uses the term $R(t)$ to represent the instantaneous rate of traffic. The amount of traffic $A(x,y)$ delivered by a regulated traffic source in the interval (x,y) is then written, in bounded form, as

$$A(x, y) \equiv \int_x^y R(t)dt \le \sigma + \rho(y - x) \tag{6–6}$$

He calls such traffic $R\text{~}(\sigma,\rho)$-regulated. We will use the representation $A\text{~}(\sigma,\rho)$ instead, the notation adopted by Parekh and Gallager in their work.

Using equations (6–4) or (6–6), Cruz is able to bound the burstiness, delay, and rate of flow at the output of a variety of idealized network elements. From these results, bounds can be obtained on end-to-end delay. We only discuss some of his individual element bounds here; for the end-to-end bounds we move to the Parekh-Gallager work.

Consider, as the first example, the pure delay element of Figure 6–6a. This element simply takes traffic coming in and delays it for some time, bounded by a given value $\overline{D}$. Then it is left for the reader to show that the effect of the delay is to increase the traffic burstiness by a factor $\rho\overline{D}$. The output traffic is then A_{out}-regulated, with

$$A_{\text{out}} \text{~} (\sigma + \rho\overline{D},\rho) \qquad (6\text{–}7)$$

as indicated in Figure 6–6a.

The second example is a pure adder, with the output traffic simply the sum of input traffic streams. The output burstiness and rate parameters are both the sums of the input burstiness and rate parameters, respectively, as indicated in Figure 6–6b.

Now consider a more interesting example, that of a work-conserving element (a queue for example) delivering traffic to its output at a rate $C > \rho$, whenever traffic is present. (The term "work conserving", mentioned earlier in discussing stop-and-go queueing, means that any traffic ready to be served or transmitted must be served. There can be no holding back, as was possible with stop-and-go queueing.). Then, with $A \text{~} (\sigma, \rho)$-regulated traffic applied at the input, there is a maximum delay $\overline{D}$ the traffic can undergo in moving through the device given by

$$\overline{D} = \sigma/(C - \rho) \qquad (6\text{–}8)$$

The proof of this result is quite simple. Consider a busy period of the element, defined to be any interval between times at which the element (a queue say) is empty. Figure 6–7 provides a typical example, assuming continuous-flow-type traffic for simplicity. Say this interval is τ sec long. (The interval will generally be randomly varying.) Then the total amount of traffic delivered to the output must be τC units. But because of the regulated character of the traffic at the input, the total amount of traffic $A(t, t + \tau)$ entering the element during the interval must be bounded by $\sigma + \rho\tau$. We must thus have

$$\tau C \leq \sigma + \rho\tau$$

or

$$\tau \leq \sigma/(C - \rho) \qquad (6\text{–}9)$$

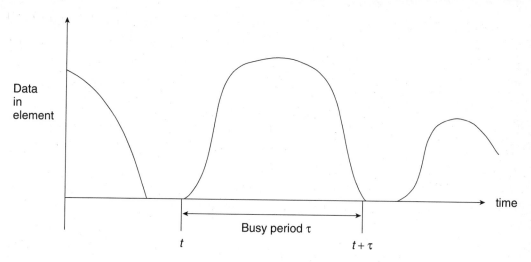

FIGURE 6–7 ▪ Busy period, work-conserving element.

This provides a bound on the maximum busy period. But the maximum delay any traffic unit can suffer is the maximum busy period. (Why is this so?) Hence, equation (6–9) provides a bound on the maximum delay, as indicated earlier by equation (6–8). Note that equations (6–8) and (6–9) both have the common queuing delay form, with the delay increasing rapidly as the input rate (here a bound on the rate) approaches capacity. Note also, that the larger the burstiness facor σ, the larger the delay bound, since, as is apparent from the derivation of equation (6–9), the larger σ is, the longer the maximum time required to clear a busy period and hence the longer the interval. But note again that equations (6–8) and (6–9) represent bounds on maximum delay, not the average delay arising in studies of queueing phenomena. The queueing delays usually discussed are average stochastic delays. The bounds appearing here are maximum (worst-case), hence deterministic, delays.

Finally, to conclude this brief introduction to Cruz's work on delay bounds for regulated traffic, consider the work-conserving multiplexer of Figure 6–6d. This device represents the logical extension of the work-conserving element of Figure 6–6c to the case of two or more traffic streams multiplexed together. Although two regulated traffic streams only are shown multiplexed in Figure 6–6d, the bound, to be stated below, is obviously easily extended to any number of regulated traffic streams. The two streams are shown entering the multiplexer on links of capacity C_1 and C_2, respectively. Then the following result, extending equation (6–8), may be shown to hold [CRUZ 1991]: Given the input traffic streams regulated, respectively, as

$$A_1 \sim (\sigma_1, \rho_1) \qquad \text{and} \qquad A_2 \sim (\sigma_2, \rho_2)$$

the maximum delay through the device is bounded by

$$\overline{D}_{\text{mux}} = \frac{\sigma_1 + \sigma_2}{C - \rho_1 - \rho_2} = \frac{\sigma}{C - \rho}$$

(6–10)

$$\sigma = \sigma_1 + \sigma_2 \quad \rho = \rho_1 + \rho_2$$

So the burstiness and rate factors add in determining the bound. The bound given by equation (6–8) is just a special case of this result. Interestingly, this result is independent of the input capacities C_1 and C_2, even if $C_i > C$, $i = 1, 2$; that is, the input capacities can be higher than the output capacity. But clearly we must have $\rho = \rho_1 + \rho_2 < C$ for the result to be meaningful.

The output traffic streams are found to be burstier in the regulated sense, just as was found to be true for the pure delay element of Figure 6–6a:

$$A_{i\text{out}} \sim (\sigma_i + \rho_i \overline{D}_{\text{mux}}, \rho_i), \qquad i = 1, 2$$

(6–11)

The delay through the multiplexer thus adds to the burstiness, although note again that this result is to be interpreted strictly in the maximum bound sense. Finally, the total output stream of the multiplexer of Figure 6–6d is found to be a regulated stream with burstiness and rate parameters added, as might be expected:

$$A_{\text{out}} = A_{1\text{out}} + A_{2\text{out}} \sim (\sigma_1 + \sigma_2 + (\rho_1 + \rho_2) \overline{D}_{\text{mux}}, \rho_1 + \rho_2)$$

(6–12)

Cruz's definition of regulated traffic has been used by Parekh and Gallager in establishing worst-case (that is, maximum) delay bounds for a service discipline they call *generalized processor sharing* (GPS). This queue service discipline, to be applied at each node in a network, is one of many such disciplines that have been proposed to provide delay, throughput, and packet (cell) loss guarantees for traffic in an integrated services network. Stop-and-go queueing, discussed earlier, is one such example. GPS is based on, and extends, an earlier service discipline called *fair queueing* [DEME 1989]. A related earlier service discipline is called *Virtual Clock* [ZHANL 1980]. These two service disciplines, as well as a number of others, including stop-and-go queueing, are briefly summarized and compared in [ZHANH 1991]. Since our focus here is on studying worst-case, deterministic, delay bounds end-to-end in a network, we focus on generalized processor sharing only. Readers inter-

[DEME 1989]   Demers, A., S. Keshav, and S. Shenker, "Analysis and Simulation of a Fair Queueing Algorithm," *Proc. ACM SIGCOMM 89*, Sept. 1989: 3–12.

[ZHANL 1980]   Zhang, L., "A New Architecture for Packet-Switch Network Procotols," *Ph.D. dissertation*, MIT, July 1980.

[ZHANH 1991]   Zhang, H., and S. Keshav, "Comparison of Rate-Based Service Disciplines," *Proc. ACM SIGCOMM 91*, Zurich, Switzerland, Sept. 1991.

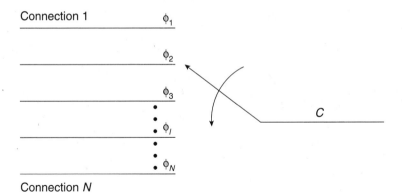

Connection 1

Connection N

FIGURE 6–8 ▪ Schematic representation of generalized processor sharing.

ested in delving further into the area of queue service disciplines are referred to [ZHANH 1991] and references contained within it.

Fair queueing is a service discipline designed to allocate link capacity (bandwidth) equally and fairly among multiple connections sharing a link. It does this by emulating round-robin service of the various connections. General processor sharing (GPS) provides similar service: Say the capacity on a given link is C cells/sec. Say there are N connections sharing the link. Connection i, $1 \leq i < N$, is assigned a parameter Φ_i such that it is guaranteed service at a rate g_i given by

$$g_i = \Phi_i C \Big/ \sum_{j=1}^{N} \Phi_j \qquad (6\text{–}13)$$

The guaranteed rate of service of connection i is thus proportional to Φ_i, which is called the proportional rate parameter. In addition, GPS is defined to be work conserving, in the sense that if one connection has traffic ready to be served, while another has none, capacity from the latter will be used to serve the former. As a result, the actual connection i traffic, served in an interval (τ, t), denoted by $S_i(\tau, t)$, will obey the condition

$$S_i\,(\tau, t)/S_j\,(\tau, t) \geq \Phi_i/\Phi_j \qquad j = 1, \ldots N \qquad (6\text{–}14)$$

Thus, g_i is the minimum service rate for connection i. GPS is diagrammed schematically in Figure 6–8. (Note that if $\Phi_i = 1/N$, all i, GPS reduces to round-robin sharing.)

The results of the use of this procedure may be summarized as follows:

1. Let r_i be the *average* connection-i service rate. Then, so long as $r_i \leq g_i$, service rate g_i is guaranteed, independent of other connections.

2. The maximum delay of traffic on a given connection can be bounded, based on its own characteristics, independent of other sessions. Thus, given the guaranteed service rate g_i and an assumption of regulated traffic, to be discussed below, the end-to-end delay of connection i will be bounded independent of all other sessions. This is discussed further later.

3. GPS allows some flexibility in service assignment to be introduced as well. Thus, say one connection is relatively delay-insensitive. Its guaranteed rate g_i may then be reduced, with additional capacity then allocated to other connections. This is possible so long as

$$\sum_i r_i < C$$

It turns out that the delay of this connection may only be impacted slightly, but with delay improvement obtained for the other connections [PARE 1993].

Now consider the special case in which each connection on a link is regulated in the Cruz sense of equations (6–4) or (6–6), that is, leaky bucket flow-constrained, with

$$A_i \sim (\sigma_i, \rho_i) \qquad \text{or} \qquad A_i(\tau, t) \le \sigma_i + \rho_j(\tau - t) \tag{6–15}$$

Assuming GPS service, one can then find worst-case, end-to-end bounds on connection delay and backlog for each connection. These bounds will turn out to be tighter than those provided by stop-and-go queueing. As in the case of stop-and-go queueing, let connection-i traffic follow a path consisting of m nodes end-to-end. Consider node l on that path with capacity C_l on the outgoing link of that path. (We use the same notation, where possible, as used previously in discussing stop-and-go queueing. See Figure 6–4 for example.)

Let $A_i^l(0,t)$ represent the connection-i traffic arriving at node l in the interval $(0,t)$, while $S_i^l(0,t)$ represents the connection-i traffic served at that node, using GPS, during the same interval. The connection-i backlog at node l, that is, the number of cells not yet served, is then of course given by

$$Q_i^l(t) = A_i^l(0,t) - S_i^l(0,t) \tag{6–16}$$

The total connection i backlog, on all nodes along the path, is then

$$Q_i(t) = \sum_{l=1}^{n} Q_i^l(t) \tag{6–17}$$

This represents all the connection-i traffic buffered along the m-hop path. (We neglect in this discussion, traffic moving on the links themselves. In wideband, long-propagation networks, this traffic can easily dominate the buffered traffic. But since we are principally interested in delay along the path, the effect of this traffic appears in the propagation delay, which we will include later in the discussion.)

Now let $D_i(t)$ be the total time spent in the network by a connection-i cell arriving at time t, excluding propagation delay. (As noted above, this term will be included later.) $D_i(t)$ depends, in general, on traffic arrivals of all connections A_j in the network. Let D_i^* be the maximum delay end-to-end for connection i, maximized over all time and over all network connections:

$$D_i^* = \max_{\text{all } A_j} \quad \max_{t \geq 0} D_i(t) \tag{6-18}$$

Similarly, let Q_i^* be the *maximum* backlog of connection-i traffic, end-to-end:

$$Q_i^* = \max_{\text{all } A_j} \quad \max_{t \geq 0} Q_i(t) \tag{6-19}$$

These can be bounded simply for a stable network, with a simple, stability-like condition for each connection.

Specifically, consider the link utilization u_l on link l along the path. Call the full set of connections on that link $I(l)$. Then, since connections are leaky-bucket controlled with rate ρ_j for the connection j, the link utilization u_l, assumed to be less than 1, is given by

$$u_l = \sum_{k \in I(l)} \rho_j / C_l < 1$$

Let g_i be the *minimum* service rate (or backlog clearing rate) of service i along its path:

$$g_i = \min_l \; g_i^l \tag{6-20}$$

Now assume that this minimum service or backlog clearance rate for connection i is at least as much as its leaky bucket constrained arrival rate ρ_i:

$$g_i \geq \rho_i \tag{6-21}$$

Then the following worst-case backlog and delay bounds are readily established:

$$Q_i^* \leq \sigma_i \tag{6-22}$$

and

$$D_i^* \leq \sigma_i / g_i \leq \sigma_i / \rho_i \tag{6-23}$$

The worst-case backlog (cells buffered) end-to-end is thus bounded by the burstiness parameter of the regulated traffic, while the maximum delay end-to-end (exclusive of propagation delay) depends on the ratio of that parameter to the regulated rate ρ_i.

The proof of equation (6–22) and, then, equation (6–23), is quite simple. Let (τ, t) be an interval within a connection-i network busy period beginning at time τ. Connection-i traffic leaving the network during that time is given by $S_i^m (t, \tau)$. (Recall that the connection-i path is assumed to have m hops). But this amount of traffic must be at least $g_i \bullet (\tau - t)$, since g_i is the minimum service rate of connection i along its path. We thus have

$$S_i^m(t,\tau) \geq g_i \bullet (t - \tau) \geq \rho_i \bullet (t - \tau) \qquad (6\text{–}24)$$

by our assumption of equation (6–21) above. But now let t be the time at which the maximum backlog of connection-i traffic, end-to-end, is achieved; that is, $Q_i(t)$ at this time is Q_i^* (see equation (6–19)). The backlog, end-to-end, is the difference between the traffic arrivals $A_i(t - \tau)$ into the network in the interval (t,τ) and the traffic leaving the network $S_i^m (t - \tau)$. We thus have

$$Q_i^* = A_i (t - \tau) - S_i^m (t - \tau) \qquad (6\text{–}25)$$

But connection-i traffic has been assumed to be regulated according to equation (6–15). Using equations (6–15) and (6–24) in equation (6–25), we find the maximum backlog, end-to-end, bounded, as noted earlier, by equation (6–22):

$$Q_i^* \leq \sigma_i \qquad (6\text{–}22)$$

The delay, end-to-end, excluding propagation delay, experienced by an arriving unit of traffic (say a cell) must be due, at worst, to the time required to serve the maximum end-to-end backlog Q_i^*. (This is similar to the observation used earlier in deriving Cruz's delay bound of equation (6–8) for this work-conserving element, using the bound of equation (6–9) on the maximum busy period.) Since the minimum service or backlog clearing rate is g_i, we then have,

$$D_i^* \leq Q_i^*/g_i \qquad (6\text{–}26)$$

Using equations (6–22) and (6–21), we get, finally,

$$D_i^* \leq \sigma_i/\rho_i \qquad (6\text{–}23)$$

Adding the propagation delay to D_i^* in equation (6–23), one gets the worst-case (maximum) bound, end-to-end, on the delay experienced by regulated connection-i traffic, with GPS service used at every node. The bound on the total amount of connection-i traffic, end-to-end, is also found by modifying Q_i^* to include the traffic enroute along the propagation path [PARE 1993].

There is, however, a problem with applying the GPS delay bound in practice. GPS is not a realizable service discipline, since, by abstractly assigning numbers Φ_i to each connection and using these to determine the guaranteed rate g_i, as posited in equation (6–13), it essentially requires each connection to be served in parallel. (Round-robin service on a bit-by-bit service is similarly impractical, leading to fair queueing [ZHANH 1992].) Parekh and Gallagher instead propose the use of a realizable extension of GPS they call *packet GPS* or PGPS [PARE 1993]. This is similar to an earlier, "virtual time," scheme. PGPS is summarized as follows: Let F_p be the time a packet (cell) would finish service under GPS. The PGPS rule is to then service packets in increasing order of F_p, maintaining work conservation at all times. Thus, when a link server becomes free at time τ, it picks, for its next service, the first packet that would have completed GPS service if no other packets were to arrive after time t.

Let L_{max} be the maximum packet length. (In the case of ATM cells this is 53 octets or 424 bits.) Parekh and Gallager then prove that a PGPS packet can depart no later than L_{max}/C sec after its GPS departure time. (The proof involves noting that since both GPS and PGPS are work-conserving, their busy periods are the same). Because of this result, they obtain the following bound on PGPS end-to-end delay, over an m-hop path, again neglecting the propagation delay [PARE 1993]:

$$D_i^*\Big|_{PGPS} \le \frac{\sigma_i + (m-1)L_{max}}{\rho_i} + \sum_{l=1}^{m} L_{max}/C_l \qquad (6\text{–}27)$$

Here, C_i is the total link capacity on link l. This expression is to be compared to equation (6–23) for the bound on GPS delay. Note that for high-capacity links, which would normally be the case in B-ISDN networks, the second term involving C_l would be expected to be negligible. The first term is quite similar to equation (6–23), with the addition of a maximum packet-length term L_{max} for each hop.

What are the delays predicted by the bound of equation (6–27) in practice? How do they compare with stop-and-go queueing, as well as with ordinary statistical multiplexing (FIFO service) at each node along a path? Yates et al. have carried out a simulation study of the end-to-end delay incurred by real-time (voice) packets over a 5-hop path in a network [YATE 1993]. They have modeled 32-kbps voice, taken to be periodically generated at the rate of 32 bits/msec. The voice samples are packetized into 512-bit (64-octet) packets, periodically generated at the rate of 32,000/512 = 62.5 packets/sec. Voice source talk spurt, silence (on-off) characteristics were ignored for this study. Since the voice packets are periodically generated, the voice traffic appears as naturally regulated (that is, no leaky bucket is needed). There is no bursti-

[YATE 1993] Yates, D., et al., "On per-session end-to-end delay distribution and the call admission problem for real-time applications with QoS requirements," *Proc. ACM SIGCOMM 93*, San Francisco, Sept. 1993.

ness (σ = 1 packet in the regulated form of equation (6–15)), and the rate bound ρ = 62.5 packets/sec. T1 link speeds of C_l = 1.54 Mbps were assumed to be used throughout the network.

They then show, through simulation, that the measured delay distribution obtained using statistical multiplexing at each node provides delay values far below the worst-case deterministic bounds found using both PGPS and stop-and-go queueing. Specifically, consider PGPS first. Applying equation (6–27) to this example, and using L_{max} = 1 packet to agree with the units of σ (1 packet) and ρ (62.5 packets/sec), the delay bound expression, ignoring propagation delay, turns out to be

$$D_i^*\big|_{PGPS} \leq 81.7 \text{msec}$$

Now compare this result with that of stop-and-go queueing using equation (6–3), but ignoring the propagation delay term. (Since propagation delay appears additively in evaluating the end-to-end delay of all schemes, it can be ignored in comparing them.) Recall, from our discussion of stop-and-go queueing, that the frame size T can be no smaller than the maximum packet size. For the 512-bit voice packets under consideration here, generated periodically at a rate of 62.5 packets/sec, $T \geq 1/62.5$ = 16 msec. Choosing T = 16 msec to provide the best advantage to stop-and-go queueing in this case, we have

$$64 \text{ msec} < D_p < 176 \text{ msec}$$

with the propagation delay ignored.

The PGPS bound is thus somewhat above the minimum bound for stop-and-go queueing, but less than one-half of the maximum bound. Both PGPS and stop-and-go queueing bounds are, however, far above the maximum delay experienced by any packet in the simulation in this case.

What does the PGPS service discipline predict for nonreal-time-traffic? For this purpose we take an example calculated in Chapter 4 in evaluating the leaky bucket algorithm. Specifically, consider example 2 in section 4.3, that for a bursty image source. Recall that the average burst interval was chosen as $1/\beta$ = 0.5 sec, with the average off time $1/\alpha$ = 11 sec. The image transfer rate was taken as R_p = 5200 cells/sec. Using a leaky bucket design rule of loss probability $P_L = 10^{-9}$ at these normal design values, with P_L increasing to 0.07 for the transfer rate 20% higher than the design rate, we found that the token arrival rate was r = 5150 tokens/sec while the token buffer size was B = 400 cells. In the notation used here, this translates to ρ = 5150 and σ = 400. Assuming very high capacity links so that L_{max}/C_l in equation (6–27) is negligible, and neglecting $(m - 1) L_{max}$ as well in comparison with σ, the delay bound for PGPS turns out to be exactly that of GPS and is given by

$$D_i^* \leq \sigma/\rho = 78 \text{ msec}$$

This is obviously quite tolerable for the image traffic assumed here, particularly since this delay bound is much smaller than the image transfer time of 0.5 sec.

The deterministic worst-case delay bound for GPS leads to looser bounds than would be the case if stochastic bounds were to be used. Recent work has been carried out on statistical bounds for GPS at a single node, focusing on its asymptotic behavior when each traffic stream is confined to its own buffer [VECI 1994]. We discuss statistical bounds further in the next section.

6.2 ▪ STOCHASTIC BOUNDS AND EFFECTIVE CAPACITY

The previous section introduced the concept of an absolute bound on end-to-end delay in integrated networks and discussed two service strategies, stop-and-go queueing and general processor sharing, designed specifically to bound the delay. These are deterministic, worst-case bounds, in the sense that the end-to-end delay of any packet (or cell) in the traffic class being serviced in this manner is guaranteed never to exceed this bound. This is, of course, a useful property when dealing with traffic requiring a delay QoS. The problem is that deterministic control of the delay may lead to sizable delays end-to-end, or, alternatively said, invoking an absolute guarantee of maximum delay may lead to looser bounds than could otherwise be obtained. A requirement, say, that 95% or 97% of the packets should not experience more than a specified delay, end-to-end, might then be preferable. Such a delay bound is an example of a *stochastic delay bound*. In fact, much of traffic analysis and engineering design in both circuit-, and packet-switched networks deals with stochastic performance guarantees. Delay and delay jitter performance guarantees are, in practice, often couched this way. This point was made at the beginning of this chapter.

Some work on end-to-end stochastic delay bounds has recently appeared in the literature [KURO 1992], [CHAN 1992], [CHAN 1994]. We focus here on the work of Chang, which parallels Cruz's regulator approach although in a stochastic sense. It thus follows naturally on our discussion of

[VECI 1994]   De Veciana, G., and G. Kesidis, "Bandwidth Allocation for Multiple Qualities of Service Using Generalized Processor Sharing," *Tech. Rpt. SCC-94-01.* U. of Texas at Austin, March 1994.

[KURO 1992]   Kurose, J., "On Computing Per-Session Performance Bounds in High-Speed Multi-Hop Computer Networks," *Performance Eval. Review, 20,* 1 (June 1992): 128–139.

[CHAN 1992]   Chang, C. S., "Stability, Queue Length, and Delay, II: Stochastic Queueing Networks," *Rpt. RC 17709,* IBM Research, Yorktown Hts., NY 10598, Feb. 1992.

[CHAN 1994]   Chang, C. S., "Stability, Queue Length, and Delay of Deterministic and Stochastic Queueing Networks," *IEEE Trans. on Auto. Control, 39,* 5 (May 1994): 913–931.

regulated traffic in the previous section. Although Chang has addressed stochastic bounds on delay, end-to-end, in a network, we summarize some of his work at a single node only. This is done because it turns out that the concept of effective or equivalent capacity, first introduced in this book in an ad hoc manner in discussing admission control in section 4.1, falls out of this analysis quite naturally! In particular, we come up with a closed-form expression for effective capacity that a number of investigators have recently obtained using other approaches, which has the property that the effective capacities of multiple traffic streams sharing a buffer add. A special case for two-state on-off sources appeared earlier in section 4.1, and was stated in equation (4–30).

Chang's approach is to show that queue length and the corresponding delay at a node can be bounded exponentially for different stochastic traffic types, providing a stability condition is met. It turns out that this stability condition involves precisely the equivalent or effective capacity of the sources sharing the buffer. For the special case of two-state, on-off sources discussed at length in section 4.1, this gives rise to equation (4–30).

Consider the infinite queue model of Figure 6–9 which represents the buffer driving a link of capacity C cells/sec in an integrated network. K independent traffic streams are shown sharing this buffer. This is, of course, the same model we have used a number of times in previous chapters of this book. The one difference is that we now use discrete-time analysis, with the buffer occupancy $q(t)$ defined at discrete intervals of time t. We take as the unit of time, the time required to serve C units of capacity. Thus, the time could be given in seconds, with C cells served per second, or in msec, with C cells served per msec. Consider now the unit interval $[t - 1, t)$ shown in Figure 6–10. This notation implies inclusion of $(t - 1)$, but not t. Let the number of arrivals (cells) in this interval from source k be some random number $a_k(t)$. The total number of arrivals in $[t - 1, t)$ is then

$$a(t) = \sum_{k=1}^{K} a_k(t)$$

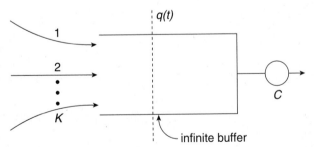

FIGURE 6–9 ■ Queue model for effective capacity analysis.

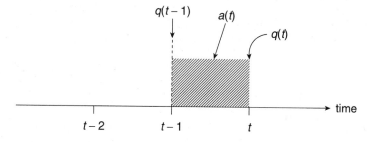

FIGURE 6–10 ■ Discrete-time analysis.

Note that this is really a *rate*, since it represents the number of arrivals in one unit of time.

The total number of arrivals from source k in the interval $[t_1, t_2)$ is then another random variable

$$A_k(t_1, t_2) = \sum_{t=t_1}^{t_2-1} a_k(t)$$

The total number of arrivals from all sources during this time interval is a random variable

$$A_k(t_1, t_2) = \sum_{k=1}^{K} A_k(t_1, t_2)$$

The queue length $q(t)$ depends, of course, on these arrivals. To bound $q(t)$ in a statistical sense, that is, to ensure a stable queue, we have to bound the number of arrivals $a(t)$ in a unit interval, as well as the number $A(t_1, t_2)$ in the larger interval $[t_1, t_2)$.

We choose to use statistical bounds now, rather than the absolute (regulated) bounds of the previous section. A number of such bounds have been defined and have been found quite useful [PAPO 1991]. For our purposes, following Chang, a bound in terms of the moment-generating functions of the random variables $A_k(t_1, t_2)$ is most useful. (This choice of bound can also be justified using a discipline called large-deviation theory [BUCK 1990], as will be noted later). Recall, from Chapter 5, that the moment-generating function was defined to be the transform of the random variable. In that chapter [see

[PAPO 1991]   Papoulis, A., *Probability, Random Variables, and Stochastic Processes*, 3rd ed. NY: McGraw-Hill, 1991.

[BUCK 1990]   Bucklew, J., *Large-Deviation Techniques in Decision, Simulation, and Estimation*, New York: John Wiley, 1990.

equation (5–8)], we defined it specifically as the z-transform. Here it turns out to be more useful to use the Fourier transform. Given a random variable $x(t)$, then, we define the mgf of x to be $E[e^{\theta x(t)}]$, with θ the transform variable. This is equivalent to the z-transform of equation (5–8), with $e^{\theta} \equiv z$. In all the examples following equation (5–8), one simply replaces z by e^{θ} to obtain the Fourier transform form of the moment-generating function.

Using this form, then, the mgf of the arrival process k is given by $E[e^{\theta A_k(t_1, t_2)}]$. Arrival process k is then stochastically bounded in the sense that

$$E\left[e^{\theta A_k(t_1, t_2)}\right] \le e^{\theta \hat{A}_k(\theta, t_2 - t_1)} \tag{6–28}$$

All arrival processes we shall consider have this attribute. The moment-generating function is assumed exponentially-bounded. An equivalent bound is to take natural logs of both sides of equation (6–28). We then get

$$\ln E\left[e^{\theta A_k(t_1, t_2)}\right] \le \theta \hat{A}_k(\theta, t_2 - t_1) \tag{6–29}$$

The logarithm of the moment-generating function is thus bounded by a function of θ and $(t_2 - t_1)$. The parameter θ appearing will be related later to the survivor function $G(x)$, the probability the buffer of Figure 6–9 exceeds a value x. This was the function first introduced in Chapter 3 (see equation (3–38) and the subsequent discussion for example).

The (deterministic) function on the right-hand side of equation (6–28) is called an *envelope process* of $A_k(t_1, t_2)$ [CHAN 1992]. Note that this envelope process is assumed stationary in time, depending on $(t_2 - t_1)$ only, and not on the times t_1 and t_2 individually. As a special case, and the one with which we will be dealing most specifically, let

$$\hat{A}_k(\theta, t_2 - t_1) = \hat{a}_k(\theta)(t_2 - t_1) + \hat{\sigma}_k(\theta) \tag{6–30}$$

This is called a *linear envelope process*, and is analogous to Cruz's $\rho t + \sigma$ in the deterministic bound case. Note that $\hat{a}_k(\theta)$ is a rate parameter. Informally, this says that $A_k(t_1, t_2)$ has in some sense (although expressed probabilistically) a maximum arrival rate bounded by $\hat{a}_k(\theta)$. This will, in fact, turn out to be a bound on the effective capacity C_k of source k!

With this bound on the moment-generating function of $A_k(t_1, t_2)$, we are now in a position to proceed with our discussion of a bound on the time-varying queue occupancy $q(t)$, which will lead directly to the definition of the effective capacity of traffic stream k. To do this we must relate $q(t)$ to the total arrival process $a(t) = \sum_{k=1}^{K} a_k(t)$. It is left to the reader to demonstrate that the equation describing the evolution of $q(t)$ is precisely that of equation (5–35) in Chapter 5. We change equation (5–35) slightly, however, to show the capacity C appearing explicitly:

$$q(t) = \max(0, q(t-1) + a(t) - C) = (q(t-1) + a(t) - C)^{+} \tag{6–31}$$

(Recall that a unit time interval here was defined to be one corresponding to C units of traffic served.)

Following Chang and a suggestion made by Professor G. Kesidis of the University of Toronto,[1] we expand $q(t)$ recursively, starting with an empty queue at time $t = 0$ $[q(0) = 0]$. Thus,

$$q\,(1) = (q\,(0) + a\,(1) - C)^+ = \max\,(0, a\,(1) - C)$$

since $q(0) = 0$. Then

$$q\,(2) = (q\,(0) + a(2) - C)^+ = \max\,(0, \max\,(0, a(1) - C) + a(2) - C)$$

$$= \max\,(0, a(2) - C, a(2) + a\,(1) - 2C)$$

using $q(1)$. Continuing,

$$q\,(3) = (q\,(2) + a(3) - C)^+$$

$$= \max\,(0, \max\,(0, a(2) - C, a(2) + a(1) - 2C) + a(3) - C)$$

$$= \max\,(0, a(3) - C, a(3) + a(2) - 2C, a(3) + a(2) + a(1) - 3C)$$

Finally, at time t,

$$\begin{aligned} q\,(t) = \max\,(0, a\,(t) - C, a\,(t) + a\,(t-1) \\ - 2C, \dots, a(t) + a(t-1) + \dots + a(1) - tC) \end{aligned} \tag{6–31a}$$

We now rewrite equation (6–31a) in terms of the aggregate number of arrivals $A(t_1, t_2)$ in the interval $[t_1, t_2)$. Note, first, that $A(t-1, t) = a(t)$, since $a(t)$ is the number of arrivals in $[t-1, t)$, by definition. Also, $A(t-2, t) = a(t-1) + a(t)$, etc. Then it is clear that $q(t)$ may be rewritten as

$$q\,(t) = \max\,(0, A\,(t-1, t) - C, A\,(t-2, t) - 2C, \dots, A\,(0, t) - tC)$$

$$= \max_{s}\,(A\,(t-s, t) - sC) \qquad A\,(t, t) = 0 \tag{6–31b}$$

We now take the moment-generating function (mgf) of $q(t)$, just as was done in Chapter 5, and write it using equation (6–31b). Thus,

$$E[e^{q(t)\theta}] = E[e^{\max_{s} \theta\,(A\,(t-s,t)-sC)}]$$

$$= \max_{s} E[e^{\theta\,(A\,(t-s,\,t)\,-\,sC)}] \tag{6–32}$$

(It is left to the reader to show that one can interchange the operations max and expectation $E(\ )$). We can eliminate the max operation by using the following obvious inequality:

$$\max\,(x_1 + x_2 + \dots + x_n) \le \sum_{j=1}^{n} x_j, \quad x_j \ge 0 \tag{6–33}$$

---

[1] Personal communication.

Since the moment-generating function is nonnegative, we use equation (6–33) in (6–32) to get the inequality

$$E\left[e^{q(t)\theta}\right] \le \sum_{s=0}^{t} E\left[e^{\theta(A(t-s,t)-sC)}\right] \tag{6–34}$$

Why have we chosen to use the mgf of $q(t)$ and to bound it? Because we can now use the bound of equation (6–28) we assumed for the aggregate arrival process $A_k(t_1,t_2)$. In particular, recall that we assumed all K arrival processes were independent. Then, since

$$A(t_1,t_2) = \sum_{k=1}^{K} A_k(t_1,t_2)$$

We have

$$E\left[e^{\theta(A(t-s,t)-sC)}\right] = \left\{\prod_{k=1}^{K} E\left[e^{\theta A_k(t-s,t)}\right]\right\} e^{-\theta sC} \le \left[\prod_{k=1}^{K} e^{\theta \hat{A}_k(\theta,s)}\right] e^{-\theta sC} \tag{6–35}$$

using equation (6–28) and noting that the constant term $e^{-\theta sC}$ can be taken out of the expectation.

We now define the composite envelope function

$$\hat{A}(\theta,t) = \sum_{k=1}^{K} \hat{A}_k(\theta,t)$$

This enables us to simplify equation (6–35):

$$E[e^{\theta(A(t-s,\,t)-sC}] \le e^{\theta\,[\hat{A}\,(\theta,\,s)-sC]} \tag{6–35a}$$

Consider again the special case of a linear envelope process

$$\hat{A}_k(\theta,\,t) = \hat{a}_k(\theta)\,t + \hat{\sigma}_k\,(\theta) \tag{6–36}$$

Then the composite envelope process $\hat{A}\,(\theta,\,t)$ may also be written as a composite linear envelope process

$$\hat{A}\,(\theta,\,t) = \hat{a}\,(\theta)\,t + \hat{\sigma}\,(\theta) \tag{6–37}$$

with

$$\hat{a}(\theta) = \sum_{k=1}^{K} \hat{a}_k(\theta) \tag{6–38}$$

and

$$\hat{\sigma}(\theta) = \sum_{k=1}^{K} \hat{\sigma}_k(\theta) \tag{6–39}$$

Returning to equation (6–34) involving the mgf of the queue occupancy, we get, using equation (6–35a), and then, the composite linear envelope process representation,

$$E\left[e^{q(t)\theta}\right] \leq \sum_{s=0}^{t} e^{\theta[\hat{A}(\theta,s)-sC]} = \sum_{s=0}^{t} e^{\theta[\hat{a}(\theta)s+\sigma(\theta)]}e^{-\theta sC} \qquad (6\text{–}34a)$$

Rewriting this expression in a somewhat different form, we have

$$E\left[e^{q(t)\theta}\right] \leq e^{\hat{\sigma}(\theta)\theta}\sum_{s=0}^{t} e^{\theta s[\hat{a}(\theta)-C]} \qquad (6\text{–}34b)$$

Now let $t \to \infty$. The sum on the right-hand side of equation (6–34b) will diverge if $\hat{a}(\theta) \geq C$. It is thus clear that the mgf of $\theta(t)$ will be bounded if and only if

$$\hat{a}(\theta) < C \qquad (6\text{–}40)$$

Let us stop for an instant to examine the meaning of this equation. Note from equations (6–36) to (6–38) that $\hat{a}(\theta)$ represents the rate term of the linear envelope process. Equation (6–40) states that the queue will be stochastically bounded in the sense of a bound on the mgf of $q(t)$ if and only if that rate $\hat{a}(\theta)$ is less than the link capacity C. We shall see shortly that $\hat{a}(\theta)$ is, in turn, a bound on a quantity we shall call the effective or equivalent capacity of the composite traffic stream accessing the buffer. This effective capacity will be shown to agree precisely with the one found and discussed for the two-state traffic source model used extensively in Chapter 4. More generally, it will enable us to define the equivalent or effective capacity of any traffic source satisfying some simple conditions. Equally important, the form of equation (6–38) indicates that the equivalent capacity of independent sources will be expected to add. This will of course be shown to be the case. Hence, one need only calculate the equivalent capacity of individual source models and simply add the capacities to obtain the equivalent capacity of the much more complicated composite source model. Equation (4–30) in Chapter 4 is a special case of this result. That result was stated there without proof since it involved a rather complex analysis of the special case of two-state fluid-flow models. The result we obtain here is more general.

But all of this must be said with some caveats: The result of equation (6–40) and the equivalent capacity result based on it, to be developed shortly, apply to one queue only. All traffic inputs to the queue are assumed to have the same desired QoS (probability of loss and delay through the queue). The equivalent capacity expression will also turn out to be a *conservative* estimate of capacity, as noted already in Chapter 4, since, as will be shown, it ignores the smoothing or bandwidth reduction effect implicit in statistical multiplexing.

With equation (6–40) satisfied, the queue of Figure 6–9 is bounded in the sense that the mgf of $q(t)$, $E[e^{q(t)\theta}]$, is bounded in the limit as $t \to \infty$. Taking the limit, as $t \to \infty$, of both sides of equation (6–34b), with equation (6–40) satisfied, we have, very simply,

$$E[e^{q\theta}] = \lim_{t \to \infty} E[e^{q(t)\theta}] \le \beta(\theta) \tag{6–41}$$

where

$$\beta(\theta) \equiv e^{\hat{\sigma}(\theta)\theta} \sum_{s=0}^{\infty} e^{\theta s[\hat{a}(\theta)-C]} = e^{\hat{\sigma}(\theta)\theta} \Big/ \left[1 - e^{-\theta(C-\hat{a}(\theta))}\right] \tag{6–42}$$

The left-hand side of equation (6–41) is the mgf of the *stationary* statistics of the queue length q, and equation (6–41) states that this mgf is bounded if $\hat{a}(\theta) < C$.

We now show how this discussion on stochastically bounding the (stationary) queue length q ties in naturally to the effective (equivalent) bandwidth concept based on maintaining a specified cell loss probability P_L. To do this we have to invoke the so-called *Chernoff bound* [PAPO 1991]. This is a bound relating the probability a random variable exceeds some fixed value to its moment-generating function. It is in the class of bounds related to the Tchebycheff inequality [PAPO 1991]. In the notation we have been using here, with q a random variable, the Chernoff bound is given by

$$P\,[q > x] \le e^{-\theta x}\, E[e^{q\theta}] \tag{6–43}$$

The bound thus states that the tail probability of a random variable (the probability it exceeds a value x), decreases exponentially with x, the proportionality factor being just the mgf $E[e^{q\theta}]$. The bound is often used to study the asymptotic values of random variables. This is precisely what we shall do here, since, in our notation, $P[q > x]$ is the survivor function $G(x)$, the probability the queue length q of the buffer of Figure 6–9 exceeds a value x.

In particular, referring to the buffer of Figure 6–9 and assuming the linear envelope rate $\hat{a}(\theta) < C$, so that equation (6–41) is satisfied, we have, inserting equation (6–41) in equation (6–43),

$$G\,(x) \equiv P\,[q > x] \le \beta(\theta)\, e^{-\theta x} \tag{6–44}$$

The probability that the occupancy of the (infinite) buffer of Figure 6–9 exceeds some value x, thus decreases exponentially with x. Note that the asymptotic, fluid-flow, approximation of equation (3–38) or (3–43) agrees with this more general result, based on the Chernoff bound.

We know from our earlier discussion in Chapter 4 that the survivor function $G(x)$ is a good approximation to the cell loss probability P_L of a finite buffer, if that probability is "small enough". Hence, letting $P_L \sim G(x)$, equation (6–44) gives us an exponential bound on the cell loss probability. (Since buffer cell delay is directly proportional to the buffer occupancy, another interpretation of equation (6–44) is that the probability the buffer cell delay exceeds some value t, say, is exponentially decreasing in t. This is the stochastic delay bound mentioned in the last section. Replacing $G(x)$ by P_L, then, we have, from equation (6–44),

$$P_L \leq \beta\,(x)\,e^{-\theta x} = e^{-\theta x + \ln \beta\,(\theta)} \qquad (6\text{–}45)$$

Taking $\theta x \gg 1$ and $P \ll 1$, we have

$$P_L \rightarrow e^{-\theta x}, \qquad \theta x \gg 1, \qquad P_L \ll 1 \qquad (6\text{–}45a)$$

The cell loss probability, when "small enough," is thus bounded by a simple decreasing exponential in x. This asymptotic approximation for P_L is discussed in detail in [ELWA 1993]. Note that this is precisely the approximation we discussed in Chapter 4, in first encountering the equivalent (effective) capacity of a source, when we replaced the fluid-flow asymptotic approximation equation (4–22), [or equation (3–43) in Chapter 3] for $G(x)$ or P_L by the simple exponential equation (4–25). We noted there, that neglecting the terms in front of the exponential in x resulted in a conservative estimate for the capacity. Equation (6–45), with the corresponding condition $\hat{a}(\theta) < C$, generalizes the fluid-flow result of Chapter 4 to more general source models and to multiplexed sources as well.

Although the asymptotic form of equation (6–45a) implies that $P_L \rightarrow e^{-\theta x}$ for P_L "small enough" (or x "large enough"), it is not clear how small P_L has to be (or x, large enough) for this asymptotic form to be valid. The exponential bound of equation (6–45a) could be quite poor even for $P_L \sim 10^{-9}$, if $\beta(\theta)$ were significantly different from 1. Choudhury et al. have studied the simple exponential approximation for P_L obtained above and have shown, with specific examples, that it can sometimes be a poor approximation [CHOU 1993].

Despite this caveat concerning the simple exponential approximation of equation (6–45a) for P_L, with $\beta(\theta)$ taken to be equal to 1, we proceed to use it anyway. In particular, it enables us to find a value for the parameter θ in terms of P_L and x. Thus, from equation (6–45a), we have

$$\theta = \frac{1}{x}\,\ln\,(1/P_L) \qquad (6\text{–}46)$$

This will be used in relating the linear envelope rate $\hat{a}(\theta)$ to a bound on the effective capacity. Note again that this is similar to what we did in Chapter 4 in using the exponential approximation of equation (4–25) to the fluid-flow loss

[ELWA 1993]   Elwalid, A. I., and D. Mitra, "Effective Bandwidth of General Markovian Traffic Sources and Admission Control of High-Speed Networks," *IEEE/ACM Trans. on Networking*, 1, 3 (June 1993): 329–343.

[CHOU 1993]   Choudhury, G. L., et al., "Squeezing the Most out of ATM," AT&T Bell Labs. paper, May 28, 1993.

probability to find the effective (equivalent) capacity. Equation (4–26) in that chapter parallels equation (6–46) here.

We return now to equation (6–40), the basic requirement for the exponential approximation discussed above to be valid. We now show how the effective capacity of an individual source is obtained using this relation, thus generalizing the effective (equivalent) capacity concept first introduced in Chapter 4. Note first that the condition $\hat{a}(\theta) < C$ is a rather nebulous one. Given a *particular* set of traffic sources accessing the buffer of Figure 6–9, how *does* one find the linear envelope rate $\hat{a}(\theta)$? What is this quantity for a real physical system?

We relate this quantity to the statistics of the real system by going back to the definition of the linear envelope process. Recall that this process was introduced as a special case of the composite envelope process $\hat{A}(\theta,t)$, defined as the sum of individual envelope processes $\hat{A}_k(\theta, t)$, defined in turn by equation (6–28) or (6–29) as a way of bounding the number of arrivals $A_k(0,t)$ in the interval $(0,t)$ of arrival process k. It is the statistics of the individual arrival processes accessing the buffer of Figure 6–9 that has physical meaning and is assumed given. We must thus relate the buffer stability condition $\hat{a}(\theta) < C$ to these known processes. To do this we first assume the individual processes accessing the buffer of Figure 6–9 are each stationary with time. We thus have

$$A_k\,(t_1, t_2) = A_k\,(t_2 - t_1)$$

that is, the arrival statistics depend only on the interval of time, not on the specific time at which measured. Then, from equation (6–29), we have, focusing on the interval $(0,t)$,

$$\hat{A}_k(\theta,t) \geq \frac{1}{\theta}\,\ln E\!\left[e^{\theta A_k(t)}\right] \tag{6–47}$$

But recall, from equation (6–30), that for a linear envelope process taken over the interval $(0,t)$, we have

$$\hat{A}_k\,(\theta,t) = \hat{a}_k\,(\theta)\,t + \hat{\sigma}_k\,(\theta) \tag{6–48}$$

Taking the limit as $t \to \infty$, and focusing on the rate $\hat{a}_k(\theta)$, it is apparent that $\hat{a}_k(\theta)$ must then be given by

$$\hat{a}_k(\theta) = \lim_{t\to\infty}\frac{1}{t}\hat{A}_k(\theta,t) \geq \lim_{t\to\infty}\frac{1}{t}\frac{1}{\theta}\ln E\!\left[e^{\theta A_k(t)}\right] \tag{6–49}$$

from equations (6–48) and (6–47).

But note now that the composite linear envelope rate $\hat{a}(\theta)$ was defined as the sum of the individual rates $\hat{a}_k(\theta)$ [see equation (6–38)]. Using equation (6–49), we finally obtain the desired connection between the linear envelope rate $\hat{a}(\theta)$ and the actual arrival statistics of the traffic processes inputting the buffer of Figure 6–9. This is given by the inequality

$$\hat{a}(\theta) = \sum_{k=1}^{K} \hat{a}_k(\theta) = \lim_{t \to \infty} \frac{1}{t} \hat{A}(\theta,t) \ge \lim_{t \to \infty} \frac{1}{t} \frac{1}{\theta} \ln\left[Ee^{\theta A(t)}\right] \qquad (6\text{–}50)$$

since $\hat{A}(\theta,t) = \sum_{k=1}^{K} \hat{A}_k(\theta,t)$, as noted earlier, and $A(t) = \sum_{k=1}^{K} A_k(t)$, with the individual arrival processes $A_k(t)$, $1 \le k \le K$, assumed independent of one another. [Recall that this assumption of independent arrival processes was used earlier in obtaining equation (6–35)].

We now use the inequality of equation (6–50) connecting the linear envelope rate $\hat{a}(\theta)$ to the composite traffic arrival rate to connect that composite arrival rate to the output link capacity C of the buffer (statistical multiplexer) of Figure 6–9. Specifically, since we showed earlier that we must have $\hat{a}(\theta) < C$ as a condition for the stability of the queue, we must have, combining this condition with equation (6–50),

$$\lim_{t \to \infty} \frac{1}{t} \frac{1}{\theta} \ln\left[Ee^{\theta A(t)}\right] \le \hat{a}(\theta) < C \qquad (6\text{–}51)$$

The left-hand-side of this inequality is what we now define to be the equivalent or effective capacity C_e of the composite traffic source assessing the statistical multiplexer buffer of Figure 6–9. For if the composite traffic sources additively accessing the buffer of Figure 6–9 have the property that the left-hand side of equation (6–51) is less than the output link capacity C, then stability of the buffer is assured. Thus, we have, as the effective capacity of the traffic sources, by definition,

$$C_e \equiv \lim_{t \to \infty} \frac{1}{t} \frac{1}{\theta} \ln\left[Ee^{\theta A(t)}\right] \qquad (6\text{–}52)$$

Since $A(t) = \sum_{k=1}^{K} A_k(t)$, with the K individual traffic sources all independent of one another by assumption, we can also write

$$C_e = \sum_{k=1}^{K} C_k \qquad (6\text{–}53)$$

with C_k the effective capacity of source k, given by

$$C_k \equiv \lim_{t \to \infty} \frac{1}{t} \frac{1}{\theta} \ln\left[Ee^{\theta A_k(t)}\right] \qquad (6\text{–}54)$$

This is the effective capacity expression to which we have been alluding throughout this section. Note that the effective capacities of individual, independent, sources add. This is obviously a very useful property. This generalizes the result stated earlier in Chapter 4, without proof, for the special case of on-off sources [see equation (4–30)]. We shall, in fact, use the on-off source model shortly as an example of the applicability of equations (6–53) and (6–54). One need only calculate the effective capacity of individual sources and add the results. Although we have derived equations (6–54) and (6–53) using discrete-time analysis [see equation (6–31) for example], it turns out that these expressions are valid for continuous-time sources as well [KESI 1993]. In the examples given later, we shall consider both discrete-time and continuous-time sources.

How do we apply equations (6–54) and (6–53) in practice? First, recall that the parameter θ was related earlier, by equation (6–46), to the buffer size x and the cell loss probability P_L. Given P_L and x, we find θ from equation (6–46) and then use equation (6–54) to calculate the individual capacity C_k of the kth source. Adding the capacities, we then get the effective capacity C_e of all K sources. This result is then applicable to admission control at a single ATM, as first discussed in Chapter 4. For, given a new connection to be made, we simply determine whether that new connection will overload the buffer (that is, whether $C_e > C$), in which case we deny admission; or, if the resultant $C_e < C$, we allow the connection to be set up.

But note again that, although this technique is conceptually simple, and easy to implement, assuming C_k can be calculated for any given source, it requires all sources to have the same quality of service descriptors P_L and x (x, a measure of allowable maximum delay through the buffer). We also stress that this measure of effective capacity may turn out to provide conservative estimates of capacity, as was shown in the examples discussed in Chapter 3. It requires the loss probabiliy P_L to be asymptotically small—how small it should be, or how large x should be, depends on the individual source characteristics, and is not clearly established. Finally, note that this effective capacity result was obtained by neglecting the term $\beta(\theta)$ in front of the exponential bound of equation (6–44), the argument being made that with P_L "sufficiently small," or buffer size x "sufficiently large", the effect of $\beta(\theta)$ vanishes in the limit. But taking $\beta(\theta) = 1$ effectively eliminates the statistical multiplexing advantage of adding the K sources of Figure 6–9. This is, in fact, implied by the simple addition of effective capacities to obtain the composite effective capacity. This additive (linear) result leads to a simple expression to be used for admission control, but bypasses the smoothing effect (the law of large numbers) implicit in multiplexing K disparate and independent sources. One would expect a "smooth" signal to have a smaller bandwidth (capacity) than obtained by adding the individual bandwidths (capacities) of individual sources. This is the basic reason for the conservative estimate of capacity that may be obtained using the effective capacity concept.

[KESI 1993]   Kesidis, G., J. Walrand, and C. S. Chang, "Effective Bandwidths for Multiclass Fluids and other ATM Sources," *IEEE/ACM Trans. on Networking, 1,* 4 (Aug. 1993): 424–428.

These caveats notwithstanding, the concept of the effective capacity of a traffic source accessing a buffer, conditioned on the desired loss probability P_L and maximum buffer size x, has received a lot of attention in the technical literature. Kesidis et al. have derived equation (6–54), as well as the related expression (6–53), using theorems from large-deviation theory [KESI 1993], [BUCK 1990]. This is the theory used to study the probabilistic behavior of large excursions or deviations of random variables from their mean values. It is clearly useful in studying tail probabilities of random variables, and in obtaining estimates of their asymptotic behavior. This technique has been applied to a variety of problems in decision and estimation theory [BUCK 1990], as well as to information theory, among other areas of science and technology [COVE 1991]. Kesidis et al. have shown the existence of effective bandwidths for a variety of traffic sources using theorems from large-deviation theory, while obtaining (6–54) and (6–53) thereby, as noted above [KESI 1993].

Effective bandwidths for a variety of traffic models and sources have been obtained by a host of other investigators as well. Included, for example, is work by F. P. Kelly, who found that the notion of an effective bandwidth exists for an *M/G*/1 queue shared by multiple classes of traffic [KELL 1991]; Gibbens and Hunt, who have extended the fluid-flow analysis of Anick et al. described in Chapter 3 ([ANIC 1982] and [KOST 1984]) to show that the notation of additive effective bandwidth exists for a set of heterogeneous on-off sources jointly accessing a channel [GIBB 1991]; and Elwalid and Mitra [1993], who obtained the effective bandwidth of continuous-time Markov sources. All of these examples turn out to be obtainable as special cases of equations (6–53) and (6–54).

We now consider some examples of the application of equation (6–54). We start with the most trivial case, that of a continuous bit rate (CBR) source of rate R_p packets/sec. This is a deterministic source. The number of arrivals in the interval $[0,t)$ is $A(t) = R_p t$. Applying equation (6–54), its effective capacity is just R_p! This is clearly as expected, at least validating the results of equation (6–54) and (6–53) (for a number of such sources) in the case of CBR sources.

The next example is that of a Poisson source of average rate λ_k cells/sec. In Chapter 5 we showed the moment-generating function of a Poisson variable n, using z-transforms, was

---

[COVE 1991]   Cover, T. M., and J. A. Thomas, *Elements of Information Theory*, New York: John Wiley, 1991.

[KELL 1991]   Kelly, F. P., "Effective Bandwidths at Multi-Class Queues," *Queuing Systems, 9* (1991): 5–16.

[KOST 1984]   Kosten, L., "Stochastic Theory of Data Handling Systems with Groups of Multiple Sources," *Proc. 2nd Internal. Symp. on Performance of Computer Commun. Systems*, North-Holland, 1984.

[GIBB 1991]   Gibbens, R. J., and P. J. Hunt, "Effective Bandwidths for the Multi-Type UAS Channel," *Queueing Systems, 9* (1991): 17–28.

$$G_n(z) \equiv E(z^n) = e^{-\lambda_k(1-z)} \tag{6-55}$$

Here we use, as noted earlier, Fourier transforms to define the mgf. Replacing z by e^θ and using $A_k(t)$ in place of the counting variable n, we get

$$E\left[e^{\theta A_k(t)}\right] = e^{-\lambda_k t(1-e^\theta)} \tag{6-56}$$

Taking the logarithm of equation (6–56) as called for in equation (6–54), dividing by t and θ, and then taking the limit as $t \to \infty$, we get, as the equivalent capacity of a Poisson source accessing a buffer,

$$C_k = \lambda_k (e^\theta - 1)/\theta \geq \lambda_k \tag{6-57}$$

Depending on the choice of θ (which in turn depends on the loss probability and maximum delay parameters chosen as the tolerable QoS), one gets an effective capacity, lower-bounded by the average Poisson rate. Note also, from equation (6–53), that the effective capacity of multiple Poisson sources, given as the sum of the effective capacities of each, is simply obtained by adding the Poisson rate parameters. This agrees again with the expected result, since the sum of Poisson arrivals is itself Poisson with the average arrival rate $\lambda = \sum_k \lambda_k$ [SCHW 1987].

Consider some examples to see the impact of the choice of cell loss probability P_L and maximum delay x on the effective capacity. Take $P_L = 10^{-5}$ at first. Then, from equation (6–46), $\theta = 11.5/x$. If we now pick $x \gg 11.5$ cells, so that $\theta \ll 1$, $C_k \doteq \lambda_k$, independent of the buffer size. Thus, for a large enough buffer, the effective capacity of a Poisson source is just the average rate of that source. But what if $x = 10$ cells, for example? Then $\theta = 1.15$ and $C_k \doteq 2\lambda_k$, from equation (6–57). The effective capacity thus doubles in this case. (But note that this is all approximate and may not even be close to the actual bandwidth of the Poisson source since we have taken $\beta(\theta)$ in equations (6–43) and (6–44) to be equal to 1.)

Now let $P_L = 10^{-9}$. Then $\theta = 20.7/x$ from equation (6–46). If we want to keep $C_k \leq 1.1\lambda_k$, that is, no more than 10% larger than the Poisson rate λ_k, we have to have $\theta \leq 0.2$ from equation (6–57), or $x \geq 100$ cells. More generally, if we want $C_k \leq 1.1\lambda_k$, $\theta \leq 0.2$, or $x > 5 \ln(1/P_L)$ cells. But note again that P_L must be small enough (or x large enough) to have $\ln\beta(\theta) \ll \theta x$.

We now consider more complex, hence more interesting and possibly more realistic, traffic models such as those discussed in earlier chapters in this book.

First consider an N-state, discrete-time Markov source. The model of this source is portrayed schematically in Figure 6–11. This is exactly the discrete-time chain used as a state model in section 3.7 [see equation (3–113)]. Transitions between states are defined as transition probability parameters r_{ij}, including self-transition r_{ii}. Given the system is in state i at time t, the

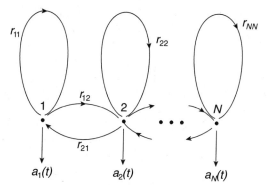

FIGURE 6–11 ■ Discrete-time Markov source.

probability of a transition to state j in the interval $(t, t + 1)$ is r_{ij}. For this model, transitions can occur at discrete-time intervals only. (Figure (6–11) shows a few adjacent-state transitions only to keep the diagram from being too cluttered.) Similarly, if the system is in state i at time t, the number of cells arriving in one interval is the number $a_i(t)$ as shown in Figure 6–11. $a_i(t)$ may be deterministic or random, with known statistics. Letting $\boldsymbol{\pi} = [\pi_1, \pi_2, \ldots, \pi_N]$ represent the vector of steady-state probabilities of being in the N states, 1 to N, as in earlier chapters, we find $\boldsymbol{\pi}$ by solving the matrix equation

$$\boldsymbol{\pi} P = \boldsymbol{\pi} \qquad (6\text{–}58)$$

the same equation as equation (3–113) in section 3–7. The transition probability matrix P is a stochastic matrix given by

$$P = \begin{bmatrix} r_{11} & r_{11} & \cdots & r_{1N} \\ r_{21} & r_{22} & \cdots & r_{2N} \\ \cdot & & & \cdot \\ \cdot & & & \cdot \\ \cdot & & & \cdot \\ r_{N1} & & \cdots & r_{NN} \end{bmatrix} \qquad (6\text{–}59)$$

Since the system stays in its own state each time interval, with probability r_{11}, or transfers out to some other states, we must have

$$\sum_{j=1}^{N} r_{ij} = 1 \qquad (6\text{–}60)$$

This is the origin of the term stochastic matrix: Each row of P must sum to 1.

Chang has shown that for this special discrete-time source, the effective capacity expression (6–54) specializes to the following closed-form expression [CHAN 1992], [CHAN 1994]:

$$C_e = \frac{1}{\theta} \log \text{sp}[P\Phi(\theta)] \qquad (6\text{–}61)$$

(We drop the dependence on k now to simplify the notation. It is henceforth understood that effective capacities add. Hence, as noted earlier, we can calculate the effective capacity of individual sources such as this one, and simply add the results). The term $\Phi(\theta)$ in equation (6–61) is defined to be the diagonal matrix whose ith component, $\Phi_i(\theta)$, is the moment-generating function of $a_i(t)$. Thus,

$$\Phi(\theta) \equiv \text{diag} \left[\Phi_i(\theta), \Phi_2(\theta), \ldots \Phi_i(\theta), \ldots, \Phi_N(\theta) \right] \qquad (6\text{–}62)$$

with

$$\Phi_i(\theta) \equiv E\left[e^{a_i(t)\theta} \right] \qquad (6\text{–}63)$$

The notation sp [A] stands for the *spectral radius*, or maximum eigenvalue of the matrix A in brackets. As an example, if $a_i(t)$ is a *deterministic* rate a_i, $\Phi_i(\theta) = e^{a_i\theta}$. If $a_i(t)$ is Poisson, with parameter λ_i (the source is then a discrete-time MMPP, just the source used to model video in section 3.7),

$$\Phi_i(\theta) = e^{-\lambda_i(1 - e^\theta)}$$

Consider now the special case of a two-state, discrete-time Markov chain. This example is portrayed diagrammatically in Figure 6–12. Then it is left for the reader to show that the maximum eigenvalue, or spectral radius, of the matrix $P\Phi(\theta)$ in this case is given by

$$z = \text{sp}[P\Phi(\theta)] = \frac{1}{2}\left[a(\theta) + \sqrt{a^2(\theta) + 4\Phi_1(\theta)\Phi_2(\theta)(r_{12}r_{21} - r_{12}r_{22})} \right] \qquad (6\text{–}64)$$

with $a(\theta) \equiv r_{11}\Phi_1(\theta) + r_{22}\Phi_2(\theta)$.

The effective capacity C_e of this source is then just

$$C_e = \frac{1}{\theta}\,\log z \qquad (6\text{–}65)$$

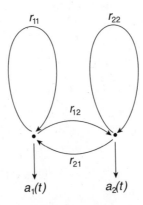

FIGURE 6–12 ■ Special case: two-state, discrete-time Markov source.

As an example, say the source is off (silent) in state 1, and transmits at a fixed rate of V cells/sec while in state 2. This is then the discrete-time version of the silence–talk spurt model for voice discussed extensively in Chapter 3, or the two-state bursty traffic model of section 3.9. For this case,

$$\Phi_1(\theta) = 1 \qquad \text{and} \qquad \Phi_2(\theta) = e^{V\theta}$$

Using these expressions in equation (6–64) and then applying equation (6–65), one finds the effective capacity of this source. For a two-state MMPP, with the source generating cells at a Poisson route of λ_i when in state i, $i = 1$, 2, one uses

$$\Phi_i(\theta) = e^{-\lambda_i(1-e^\theta)} \qquad i = 1, 2,$$

in equation (6–64).

We noted earlier that Kesidis et al have shown, using theorems from large deviation theory, that equations (6–54) and (6–53) apply not only to discrete-time sources but to continuous-time sources as well [KESI 1993]. In particular, consider the N-state Markov fluid source model of Figure 6–13. It has exponentially-distributed transition *rate* μ_{ij} between states i and j, and a constant (fluid) rate of generation of cells of λ_i cells/sec, when the system is in state i, $i = 1, \ldots, N$. This model is precisely that used in section 4.3 in studying the performance of the leaky bucket. Figure 6–13 is the same as Figure 4–23, used earlier in the leaky bucket analysis. Kesidis et al. have shown that, for this case, equation (6–54) reduces to an expression similar to that of equation (6–61) [KESI 1993]:

$$C_e = \frac{1}{\theta} z(M + \theta\Lambda) \tag{6–66}$$

Here, $z(A)$ represents the largest real eigenvalue of matrix A. M is the $N \times N$ matrix of transition rates μ_{ij} discussed extensively in Chapters 3 and 4 (see equations (3–11), (3–47), and (4–52), for example), with the properties that

$$\mu_{ii} = -\sum_{j\neq i} \mu_{ij}$$

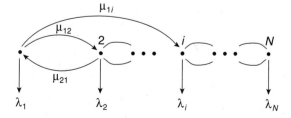

FIGURE 6–13 ■ Markov fluid model.

and

$$\pi M = 0 \qquad\qquad (6\text{--}67)$$

where π is the N-element vector of steady-state probabilities of occupancy of states 1 to N. Λ is the diagonal matrix of the N fluid-flow rates λ_1 to λ_N:

$$\Lambda = \text{diag}\,(\lambda_1, \lambda_1, \ldots \lambda_N) \qquad\qquad (6\text{--}68)$$

Elwalid and Mitra have obtained the same expression (6–66) for the effective capacity of a Markov fluid source using a different technique [ELWA 1993].

Consider the two-state, on-off fluid source model discussed extensively in Chapters 3 and 4 as an example. This model is again portrayed in Figure 6–14. We use the same notation used earlier (see Figures 3–2 and 4–24), with α representing the transition rate from the off- to the on-state, and β the rate in the reverse direction. In the on-state, the source transmits at a constant rate of R_p cells/sec.

For this example, we have

$$M = \begin{bmatrix} -\alpha & \alpha \\ \beta & -\beta \end{bmatrix} \quad \text{and} \quad M + \theta\Lambda = \begin{bmatrix} -\alpha & \alpha \\ \beta & -\beta + \theta R_p \end{bmatrix}$$

It is then left for the reader to show that the eigenvalue z, in this case, is given by

$$z = \frac{-\alpha - \beta + \theta \bar{R}_p}{2} + \sqrt{\frac{(\alpha + \beta - \theta R_p)^2}{4} + \alpha\theta R_p} \qquad\qquad (6\text{--}69)$$

The effective capacity of this source is then given by

$$C_e = z/\theta = \left(\frac{R_p}{2} - \frac{\alpha + \beta}{2\theta}\right) + \sqrt{\left[\frac{R_p}{2} - \left(\frac{\alpha + \beta}{2\theta}\right)\right]^2 + \frac{\alpha R_p}{\theta}} \qquad\qquad (6\text{--}70)$$

Comparing with equation (4–27a) of section 4.1, we note that the two expressions are identical when we replace θ by its equivalent $(1/x)\ln(1/P_L)$ from equation (6–46)! We have thus shown that the effective (or equivalent) capacity expression, obtained using rather tedious algebra in section 4.1, is a special case of the more general form of equation (6–54) or, in the Markov fluid-flow case, equation (6–66). We also know from equation (6–53) that if K heterogeneous sources of the same on-off type are multiplexed, each with its own transition rates α_i and β_i, and constant cell arrival rate R_p^i when in the

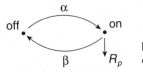

FIGURE 6–14 ▪ On-off fluid model example.

on-state, we get the sum of the effective capacities, proving equation (4–30) of section 4.1. (Note, more generally, from equation (6–53), that the sources don't all have to be the on-off type. The additivity of effective capacities applies to any set of traffic sources sharing the same delay and loss probability parameters for which one can define effective capacities.)

Our final example is that of the Markov-modulated Poisson process (MMPP), a traffic source model we first introduced in section 3.4 and then again in section 3.7. This corresponds to the model of Figure 6–13, with the one change that the rates $\lambda_1 \ldots \lambda_N$ shown there are now understood to be Poisson rates, a different one corresponding to each state. For this case, Kesidis et al. have also shown that the effective capacity expression (6–54) reduces to the determination of an eigenvalue [KESI 1993]:

$$C_e = \frac{1}{\theta} z \Big[M + \big(e^\theta - 1 \big) \Lambda \Big] \tag{6–71}$$

$z(A)$ is again the largest real eigenvalue of the matrix A. Note, as a special case, that if the source is a simple Poisson source (hence with just one state), there are no transitions between states, and one obtains equation (6–57) directly. Note also that if $\theta \ll 1$, equation (6–71) reduces to equation (6–66), the effective capacity result for a Markov-modulated fluid source. But note from our earlier discussion of the effective capacity of a Poisson source that this is the condition for which the Poisson source effective capacity is just its average rate λ. The Poisson source, or set of sources in the case of the MMPP, thus behaves effectively like a fluid source of the same (average) rate.

As an example, consider an on-off source with characteristics similar to those of Figure 4–12 of section 4.1, for which the fluid-flow effective capacity turned out to be a fairly good approximation to the actual capacity. In units of cells transmitted by the source to the multiplexing buffer, let $R_p = 100,000$ cells/sec. Say we desire $P_L = 10^{-5}$ for the buffer loss probability, as in the case of Figure 4–12, with a maximum buffer size of $x = 7000$ cells. Choose $1/\beta = 100$ msec as the average on time, with $p = 0.5$ as the probability the source is "on" (from Figure 4–12 the effective capacity expression (6–70) is a good approximation to the source capacity.) For this case $\theta = \ln(10^{-5})/x \ll 1$. The buffer is thus large enough so that an on-off Poisson-source model would provide the same resultant effective capacity.

Now consider a video source modeled as a doubly-stochastic source, examples of which were given in Chapter 3. Figure 6–15 shows the results of calculations carried out on multiplexed JPEG-type sources which have been deterministically smoothed [SHRO 1995]. A ten-state generalized histogram model has been used to represent each source, and a buffer of 1000 cells chosen to ensure the loss probability is less than 10^{-6}. (For this buffer size the sources may be modeled as Markov-modulated fluid sources.) The curve labeled "Model" indicates the number of such sources that may be multiplexed as a function of the line capacity. Also shown is the number of sources that could be multiplexed using an effective capacity calculation. This is simply given as the sum of the individual capacities. Note how conservative this result is, particularly at high capacities.

The "Model" curve for the video sources may be obtained much more simply using the Gaussian approximation approach discussed in section 4.1. Recall from our original discussion of video signal characterization in section 3.5 that variable-rate video signals do appear to have a bell- or Gaussian-shaped histogram. This is apparent from Figures 3–18, 3–20, and from the histogram of multiplexed JPEG sources sketched in Figure 3–30. On this basis it would appear that the capacity result given by equation (4–12) in section 4.1 should fit the "Model" curve of Figure 6–15. This is, in fact, readily shown to be the case. In particular, let the average bit rate of a single source

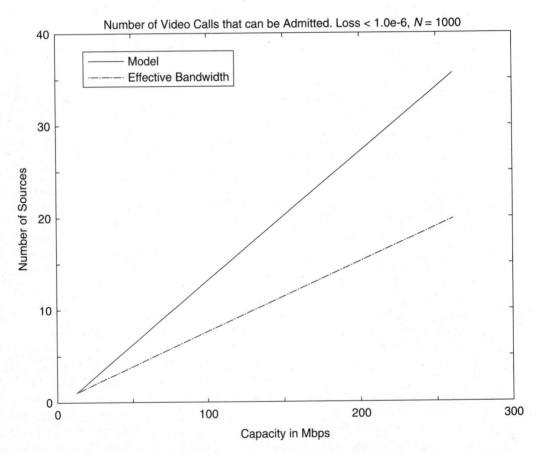

FIGURE 6–15 ■ Limitation of the effective bandwidth scheme: A demonstration with JPEG type video sources (from [SHRO 1995], Figure 4–6).

be 5.6 Mbps. (This corresponds to 235,000 bits per frame, with a frame rate of 24 frames per second. This was the number used as well in the video example of section 3.8.) Let the standard deviation be 1.67 Mbps. For a loss probability of 10^{-6} the parameter K in equation (4–13) is 5.08. It is then left for the reader to show that equation (4–12) does in fact fit the "Model" curve of Figure 6–15 quite accurately.

▪ **PROBLEMS**

6–1 Refer to the discussion of stop-and-go queueing in section 6.1. Demonstrate the following results of using this technique: the maximum offset is T sec; packets maintain their original smoothness property as they move along a given path, despite the merging of multiple connections; the maximum buffer size required at any node with outgoing link capacity C_l in bps is $3C_lT$ bits. Draw some typical end-to-end paths with at least three links (hops) in verifying these results.

6–2 Find the minimum stop-and-go queueing frame size T for the following cases: 32-kbps voice; 2-Mbps file transfer; 6-Mbps video. For each case calculate the end-to-end delay bounds for a 3-hop path covering 2000 km. Use 53-octet ATM cells in each case. Repeat for larger values of T and comment on the resultant delay bounds.

6–3 Consider the pure delay element of Figure 6–6a. Show this increases the traffic burstiness, as defined by the parameter σ of equation (6–4), by ρD, as shown in that figure and indicated by equation (6–7). Can you explain this result intuitively? Now refer to the work-conserving element of Figure 6–6c. Show the bound on maximum delay is given by equation (6–8). Why is it important to specify "work conserving"? Can you show, by example, why this bound might be violated if a nonwork-conserving discipline were used in serving a queue? Can you explain intuitively why the maximum delay bounds in the devices of Figure 6–6c and d are proportional to the traffic burstiness?

6–4 A set of files is to be delivered across an ATM network at a rate of 4800 ATM cells/sec. A leaky bucket policing mechanism is used to regulate the file transfer. The leaky bucket parameters chosen are $r = 4700$ and B (or M) = 200. Find the end-to-end delay bound using the PGPS service discipline if the path chosen across the network covers 3 hops and is 1500 km long. Repeat if B is doubled to 400. Comment on the effect of doubling B.

6–5 Can you explain intuitively why the GPS and PGPS end-to-end delay bounds are proportional to the traffic burstiness? Compare with the bounds on the devices of Figure 6–6. (See problem **6–3** above.)

6-6 Consider the infinite buffer of Figure 6-9.

   a. Show, using the definition of discrete-time varying queue occupancy $q(t)$ of Figure 6-10, that the evolution of $q(t)$ with time obeys equation (6-31).

   b. Show $q(t)$ may also be written in the form of equation (6-31b).

   c. Taking the mgf of $q(t)$ as defined by equation (6-31b), show that the bound of equation (6-34) results. Show that for the case of independent arrival processes, each stochastically bounded by a linear envelope process in the sense of equations (6-28) and (6-30), the bound of equation (6-34b) results.

6-7 A Poisson source of average rate 2000 cells/sec accesses an ATM buffer whose output link operates at a capacity of C_L = 10,000 cells/sec.

   a. Find the effective capacity of the source if the loss probability at the buffer is to be P_L = 10⁻⁶ and the maximum queueing delay is to be 4 msec. How many such sources can be multiplexed at this buffer if admission control is based on effective capacity?

   b. Repeat **a.** if the source has an average rate of 1000 cells/sec.

   c. What combinations of 1000 and 2000 cells/sec Poisson sources can be jointly multiplexed if effective capacity is used as in **a.** and **b.** to determine admission?

   d. Repeat **a.** to **c.** if the maximum queueing delay is increased to 40 msec.

6-8 The effective capacity of a discrete-time, N-state Markov source is given by equation (6-61).

   a. Show that, for a two-state source, equation (6-61) simplifies to equations (6-65) and (6-64).

   b. In each state, the source behaves as a Poisson source. The rate when in state 1 is 1000 cells/sec; when in state 2 the rate is 2000 cells/sec. When in state 1, there is a probability of 0.5 of staying in that state and a probability of 0.5 of moving to state 2. The same statistics apply when in state 2. This source accesses the ATM buffer of problem 6-7. Find the effective capacity of the source if the loss probability is to be 10⁻⁶ and the maximum queueing delay is to be 4 msec, as in problem **6-7a**. Compare with the results of problem **6-7**.

6-9 Using equation (6-66) show the effective capacity of the two-state, fluid-source model of Figure 6-14 is given by equation (6-70). Now consider N heterogeneous on-off sources multiplexed together. Each source has the same QoS parameters P_L and maximum buffer delay. The ith source has a peak transmission rate R_p^i, mean on time $1/\beta_i$, and mean off interval $1/\alpha_i$. Show the effective capacity of the multiplexed sum is given by equation (4-30) in Chapter 4.

6-10 Figure 6-15 shows the bandwidth required to multiplex a number of video sources with each source modeled as a doubly-stochastic source.

The resultant curve is labeled "Model", and is compared with the curve obtained using effective capacity analysis. A simpler way of obtaining the "Model" curve relies on the observation that the histogram of multiplexed video sources tends to approach a Gaussian distribution. This has been noted in Chapter 3. If so, the calculation of capacity in section 4.1 of Chapter 4 which assumes a Gaussian distribution should be applicable. Equations (4–12) and (4–13) are the appropriate equations to use. Consider therefore, a number of video sources to be multiplexed together. Each source requires 5.6 Mbps of capacity, on the average. Its standard deviation is 1.67 Mbps. The probability of loss at the buffer is to be 10^{-6}. Calculate the capacity required for various numbers of such sources and compare with the curve labeled "Model" in Figure 6–15. Repeat this set of calculations for other values of loss probability and compare the results.

6–11 In problem **3–24** of Chapter 3, the average number of bits per frame for the *Star Wars* video sequence of Figure 3–26 was found to be 235,000 bits. The corresponding standard deviation was found to be 52,000 bits. These are based on an eight-level histogram approximation as discussed in Chapter 3. Assuming the histogram of the multiplexed sum approaches a Gaussian distribution, repeat the calculations of problem **6–10** for these numbers and compare results. The video frame rate is 24 frames per second.

Chapter 7

Feedback Congestion Control in Broadband Networks

7.1 ▪ INTRODUCTION

We have alluded occasionally, in previous chapters, to the need for congestion control in ATM-based, high-speed networks. All communication networks, whether packet switched or circuit switched, must have some safeguards built in to prevent traffic from exceeding the network capacity, resulting in deleterious operation, leading possibly even to deadlock situations in which all buffers fill and traffic transmission ceases [SCHW 1987]. As has been noted many times in the literature, traffic congestion in communication networks is completely analogous to the traffic congestion on roads and highways that most of us experience on a daily basis, including, more often than not, deadlock situations in which nothing moves.

The admission control and policing mechanisms discussed in Chapter 4 are examples of techniques designed to reduce the possibility of congestion overtaking a network. These are examples of so-called "open loop controls," where it is presumed that, by proper "shaping" of the traffic at the source network, operation can be kept in a proper, noncongested state. Yet the use of open-loop control alone is understood not to guarantee congestionless operation. The basic leaky bucket policing mechanism, for example, only has two tunable parameters: the token arrival rate (or counter increment/decrement rate) and the maximum token buffer pool (or counter maximum/minimum, depending on how implemented). We have provided examples, in Chapter 4, of ways in which the leaky bucket controller might be designed to handle two-state traffic types such as voice or image traffic. But real traffic can be much more complex than the simple two-state model indicates. A leaky bucket mechanism cannot be expected to handle all types of traffic and guarantee congestion will not occur. This is one of the reasons for our brief introduction, in Chapter 4, to video histogram control as one possible mechanism proposed to control video congestion.

It is clear that exerting absolute *peak* control on incoming traffic, and allocating peak transmission capacity, is one possible solution to the problem of congestion, but this evades the issue: it eliminates the possibility of statistical multiplexing and makes for inefficient, costlier networks. In addition, the implementation of peak rate allocation and control, end-to-end, in a network can be quite complex in a very large wide-area network. How does one guarantee that transmission capacity within all portions of a network is sufficient to handle the combined peak rates of the possibly thousands of VC/VPs traversing it? Providing effective congestion control in the high-speed networks under discussion here is thus a necessity, yet the problems posed in carrying this out are immense and not completely understood, let alone solved, at this point.

Why *is* congestion control in high-speed networks such a problem? Why not simply adopt the congestion control strategies utilized in all existing packet-switched networks? The prime reason has to do with the relatively high bandwidths or speeds with which ATM-based networks are designed to operate. These high bit rates result in extremely short cells (measured in time), the impact of which is felt in two ways: cell processing, including congestion control actions, must be carried out in correspondingly shorter intervals of time as the bit rate increases; more cells are found moving along an end-to-end propagation path as the bit rate increases. We focus here on the second issue.

Consider a typical end-to-end path modeled by a series of queues (one for each switching node on the path) as indicated schematically in Figure 7–1. Assume, for simplicity's sake, that all link capacities are the same and equal to μ cells/sec. The physical propagation delay, end-to-end, not including queueing delay, is labeled τ_f. Let the product of propagation delay and link capacity in cells/sec ($\mu\tau_f$) be much larger than one. Thus, let

$$\mu\tau_f \gg 1 \qquad (7\text{--}1)$$

Since $1/\mu$ is the cell length, in sec, this implies that if the source is operating at its full capacity, that is, if it is sending μ cells/sec out over the path, that there may be as many as $\mu\tau_f$ cells enroute along that path. Now if the destina-

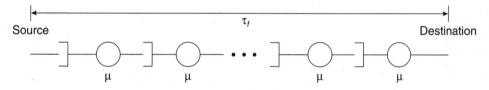

FIGURE 7–1 ■ Model, end-to-end path.

tion buffer becomes congested and attempts to signal the source to stop sending, the $\mu\tau_f$ cells already enroute cannot be controlled unless they are dropped. In addition, if it takes τ_b sec for a feedback message from the destination to arrive back at the source, an additional $\mu\tau_b$ cells will be launched before the control message arrives at the source. (We assume, to be general, that the feedback control messages, either transmitted as part of data cells, or as acknowledgments of cells received in the forward directions, may follow a different path than the data path shown in Figure 7–1.) The total number of cells already sent before any control can take place is thus

$$\mu(\tau_f + \tau_b) = \mu\tau \gg 1 \qquad (7\text{--}2)$$

with τ the round-trip propagation delay. This product is called the delay-bandwidth product. It is a large number for high-speed networks and leads to the basic difficulty in handling congestion in such networks: the task of how to handle the cells already in the round-trip "pipe" before any control action can begin.

Consider some specific numbers to make this problem more concrete. Let the transmission capacity be 45 Mbps to start. This says that the time to transmit one 53-octet cell is 9.4 μsec, or μ = 106,000 cells/sec is the transmission capacity in units of cells/sec. If the round-trip propagation path is 1000 km long, with a propagation delay of 5 μsec/km along that path (this value is fairly typical for high-speed fiber-, or cable-based links), τ is 5 msec. Then $\mu\tau = 53$. In a system operating at full capacity, over 500 cells will thus have been launched before any control action initiated by the destination is reflected back at that point!

Let the transmission rate now be increased to 150 Mbps. The corresponding delay-bandwidth factor now rises to $\mu\tau = 1800$. If the rate is increased further to 600 Mbps, $\mu\tau = 7100$! If it is raised to 2.4 Gbps, $\mu\tau = 28,000$. (The corresponding ATM cell length is $1/\mu = 177$ nsec, or 0.177 μsec.) Note that all of these capacity values are values cited for use in B-ISDN, and were mentioned in our initial discussion of B-ISDN in Chapters 1 and 2.

Since so many cells are potentially enroute in high-speed wide-area networks, it has become a debatable issue as to whether feedback, or closed-loop control, can be effectively used in these networks for congestion control. It is clear that unstable situations could easily arise if improper controls were used. It is for this reason that some workers in the field of B-ISDN and ATM networks have advocated staying strictly with open-loop, or traffic shaping,

[ECKB 1990]   Eckberg, Jr., A. E., et al., "Bandwidth Management: A Congestion Control Strategy for Broadband Packet Networks—Characterizing the Throughput-Burstiness Filter," *Computer Networks and ISDN Systems, 20* (1990): 415–423.

[ECKB 1991]   Eckberg, Jr., A. E., et al., "Controlling Congestion in B-ISDN/ATM: Issues and Strategies," *IEEE Commun. Mag., 29,* 9 (Sept. 1991): 64–70.

techniques such as those discussed in Chapter 4. It has been advocated as well that open-loop control be coupled with a procedure called *violation tagging* to control the possible onset of congestion in a network [ECKB 1990], [ECKB 1991]. In this technique, cells are divided into two groups, those that must get through and those for which "best effort" delivery suffices. In the event of congestion occurring anywhere along a transmission path through the network, cells with a violation tag bit set are dropped. The ATM cell header CLP bit (Figure 2–2 in Chapter 2) could be used for this purpose.

Digitized voice to be transmitted over an ATM network provides a simple example of this technique. Eight-bit voice samples are divided into two groups consisting, respectively, of the four most-significant bits and the four least-significant bits. Successive most-significant bit samples are then combined to form one set of ATM cells; the least-significant bit samples are correspondingly combined to form another set of cells. The ATM cell header CLP bit can then be set for the least-significant bit cells. In the event of congestion occurring within a network, these cells can be dropped. Similar schemes have been proposed for video traffic, with the video signals coded using *layered* or *hierarchical coding*, in which bits are grouped into multiple levels of significance. Lesser significant bits can be dropped, if necessary, reducing the picture quality and/or resolution, but allowing relatively good images to still get through. It has been proposed as well that the leaky bucket policing mechanism be augmented to conditionally allow cells violating the policing constraints into a network rather than dropping them outright. Should they encounter congestion later in the network, they would be dropped. (This can become a controversial issue of course, since these very cells might then be the cause of congestion.)

Despite misgiving posed by some workers in the field of ATM as to the efficacy of closed-loop controls, a consensus has developed to at least provide feedback control for "best-effort" or "available bit rate" (ABR) traffic (see Chapter 2). The ATM Forum, in particular, has approved the adoption of a proposal to provide feedback control to help manage ABR traffic in ATM networks. The ATM Forum is an influential, private organization comprised of most companies worldwide with interests in ATM networking. It was set up to expedite the introduction of ATM technology into the telecommunications field.

Simulation studies carried out in conjunction with the ATM Forum deliberations indicate that feedback control can be a useful technique for controlling ABR congestion in both ATM-based LANs and wide-area, high-speed networks, despite the issue raised earlier of the potential for instability due to the large delay bandwidth products arising in the wide-area networks. The simulations, together with simplified models and analyses of proposed control mechanisms, indicate that, even with large delay-bandwidth products, feedback control can be effective in controlling congestion. These models will be discussed later in this chapter.

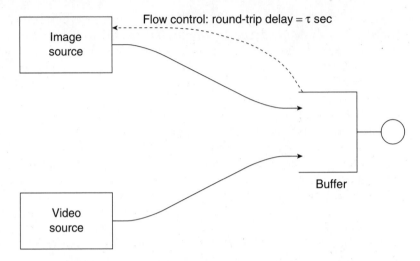

FIGURE 7–2 ■ Example where feedback control can be effective.

In addition, there exist some traffic situations in which the relatively large propagation delay encountered in communicating over wide-area networks should not pose a problem since the traffic variation that could potentially lead to congestion is predictable in advance, and hence control signals can be fed back early enough to take action, if necessary.

A simple example involves the combined transmission of real-time video and nonreal-time traffic sources such as file transfer or images. The simplified picture for this example appears in Figure 7–2. We noted earlier, in Chapter 3, that video, even in compressed form, retains some correlation over multiple frames (see Figures 3–19 and 3–26, for example). Since frames are transmitted at 33–40 msec intervals, it appears that good estimates of the frame cell content should be available for at least 100 msec or more in advance. For round-trip propagation delays up to this value (corresponding to a round-trip propagation path of 20,000 km or less), one should thus be able to signal the image (or file) source shown in Figure 7–2 to reduce its flow, or shut off completely, in enough time to keep the buffer shown from becoming too congested. This example has been studied in detail and results obtained indicate that such feedback control does work and provides a quantifiable gain in image traffic throughput over the noncontrolled case [SKEL 1994].

There exist two distinct ways of having a source reduce its traffic flow in response to congestion control messages fed back through a network. In the window-, or credit-based procedure, a source is allotted a maximum number

[SKEL 1994] Skelly, P. A., et al., "A Cell and Burst Level Control Framework for Integrated Video and Image Traffic," *Proc. IEEE Infocom 94*, Toronto, June 1994: 334–341.

of packets or cells it can transmit into the network before receiving an acknowledgment of correct reception at the destination. Control messages from either the destination or from a congested point within the network are then used to reduce the window size or credit of outstanding packets. In the rate-based procedure, the rate of transmission of packets or cells into the network is controlled by feedback messages. Both methods have been used in data networking. The ATM Forum chose to adopt a rate-based scheme, although a credit-based proposal was considered as well.

In the rest of this chapter we consider both types of control mechanisms, focusing on the dynamics of their operation where possible. In section 7.2 we define more carefully what is meant by congestion and describe the two control mechanisms in somewhat more detail, with emphasis on window control since this has been the technique more commonly adopted in currently operating data networks. In section 7.3 we focus on examples of window controls in existing networks or network architectures, with particular reference to TCP-IP networks and Decnet. We describe a simple model and analysis based on it which has been used to demonstrate the stability of these controls. The analysis is actually applicable to both rate-based and window-type controls since it uses a rate-based model for simplicity. In section 7.4 we describe the ATM Forum proposal for closed-loop rate control. In section 7.5 we return to window control, describing and carrying out an analysis of a window control mechanism designed for high-speed networks.

7.2 ▪ CONGESTION AND CONGESTION CONTROL MECHANISMS

We have been using the word "congestion" quite loosely in this chapter thus far. What do we mean by congestion? Congestion manifests itself at various switches and/or buffers in a packet-switched network when the delays encountered by cells or packets begin to increase rapidly, buffers overflow and drop cells beyond a specified limit, and the throughput begins to drop, even approaching zero or deadlock. These phenomena are portrayed diagrammatically in Figure 7–3. Note that the delay and throughput indicated in that figure could represent those parameters at any node in a network, or could represent delay and throughput end-to-end. They are the typical set of curves encountered in any network, including transportation networks, which incorporates buffers or queues to store the traffic (cells in our case).

Congestion control incorporating feedback thus involves the following features:

1. Recognizes the onset of congestion. A good technique is one that recognizes possible congestion occurring *before* actual congestion is encountered and takes action to *avoid* congestion.

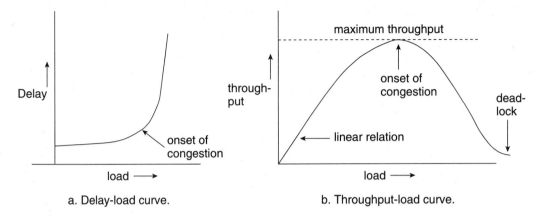

a. Delay-load curve.   b. Throughput-load curve.

FIGURE 7–3 ■ Congestion arising in a network.

2. Sends an appropriate signal back to the user(s) involved in causing the congestion.

3. Invokes an appropriate control.

One simple way of recognizing the onset of congestion in a network, adopted by a number of current packet-switched networks, is to have buffers exceed specified threshold levels [ATKI 1980]. A variation of this technique, suited for congestion *avoidance,* is to have an *average* queue length exceed a specified threshold [RAMAK 1990]. The Internet transport protocol TCP, developed originally for the predecessor ARPANET, uses a transmitter time-out (hence, presumed loss of a packet) as a measure of congestion possibly beginning [JACO 1988].

The congestion signal sent back to the source could be just one bit—congestion detected—or could contain more complete information, such as actual buffer occupancy [RAMA 1990]. It was noted earlier, in Chapter 2, in discussing the ATM cell format, that the 3-bit payload type (PT) field (Figure 2–2) can be used to indicate congestion. Two-bit indicators have been proposed, similar to those adopted for frame relay networks [CCITT 1992e]. One bit, labeled a Forward Explicit Congestion Notification (FECN) bit, would be set at any node at

[ATKI 1980]   Atkins, J. D., "Path Control: The Transport Network of SNA," *IEEE Trans. on Commun. COM-28,* 4 (April 1980): 527–538.

[RAMAK 1990]   Ramakrishnan, K. K., and R. Jain, "A Binary Feedback Scheme for Congestion Avoidance in Computer Networks," *ACM Trans. on Computer Systems, 8,* 2 (May 1990): 158–181.

[JACO 1988]   Jacobson, V., "Congestion Avoidance and Control," *Proc. ACM SIGCOMM 88,* Stanford, CA, Aug. 1988: 314–329.

[CCITT 1992e]   "Recommendation Q.922, ISDN Data Link Layer Specification for Frame Mode Bearer Service," Annex A, "Core Aspects of Q.922, for Use with Frame Relaying Bearer Service." CCITT, Geneva, 1992.

which congestion was encountered. The cell carrying this bit then moves to the destination, at which point a message must be generated to be returned to the source to indicate congestion. A second bit, a Backward Explicit Notification (BECN) bit, indicates a more severe congestion condition, and would be set in a cell moving in the *reverse* direction, back to the source. This indication should thus arrive at the source sooner, for quicker action.

Two types of control mechanisms have been used to control congestion, as noted in the previous section. Window control is the more common technique; rate control has also been used and/or proposed. In the case of window control, a maximum number of cells (or packets) is specified that a source can transmit, without acknowledgment from the destination. (It is worthwhile stressing here that by source and destination pair we mean a particular end-to-end connection, whether a VC in the case of ATM or a transport connection in the case of TCP.) Once the number of cells allotted in a window has been transmitted without any acknowledgment, transmission must stop. The window size thus limits the maximum number of cells, and hence the source throughput, that can be transmitted in a round-trip interval. Congestion control implies reducing this window size in some specified manner.

Rate control is a second method used for congestion control and is the method implicitly proposed for the feedback control shown in Figure 7–2. Rate control can be used in conjunction with a leaky bucket policing mechanism, and analysis has been carried out of such a proposed scheme [WONG 1990]. In this type of procedure, the leaky bucket token arrival rate is varied in accordance with the congestion control information arriving at the source. Since varying the window size varies the number of cells that may be transmitted in a round-trip interval, window control in some sense corresponds to rate control. There is overlap between the two techniques. We shall, in fact, see that some control analyses model the effect of varying the window size as a form of rate control.

In the next section we focus more specifically on window control. We first summarize some early work done on analyzing the performance of fixed-size window controls, and then discuss some adaptive window control mechanisms both utilized, and proposed for use, in practice. This early work is geared to lower-speed networks where the delay-bandwidth product is not too large, and where the propagation delay is not too much of a problem. We then invoke a simple analytical model of one of these adaptive window control mechanisms which explicitly takes propagation into account and indicates the impact of increasing propagation delay. This work indicates that feedback window control is stable, but oscillations will occur as propagation delay increases.

[WONG 1990]   Wong, L. N., and M. Schwartz, "Access Control in Metropolitan Area Networks," *IEEE ICC 90,* Atlanta, GA, April 1990.

7.3 ■ CURRENT WINDOW CONTROL MECHANISMS FOR DATA NETWORKS

Window control mechanisms have been used to control congestion since the inception of packet switching in the 1960s. They appear in X.25 networks [SCHW 1987], in SNA, IBM's pioneering computer networking architecture [ATKI 1980], [SCHW 1987], and, more recently, in TCP/IP networks such as those associated with the Internet [JACO 1988], and in DECs DECNET [RAMA 1990].

A simple model of a sliding window control for a single virtual circuit end-to-end, from source to destination, appears in Figure 7–4. The sliding window control is one in which each packet is individually acknowledged, allowing the window to move forward or "slide" by one once the acknowledgment arrives back at the source. Figure 7–4a is a model of the virtual circuit (or any other end-to-end connection). Note that this model is the same as the one shown in Figure 7–1, except that this model now explicitly indicates the traffic load λ impinging on the end-to-end path, as well as the fact that the model is assumed to consist of M hops, with M buffers end-to-end. Figure 7–4b portrays the resulting model of the sliding window, with the window size given as W [PENN 1975], [SCHW 1987]. Note that this resultant model is that of a closed queueing network, similar to the first leaky bucket model discussed earlier in Chapter 4 (see Figure 4–16).

If propagation delay is neglected and the M tandem queues of Figure 7–4 are assumed to be independent, the queueing delay-throughput characteristic of the sliding window control is readily obtained. It is then shown that if the ratio of throughput to delay is to be maximized (this ratio is termed the "power"), the optimum window size is $W = M$, that is, the window size should be equal to the number of hops along the end-to-end path [SCHW 1982], [SCHW 1987]. Lazar has carried out a study of the optimum congestion control mechanism, again neglecting propagation delay, in the sense of maximizing the path throughput with the average time delay, constrained to be some specified value. He has shown that the sliding window results [LAZA 1983a], [LAZA 1983b].

These studies demonstrate that the sliding window control has some nice properties under conditions of *equilibrium*. They do not address the question of how to vary the window size as traffic conditions change, of the infor-

[PENN 1975]   Pennotti, M. C., and M. Schwartz, "Congestion Control in Store and Forward Links," *IEEE Trans. on Commun., COM-23,* 12 (Dec. 1975): 1434–1443.

[SCHW 1982]   Schwartz, M., "Performance Analysis of the SNA Virtual Route Pacing Control," *IEEE Trans. on Commun., COM-30,* 1 (Jan 1982): 173–184.

[LAZA 1983a]   Lazar, A., "The Throughput-Time Delay Function of an M/M/1 Queue," *IEEE Trans. on Info. Theory, IT-29,* 11 (Nov. 1983): 914–918.

[LAZA 1983b]   Lazar, A., "Optimal Flow Control of a Class of Queueing Networks in Equilibrium," *IEEE Trans. on Automatic Control, AC-28,* 8 (Aug. 1983): 1001–1007.

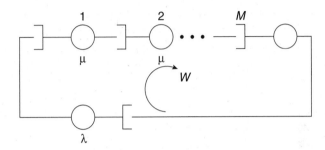

a. End-to-end virtual circuit model.

b. Window control incorporated.

FIGURE 7–4 ■ Sliding window control.

mation to be fed back in making the window adaptive, nor of the stability of the resultant window mechanism as the propagation delay is introduced, resulting in *delayed* feedback. These questions are addressed in more recent work that we now discuss.

Consider, first, the question of the window adjustment needed to either avoid congestion or to reduce it if deemed present. One possibility is to invoke congestion control in phases, reducing the window size gradually if "mild congestion" is detected; then slamming the window shut or reducing it abruptly, to a minimum value, if "severe congestion" is experienced. "Mild" or "severe" congestion could correspond, respectively, to different queueing thresholds at a nodal buffer. This is the method adopted many years ago in IBMs Systems Network Architecture (SNA)[ATKI 1980]. To avoid having two thresholds to consider, involving measures of "mild" and "severe" congestion, more recent congestion control mechanisms have focused on exponential reductions of window size when congestion is to be either avoided or controlled when it occurs. Letting W represent the window size, as in Figure 7–4, an exponential reduction is represented by the expression

$$W \leftarrow dW \qquad d < 1$$

As the congestion persists, W rapidly goes to zero, or to some specified minimum value.

One argument given for this exponential reduction in window size, when congestion is determined to either be present or imminent, is that the queue size tends to grow rapidly at the onset of congestion [JACO 1988]. Thus the queue size $q \propto 1/(1 - \rho)$, ρ the utilization. Only a correspondingly sharp reduction in window size can counter this potentially rapid increase in queue size.

On the other hand, when measurements indicate congestion is not present, the window can be incremented linearly to some maximum value: $W \leftarrow W + b$. A typical increment is $b = 1$. There is, thus, a slow, linear increase of window size when congestion is not present; a rapid, exponential (or nonlinear) decrease when it is deemed to be present.

What should the measure of congestion be? One possibility already mentioned is to have a nodal buffer size q equal or exceed some specified threshold. More generally, we can write $Q(q) \geq L$, with $Q(q)$ some function of the queue size and L a threshold. Summarizing the window control mechanism proposed then, we have

$$\left. \begin{array}{ll} W \leftarrow dW, & Q\,(q) \geq L \\ W \leftarrow W + b, & Q\,(q) < L \end{array} \right\} \tag{7–3}$$

What are some specific mechanisms used or proposed in practice? Ramakrishnan and Jain propose an "explicit binary feedback scheme" (similar to the FECN method mentioned earlier) for congestion avoidance, in which a single bit is set in a packet moving toward the destination user if congestion is deemed imminent [RAMA 1990]. This single-bit indication is then fed back through an acknowledgment to the source(s) of possible congestion. This bit is set at any node whose *average* queue length $\bar{q}$ equals or exceeds a value of 1. The average queue length is measured over a time T taken equal to the last (busy plus idle) cycle time, plus the busy period of the current cycle. This interval is shown in Figure 7–5. Their window update policy is to update the window only after two windows worth of acknowledgments have been received. If W_c is the current window value, and W_p the previous window value, the number of acknowledgments used in determining a window update is $(W_p + W_c)$. The update decision is to then count the bits set in the last W_c acknowledgments returned. If at least 50% of the bits have been set, then

$$W_c \leftarrow 0.875 W_c$$

otherwise,

$$W_c \leftarrow W_c + 1$$

The parameters d and b are thus 0.875 and 1, respectively. A similar strategy has been proposed for frame relay networks [CCITT 1992d]. The policy chosen for TCP over Internet is to have $d = 0.5$ whenever a time-out occurs at the transmitter [JACO 1988]. This results in a much more rapid decrease in window size if traffic congestion is encountered. (Note also that there is no explicit congestion feedback signal transmitted in this case. The loss of packets, as exemplified by transmitter time-outs occurring, triggers the window reduction. The TCP mechanism is meant to reduce congestion when it is encoun-

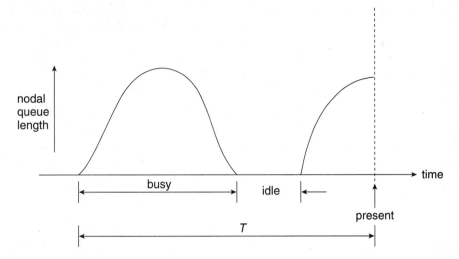

FIGURE 7–5 ■ Interval used to measure average queue length.

tered; the Ramakrishnan-Jain procedure is specifically designed to *avoid* congestion. The TCP window variation also includes a "slow-start" procedure to recover from window reduction when it occurs [JACO 1988].)

    We return now to the discussion of the Ramakrishnan-Jain window control procedure. They indicate that the choices of $d = 0.875$ and $b = 1$ noted above are based on maximizing the "power," the function referred to earlier as the ratio of throughput to average delay at a node. A typical delay-throughput curve appears in Figure 7–6. Note that, as true with any queueing curve, the

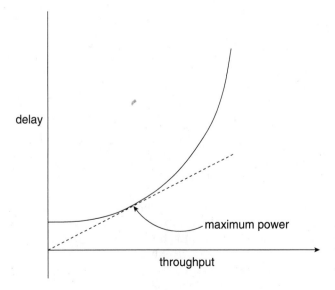

FIGURE 7–6 ■ Maximizing power = throughput/delay.

delay remains relatively constant, not increasing very much while the throughput increases significantly, until a point referred to as the "knee" of the curve is reached; at this point the delay begins to increase significantly while the throughput levels off. This is the point at which the power is maximum.

Consider an infinite $M/M/1$ queue as an example. Its average arrival rate or load is λ, its service rate is μ. The average queueing delay is then

$$E(T) = \frac{1}{\mu}\frac{1}{1-\rho} \qquad \rho \equiv \lambda/\mu \qquad\qquad (7\text{--}4)$$

Since the throughput γ is just the load λ for an infinite queue, the power is given by

$$\text{Power}|_{M/M/1} = \lambda/E(T) = \rho\mu^2\,(1-\rho) \qquad\qquad (7\text{--}5)$$

It is left to the reader to show this is maximum at a utilization of $\rho = 0.5$. An alternate interpretation of the knee of the curve is the point at which a straight line drawn from the origin is tangent to the curve of $E(T)$ vs. λ. This is indicated in Figure 7–6. This is left for the reader to show as well.

A second example is that of the infinite $M/D/1$ queue, more appropriate to ATM-based networks with fixed packet (cell) size. The average queueing delay in this case is

$$E(T) = \frac{1}{\mu}\left(1-\frac{\rho}{2}\right)/(1-\rho) \qquad\qquad (7\text{--}6)$$

It is left to the reader to show, both by calculating the maximum of the power $\lambda/E(T)$ and by finding the point at which the straight line from the origin is tangent to the $E(T)$ vs. λ curve, that the utilization at which the power is maximum is $\rho = 2 - \sqrt{2} = 0.586$. (It is interesting how this value of ρ crops up in unexpected places! See equation (5–51) in Chapter 5, for example).

Returning now to the infinite $M/M/1$ queue example, consider the distribution of queue size. For this queue,

$$P(q = k) = (1-\rho)\rho^k \qquad\qquad (7\text{--}7)$$

The probability the queue length equals or exceeds a value n is then

$$P[q \geq n] = (1-\rho)\sum_{n}^{\infty}\rho^k = \rho^n \qquad\qquad (7\text{--}8)$$

If we now take $\rho = 1/2$, the utilization at which the power is maximum, and set $n = 1$, we get $P(q \geq 1) = 0.5$. This says that at the value of utilization at which the power is maximum, there is a 50% probability that the queue length will equal or exceed 1. Ramakrishnan and Jain [RAMAK 1990] have used this simple analysis to select the parameters for their window control: If buffers are operating at the desired point of maximum power, the respective queues should be at or greater than an average of on 50% of the time. Congestion bits set in packets passing through will then also be set at least 50% of the time. This accounts for their choice of the test as to when to reduce the window size and avoid congestion, that is, avoid going above the knee of the delay-throughput curve. They indicate that simulation verifies this result. Note also that since the $M/D/1$ analysis gives a value of $\rho = 0.586$ as being at the knee of the curve, the choice of the $M/M/1$ queue as the model used is not too critical.

Because a source experiences a delay in receiving the congestion information fed back (one bit set in the work of Ramakrishnan and Jain, as well as in the FECN/BECN indicators noted earlier or the time for a timer to expire in the TCP case) it is expected that oscillations in the window size will occur. Two methods can be used to dampen them. One approach is to take action based on an average queue threshold exceeded, rather than basing congestion notification on an instantaneous queue threshold exceeded. This is the method chosen by Ramakrishnan and Jain as explained above [RAMA 1990]. One can also dampen the oscillatory behavior of the window mechanism by reducing the window size at a smaller rate, that is, increasing d in equation (7–3). This is the reason why Ramakrishnan and Jain have selected $d = 0.875$. The price paid for reducing the window oscillations is to slow down the congestion response. There is thus the usual tradeoff between desired rapid response to a control signal and the concurrent oscillation (overshoot) in the response.

A critical issue, however, in using feedback to adjust window size in response to congestion, is the issue of stability, as noted at the beginning of this chapter. Can one ensure that the congestion control mechanisms adopted, despite having to operate over potentially long delays, do result in stable operation, albeit with unavoidable oscillatory behavior? Some recent theoretical studies, using admittedly simple models for their analysis, indicate that the window adjustment mechanism discussed here is a stable one. Studies of a somewhat different window adjustment algorithm (to be described in section 7.5) and designed specifically for the large delay-bandwidth product environment indicate that algorithm is stable as well. These studies all analyze continuous-time rate control mechanisms, rather than window control explicitly, since a time-varying window control mechanism is difficult to model analytically. Note, however, that a connection can be made between the two. Given a window size of W packets or cells, and round-trip acknowledgment time τ, the maximum throughput, or rate at which a source generates packets (cells) is just W/τ. By varying W, we effectively vary the rate.

The simplest model describing feedback control for congestion avoidance/reduction appears in Figure 7–7 [BOLO 1990]. It shows a single queue

[BOLO 1990]   Bolot, J. C. and A. V. Shankar, "Dynamical Behavior of Rate-Based Flow Control Mechanisms," *ACM Computer Communication Review* (April 1990): 35–49.

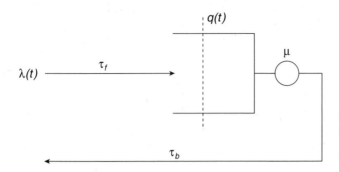

FIGURE 7–7 ■ Simple model, congestion-control mechanism (from [BOLO 1990], Figure 1, by permission).

with time-varying queue occupancy (length) $q(t)$. Traffic of rate $\lambda(t)$ is transmitted to this queue, but, because of propagation delay, only arrives at the queue τ_f sec later. To close the loop and provide feedback to the source, a measure of the queue occupancy is fed back to the source, arriving there τ_b sec later. The single queue thus represents the effective queueing delay introduced along a complete path in the network. It could also represent the "bottleneck" queue on the path, the one at which congestion is encountered, all other buffers on the path assumed to be effectively empty. Such single-queue models have often been used to capture the gross queueing effects along the route through a network. See [SUNS 1977] for example.

Bolot and Shankar have carried out a simple analysis of this basic model, assuming fluid-flow conditions prevail [BOLO 1990]. The rate $\lambda(t)$ is thus taken to be deterministic, although time-varying, as is the queue size $q(t)$. Their model and analysis, focusing on controlling the source rate by a signal fed back from the queue, capture the exponential reduction in source rate if the queue occupancy tends to grow, and linear increase in the rate if the queue is empty. The model thus approximates the control algorithm of equation (7–3), albeit through rate control rather than window control directly. The analysis shows, as expected, that the source rate does vary in an oscillatory manner, but the mechanism is stable.

Their analysis consists of representing the control by two coupled linear differential equations which are readily solved to obtain the parameters of interest. Specifically, say that a signal is fed back increasing the source rate $\lambda(t)$ linearly if the queue is empty, while the rate is reduced exponentially if the queue is at all occupied. (This compares with the window control discussed above in which the window is reduced exponentially if the average queue occupancy exceeds 1.) This control signal arrives at the source τ_b sec after being out. The rate control is then represented by the following equation:

[SUNS 1977]   Sunshine, C. A., "Efficiency of Interprocess Communication Protocols for Computer Networks," *IEEE Trans. on Commun. COM-25*, 2 (Feb. 1977): 287–293.

$$\frac{d\lambda(t)}{dt} = \alpha \qquad\qquad q(t - \tau_b) = 0$$

$$\qquad\qquad = \frac{-\lambda(t)}{\beta} \qquad\qquad q(t - \tau_b) > 0 \qquad\qquad (7\text{--}9)$$

Note that the linear increase parameter α is comparable to b in the window control of equation (7–3), while β plays the role of d in the exponentially-decreasing control of equation (7–3). (As β increases, the control effect is reduced; as β decreases, the control is strengthened. The parameter d in equation (7–3) operates in the same manner.)

Now consider the effect on the queue of changes in the traffic arrival rate $\lambda(t)$. So long as the traffic rate, as seen at the queue, is less than the service rate μ, the queue tends to empty and stays empty once it reaches that position. If the rate λ exceeds μ, however, the queue size increases at a rate proportional to the difference between the arrival rate and m. Specifically, then,

$$\frac{dq(t)}{dt} = 0 \qquad \text{if } \lambda(t - \tau_f) < \mu \quad \text{and} \quad q(t) = 0$$

$$\qquad\qquad = \lambda(t - \tau_f) - \mu \qquad\qquad \text{otherwise} \qquad\qquad (7\text{--}10)$$

Here, the time shift $(t - \tau_f)$ indicates that the effect of the rate $\lambda(t)$ at the source is only felt at the queue (that is, the congested node in a network) τ_f sec later.

Equations (7–9) and (7–10) may be solved simultaneously quite simply. The details are left to the reader. Typical curves for $\lambda(t)$ and $q(t)$ appear in Figure 7–8. Note that these curves capture the expected effects. Assuming the buffer starts off empty, the source rate tends to increase linearly, starting from zero, with rate of increase α. As it reaches and crosses the value μ, the buffer will tend to start filling. But that can only happen τ_f sec later, as the traffic flowing at a rate $\geq\mu$ reaches the buffer. At this point, the control comes into play, signaling the source to start reducing its rate following the rule of equation (7–9). But this reduction can only begin τ_b sec later, as is apparent from the curve of Figure 7–8. In the meantime, the reduction begins to be felt at the queue τ_f sec later, at which time the rate of increase of the queue size begins to decrease. At time t_2, as shown in Figure 7–8, $\lambda(t)$ crosses and drops below the buffer service rate μ. This point is felt at the buffer τ_f sec later, at which time the buffer, having reached its maximum value, starts emptying. Once the queue empties completely, a signal is again sent back to the source, arriving τ_b sec later, indicating the source should start increasing its rate. The cycle just outlined then repeats, continuing on indefinitely, except for the initial start-up (transient) interval shown in Figure 7–8. The oscillatory behavior of the control, as noted above, is apparent, and is of course due to the delay in responding to both traffic increases and control signals sent out from the buffer.

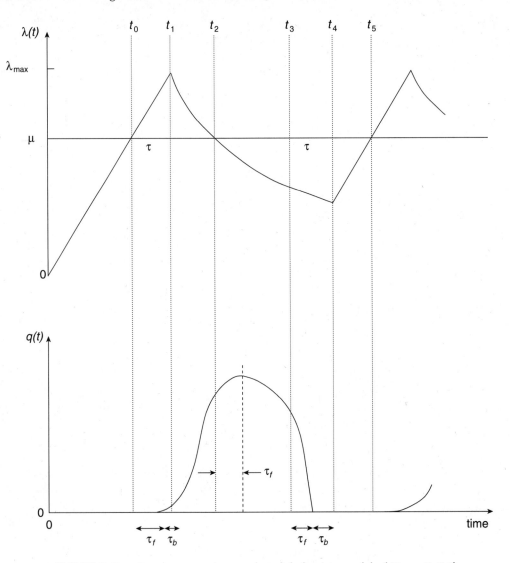

FIGURE 7–8 ■ Source rate and queue length behavior, model of Figure 7–7 (from [BOLO 1990], Figure 2, by permission).

The oscillatory, steady-state behavior of both the source rate $\lambda(t)$ and the queue occupancy $q(t)$ are given quantitatively by the following equations which are solutions of equations (7–9) and (7–10) in any one cycle [BOLO 1990]. It is left to the reader to derive these results.

1. $\lambda(t)$ decreasing in each cycle

$$\lambda(t) = (\mu + \alpha\tau)e^{-(t-t_1)/\beta} \qquad t_1 \leq t \leq t_4 \qquad (7\text{–}11)$$

2. $\lambda(t)$ increasing in each cycle

$$\lambda(t) = \alpha(t - t_4) + \lambda_{min} \qquad t_4 \le t \le t_1 + T \qquad (7\text{--}12)$$

with $\lambda_{min} = \lambda(t_4) = \lambda(t_3 + \tau)$ in equation (7–11), and T the period of the full cycle. The time-varying expression for the queue occupancy is, in turn, given by

$$q(t) = \int_{t_0}^{t} \left[\lambda(t - \tau_f) - \mu\right] dt \qquad (7\text{--}13)$$

from equation (7–10).

The times t_0, t_1, t_3, and t_4 appearing in these equations are those shown indicated in Figure 7–8. (Equations (7–11) to (7–13) refer explicitly to the first cycle only, as shown in Figure 7–8. These same equations apply in each cycle thereafter, however, as already noted.) Some performance parameters of interest may be obtained from these equations and by reference to Figure 7–8 [BOLO 1990]. Specifically, we have

$$\lambda_{max} = \mu + \alpha\tau \qquad (7\text{--}14)$$

since $\lambda(t)$ increases linearly in the range t_0 to t_1, with $(t_1 - t_0) = \tau$. It is left to the reader to show that

$$q_{max} = \frac{\alpha\tau^2}{2} + \alpha\beta\tau + \mu\beta\ln\left[\mu/(\mu + \alpha\tau)\right] \qquad (7\text{--}15)$$

Finally

$$T = 2\tau + (t_3 - t_1) + (\mu - \lambda_{min})/\alpha \qquad (7\text{--}16)$$

with

$$(t_3 - t_1) = \beta x \qquad (7\text{--}17)$$

x, in turn, the solution to the equation

$$1 - e^{-x} = \left(\frac{\mu}{\mu + \alpha\tau}\right) x - \frac{\alpha\tau^2}{2\beta(\mu + \alpha\tau)} \qquad (7\text{--}18)$$

Some tradeoffs become apparent from these equations and from numerical results appearing in [BOLO 1990]. First, the length of the transient period, the time t_0 in Figure 7–8, is reduced by increasing the parameter α. [This is then comparable to increasing the parameter b in the window control of equation (7–3).] Note, in particular, that $t_0 = \mu/\alpha$. But increasing α increases λ_{max} and q_{max} as well, while the period T is reduced somewhat. Note also that the maximum queue size is proportional to τ^2, so that as the round-trip delay increases, the maximum buffer occupancy increases considerably.

A considerable simplification of the analysis results if one assumes that the control in the congested region is linear rather than exponential and decreases the source rate at the same rate as it is increased in the noncongested region [BOLO 1990]. Thus, let

$$\frac{d\lambda(t)}{dt} = \alpha \qquad q(t - \tau_b) = 0$$

$$= -\alpha \qquad q(t - \tau_b) > 0 \tag{7-19}$$

(This amounts to linearizing equation (7–9), assuming $\lambda(t)$ does not vary very much from its desired value μ. Then $\lambda(t)/\beta \doteq \mu/\beta$ in equation (7–9) is replaced by the constant value α.) The performance parameters are then given by the following simple expression in [BOLO 1990]:

$$q_{max} = \alpha\tau^2 \tag{7-20}$$

$$T = 2\tau(2 + \sqrt{2}) \tag{7-21}$$

(It is assumed, in deriving these, that $\lambda_{min} > 0$.) Note that the period T is now independent of the parameter α, but that q_{max} is still proportional to α as well as to τ^2. Numerical calculations indicate that the results of the linearized control do not differ very much from those of the exponential-reduction control if the control parameters are chosen so that $\alpha\beta = \mu$ [BOLO 1990].

A different analysis using a probabilistic rather than a deterministic approach has been carried out and comes to essentially the same conclusions as these presented above, using a simple deterministic approach. In the probabilistic approach, both the queue length $q(t)$ and $\lambda(t)$ are described as random variables [MUKH 1991]. The linear-increase/exponential-decrease adaptive rate control algorithm is then embedded in a standard Fokker-Planck or forward diffusion equation, which is used to describe the evolution in time of the probability density functions for Markov processes [PAPO 1990]. Their results indicate that feedback delay introduces oscillations, but that these oscillations become periodic, approaching a limit cycle. The controlled system is thus oscillatory but stable. The same tradeoffs noted above appear in this analysis as well: Increasing the control variables α and λ/β results in a faster response, which is desirable, but increases the oscillations, which is undesirable.

These oscillations introduced by the congestion control mechanisms have been observed in both simulation studies and measurements of real traffic [RAMAK 1990], [JACO 1988].

In the next section, we discuss the ATM Forum proposal for a rate-based, closed-loop flow control mechanism. It turns out the analysis discussed in this

[MUKH 1991]   Mukherjee, A., and J. C. Strikwerda, "Analysis of Dynamic Congestion Control Protocols—A Fokker-Planck Approximation," *Proc. ACM SIGCOMM 91,* Zurich, Switz., Sept. 1991: 159–169.

section agrees with some of the simulations carried out of that mechanism. These simulations indicate the rate-based mechanism is stable, although it too exhibits the expected oscillations about the stable, controlled, point.

In section 7.5 we return to a window control, discussing an adaptive window control algorithm designed specifically for networks with very large delay-bandwidth products. Analysis of this algorithm indicates that, although oscillations will be present, they can be controlled.

7.4 ■ CLOSED-LOOP, RATE-BASED TRAFFIC CONTROL: ATM FORUM PROPOSAL

As noted earlier, the ATM Forum, a voluntary private organization comprised of most companies involved with ATM technology, has proposed using a rate-based closed-loop approach to manage available bit rate (ABR) traffic over ATM networks. The specific algorithm adopted by the Forum is called the "enhanced proportional control algorithm" (EPRCA) [ATM 1994a], [BONO 1995]. The rate-based algorithm was selected after consideration of a credit-based scheme [ATM 1994b], [KUNG 1995]. Both algorithms were extensively studied, using simulation, by members of the ATM Forum traffic management subworking group. The credit-based scheme requires link-by-link flow control, using a variant of the sliding window mechanism. The rate-based mechanism, to be discussed in some detail in this section, is an end-to-end flow control scheme. A comparative study of the two strategies indicates the rate-based approach is relatively simpler to implement, since the credit-based approach requires per VC queue management at each node of a network [HSIN 1994].

The rate-based flow control mechanism underlying EPRCA is easily described in words. Consider a source transmitting on a virtual connection (VC) to a destination. It does so at some allowed cell rate (ACR), ranging between minimum and maximum (peak) values that have been previously established during call connection setup. It is this cell rate that is varied, depending on congestion conditions experienced along the path or paths the cells will take between source and destination.

[ATM 1994a] *Closed-Loop Rate-Based Traffic Management,* Document Number ATM Forum/94-0438R2 (September 1994).

[BONO 1995] Bonomi, F., and K. W. Fendick, "The Rate-Based Flow Control Framework for the Available Bit Rate ATM Service," *IEEE Network, 9,* 2 (March/April 1995): 25–39

[ATM 1994b] *Credit-Based FCVC Proposal for ATM Traffic Management* (revision A2), ATM Forum/94-0632 (July 1994).

[KUNG 1995] Kung, H. T., and R. Morris, "Credit-Based Flow Control for ATM Networks," *IEEE Network, 9,* 2 (March/April 1995): 40–48.

[HSIN 1994] Hsing, D. K., and F. Vakil, "A Discussion on the ATM Forum Flow Control Proposals," *TM-24456,* Bellcore, September 19, 1994.

Specifically, data cells are sent spaced 1/ACR units of time apart, with the rate ACR reduced by an amount ADR after each cell is sent. (The choice of these parameters will be discussed later.) The system thus tends to drive the rate ACR down to the minimum possible value. Every Nrm cells, however (with Nrm an implementation parameter), the source generates a special cell called a *resource management* (RM) cell transmitted in the forward direction to the destination. On arriving at the destination, this cell causes a backward-direction RM cell to be sent back to the source. If this backward-direction RM cell is received at the source with no indication of congestion encountered, the source rate is incremented by Nrm∗ADR, plus an additional bias. This is designed to undo the decrease in the source rate accumulated by the transmission of the previous Nrm data cells.

The algorithm is in essence a fail-safe one: It continually reduces the source rate toward the minimum value, unless it receives a signal, once every Nrm cells sent, to bring the rate back up (and possibly beyond) to at most the maximum allowed value. If the backward-direction RM cell is lost, or arrives at the source with an indication of congestion encountered, the source rate is not incremented and continues to be reduced after each data cell sent.

The ATM Forum proposal for the RM cell format appears in Table 7–1 [ROBE 1994]. Note first, that what distinguishes this cell type from the normal ATM cell is the 3-bit PT field (Figure 2–2, Chapter 2), in the fourth octet of the 5-octet header. This field is set to 110 (the number 6) for an RM cell. (The first

TABLE 7–1 ■ RM Cell Format (from [ROBE 1994], by permission)

Octet no.	Bits	Field & Name	Set by		
			Source	Network	Destination
1–5		ATM Header	PT=110		
6		Protocol id	0		
7	1	DIR, direction bit	0=forward		1=backward
7	2	CI, congestion indication	0	1, if congest.	1, if EFCI = 1
7	3	BS, block start			
7	4	Reserved			
7	5–8	N	$\log_2 Nrm$		
8,9		Reserved			
10,11		CCR, current cell rate	ACR		
12,13		MCR, min.cell rate			
14,15		ER, explicit cell rate	PCR	Explicit cell rate	may be set, if EFCI=1
52,53		CRC, cyclic check	CRC,16	CRC,16	CRC,16

[ROBE 1994]   Roberts, L., "RM Cell Format Proposal," ATM Forum/94–0973R1, Traffic Management Sub-Working Group, ATM Forum Technical Committee, Nov. 10, 1994.

bit of this field is always a 0 for data cells.) The first bit of the seventh octet is set to 0 for RM cells moving in the forward direction; to 1, if moving in the backward direction. If congestion is detected anywhere along the source-destination path in the network, the congestion indication (CI) bit, the second bit of octet 7, is set to 1. The setting of this bit is an indication to the source, on receiving the backward-direction RM cell, not to increment its cell rate.

Note that Table 7–1 also indicates that the CI bit is set to 1 "if EFCI=1". The term EFCI refers to the congestion indication bit of the data cells moving in the forward direction. This is the second bit in the data cell PT field (Figure 2–2, Chapter 2). This bit is normally set to 0 by the source. A network switch experiencing congestion will change this bit to 1 on all relevant data cells passing through it. (Depending on the implementation, the congestion could refer to *all* data cells, or to those on a particular VC or set of VCs.) On reaching the destination, a cell with a bit so set will cause the next backward-direction RM cell for that VC to have its CI bit set to 1 as well. As noted above, this is then an indication to the source not to increase the cell rate. This congestion notification mechanism is similar to the FECN method mentioned earlier in section 7.2. A backward-moving RM cell with CI=0 can have that bit changed to 1 as well by any switch experiencing congestion along the path back to the source. Congestion notification by a switch can also be speeded up, as done with the BECN method mentioned in section 7.2, by setting CI=1 in a backward RM cell passing through it in response to a forward data cell with its EFCI bit set to 1. The switch changes EFCI in the data cell to 0 as well, so that the process is not further repeated at the destination.

Octets 10,11 and 14,15 in the RM cell format of Table 7–1 can be used to invoke two additional control features, if so desired. These two features represent enhancements to an earlier proposal for a rate-based algorithm. The ER (explicit rate) octets 14,15 are initially set to the peak (maximum) cell rate (PCR) by the source. Any intermediate switch along the path to the destination can then reduce this rate to a rate ER if it cannot, for some reason, handle the current source cell rate. (Added connections through that switch coming on quickly may, for example, require a fast response by the source.) The backward RM cell arriving at the source then carries the smallest or bottleneck ER set along the path, and the source, in setting its allowed cell rate ACR, uses ER if smaller than the newly calculated ACR. The value of ACR appearing in octets 10,11 of the RM cell is not modified by intermediate switches, but may be used to selectively increase or decrease rates on different connections to help reduce congestion, more equitably allocate link rates, or provide increased throughput where possible.

Following is a more detailed description of the rate-based algorithm appearing in [ATM 1994a]:

Network assigns values of PCR (peak cell rate), ICR (initial cell rate), MCR (minimum cell rate), MDF (mutiplicative decrease factor), Nrm.

1. Initialize, with ACR set to ICR. Thus,

$$MCR \leq ACR = ICR \leq PCR$$

Set

$$ADR = ACR/2^{MDF}$$

2. If the current time is at least the next cell transmission time, and ACR > ICR or a cell has been sent, set

$$ACR = \max(ACR - ADR, MCR)$$

The next cell transmission time at which a cell will be sent, if available, is then 1/ACR units of time later.

3. Every Nrm cells the forward RM cell is sent, and the additive decrease rate ADR changed to

$$ADR = ACR/2^{MDF}$$

4. On receiving a backward RM cell, the source does the following:

if CI = 0,

$$ACR = ACR + Nrm*ADR + AIR$$

$$ACR = \min(ACR, ER, PCR)$$

$$ACR = \max(ACR, MCR).$$

As noted earlier, the allowed cell rate (ACR) decreases by the rate $ACR/2^{MDF}$ each data cell time, but increases by the rate Nrm*ARD + AIR every Nrm cells, if congestion is not present. The parameter AIR is established at connection setup time and is the bias term mentioned earlier.

Extensive simulations of the algorithm for a variety of network architectures and topologies have been carried out, as noted previously. The configurations chosen range from small propagation delay LANs to long propagation delay wide-area networks (WANs), as well as combinations of these. All indicate the algorithm is stable, although oscillations do appear, as expected. We focus here on one set of simulations and compare its results to the simple analysis discussed in the previous section. Interestingly, we find ballpark figure agreement between simulation and analysis in the case of a moderate-sized network simulation. This is actually almost unexpected, considering the simplifying assumptions made in carrying out the analysis. As we shall see, the simulation and analysis agree reasonably well on the period (cycle time) of the control oscillations, on maximum queue lengths, the time delay or phase difference between onset of the peak values of the source transmission rate and the queue length (see Figure 7–8), and other parameters of interest.

The particular set of simulations on which we focus has five sources connected to five destinations through two tandem ATM switches [BARN 1994]. Traffic from the five sources is multiplexed at the first switch over individual links varying in length from 1 to 50 km. The traffic is demultiplexed at the second switch and transmitted to the destinations over individual links with the same length variation. A backbone, bottleneck, link connects the two switches. All line rates were taken to be 149.76 Mbps, with a corresponding cell transmission time of 2.8 μsec. Two different cases were simulated, a MAN (metropolitan area network), with a backbone link length of 50 km, and a WAN, with a backbone link length of 1000 km. The maximum round-trip path length was thus 300 km in the MAN case and 2200 km in the case of the WAN. The topological form of this model was specifically chosen to determine how well the algorithm in the MAN case performed when presented with such a wide variation in path lengths, and hence propagation delays, among the source-distance pairs. (Using a propagation delay factor of 4 μsec/km, the round-trip propagation delay varied about three to one in the MAN case, from 0.416 msec to 1.2 msec. This, in turn, affects the times at which the rate parameter ACR is adjusted on the different source-destination pairs by backward-moving cells.)

In running the simulations, the peak cell rate (PCR) was chosen to be 353,000 cells/sec, the initial cell rate (ICR) was set to PCR/20, and the minimum cell rate (MCR) was taken as PCR/1000, or 353 cells/sec. The parameter MDF was set to 8, so that the rate change was ADR = $ACR/2^8$ = ACR/256. Simulations were carried out for a variety of source types, including variable load, persistent load, staggered load, and bursty load sources [BARN 1994]. Times between cells and bursts were exponentially distributed in the variable load and bursty load cases, respectively.

The rate-control scheme was found to perform quite well. After initial transient periods, stable limit cycles were obtained, with constrained (controlled) limits on the oscillatory behavior. (A comparison between the rate control algorithm under discussion here and an equivalent one using a timer-based approach showed the former to be dramatically superior in terms of peak buffer occupancy.)

We focus now on a rough comparison of the simulation results with analytical ones obtained using the Bolot/Shanker model of the previous section adapted to the example networks described here. Consider the MAN case first. To apply the analytical model here, we first replace the five traffic sources by one equivalent stream, assumed transmitted over the longest-delay propagation path, end-to-end. We use the linearized rate adjustment case of equation (7–19) of the previous section for simplicity, with the

[BARN 1994]   Barnwell, A. W., "Baseline Performance Using PRCA Rate-Control," ATM Forum/94-0597, Traffic Management Sub-Working Group, ATM Forum Technical Committee, July 1994.

up/down rate adjustments taken to be the same. Note that with MDF = 8, so that ACR is reduced by ACR/256 each cell time with the EPRCA algorithm, the "down" adjustment is in fact a small one, as required by the linear analytic model. But the linear model obviously does not capture the larger "up" adjustment every Nrm cell times when there is no congestion. However, this may not be too much of a problem for very large cell transmission rates and relatively small propagation delays if Nrm is not too large. The analytic model assumes continuous rate adjustment rather than adjustment at discrete intervals, as is always the case in reality. However, with cells transmitted every few microseconds at high link utilization and at the bit rates assumed in the simulations, continuous-rate adjustment is probably a good approximation. The analytic model of equation (7–19) indicates, however, that a rate reduction signal is sent back every time the bottleneck queue level exceeds zero. In the simulations, a double-threshold congestion control scheme was adopted, the onset of congestion being marked, and hence rate reduction being signaled, whenever the queue occupancy exceeded 550 cells: Congestion cleared whenever the occupancy dropped below 450 cells. In the simulations, maximum queue sizes of 10,000 cells were used, with maximum occupancy found, in most of the simulations, to hover just below 1000 cells.

Despite the differences in some of the analytic model and simulation assumptions, it is interesting that results of analysis and simulation are found to have a measure of agreement, as noted earlier. To demonstrate this, we must show how equation (7–19) is applied here. We first replace the derivative $d\lambda/dt$ appearing in that equation by the discrete approximation $\Delta\lambda/\Delta t$, and set $\Delta\lambda$ equal to ACR/256 and Δt equal to 1/PCR. The implication here is that we potentially adjust the rate at intervals spaced 1/PCR units of time apart. This is then the approximation to the actual "down" adjustment every 1/ACR units, with ACR verying slowly. This is presumably a conservative approximation. Since $d\lambda/dt = \pm\ \alpha$ in equation (7–19), we then have $\alpha =$ $(\text{PCR})^2/256$ applied to the case here. With PCR the maximum or peak cell transmission rate, the link capacity μ must be this value. We thus have, from equation (7–9), assuming the linear approximation holds, $\alpha = \mu/\beta$, or $1/\beta =$ PCR/256. In particular, using the value of PCR = 353,000 cells/sec chosen for the simulations, we have $\alpha = 4.9*10^8$ cells/sec^2 and $\beta = 0.725$ msec.

Equation (7–21) of the previous section now predicts the steady-state period or cycle time T of the limit cycle of both the cell transmission rate λ and queue size q will be $T = 2\tau(2+\sqrt{2}) = 6.8\tau$. Using $\tau = 1.2$ msec (the maximum round-trip propagation delay for the MAN simulations), we get $T = 8.2$ msec. The simulations have periods of oscillation varying from 8.8–9.4 msec ([BARN 1994], Figures 5, 6, 8, 9, 11). Equation (7–20) indicates the maximum queue occupancy, assuming an infinite buffer, should be $q_{max} = \alpha\tau^2 \approx 700$ cells, using the values calculated above for α and τ. The measured maximum queue occupancy varies from 850–900 cells, agreeing reasonably well with the figure obtained from analysis, considering, in particular, the gross simplifying assumptions made.

Now consider the maximum rate of cell transmission at the source, as controlled by the flow control algorithm. Even though the design goal is to keep the allowable cell rate (ACR) below the peak cell rate (PCR), the actual value of source transmission rate will overshoot the peak value because of the delay in receiving control information from any congested queue. This is apparent from the simple, single bottleneck model of Figure 7–7 and the resultant periodic curve of transmission rate appearing in Figure 7–8. Equation (7–14) demonstrates this phenomenon as well, showing, for the simple model used in that analysis, that the maximum rate of transmission increases with propagation delay τ. Applying equation (7–14) to the example under discussion here, with the numbers obtained above, we get $\alpha\tau = 588,000$ cells/sec, so that $\lambda_{max} = 353,000 + 588,000 = 940,000$ cells/sec. The simulations show a much wider swing, however, to $1.4*10^6$ cells/sec.

Finally, consider the time delay or phase difference between the rate and queue-length oscillations. From Figure 7–8, the peaks of the two oscillations appear out of phase by $[(t_2 - t_1) + \tau_f]$ sec, using the notation of that figure. It is left to the reader to show that $(t_2 - t_1) = \beta\log_e(\lambda_{max}/\mu) = 0.725$ msec for the numbers used here. Assuming the first switch which multiplexes the five sources is the bottleneck one, and calculating the forward propagation delay using the maximum source-switch link length of 50 km, we have $\tau_f = 0.2$ msec. The predicted phase delay is thus $0.725 + 0.2 = 0.9$ msec. The measured delay is somewhat difficult to determine using the curves in [BARN 1994], but appears to be somewhat less than 2 msec.

Most of the quantitative numbers for the MAN case thus agree surprisingly well between analysis and simulation, considering all the approximations made. The quantitative comparison turns out to be much poorer, however, in the case of the WAN simulations. Qualitatively, the simulation results obtained bear out the expected intuitive results and are similar to those just discussed for the MAN case: Both the source rate of transmission and queue length vary cyclically because of the delay between sending and receiving control signals. The rate and queue-length oscillations differ in phase because of the control delay. But the quantitative analytical results do differ substantially from those obtained through simulation. The predicted maximum cell transmission rate, for example, is 4.7×10^6 cells/sec; the measured rate is 1.4×10^6 cells/sec. The maximum queue length, analytically, turns out to be 35,000 cells, assuming an infinite buffer. But the simulation had a buffer accommodating at most 10,000 cells, with no discernible loss. The measured period of oscillation was 42 msec. The analytical calculation gives 59 msec. These differences between analysis and simulation at the much longer propagation delays may be due to the fact that the assumptions made in approximating the real control mechanism by an equivalent linear model are no longer valid. The rate increases, occurring at most once every Nrm cells, may now no longer be ignored at these long delays, for example.

7.5 ▪ WINDOW CONTROL IN A LARGE DELAY-BANDWIDTH ENVIRONMENT

In section 7.3 we summarized some studies of window- and rate-controlled congestion avoidance techniques designed for moderate-speed networks. They showed that the control mechanisms tend to produce oscillatory, yet stable, behavior as round-trip propagation delay increases. The simulation studies carried out on the ATM rate-based control technique concurs with these earlier results. Recent work on window control for high-speed networks indicates that this congestion control mechanism does maintain its stability, although again with oscillations possibly occurring, as the delay-bandwidth product becomes extremely large. These studies indicate that it is, in fact, possible to control the window size to provide optimum performance in the sense of operating at a maximum "power" point, or knee of the delay throughput curve, similar to that in the procedure proposed in section 7.3.

This work is due to Mitra of AT&T Bell Laboratories [MITR 1992]. He and his colleagues have carried out a static analysis, buttressed by simulation, of window control in this high-speed, very large delay-bandwidth product environment [FEND 1991], [MITR 1990]. Dynamic analyses have shown that the window control algorithm proposed is stable, albeit possessing oscillatory behavior [FEND 1992], [FEND 1991]. We summarize the results of the analysis first, then discuss, briefly, the dynamic analysis leading to the conclusion that the algorithm proposed is stable. We conclude this section with a more detailed description of Mitra's analysis of window control for the large delay-bandwidth case.

Mitra's analysis begins with the window control model of Figure 7–4b. The service rate μ is assumed to be the net, or reduced, rate, after other connections at a given node have been accounted for. (More generally, there will then be a net rate of μ_i at node i, but simplicity of analysis dictates the same net capacity μ at all nodes.) Now add two-way propagation delay over each link on the path, to account for the forward, data propagation delay, and the backward, acknowledgment propagation delay. (Acknowledgment queueing

[MITR 1992]   Mitra, D., "Asymptotically Optimal Design of Congestion Control for High-Speed Data Networks," *IEEE Trans. On Commun., 40,* 2 (Feb. 1992): 301–311.

[FEND 1991]   Fendick, K. W., et al., "An Approach to High-Performance, High-Speed Data Networks," *IEEE Commun. Mag., 29,* 10 (Oct. 1991): 74–82.

[MITR 1990]   Mitra, D., and J. B. Seery, "Dynamic Adaptive Windows for High-Speed Data Networks: Theory and Simulations," *Proc. ACM SIGCOMM 90,* Philadelphia, Sept. 1990: 30–40.

[FEND 1992]   Fendick, K. W., et al., "Analysis of a Rate-Based Control Strategy with Delayed Feedback," *Proc. ACM SIGCOMM 92,* Baltimore, Aug. 1992: 136–148.

delay is thus neglected. Alternatively, the *M*-hop path shown could be the round-trip path.) In addition, assume operation is in the heavy-traffic (congested) case in which a packet (or ATM cell) is always available for transmission and is limited only by the window control. This amounts to having $\lambda \gg \mu$ or $\lambda \to \infty$, in Figure 7–4. The resultant high-traffic, window control model appears in Figure 7–9a. (It is left to the reader to show that with $\lambda \to \infty$, the λ server and queue of Figure 7–4b disappear. See [SCHW 1987], Chapter 5.)

Because of the linearity of the model of Figure 7–9a, one can lump all the propagation delay together, leading to the final model of Figure 7–9b. We now focus on the large delay-bandwidth product case $\mu\tau \gg 1$ [see equation (7–2)]. The delay-bandwidth product will play a key role in the control analysis so it is appropriate to give it its own symbol. Mitra has chosen to call it λ, not to be confused with the traffic arrival rate λ we have just set at a very high rate. To avoid confusion in this book, however, we shall use the symbol Γ here to represent the delay-bandwidth product. Thus, we have

$$\Gamma \equiv \mu\tau \gg 1 \tag{7–22}$$

As noted in the introductory section 7.1, Γ represents the number of cells (or packets) enroute over the complete round-trip path, from source to destination, and return.

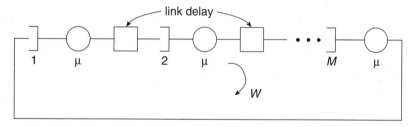

a. Sliding window control, heavy-traffic case, propagation delay included.

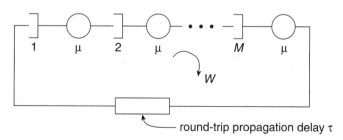

b. Equivalent model.

FIGURE 7–9 ■ Sliding window control, heavy-traffic case.

Recall from the examples chosen in section 7.1 that Γ can range from a value of 53 for ATM cells traversing a 1000-km, 45 Mbps path, to 28, 000, for a 2.4 Gbps 1000-km path. Longer-distance paths produce correspondingly higher values of Γ.

Now define R to be the round-trip response time T_r, normalized to the round-trip propagation delay τ. R is thus the normalized propagation delay plus the normalized queueing delay of the M nodes shown in Figure 7–9:

$$R \equiv T_r/\tau = 1 + \text{queueing delay}/\tau \qquad (7\text{–}23)$$

Let γ be defined to be the delay-*throughput* product; that is, it is the actual throughput γ' across the M-hop path, in cells (packets) per sec, multiplied by the round-trip propagation delay τ. Thus,

$$\gamma \equiv \gamma' \, \tau \le \Gamma \qquad (7\text{–}24)$$

since the throughput along the path cannot be greater than the capacity (bandwidth) μ.

The result of Mitra's analysis with $\Gamma \gg 1$, may be summarized by the response time-throughput curve appearing in Figure 7–10 [MITR 1992]. As the window W (Figure 7–9) is increased, the response time remains essentially constant, with negligible queueing delay, until the "moderate usage region" is reached. This is the region just before congestion takes over, in which case the response rises very sharply. It is the region corresponding to the "knee" of the response time-throughout curve, beyond which the throughput saturates at its maximum value while the response time R continues to rise, as already noted. It turns out that the point at which the power γ/R is maximized lies within this

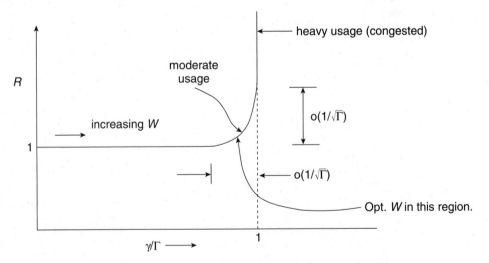

FIGURE 7–10 ■ Asymptotic performance, window control, $\Gamma \gg 1$.

region. (Recall that "power" was defined earlier to be the ratio of throughput to delay and has been used as a single performance parameter in studies of network congestion. See equation (7–5), for example. Normalizing the throughput and delay to the constant parameter τ (the round-trip propagation delay), does not affect the operating point, in this case the size of the window W, at which the power is maximum.) These results are all asymptotic, in the sense that they require $\Gamma \gg 1$, that is, the large delay-bandwidth product case. Note from Figure 7–10 as well, that the width of this region is $o(1/(\sqrt{\Gamma}))$, that is, the knee of the curve of Figure 7–10 is quite sharp. It turns out from simulation studies that a simple adaptive window control algorithm suffices to keep the system (the M-node path) in the desired moderate usage region [MITR 1990].

More specifically, the results of the analysis may be summarized as follows. (Details will be presented at the end of this section, as noted earlier.) The optimum operating point of the window-controlled, M-node path, in the sense of maximizing the power $P = \gamma/R$, is given by

$$W^* \equiv W_{\text{opt}} \sim \Gamma - \alpha^* \sqrt{\Gamma}$$

$$\text{with} \quad \alpha^* \sim -1/2\sqrt{M} \tag{7–25}$$

The optimum window size is thus

$$W \sim \Gamma + \frac{1}{2}\sqrt{\Gamma/M} \tag{7–25a}$$

Since the delay-bandwidth factor Γ represents the number of cells (packets) that may be accommodated along the round-trip propagation path at the given path capacity, the optimum window size W^* is approximately that same number. Thus, if $\Gamma = 500$, the window size should be set at about this value; if $\Gamma = 20{,}000$, it should be set at this value. If the window size drops below this optimum value, the throughout suffers (Figure 7–10); if it increases beyond this value, the response time (delay) increases rapidly, with negligible improvement in throughput. A simple algorithm to be described shortly suffices to keep the window size at the desired value.

What are the resultant response time and throughout at this desired operating point? The values attainable are almost obvious from the curve of Figure 7–10. But quantitatively, the values are as follows:

The normalized throughput is found to be given by

$$\gamma^* = W^* \left[1 - \sqrt{\frac{M}{W^*}} \right]$$

$$\sim \Gamma \left[1 - \sqrt{\frac{M}{\Gamma}} \right] \tag{7–26}$$

using the value $W^* \sim \Gamma$ to approximate the window size at the optimum operating point. The response time R^* at the operating point is then given by

$$R^* = \frac{W^*}{\gamma^*} = 1 / \left[1 - \sqrt{\frac{M}{W^*}} \right] \sim 1 + \sqrt{\frac{M}{\Gamma}} \qquad (7\text{-}27)$$

since

$$W^* \sim \Gamma \gg 1$$

(Recall, as noted in a previous section, that the throughput is just the window size divided by the round-trip response time. Alternatively, Little's formula applied to Figure 7–9 may be invoked to obtain this relation. Details are left to the reader.)

Equation (7–27) has an interesting physical interpretation. From equation (7–23) (the definition of the normalized round-trip response time R), R is made up of two components, the round-trip propagation time and the queueing delay on the M nodes along the M-hop path. Equation (7–27) implies that as the bandwidth of the network increases, increasing Γ, the queueing delay decreases relative to the propagation delay. Thus, queueing delay plays a smaller and smaller role, with the propagation delay dominating the overall round-trip response time. This was noted in the last chapter as well. This is just the reverse of the case with the traditional packet-switching networks, where the longer packet lengths and much smaller link capacities (54 kbps – 1.5 Mbps) dictate that queueing delays represent the major source of delay. Another result of this relative reduction in queueing delay in networks with large delay-bandwidth products is that relatively fewer cells (packets) are enqueued at the individual buffers. (From equation (7–27), most of the cells are arrayed on the links, enroute from node to node.) This is readily demonstrated as follows. For a homogeneous M-node network, as assumed here, the average queueing delay $E(T)$ at each node, normalized to the round-trip propagation delay τ, must be given by

$$E(T) \doteq \frac{1}{M} \sqrt{\frac{M}{\Gamma}} = 1 / \sqrt{M\Gamma} \qquad (7\text{-}28)$$

using equation (7–27). From Little's theorem [SCHW 1987], we then have, as the average number of cells (packets) buffered at a node (including the one in service),

$$E(N) = \gamma^* E(T)$$

$$= \Gamma / \sqrt{M\Gamma} = \sqrt{\Gamma / M} \qquad (7\text{-}29)$$

This result agrees with that obtained from the asymptotic analysis [MITR 1992], as will be shown later.

Finally, analysis indicates that the standard deviation σ of the number of cells enqueued at a node is very close to the average number $E(N)$. It is given by

$$\sigma^* \sim \sqrt{W^*/(M+1)} \sim \sqrt{\Gamma/(M+1)} \qquad (7\text{–}30)$$

As an example, say $\Gamma = 10{,}000$ and $M = 4$ is the number of hops along the path. Then there are 10,000 cells on the round-trip propagation path, but only $\sqrt{M\Gamma} = 200$ cells queued along the path, on the average. There are thus $E(N) \doteq 50$ cells queued at each of the four buffers, on the average. As either the propagation path length or the capacity (bandwidth) increase, the number of cells enroute increases linearly with Γ, while the number queued, on the average, only increases as $\sqrt{\Gamma}$. The number on queue thus decreases relative to the number in transmission.

Table 7–2 shows examples of the application of these asymptotic results, all for a 4-hop ($M = 4$) path. Note how the ratio of average number on queue to window size (maximum number along the path) decreases as Γ increases.

Figure 7–10 indicates that the moderate usage region where one would like to locate the operating point of the window control is quite sharply defined and reduces as $1/\sqrt{\Gamma}$ as Γ increases. Mitra and his colleagues have proposed a simple adaptive algorithm to control the window size and keep it at the desired operating point as traffic conditions change along the M-hop path [MITR 1990]. Equation (7–27) for the throughput may be rewritten as

$$R^* \sim 1 + \sqrt{M/W^*} \qquad (7\text{–}27a)$$

Writing this in an alternate form, one gets

$$(R^* - 1)\sqrt{W^*} \doteq \sqrt{M} \qquad (7\text{–}31)$$

This equation indicates that as the throughput increases, one should reduce the window size W; as the throughput decreases, one should increase the window. The algorithm proposed, and checked by simulation, adapts the window

---

TABLE 7–2 ■ Window Control Performance of Optimum Operating Point, High-Speed Network, $M = 4$ nodes

$\Gamma \rightarrow$	45	500	10,000
Window size W^*	47	506	10,025
Normalized response time R^*	1.3	1.09	1.02
At each node —			
$E(N)$	3.4	11.2	50
σ^*	3.1	10.1	45
$E(T) = E(N)/W^*$ (normalized delay)	0.075	0.022	0.005

size on a packet-by-packet (cell-by-cell) basis, using the result of equation (7–31) to keep the window at the desired operating point. Let n represent the nth packet (cell) acknowledged at the source as having been received correctly at the destination. Let R_n indicate the measured round-trip response time for that packet (forward time to the destination plus time for the acknowledgment to return to the source). Let W_n be the window size when the acknowledgment is received. Then, to drive the window size to the value indicated by equation (7–31), it suffices to have the window change as following:

$$W_{n+1} = W_n - a'\left[(R_n - 1)\sqrt{W_n} - \sqrt{M}\right] \qquad (7\text{–}32)$$

Here $a' \ll 1$ is a control parameter whose setting determines the speed of adaptation. (Increasing a' speeds up the adaptation time but may lead to oscillations. Reducing a' reduces the oscillations, but results in a longer adaptation time.) Letting

$$X_n = (R_n - 1)\sqrt{W_n} - \sqrt{M} \qquad (7\text{–}33)$$

it is clear that if $X_n < 0$, the window is to be increased. If $X_n > 0$, meaning the response time has increased, due presumably to added queueing delay or congestion, the window is to be reduced. A simplified version of the algorithm tested successfully in simulations [MITR 1990] begins to look like a linearized version of the window adjustment algorithm (7–3) discussed previously in section 7.3:

$$
\begin{aligned}
W_{n+1} &= W_n + 1 & \text{if } X_n < 0 \\
&= W_n - 1 & \text{if } X_n > 0 \\
&= W_n & \text{if } X_n = 0
\end{aligned}
\qquad (7\text{–}34)
$$

Note that this algorithm uses response-time information, on a packet-to-packet basis, to adjust the window dynamically. This is to be contrasted with the TCP window adjustment algorithm which adapts on the basis of a timer expiring with no packet acknowledgment received [JACO 1988], or the explicit bit feedback approach in which adaptation is based on average sizes being greater then 1 at least 50% of the time [RAMA 1990]. A simplified, single-queue fluid model analysis similar to the analysis discussed in the previous section has been used to validate the stability of the algorithm discussed here [FEND 1992], [FEND 1991].

Specifically, recall our comment in the previous section that the source rate of transmission is approximated by the window size W divided by the round-trip propagation delay τ. (Instead of τ we should actually use the round-trip response time T_r which includes the queueing delay, but note, from our discussion above, that for large Γ, the propagation delay dominates.) Thus, we have

$$\lambda \doteq W/\tau \tag{7-35}$$

with λ the source rate of transmission previously shown in Figure 7–4. We now use this equivalence between window and rate to convert the window control algorithm (7–32) to an equivalent differential equation governing the rate λ. We use the same single-queue representation of the end-to-end path as used in section 7.3, and as shown in Figure 7–7.

To capture the basic window control algorithm (7–32) in terms of an equivalent source rate control, we proceed as follows. Focus first on the equilibrium equation (7–31) at which we would like the system to operate. Note that the difference term $(R - 1)$ represents the normalized difference between the actual round-trip response time and the round-trip propagation delay, assumed constant here. Thus, in terms of the unnormalized quantities this is just $(T_r - \tau)$. But this difference must be just the queueing delay, and, in terms of the single-queue network representation of Figure 7–7, the queueing delay is just the queue length q divided by the service rate μ. We indicated that the normalized round-trip response time R_n was information carried by the nth acknowledgment received at the source. Say this acknowledgment packet (or cell) arrives at time t. If there were no queueing delay, it would have arrived precisely τ sec after the packet (cell) being acknowledged had been sent. Instead, it arrives at a later time due to the queueing delay at the single queue of Figure 7–7, as measured τ_b sec before (see equation (7–9) and Figure 7–7). We thus have

$$T_r|_n - \tau = q(t - \tau_b)/\mu,$$

or, in normalized form,

$$R_n - 1 = q(t - \tau_b) / \tau\mu$$
$$= q(t - \tau_b) /\Gamma \tag{7-36}$$

In particular, if the queue were empty τ_b sec before the arrival of the ack, the measured round-trip response time would be just τ, or $R_n = 1$.

Using equation (7–36), we are now in a position to motivate the replacement of the window control algorithm (7–32) by an equivalent continuous-time rate control equation for the single-queue example of Figure 7–7. Following [FEND 1991] and [FEND 1992], this equation is given simply by

$$\frac{d\lambda(t)}{dt} = -a\left[\frac{q(t - \tau_b)}{\sqrt{\Gamma}} - 1\right]\mu, \qquad q(t - \tau_b) > 0$$
$$= a\lambda(t - \tau) \qquad q(t - \tau_b) = 0 \tag{7-37}$$

We have taken $M = 1$ in equation (7–32), and, since the system is presumed to be operating near equilibrium, we have replaced W_n by Γ (equation (7–25)).

The terms $\lambda (t - \tau)$ and μ in equation (7–37), represent the fact that in this algorithm control adjustments are made for every ack received. The rate $d\lambda(t)/dt$ at which $\lambda(t)$ is changed is thus proportional to μ, the queue service rate if the queue is nonempty; to $\lambda(t - \tau)$, the packet transmission rate τ sec before receipt of the acks, if the queue is empty. The proportionality parameter a corresponds to a' in the original window control algorithm. Equation (7–37) is to be compared to equation (7–9) in section 7.3.

To complete the set of equations representing the rate control equivalent of window control algorithm (7–32), we simply repeat equation (7–10) of section 7.3, which represents the rate at which the queue length changes in response to source-rate changes:

$$\frac{dq(t)}{dt} = 0 \qquad \text{if } \lambda(t - \tau_f) < \mu \qquad \text{and} \qquad q(t) = 0$$

$$= \lambda(t - \tau_f) - \mu \qquad \text{otherwise}$$

$$(7–10)$$

Equation (7–37) thus replaces equation (7–9) in the window control mechanism of section 7.3.

Fendick et al. have analyzed a class of delayed-feedback, rate-control strategies of which equation (7–37) is a special case [FEND 1992]. They find results similar to those found for the analysis of equations (7–9) and (7–10) in section 7.3. In particular, there exists an unstable equilibrium point ($q = \sqrt{\Gamma}$, $\lambda = \mu$) about which the system oscillates, oscillations having a period on the order of τ, the round-trip propagation delay. However, the oscillations are bounded, in the sense that the source rate λ fluctuates in a region about the service rate μ bounded by $\pm o(\sqrt{\Gamma})$, while the queue size varies between empty ($q = 0$) and $o(\sqrt{\Gamma})$. The throughput is thus within $o(1/\sqrt{\Gamma})$ of its maximum value μ; the response time is at most $\tau + o(1/\sqrt{\Gamma})$, which, for large Γ, is close to the absolute minimum τ.

These results agree, interestingly, with the static window control results obtained by Mitra. Note, from Figure 7–10, that, at the optimum window operating point, the normalized round-trip response time is $R \sim 1 + 1/\sqrt{\Gamma}$ [see also equation (7–27)], and that the window control algorithm equation (7–32) tends to drive the operating point to this value. The normalized throughput at the optimum window operating point is $\gamma/\Gamma \sim 1 - o(1/\sqrt{\Gamma})$ (see equation (7–26) also), or the actual throughput is approximately $\mu [1 - o(1/\sqrt{\Gamma})]$. The average queue size and standard deviation of the queue length are, from equations (7–29) and (7–30), respectively, $E (N) \doteq \sqrt{\Gamma}$ and $\sigma \doteq \sqrt{\Gamma/2}$, agreeing with the dynamic analysis. (Note again that that analysis has $M = 1$.) So the conclusions here, in agreement with those obtained in sections 7.3 and 7.4, are that feedback control *can* be utilized in a high delay-bandwidth environment. It is expected that the control mechanism will display oscillations or jitter, the extent of the jitter increasing with propagation delay. For, as noted previously, the control tends to overshoot because of the delayed response. But the oscillations are bounded and appear manageable. These conclusions have been borne out by simulation [MITRA 1990]. We conclude this section by deriving the results of the window control mechanism discussed thus far. For this purpose we follow the analysis appearing in [MITR 1992].

Consider the heavy-traffic ($\lambda \to \infty$), sliding window control model of an M-node path given by Figure 7–9b. For the purposes of analysis, particularly since we are principally interested in the large delay-bandwidth case $\Gamma \equiv \mu\tau >> 1$, we normalize both the link capacities and the propagation delay to τ, obtaining the equivalent heavy-traffic, sliding window control of Figure 7–11. The box representing the propagation delay has been labeled node 0. This window control model is an example of a closed queueing network (with no exogenous or external flows in or out), which, under a variety of conditions, can be shown to be of the *product form* type [SCHW 1987]. Product form means that the joint probability $P(n_0, n_1, \ldots, n_M)$, for an $(M+1)$-node network, that node i has n_i, $0 \le i \le M$, packets on queue (including one in service) is given by

$$P(n_0, n_1, \ldots, n_m) = K \prod_{i=0}^{M} P_i(n_i) \qquad (7\text{--}38)$$

where $P_i(n_i)$ is the probability that node i, in isolation, and analyzed by itself, has n_i packets (customers) on queue. The parameter K is a normalization constant. The overall system, or network, behaves as if the nodes (or queues) may be analyzed independently of one another, even though they are clearly dependent and coupled together.

As an example, refer to Figure 7–11. Model the propagation delay box, node 0, by the infinite-server queue of Figure 7–12. This says that no matter how many packets (cells) are en route along the path, there is no "queueing" delay. There is only the average "service" delay $1/\mu_0$, which is actually τ in our representation, but taken as $1/\mu_0 = 1$ in the normalized representation of Figure 7–11. This model has often been used as a "queueing"-equivalent representation of propagation delay. Now say that the arrivals are Poisson, with average value λ_0 as shown. It is then known that the constant propagation delay case is well-approximated by a processor-sharing (round-robin) model whose queue-distribution solution is the same as that for the exponential ser-

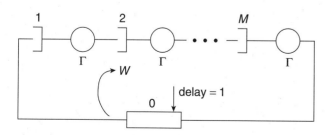

FIGURE 7–11 ▪ Sliding window control of Figure 7–9, normalized to propagation delay τ.

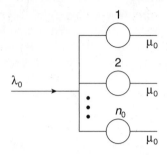

FIGURE 7–12 ■ Infinite-server model, node 0 (propagation delay) of Figure 7–11.

vice time, $M/M/n_0$, queue [KLEI 1976]. Specifically, then, for the model of Figure 7–11, we have

$$P_0(n_0) = K_0\, \rho_0^{n_0}/n_0! \qquad \rho_0 = \lambda_0/\mu_0 \tag{7–39}$$

(See [SCHW 1977], [KLEI 1975]), or any book on queueing for the $M/M/n_0$ analysis.) K_0 is the usual normalization constant.

Now focus on the other M queues, $1 \le j \le M$. We model these as FIFO queues with exponential service; that is, as already stated in introducing the Mitra model and analysis at the beginning of this section, packets (cells) are assumed to be exponential in length. Queues of this type turn out to have product-form solutions. The probability $P_i(n_i)$ in this case, is simply the $M/M/1$ solution

$$P(n_i) = K_i\rho_i^{n_i} \tag{7–40}$$

with $K_i = (1 - \rho_i)$ the normalization constant in this case. But note from Figure 7–11 that the arrival rate at each queue is the same and must be the same as that of node 0, the propagation delay node, from flow continuity considerations. We then have, in equation (7–40), $\rho_i = \lambda_0/\Gamma$, $1 \le i \le M$. The final product-form solution for the closed queueing network of Figure 7–11 is thus

$$P(n_0, n_1, \ldots, n_m) = \frac{1}{G(W, M)} \frac{\rho_0^{n_0}}{n_0!} \prod_{i=1}^{M} \rho_i^{n_i} \tag{7–41}$$

Here the term $1/G(W, M)$ is used to represent the normalization constant subsuming K, K_0, and the K_i's of equations (7–38) to (7–40). This quantity is found simply from the condition that all the probabilities sum to 1, with the added constraint, in the heavy-traffic case ($\lambda \to \infty$), that the total number of packets along the round-trip, end-to-end path must fill the window W:

$$\sum_{\substack{\text{all } n_i, \\ \sum_{i=0}^{M} n_i = W}} P(n_0, n_1, \ldots n_M) = 1 \tag{7–42}$$

[KLEI 1976]   Kleinrock, L., *Queueing Systems, Vol. II: Computer Applications*, New York: John Wiley, 1976.

From equations (7–42) and (7–41) we thus have

$$G(W, \ M) = \sum_{\substack{\text{all } n_i, \\ \sum_{i=0}^{M} n_i = W}} \frac{\rho_0^{n_0}}{n_0!} \left(\frac{\lambda_0}{\Gamma}\right)^{n_1+n_2+\ldots+n_M} \tag{7–43}$$

We have made use of the fact here, as stated above, that $\rho_i = \lambda_0/\Gamma$, $1 \le i \le M$. Note from Figure 7–11 that the total number of packets circulating in the closed queueing network (the round-trip, end-to-end path) is just the window size W, in agreement with the constraint noted above. This packet (or customer) conservation constraint always shows up in any closed queueing network model, since, by definition of "closed", there are no external arrivals or departures.

Once we have the solution $P(n_0, n_1, \ldots, n_M)$ for the probability distribution of the packets in the closed queueing network, it should be clear that, at least theoretically, one can find all statistical quantities of interest from this distribution. This would include the throughput of the window-controlled M-node path modeled by Figures 7–9b or 7–11, the round-trip response time, the average number buffered in any node along the path, etc. It turns out, however, that these quantities are all obtainable from the normalization constant $G(W, M)$ [SCHW 1987]. This is one of the advantages of a product-form solution. As an example, the throughput γ_i of the ith node is found to be given by

$$\gamma_i = \lambda_i G \ (W - 1, M) \ /G \ (W, \ M) \tag{7–44}$$

with λ_i the average rate of input to node i, and $G(W-1, M)$ the value of $G(W, M)$ with the window size reduced by one [SCHW 1987]. So all we have to do is to calculate $G(W, M)$ for various values of W, using equation (7–43), and from this determine the throughput and any other statistical parameters of interest. We thus focus on the calculation of $G(W, M)$, and in particular, its value for large values of Γ ($\Gamma \gg 1$).

Before proceeding, we can simplify the basic equation (7–43). Since we are dealing with a closed queueing network, with no external arrivals or departures, the arrival rates λ_i and λ_0 appearing in equation (7–43) and in Figure (7–12) can be chosen arbitrarily. The throughput γ_i at node i is *not* an arbitrary quantity, however. It is the average number of packets/sec actually processed at that node. Since λ_i in equation (7–44) may be arbitrarily chosen, but γ_i is an actual measurable quantity, this must imply that the normalization constant $G(W, M)$ changes as the choice of λ_i changes, with γ_i in equation (7–44) remaining constant. This is, in fact, the case. The important thing to note is that, although the traffic intensity parameters λ_i in any closed queueing network are not defined absolutely, the relations between them at the different nodes in a network must obey flow conservation laws. As an example, in our case of the window-controlled model of Figure 7–11, it is clear from the figure, as has already been noted above in writing equation (7–43), that $\lambda_i = \lambda_0$, $1 \leq i \leq M$; that is, since all $(M + 1)$ queues are connected in series, a flow out of one queue must represent a flow into the next queue, with all flows thus the same. (See [SCHW 1987] for more general examples, where the output of a queue may, in turn, combine at the input of one queue. The closed queueing network of Figure 7–11 is a special case of the more general mesh-type queueing network that has been used to model multiprocessor computer systems and computer networks, among other examples.)

Since λ_0, in equation (7–43), is arbitrary (as noted, we have already set $\lambda_i = \lambda_0$, $1 \leq i \leq M$, because of the flows in Figure 7–11), we should choose λ_0 to simplify equation (7–43) as much as possible. It is apparent that a good choice is $\lambda_0 = 1$, so that $\rho_0 = \lambda_0/\mu_0 = 1$ as well. (Recall that in normalized form, $1/\mu_0$, the average propagation delay, is 1.) We thus have, for this choice of λ_0,

$$G(W, \ M) = \sum_{\substack{\text{all } n_i, \\ \sum_{i=0}^{M} n_i = W}} \frac{1}{n_0!}\left(\frac{1}{\Gamma}\right)^{n_1+n_2+\ldots+n_M} \tag{7–45}$$

The corresponding (normalized) throughput γ is then given by

$$\gamma = G\,(W - 1, M) \,/\, G\,(W, M) \tag{7–46}$$

from equation (7–44), noting that $\gamma_0 = \gamma_i = \gamma$ because of flow conservation. (The actual throughput across the M-node virtual path is then $\gamma' = \gamma/\tau$, in units of the average number of packets/sec moving through that path.) It is equation (7–45) on which we then focus in calculating $G(W, M)$, to obtain the throughput γ and other statistical parameters of interest. We thus set about simplifying equation (7–45), emphasizing in particular the large delay-bandwidth case $\Gamma \gg 1$. We follow Mitra [MITRA 1992] in carrying out the simplification, as already noted.

The first simplification is obtained by replacing the sum of the packets in the M queues along the path by a single parameter S. We thus set $n_1 + n_2 + \ldots + n_M = S$ in equation (7–45). Since the sum over all possible values of n_i, $0 \leq i \leq M$ must be the window size W, we thus have $S + n_0 = W$. Equation (7–45) may thus be rewritten as

$$G(W, \ M) = \sum_{\substack{\text{all } n_i, \\ S+n_0=W}} \frac{1}{n_0!}\left(\frac{1}{\Gamma}\right)^{S} \tag{7–45a}$$

The sum over all n_i in equation (7–45a) may now be found by first summing over all values of S. But this is just the same as keeping S fixed and finding how many possible ways there are of obtaining this sum. A little thought will indicate that this is identical to the classical combinatorial problem of determining the number of ways in which S balls may be placed in M urns. It is left to the reader to show that the solution to this problem is just

$$\binom{M-1+S}{M-1} = \binom{M-1+S}{S} = \frac{(M-1+S)!}{S!(M-1)}$$

Here $(a/b) \equiv a!/(a-b)! \, b!$ is the usual symbol representing the number of combinations of a elements taken b at a time. Equation (7–45a) may thus be simplified to

$$G(W, M) = \frac{1}{(M-1)!} \sum_{S+n_0=W} \frac{1}{n_0!}\left(\frac{1}{\Gamma}\right)^S \frac{(M-1+S)!}{S!} \qquad (7\text{–}45b)$$

The sums over all n_i, $0 \le i \le M$, have now been reduced to sums over n_0 and S, with $S + n_0 = W$.

We continue the further reduction of equation (7–45b), leaving details to the reader. In particular, we can replace the sums appearing in equation (7–45b) by an equivalent integral, which is much easier to handle than summations. To do this we note that the factorial function has an integral representation in terms of the so-called Gamma function:

$$n! = \int_0^\infty e^{-u} u^n \, du \qquad (7\text{–}47)$$

Replacing $(M - 1 + S)!$ in equation (7–45b) by this integral form, interchanging the order of summation and integration (a common trick!), and recognizing that

$$\sum_{n_0+S=W} \frac{W!}{n_0! S!}\left(\frac{u}{\Gamma}\right)^S = \sum_{S=0}^{W} \frac{W!}{(W-S)! S!}\left(\frac{u}{\Gamma}\right)^S$$

$$= \left[1 + \left(\frac{u}{\Gamma}\right)\right]^W \qquad (7\text{–}48)$$

we obtain $G(W, M)$ in the following equivalent integral form:

$$G(W, M) = \frac{1}{W! \, (M-1)} \int_0^\infty e^{-u} u^{M-1}\left[1 + \left(\frac{u}{\Gamma}\right)\right]^W du \qquad (7\text{–}45c)$$

We now make use of the fact that we want $\Gamma \gg 1$, and that we will be operating in the moderate usage region (Figure 7–10), $W/\Gamma \sim 1$. Specifically, we define the following relation between the window size W and the delay-bandwidth product Γ:

$$W = \Gamma - \alpha\, \Gamma^{1/2} \qquad (7\text{--}49)$$

with α a parameter to be found. (This connection between W and Γ is not an obvious one of course. The reader is asked to understand that this relation, its use in equation (7–45c), and the further simplification of equation (7–45c) to follow, have been obtained after considerable prior study of equation (7–45c). We are just attempting to motivate the results to be obtained, not to show how a connection like equation (7–49) has been found in the first place.)

Following [MITR 1992], we now change variables in equation (7–45c), writing $u = \Gamma^{1/2}v$. We then get

$$G\,(W,\ M) = \frac{\Gamma^{\frac{M}{2}}}{W!\ (M-1)!} \int_0^\infty e^{-v\Gamma^{1/2}} v^{M-1} \left(1 + \frac{v}{\Gamma^{1/2}}\right)^W dv \qquad (7\text{--}45\text{d})$$

We now write

$$\left(1 + \frac{v}{\Gamma^{1/2}}\right)^W = \exp\left[W \log_e\left(1 + \frac{v}{\Gamma^{1/2}}\right)\right]$$

and replace W by its equivalent equation (7–49). We also use the series expansion, $\log_e(1 + x) = x - x^2/2 + x^3/3 - x^4/4 + \ldots$, $x < 1$, to expand $\log_e(1 + v/\Gamma^{1/2})$ in a series in $v/\Gamma^{1/2}$, with $\Gamma \gg 1$. The resultant expression for $G(W,\ M)$ now becomes, after some simplification, with terms of the same power of Γ collected together,

$$G(W,\ M) = \frac{\Gamma^{\frac{M}{2}}}{W!\ (M-1)} \int_0^\infty v^{M-1} e^{-\alpha v - v^2/2} \left[1 + \frac{1}{\Gamma^{1/2}}\left(\alpha v^2/2 + v^3/3\right) + o(1/\Gamma)\right] \qquad (7\text{--}45\text{e})$$

The expression $o(1/\Gamma)$ means that the rest of the terms decrease at least at the rate of $1/\Gamma$.

Equation (7–45e) may now be written in its final, simplified form by defining the following integral function $W_M(\alpha)$ [MITR 1992]:

$$W_M(\alpha) \equiv \int_0^\infty v^M e^{-\alpha v - v^2/2} dv \qquad (7\text{--}50)$$

Using this functional notation we get

$$G(W,\ M) = \frac{\Gamma^{M/2}}{W!\ (M-1)!} \left[W_{M-1}(\alpha) + \frac{1}{\Gamma^{1/2}}\{\frac{\alpha}{2} W_{M+1}(\alpha)\right.$$

$$\left. + \frac{1}{3} W_{M+2}(\alpha)\} + o\left(\frac{1}{\Gamma}\right)\right] \qquad (7\text{--}45\text{f})$$

In particular, with $\Gamma \gg 1$, as assumed here,

$$G(W,M) = \frac{\Gamma^{M/2}}{W! \, (M-1)} \left[W_{M-1}(\alpha) + o\left(\frac{1}{\Gamma^{1/2}} \right) \right] \qquad (7\text{--}45\text{g})$$

Note that the normalization constant $G(W, M)$ and hence all statistical parameters of interest depend on these functions $W_M(\alpha)$ defined by equation (7–50). We use equation (7–45g) to determine the normalized throughput γ and, from this, the normalized response time R for the window-controlled virtual circuit of Figure 7–4, under conditions of heavy traffic ($\lambda \to \infty$) and large delay-bandwidth product, $\Gamma \gg 1$.

Recall from equation (7–46) that the normalized throughput, for the analysis just described, is given by the ratio of two normalization constants. For our purposes, it is more appropriate to use a somewhat different expression for the throughput obtained by applying Buzen's recursive algorithm for the calculation of the normalization constant $G(W, M)$ [BUZE 1973], [SCHW 1987]. Specifically, Buzen has shown that $G(W, M)$ may be found recursively by writing

$$G\,(W, M) = G\,(W, M-1) + \rho_M G\,(W-1, M) \qquad (7\text{--}51)$$

(The full algorithm starts with $G(W, 0) = 1$ and $G(1, M) = \rho_1^M$, and builds up all values of $G(W, M)$ following equation (7–51).) In our case, recall that we had arbitrarily taken $\rho_1 = \rho_2 = \ldots = \rho_M$ to be $1/\Gamma$. (See equation (7–45) and the discussion preceding it.) Using equation (7–51) in (7–46), then, we have

$$\gamma = \frac{G(W-1, M)}{G(W, M)} = \frac{\Gamma[G(W, M) - G(W, M-1)]}{G(W, M)}$$

$$= \Gamma \left(1 - \frac{G(W, M-1)}{G(W, M)} \right) \le \Gamma \qquad (7\text{--}52)$$

Using equation (7–45g) in (7–52), we get

$$\gamma = \Gamma \left[1 - \frac{(M-1)W_{M-2}(\alpha)}{\Gamma^{1/2} W_{M-1}(\alpha)} + o(1/\Gamma) \right] \qquad (7\text{--}53)$$

This may be written in a form more amenable to calculation by using a relationship among the $W_M(\alpha)$ functions found by Mitra [MITRA 1992]. Thus, it can be shown that

$$W_{M+1}\,(\alpha) + \alpha W_M\,(\alpha) = M W_{M-1}\,(\alpha) \qquad M = 1, 2, \ldots \qquad (7\text{--}54)$$

[BUZE 1973] Buzen, J. P., "Computational Algorithms for Closed Queueing Networks with Exponential Servers," *Commun. ACM, 16,* 9 (Sept. 1973): 527–531.

In particular, then, $(M - 1)W_{M-2}(\alpha)$ in equation (7–53) may be replaced by $W_M(\alpha) + \alpha W_{M-1}(\alpha)$, giving

$$\gamma = \Gamma\left[1 - \frac{(\alpha + M\beta(\alpha))}{\Gamma^{1/2}} + o(1/\Gamma)\right] \tag{7–55}$$

where

$$\beta(\alpha) \equiv \frac{1}{M}\frac{W_M(\alpha)}{W_{M-1}(\alpha)} \tag{7–56}$$

We can find the normalized response time R by taking the ratio of window size W to the normalized throughput γ, as was done earlier in equation (7–27). Thus we have

$$R = W/\gamma \tag{7–57}$$

(As noted earlier, it is left to the reader to provide the justification for this expression.)

Both the throughput and delay thus depend on the delay-bandwidth product Γ, and on the parameter α. Recall from equation (7–49) that α was an unknown parameter introduced to relate the window size W to the delay-bandwidth product Γ. The objective here all along has been to find the optimum window size W^* to obtain the best combination of response time and throughput. Based on our previous discussion, this "best" combination occurs when the power P, the ratio of throughput to delay, is maximum. But from equation (7–49), the optimum window size, in the sense of maximizing P, can be related to the optimum choice of α. We thus write P in terms of α and differentiate to find the best choice, α^*, of α. From equation (7–49), this then gives the optimum window size W^* as well.

Writing the expression for P, in terms of normalized throughput and response time, we have

$$P = \gamma/R = \gamma^2/W \tag{7–58}$$

from equation (7–57). Squaring equation (7–55), dividing by equation (7–49), and retaining terms in $o(1/\Gamma^{1/2})$ only, it is left for the reader to show that we get

$$P = \Gamma\left[1 - \frac{\alpha + 2M\beta(\alpha)}{\Gamma^{1/2}} + o(1/\Gamma)\right] \tag{7–59}$$

It is clear from equation (7–59) that the optimum value α^* of α, in the sense of maximizing P, must be given by the solution of the equation

$$\frac{d[\alpha + 2M\beta(\alpha)]}{d\alpha} = (1 + 2M)\frac{d\beta(\alpha)}{d\alpha} = 0 \tag{7–60}$$

Mitra has shown, using the definition of $\beta(\alpha)$ in equation (7–56) and relating this to the properties of the $W_M(\alpha)$ functions defined by equation (7–50), that the optimum value of α obtained numerically may be approximated by the following simple expression [MITR 1992]

$$\alpha^* \doteq -\frac{1}{2\sqrt{M}} \qquad (7\text{–}61)$$

The optimum window size is thus given by

$$W^* = \Gamma - \alpha^* \sqrt{\Gamma}$$
$$= \Gamma + \frac{1}{2}\sqrt{\frac{\Gamma}{M}} \qquad (7\text{–}62)$$

This is precisely equation (7–25) introduced earlier. The optimum value of $\beta(\alpha)$ is found to be approximated by

$$\beta^* \doteq 1/\sqrt{M} \qquad (7\text{–}63)$$

The optimum value of the normalized throughput, from equation (7–55), is thus given by

$$\gamma^* \doteq \Gamma\left[1 - \sqrt{\frac{M}{\Gamma}}\right] \qquad (7\text{–}64)$$

agreeing with equation (7–26). The normalized response time is in turn given by

$$R^* = \frac{W^*}{\gamma^*} \doteq 1 + \sqrt{\frac{M}{\Gamma}} \qquad (7\text{–}65)$$

as in equation (7–27).

Using the normalization constant $G(W, M)$, one can obtain other statistical parameters of interest, as already noted earlier. We can also apply Little's formula where appropriate. Consider, for example, the average number $E(n_0)$ of packets enroute along the propagation path. From Little's formula this is just

$$E(n_0) = \gamma' \tau = \gamma \qquad (7\text{–}66)$$

with $\gamma' = \gamma/\tau$ the actual throughput in packets/sec and τ the round-trip propagation delay, as noted earlier. From equation (7–64), then,

$$E(n_0^*) = \Gamma\left[1 - \sqrt{\frac{M}{\Gamma}}\right] \qquad (7\text{–}67)$$

is the number of packets along the propagation path at the optimum operating point.

But the average number $E(N)$ of packets buffered at any one of the M nodes along the path must be

$$E(N) = [W - E(n_0)]/M \tag{7–68}$$

At the operating point $W^* \sim \Gamma$, using equations (7–68) and (7–67), we then have

$$E(N^*) = \sqrt{\Gamma/M} \tag{7–69}$$

in agreement with equation (7–29), as noted earlier. To obtain the variance σ^2 of the number of packets enqueued at any node, Mitra shows that

$$E[n_1(n_1 - 1)] = \frac{2}{\Gamma^2} G(W - 2, M + 2)/G(W, M) \tag{7–70}$$

Here, n_1 represents the (random) number enqueued at node 1. But, because of the homogeneity and symmetry of the M-node virtual path, its statistics must be the same at any of the other $(M\text{-}1)$ buffers. Then

$$\sigma^2 = E(n_1^2) - E^2(n_1)$$

$$= E[n_1(n_1 - 1)] + E(n_1) - E^2(n_1) \tag{7–71}$$

$$= E[n_1(n_1 - 1)] + E(N) - E^2(N)$$

since we have used $E(N)$ to represent the average number enqueued at a node.

Using equation (7–45g), we can rewrite equation (7–70) as

$$E[n_1(n_1 - 1)] = \frac{2}{\Gamma} \frac{W(W - 1)}{M(M + 1)} \frac{W_{M+1}(\alpha)}{W_{M-1}(\alpha)} \tag{7–70a}$$

From equation (7–54) we get

$$W_{M+1}(\alpha)/W_{M-1}(\alpha) = M - \alpha \frac{W_M(\alpha)}{W_{M-1}(\alpha)} \tag{7–72}$$

But recall from equation (7–56) that $\beta(\alpha) \equiv 1/M\ W_M(\alpha)/W_{M-1}(\alpha)$. Introducing this definition of $\beta(\alpha)$ in equation (7–72), and then, in turn in equation (7–70a), we get

$$E[n_1(n_1 - 1)] = \frac{2}{\Gamma} \frac{W(W - 1)}{(M + 1)} [1 - \alpha\beta(\alpha)]$$

$$\doteq 2\Gamma[1 - \alpha\beta(\alpha)]/(M + 1) \tag{7–70b}$$

since $W \sim \Gamma$ in the moderate usage region under discussion here.

Recall, however, that at the optimum operating point $\alpha^* \doteq -1/2\sqrt{M}$ and $\beta^*(\alpha^*) \doteq 1/\sqrt{M}$. We have also shown that $E(N^*) = \sqrt{\Gamma/M}$ at the optimum operating point. Using these values in equation (7–70b) and then in turn in equation (7–71), we find for the variance of the number of packets in any buffer along the path, at the optimum window value,

$$\sigma^{*2} = \frac{\Gamma}{M+1} + \sqrt{\frac{\Gamma}{M}} \doteq \frac{\Gamma}{M+1} \qquad \Gamma \gg 1 \qquad (7\text{–}72)$$

The standard deviation of the number of packets enqueued is thus

$$\sigma^* \doteq \sqrt{\Gamma/(M+1)} \qquad (7\text{–}73)$$

in agreement with equation (7–30).

In summary, then, repeating comments made earlier in this section, by operating at the optimum window size $W^* = \Gamma - \alpha^* \sqrt{\Gamma} \doteq \Gamma + 1/2\sqrt{\Gamma/M}$, that is, with the window size held close to the delay-bandwidth product, the normalized throughput γ^* can be held close to its maximum possible value of Γ [see equation (7–64)], while the normalized response time is close to the minimum possible value of 1 [see equation (7–65)]. Both the average number and standard deviation of packets held at each buffer along the M-node path scale as the square root of the delay-bandwidth product [equations (7–69) and (7–73)], as then do the corresponding queueing delays, [see equation (7–28)], which is quite encouraging, particularly when real-time traffic with strict time constraints is to be transmitted over a relatively long-delay virtual circuit.

▪ PROBLEMS

7–1 a. Consider a typical delay-throughput curve such as that sketched in Figure 7–6. Show the "power", defined as the ratio of throughput to delay, is maximized as shown, at the point where a line drawn from the origin is tangent to the curve.

b. Specialize to the case of an infinite $M/M/1$ queue. Then the explicit expression for the power is given by equation (7–5). Show the maximum value of the power occurs at a utilization ρ of 0.5. Use equation (7–4) to sketch the delay-throughput curve in this case, and show that the maximum power does occur as indicated in **a.** above. *Note:* For an infinite queue the throughput is the load λ (why is this so?) and so varying the utilization ρ is equivalent to varying λ.

c. Consider now an $M/D/1$ queue, with fixed packet lengths of value $1/\mu$ each. The average queueing delay in this case is given by equation (7–6). Find the expression for the power in this case and show it is maximized at $\rho = 2 - \sqrt{2} = 0.586$. Plot the delay-throughput curve as well and show the maximum power occurs at the point indicated by **a.** above.

7-2 The rate control mechanism for the single, bottleneck, queue of Figure 7–7 is represented by the two equations (7–9) and (7–10). Solve these two equations simultaneously, starting at time $t = 0$ with the queue empty. Plot your results and show you get the curves of Figure 7–8. Verify equations (7–11) to (7–18).

7-3 Refer to the flow control mechanism described by equations (7–9), (7–10), and Figure 7–7. (See problem **7-2** above.) Let the forward and backward propagation delays each be 5 msec. The buffer transmission rate is $\mu = 20,000$ cells/sec. The rate control parameter α is 10^6 cells/sec^2. The parameter β is 10 msec. Find the maximum and minimum source rates λ_{max} and λ_{min}, the maximum queue size q_{max}, and the period or cycle time, T, of the oscillations. Sketch both the source rate $\lambda(t)$ and the queue size $q(t)$ over a number of cycles beginning at time $t = 0$ with the queue empty.

7-4 Repeat problem **7-3** for the linearized approximation of equation (7–19) and compare the results.

7-5 Consider the flow control mechanism described by equations (7–9) and (7–10) for the single-queue model of Figure 7–7.
  a. Let the buffer transmission rate be $\mu = 10,000$ cells/sec. Take the round-trip propagation delay to be $\tau = 10$ msec as in problem **7-3**. Try different sets of values of the control parameters α and β and compare the control performance for each set. In particular, try reducing the transient interval t_0, then the maximum buffer occupancy q_{max}, and, finally, the cycle time T. What are the resultant tradeoffs between these various performance parameters?
  b. Repeat **a.** above for different values of μ and τ. For example, take much larger values of μ such as 100,000 cells/sec and 10^6 cells/sec, and even higher. Let the propagation path vary from that of a LAN (several km at most) to a MAN (metropolitan area network of 50–100 km diameter) to a large WAN (wide-area network) covering 5000 km. Take the propagation delay to be 5 μsec/km. Comment on the control performance obtained in each case, and compare results. Can you come up with "reasonable" design values for the two control parameters for each case? One possible method of approaching the design is to start with the "linearized" control equation (7–19). This replaces the control mechanism with one parameter. Then vary the second parameter β, and determine the effect on performance.

7-6 Refer to the discussion of simulations performed for the ATM Forum flow control proposal of section 7.4. Work out the simplified analysis described there for the two cases considered, the MAN and the WAN, and check the results obtained. Thus, show first that the equivalent control parameters α and β are 4.9×10^8 cells/sec and 0.725 msec, respectively, and then determine the performance parameters T, q_{max}, and the phase delay for the two cases.

7-7 **a.** Show that Figure 7–4b captures the essence of a sliding-window control: There can be a maximum of W packets enroute along the virtual path at any one time. If W unacknowledged packets are moving along the path, the transmitting source shuts off. As soon as an acknowledgement for a packet arrives at the source, it can again transmit the next waiting packet. The model of Figure 7–4b assumes acknowledgements return from the destination to the source in zero time.

  b. Add propagation delay to the model of Figure 7–4b and then let the traffic load λ be much greater than the transmission rate μ. Show the model of Figure 7–9 results.

7-8 This problem summarizes the results of section 7.5. Note that the assumption made there is that packets are exponentially distributed in length.

  a. Using the results of that section, as given by equations (7–25) to (7–30), verify the entries of Table 7–2.

  b. Consider a virtual path of four hops covering a distance of 3000 km. The transmission rate at each node along the path is 150 Mbps, and cells (packets) are 53 octets long, on the average. (We are obviously trying to apply the results of this section to the ATM environment even though packets are taken to be exponentially distributed here.) Find the optimum window size, the actual round-trip response time, the number of cells in flight along the path, the average number enqueued at each node along the path, the standard deviation of the number enqueued at each node, and the average queueing delay at each node. The propagation delay along the path may be taken as 5 μsec/km.

7-9 Starting with the window-control algorithm of equation (7–32), show, following the approach indicated in the text, that, for a single, bottleneck queue, the control algorithm may be represented by the two equations (7–37) and (7–10).

7-10 This problem fills in the details in the analysis of the large delay-bandwidth window control mechanism discussed in section 7.5.

  a. Starting with the normalization constant $G(W, M)$ as given by equation (7–45a), show, following the method suggested in the text, that it is also given by (7–45c). In doing this, show the sum over S is obtained by solving the combinatorial problem indicated.

b. Carry out the simplification of equation (7–45c) under the large delay-bandwidth condition $\Gamma \gg 1$, again following the method suggested in the text, and show equation (7–45g) results.

c. Starting with equation (7–52), show the normalized throughput γ is given by equation (7–55). Provide the justification for the expression (7–57) relating the normalized response time R to γ and the window W. Finally, show the power P is given by equation (7–59).

Appendix

Elements of Queueing Theory

Queueing theory plays a key role in the modeling and analysis discussed in this book. The assumption is that readers will have had some elementary exposure to this subject, either through a formal course, through study in a prior quantitative course on computer networks, or through self-study. For those readers lacking this background, or for those desiring a brief review, we provide this Appendix. It should provide the introduction to the subject necessary to follow the quantitative material in the book. More details can be found in any textbook on queueing theory. A particularly well-written and comprehensive treatment appears in [KLEI 1975].

Consider the buffer shown in Figure A–1. Data packets arrive and are buffered, ready to be read out on a transmission link at the rate of C bits/sec, as indicated. In the more general queueing literature, the terms "jobs" or "customers" are used, rather than packets. A work-conserving queue is one in which packets must be transmitted or served, once admitted to the buffer, and in which the transmission link, the "server" in the queueing jargon, is never idle so long as there is at least one packet waiting for transmission. We consider work-conserving queues only in this Appendix. Examples of nonwork-conserving systems are mentioned briefly in Chapter 6.

It is clear that packets will have to be buffered or queued for service if the number arriving at the input to the buffer in some interval of time is larger than the number the link can transmit in that time. The buffer will thus display alternating intervals when the queue is nonempty or the server is "busy," and when the server is "idle," with no packets either being transmitted or waiting to be transmitted. Arrivals are generally random or stochastic, so that the number of packets in the queue is stochastic as a function of time as well. Queueing theory enables us to determine the statistics of the queue,

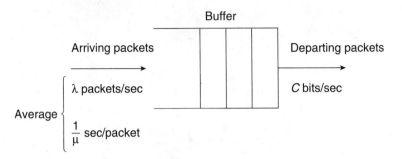

FIGURE A–1 ■ Model of buffering process.

from which such desired performance parameters as the time spent waiting in the queue or the probabilities a packet is blocked or lost, on arrival, may be found. The statistics in turn depend generally on three quantities:

1. The packet arrival process—the specific arrival statistics of the incoming packets
2. The packet-length distribution—comparable to the customer service-time distribution when discussing customer arrivals in the queueing literature
3. The number of servers and the service discipline—examples of service discipline include FIFO (first-in, first-out, or first-come, first-served) service, LIFO (last-in, last-out) service, and various types of priority service. We shall focus in this introductory treatment on FIFO service. Figure A–1 shows one output link, and hence one server. Multiple output links or servers would be represented by the servers in parallel.

The most common example of an arrival process is the Poisson process. This is the process on which we focus in this Appendix. A deterministic arrival process is one in which packets arrive equally-spaced in time. An example of such a process appears in Chapter 3, in discussing the generation of video packets. The average arrival rate of the arrival process, in packets/sec, is denoted by the symbol λ, as shown in Figure A–1. λ is also called the load on the buffer-link system of Figure A–1.

Examples of packet-length distributions include the exponential distribution and the fixed-length or deterministic distribution, among others. The packet length, in bits, is generally a random number denoted by m. Its average value is then denoted by $E(m)$. (For the deterministic distribution there is only one value, m.) The average packet length in units of time, that is, the average time required to transmit the packet out over the transmission link, is then given by $E(m)/C$, in units of seconds. We represent this time by the symbol $1/\mu$. Alternately, the parameter μ represents the average number of packets served per second. This quantity is more commonly called the capacity of the link, in units of packets/sec. The average packet length $1/\mu$ is also indicated in Figure A–1.

A more common queueing representation, and the one we henceforth use, appears in Figure A–2. The focus in this figure is on the average arrival rate or load λ and capacity μ. The circle at the output of the queue is used to represent the queue service. A two-server queue, with two links or servers, would be represented by two such output lines and circles in parallel. A little thought will indicate that the ratio of load to capacity, λ/μ, should play a critical role in the study of queues. For clearly, as this ratio increases (that is, as the load increases with respect to the capacity), the queue should build up more and the busy intervals should occur more often, while the possibility of queueing delay and the probability of queueing delay and the probability of loss both increase. This ratio of load to capacity is called the link utilization and is generally given the special label ρ. We thus have, by definition, $\rho \equiv \lambda/\mu$. We shall see that for very large buffers, approximated by infinite queues, a condition for stable operation of the queue is $\rho < 1$. For realistic finite queues the queue length is found to increase rapidly in size, with congestion setting in, as ρ approaches and exceeds the value of 1.

To determine the performance parameters of interest mentioned above, such as queueing delay or probability of packet loss, one must determine the statistics of the number of packets in the queue. The number of packets in the queue, including the one in service, is represented by the random variable n, as indicated in Figure A–2. This is also called the state of the queue. As noted above, the statistics of n depend on the arrival process, packet-length distribution, and service discipline. We focus first on the simplest type of queue, one with Poisson arrivals, exponentially distributed packet lengths, a single server as in Figure A–2, and FIFO service. We then generalize this model to one in which either the arrival process or service distribution/discipline, or both, is state-dependent. We conclude this introduction to queueing theory with a brief discussion of queues with Poisson arrivals and a general service-time distribution. A special case of particular interest in ATM networks is one in which the packet lengths are fixed or deterministic, since packets, or cells as they are called in the ATM world, are all 53 octets long. This introductory material is then followed up in the text, in Chapter 3 and elsewhere, with discussions of more complex arrival distributions used to represent traffic of var-

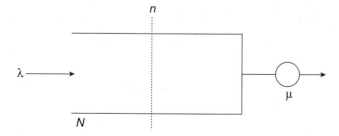

FIGURE A–2 ▪ Representation of queue.

ious types. Other subjects from queueing theory are introduced as well, where needed.

■ M/M/1 QUEUES: POISSON ARRIVALS, EXPONENTIAL SERVICE TIMES

The defining assumptions for a Poisson process are as follows: Consider a small time interval Δt, with $\Delta t \to 0$.

1. The probability of one arrival in Δt sec is then $\lambda \Delta t \ll 1$, independent of arrivals in adjacent (past or future) time slots. The assumption then is that the chance of an arrival is proportional to the time interval; λ, the proportionality constant, is thus assumed to be a fixed, known constant in this case.

2. The probability of no arrivals in Δt is $1 - \lambda \Delta t$. The process then, effectively rules out more than one arrival in Δt as $\Delta t \to 0$.

It may then be shown, through quite elementary methods, that the statistics of arrivals in a much larger interval, say T, obey the Poisson distribution [SCHW 1987]. Specifically, the probability of K arrivals in T sec is then

$$P(K) = P(K \text{ arrivals in } T \text{ sec}) = \frac{(\lambda T)^K e^{-\lambda T}}{K!} \tag{A–1}$$

$$K = 0, \ 1, \ 2, \ \dots$$

The average number of arrivals in T sec is then

$$E(K) = \sum_{K=0}^{\infty} KP(K) = \lambda T \tag{A–2}$$

So the Poisson parameter λ introduced as a proportionality factor in defining the Poisson process turns out to be the average packet arrival rate as well.

It may then also be shown that the time τ between arrivals is a continuously-distributed exponential random variable [KLEI 1975], [SCHW 1987].

$$f(\tau) = \lambda e^{-\lambda \tau} \tag{A–3}$$

Here, $f(\tau)$ is the probability density function of τ and is sketched in Figure A–3. The average time between arrivals is just

$$E(\tau) = \int_0^{\infty} \tau f(\tau) d\tau = \frac{1}{\lambda} \tag{A–4}$$

as might be expected.

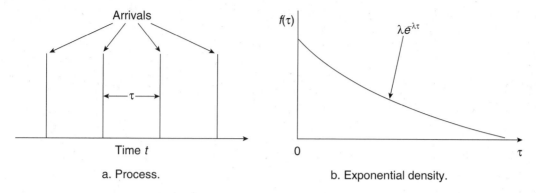

FIGURE A–3 ▪ Poisson arrivals and exponential time between arrivals.

Now consider the packet lengths. The service time, or time to complete the packet transmission, is of course intimately related to the packet lengths. (The emphasis in this application is somewhat different than in other applications of queueing theory. In those cases, one refers most commonly to *customer* arrivals, and the service time is related to the *server* characteristic. Customers are served in a statistically-varying manner because of the server characteristics. Here the server is essentially a fixed capacity outgoing line which continually outputs μ packets/sec if packets are available to be transmitted. Statistical variations then arise because the packets—the customers—are themselves varying in length.) We again invoke the simplest queueing theory assumption; packets are now assumed to be exponentially-distributed in length, with average length 1/μ. (In the queueing theory terminology, the service distribution is exponential.)

Specifically, if packets are r sec long, the probability density function of r is

$$f(r) = \mu e^{-\mu \tau} \tag{A–5}$$

and

$$E(r) = \frac{1}{\mu} \text{ sec/packet}$$

Shorter packets ($r < 1/\mu$) are then more likely than longer packets ($r > 1/\mu$). Note that this is clearly a physically implausible distribution since packets are discrete in length, whereas r in equation (A–5) is continuous. The exponential packet length assumption does provide quick results very simply, however. It allows extension to more complex models quite readily since it is the simplest service time model available and the literature is replete with applications of its use.

Note that the service time distribution is identical with that of the packet interarrival distribution of equation (A–3) and Figure A–3. A little thought will then indicate that there are Poisson-type assumptions behind the exponential service time distribution as well. Specifically, consider a packet already in service. It is then readily shown that with the exponential service time model, the probability of a packet completion in a Δt interval is $\mu \, \Delta t$, while the probability of no completion is just $(1 - \mu \, \Delta t)$. Completions from one Δt sec interval ($\Delta t \to 0$) to the next are statistically independent. The number of packet departures (service completions) in T sec obeys the same Poisson distribution as that of equation (A–1) with μ replacing λ.

Now consider the queueing model of Figure A–4: Poisson arrivals enter an infinite buffer with an exponential service time distribution. Messages are handled first-come-first-served. This queueing model is called an $M/M/1$ queue and is the simplest one available in queueing theory. The notation used is due to D. G. Kendall and has now become standardized in the queueing literature. The Kendall notation in its most general form for an infinite queue is given as $A/B/m$, with "A" a symbol denoting the arrival distribution, "B" the service discipline and "m" the number of servers used. The symbol "M" denotes Poisson or the equivalent exponential distributions. An $M/G/1$ queue would have Poisson arrivals, a general service distribution, and one server. The "D" denotes fixed (constant) service time, so a queue with this characteristic and Poisson arrivals would be written $M/D/1$ (see [KLEI 1975] for example).

We would like to find the probability $p_n(t)$ for the $M/M/1$ queue that n packets are present in the buffer at time t. This provides a state description of the buffer from which various statistical parameters (that is, average buffer occupancy, probability of exceeding a given level of occupancy, and so on) may be found. For $t \to \infty$ we should find steady-state conditions setting in and will develop the steady-state description of the buffer.

Because of the Poisson assumptions involved, a simple way of analyzing the buffer is to focus on two successive times intervals t and $t + \Delta t$ ($\Delta t \to 0$). These are shown in Figure A–5. Say that the buffer happens to be in state n at time $t + \Delta t$ as shown. With the Poisson assumptions for packet arrival and completion, it is apparent that the buffer could only have occupied one of the three states shown in Figure A–5, ($n + 1, n, n - 1$) at time t, Δt sec prior. For in the Δt sec time interval, no more than one packet could have arrived, and no

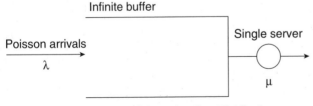

Infinite buffer

Single server

Poisson arrivals

λ

μ

Exponential service-time distribution   **FIGURE A–4** ■ *M/M/*1 queue.

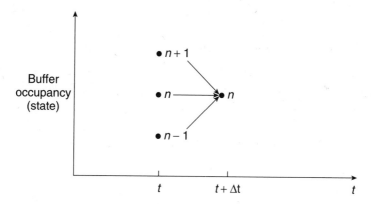

FIGURE A–5 ▪ Analysis of *M/M/*1 queue.

more than one could have had its transmission completed (service completion). $p_n(t + \Delta t)$ can then be readily found in terms of the probability of occupying each of the three states at time t, and the probabilities of arrivals and departures (the so-called transition probabilities). Specifically, we have

$$p_n(t + \Delta t) = p_n(t) \left[(1 - \mu \,\Delta t)(1 - \lambda \Delta t) + \mu \,\Delta t \,\lambda \Delta t \right]$$
$$+ p_{n+1}(t) \left[\mu \,\Delta t(1 - \lambda \,\Delta t) \right] \qquad (A–6)$$
$$+ p_{n-1}(t) \left[\lambda \,\Delta t(1 - \mu \,\Delta t) \right] \qquad n \geq 1$$

The terms in brackets multiplying $p_n(t)$ represent the probabilities of no arrivals and no departures, or one arrival and one departure—just the quantities needed to maintain the buffer at its same state. Similarly, the term in brackets multiplying $p_{n+1}(t)$ represents the probability of one departure (service completion) and no arrival, so that $n + 1$ drops to n. Finally, the last term in brackets represents the probability of one arrival and no departure.

Equation (A–6) can be used to solve for $p_n(t)$ by letting $\Delta t \to 0$. Assuming the various probabilities of state are continuous in time, one can represent $p_n(t + \Delta t)$ by the first two terms in its Taylor series:

$$p_n(t + \Delta t) \doteq p_n(t) + \frac{dp_n(t)}{dt} \Delta t \qquad (A–7)$$

Substituting equation (A–7) into (A–6), cancelling terms, and letting $\Delta t \to 0$ (second-order terms involving $(\Delta t)^2$ then vanish), one obtains a differential-difference equation governing $p_n(t)$. We shall focus on stationary statistical behavior only. Thus we assume the state probabilities are independent of time. (This implies the buffer system of Figure A–4 has been in operation for a long period of time with transient effects negligible.) This also implies $dp_n(t)/dt = 0$. From equations (A–6) and (A–7), the equation of state governing the stationary process is then readily shown to be given by

$$(\lambda + \mu)p_n = \mu p_{n+1} + \lambda p_{n-1} \qquad n \geq 1 \qquad \text{(A–8)}$$

Equation (A–8) may be diagrammed in the form of Figure A–6 which represents the two ways in which state n may be reached from $(n - 1)$ and $(n + 1)$ respectively. The solution of this difference equation with appropriate boundary conditions incorporated provides the desired expression for p_n, the probability that n packets occupy the buffer. One condition of course is that as $n \to \infty$, p_n must approach zero. For $\sum_{n=0}^{\infty} p_n = 1$. Higher states must thus have decreasingly smaller probabilities of occupancy.

Another condition relates p_1 and p_0. An equation similar to (A–6) may be written for these two states. It is then left to the reader to show that in the steady-state

$$\lambda p_0 = \mu p_1 \qquad \text{(A–9)}$$

The interpretation here, of course, is that an arrival while the queue is in state 0 (empty) moves the queue to state 0.

Equations (A–8) and (A–9) may be obtained directly in a somewhat different and instructive way that we shall find useful later in this Appendix and in the text as well. We use a technique involving so-called *balance equations*. Referring back to Figure A–6, note that we have drawn two circles encircling the origin and state n, respectively. Consider state n first. We note simply, without proof, that, in the steady-state, the rate of entering state n must equal the rate of leaving it, if the probability p_n is to have a constant value. Alternately said, the probability flux crossing the circuit surrounding state n has a net value of 0. We thus equate or balance the flux entering state n to the flux leaving it. Since μ is the rate of moving down from state n to state $n - 1$, conditioned on being in state n initially, while λ is the corresponding conditional rate of moving up to state $n + 1$, the total unconditional rate of *leaving* state n is just $p_n(\lambda + \mu)$. Now consider the unconditional rate of *entering* state n. By the same argument, this must be $\lambda p_{n-1} + \mu p_{n+1}$. Equating the two rates, we get equation (A–8)! Now focus on the circle encircling the origin. The flux leaving state 0 is just λp_0 while the flux entering it, from state 1, is μp_1. Again equating or balancing the two rates, we get equation (A–9). As noted above, we shall apply this same technique shortly, in this Appendix, in extending the *M/M/1* queue model to another type of queue model. We also use the concept of balance equations in various places in the text as well.

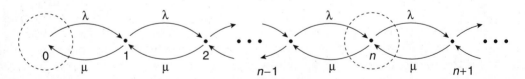

FIGURE A–6 ■ State representation of steady-state *M/M/1* queue.

Returning now to equation (A–8), one simple method of solving this equation for p_n starts with equation (A–9) and then uses (A–8) recursively. Thus, from (A–9), we have

$$p_1 = \frac{\lambda}{\mu} p_0 = \rho p_0 \tag{A–10}$$

with $\rho \equiv \lambda/\mu$, the link utilization parameter introduced earlier.

From equation (A–8) with $n = 1$, we find

$$p_2 = (\rho + 1)p_1 - \rho p_0 = \rho^2 p_0 \tag{A–11}$$

using equation (A–10). Repeating, the general expression for p_n is readily shown to be given by

$$p_n = \rho^n p_0 \tag{A–12}$$

It is apparent that we must have $\rho = \lambda/\mu < 1$ from the comment above that the state probabilities must decrease with n. This agrees with our intuitive notion that the average number of arrivals per unit time, λ, must be less than the system capacity μ. Otherwise, the buffer begins to build up indefinitely. This is precisely the comment we made earlier in defining the utilization ρ as the ratio of average arrival rate or load to capacity. In this case of an infinite queue, a steady-state solution of equation (A–6) only exists if $\rho < 1$. The queue is unstable otherwise. In the case of a finite buffer, to be discussed shortly, the utilization can be 1 or greater, but the buffer is then full more often and packets begin to be dropped on arrival.

To complete the analysis we must now find the unknown quantity p_0 in equation (A–12). This is simply done by invoking the rule that the state probabilities must sum to 1.

Since

$$\sum_{n=0}^{\infty} p_n = 1 = p_0 \sum_{n=0}^{\infty} \rho^n = \frac{p_0}{1-\rho} \tag{A–13}$$

we also find

$$p_0 = (1 - \rho) \tag{A–14}$$

and

$$p_n = (1 - \rho)\rho^n \tag{A–15}$$

This again indicates that we must have $\rho < 1$. It also indicates that as ρ increases, the higher states become relatively more probable.

Note the physical interpretation of ρ provided by equation (A–14): $\rho = (1 - p_0)$ is the probability that the buffer is not empty.

Equation (A–15), representing the probability of occupancy of the various states of the *M/M/*1 queue, may be used to find all statistical quantities of interest for the queue. Specifically, the average queue size is given by

$$E(n) = \sum_{n=0}^{\infty} np_n = \frac{\rho}{1-\rho} \qquad \text{(A–16)}$$

The average queue occupancy thus increases beyond bound as $\rho \to 1$. This implies the queue becomes unstable as $\rho \to 1$, just the comment we made above. There is no steady-state solution of equation (A–6) for this case when the queue is infinite in size. $E(n)$ is sketched in Figure A–7. For $\rho < 0.5$ the average number of packets in the queue is less than 1. For $\rho > 0.5$ the number increases rapidly. Thus for $\rho = 0.75$, $E(n) = 3$; for $\rho = 0.8$, $E(n) = 4$; for $\rho = 0.9$, $E(n) = 9$; and so on.

The average queue occupancy can be used quite simply to find an expression for the overall delay experienced by a packet (more generally, a customer) in first waiting for service and then being transmitted (served). Specifically, a theorem called *Little's formula* relates the delay directly to the average queue occupancy [LITT 1961], [KLEI 1975], [SCHW 1987]. This theorem says that for any work-conserving queueing system, the average occupancy of the system must equal the average delay for the system multiplied by the average arrival rate. In equation form, Little's formula is given by

$$\lambda E(T) = E(n) \qquad \text{(A–17)}$$

The parameter λ is the arrival rate to the queueing system, $E(T)$ is the delay through the system, and $E(n)$ is the average number of customers in the system. The system in question can be a queue such as that of Figure A–2, with any arrival and service distributions and any work-conserving service disciple. $E(T)$ is then the queueing delay, including service (transmission) time, through the

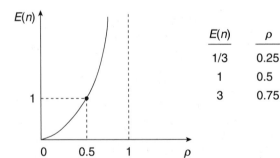

$E(n)$	ρ
1/3	0.25
1	0.5
3	0.75

FIGURE A–7 ■ Average queue occupancy, *M/M/*1 queue.

[LITT 1961]   Little, D. C., "A Proof of the Queueing Formula: $L = \lambda W$," *Operations Research, 9* (1961): 383–387.

queue, and $E(n)$ is the average number in the buffer, including the one in service, just the expression equation (A–16) found for the $M/M/1$ case. The system can just as well be a network of queues or it can be a portion of a queue such as its "waiting room", the buffer portion, excluding the service section.

Applying equation (A–17) to the $M/M/1$ result of equation (A–16), in particular, we have

$$E(T) = \frac{E(n)}{\lambda} = \frac{1}{\mu(1-\rho)} = \frac{1}{\mu - \lambda} \tag{A–18}$$

This says that for low utilization, or the load $\lambda \ll \mu$, the capacity, the average delay is just the average transmission time $1/\mu$. As the utilization increases, the delay increases correspondingly. At $\rho = 0.5$, for example, the delay is twice the transmission time. This indicates the delay in the buffer waiting for service is the same as the transmission time at this point. Above this value for ρ, the delay begins to increase rapidly, tracking the corresponding increase in the average queue size, as shown in Figure A–7. At $\rho = 0.8$, the average delay becomes five times the average transmission time, and at $\rho = 0.9$, ten times the average transmission time.

It is often of interest to know the probability that the queue exceeds a specified number. We use this calculation in some places in the book in determining the buffer size needed for a prescribed probability of buffer overflow. From equation (A–15) the probability that the number of packets waiting in an $M/M/1$ queue exceeds some number N is given by

$$P(n > N) = \sum_{n=N+1}^{\infty} p_n = (1-\rho) \sum_{n=N+1}^{\infty} \rho^n = \rho^{N+1} \tag{A–19}$$

after using the geometric sum formula.

As an example, the following table indicates $P(n > N)$ for $\rho = 0.6$ and various N:

N	$P(n > N)$
1	0.36
3	0.13
9	6.1×10^{-3}
19	3.7×10^{-5}

The probability decreases exponentially with N as shown by equation (A–19). Recall that the *average* occupancy for $\rho = 0.6$ is $E(n) = 0.6/(1 - 0.6) = 1.5$. It is apparent from the table above that the chance of exceeding ten times the average buffer occupancy is less than 10^{-3}. A buffer capable of holding fifteen packets would then appear effectively like an infinite buffer for this value of ρ.

As a check, consider a *finite* buffer now with Poisson arrivals and exponential packet lengths holding at most N packets, including the one in service. This queueing system is called the *M/M/1/N* queue. (The Kendall notation, extended to include finite queues, is written as *A/B/m/N*.) The derivation of equation (A–12) for the steady-state probability of state occupancy didn't really involve the infinite buffer assumption. The solution for p_n is thus still appropriate in the finite buffer case. The only difference now is that the probabilities of the finite set of states must sum to 1. Thus, we have

$$\sum_{n=0}^{N} p_n = 1 = p_0 \sum_{n=0}^{N} \rho^n = p_0 \left[\frac{1-\rho^{N+1}}{1-\rho} \right] \tag{A–20}$$

again using the geometric sum formula.

We thus have in this case

$$p_0 = \frac{1-\rho}{1-\rho^{N+1}} \tag{A–21}$$

and

$$p_n = \frac{(1-\rho)p^n}{1-\rho^{N+1}} \tag{A–22}$$

For $\rho^N \ll 1$ it is apparent that this result reduces to the infinite buffer result of equation (A–15). The probability that the buffer is *filled* and that packets are turned away (blocked) is simply the probability that there are N packets in the buffer or

$$p_N = \frac{(1-\rho)\rho^N}{1-\rho^{N+1}} \tag{A–23}$$

(In the text we refer quite often to cell *loss probability*. In general, this differs somewhat from *blocking probability*. The former is measured by the fraction of cell, or packet, arrivals that are lost over a specified interval of time. The latter is given by the probability, as calculated here, that the buffer is full at a packet arrival. It turns out that for the case of Poisson arrivals both quantities are the same. See [SCHW 1987] for a detailed discussion and comparison of the two probability measures.)

This expression for blocking probability may be substantiated in an instructive fashion that focuses on average packet throughput. In this approach, the average net rate of packet arrivals, or packet throughput, is equated to the average packet departure rate. Statistical equilibrium is of course presumed to prevail. To derive the blocking probability of equation (A–23), consider the finite *M/M/1* queue of Figure A–8. (This is also readily generalized to more general queueing structures.) λ packets/sec on the average are assumed to arrive at

$$\lambda(1 - P_B) \longrightarrow \boxed{\begin{array}{c}\text{Finite queue,}\\ N \text{ packets}\end{array}} \longrightarrow (1 - p_0)\mu$$

FIGURE A–8 ■ Blocking probability and average throughput, *M/M*/1 queue.

the input to the queue capable of holding, at most, N packets only. If the blocking probability is P_B, the *net* arrival rate *into* the queue must be $\lambda(1 - P_B)$. For equilibrium to exist, this must equal the average packet departure rate and is just the system throughput. Now the probability of a packet departure in an interval Δt is just $\mu\Delta t$ if there is a packet waiting in the queue. The probability that a packet is waiting is just the probability $(1 - p_0)$ that the queue is non-empty. The average departure *rate* is thus $(1 - p_0)\mu$, and we have

$$\lambda(1 - P_B) = (1 - p_0)\mu \tag{A–24}$$

This is indicated in Figure A–8.

In particular, for the finite *M/M*/1 queue, p_0 is readily found from equation (A–22). Substituting this into equation (A–24), noting that $\rho = \lambda/\mu$, and solving for P_B, we find exactly equation (A–23) arising. As a check, for an infinite queue we must have, from equation (A–24), $\rho = (1 - p_0)$, if $P_B = 0$ which agrees with equation (A–14).

Equation (A–24) is a general expression for the *throughput* (as contrasted to the load λ) in queueing structures with finite buffer ("waiting room") space. It does assume, however, that the arrival rate is state-independent, and that there is only one server in the system. In the next section discussing state-dependent queues, we generalize this throughput expression.

■ QUEUES WITH DEPENDENCE ON STATE OF SYSTEM

The *M/M*/1 queue results given in the previous section may be generalized readily in a few cases of specific interest. One such case involves the multiserver situation in which additional servers or transmission links are added as the state occupancy increases. Another case has the packet arrival rate decreasing with queue occupancy to keep the average occupancy down. Both of these are special cases of a queue in which arrivals and departures, although based on Poisson-type assumptions, depend on the state of the system.

We shall discuss these cases briefly here. All of these Poisson-type processes are examples of generalized birth-death processes in which the probability of an arrival (birth) in an interval Δt is proportional to Δt, $\Delta t \to 0$, while the corresponding probability of a departure (death) is proportional to Δt as well [COX 1965]. The generalization consists of relating the proportionality constants to the state of the system.

[COX 1965] Cox, D. R., and H. D. Miller, *The Theory of Stochastic Processes,* London: Methuen & Co., 1965.

Thus, let the arrival coefficients be called λ_n and the departure coefficients be μ_n, to denote their dependence on the state n. Figure A–9 is the state diagram generalizing that of Figure A–6 for the $M/M/1$ case. Assume these coefficients are independent of time and that statistical equilibrium has set in as well. It is then apparent by comparison with equation (A–8) for the $M/M/1$ case in which the coefficients are state independent that the difference equation relating p_n to p_{n-1} and p_{n+1} is now given by

$$(\lambda_n + \mu_n)p_n = \mu_{n+1}\,p_{n+1} + \lambda_{n-1}\,p_{n-1} \qquad n \geq 1 \qquad \text{(A–25)}$$

Equation (A–25) may also be obtained, as was equation (A–8), by invoking the balance condition about state n. Note from Figure A–9 that the left-hand side of equation (A–25) represents the rate of leaving state n, while the right-hand side represents the rate of entering that state from its neighboring states.

This equation may be solved recursively, as was equation (A–8), by first writing an equivalent equation relating p_1 to p_0 and then continuing for higher state probabilities. It is left for the reader to show that the resultant expression for p_n is given by

$$p_n = \frac{\lambda_0\lambda_1\lambda_2\lambda_3\ldots\lambda_{n-1}}{\mu_1\mu_2\ldots\mu_n}\,p_0 \qquad \text{(A–26)}$$

The probability p_0 that the queue is empty is, in turn, found by summing all the states and setting the sum equal to 1.

As a specific case say $\mu_n = n_\mu$. This is the case of a queue with multiple servers; as a new packet (or "customer," in the queueing jargon) arrives, an additional server (link) is pressed into service. There can be a limit on the number of servers available but we shall leave that case for the reader to develop. If we assume no limit on the number of servers we have

$$p_n = \left(\frac{\lambda}{\mu}\right)^n \frac{p_0}{n!} = \frac{\rho^n}{n!}\,p_0 \qquad \text{(A–27)}$$

with $\rho \equiv \lambda/\mu$ again.

Then with

$$\sum_{n=0}^{\infty} p_n = 1 = p_0 \sum_{n=0}^{\infty} \frac{\rho^n}{n!} = p_0 e^{\rho} \qquad \text{(A–28)}$$

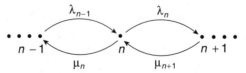

FIGURE A–9 ■ State representation, birth-death process.

we have

$$p_0 = e^{-p} \qquad \text{(A–29)}$$

and

$$p_n = \frac{\rho^n e^{-\rho}}{n!} \qquad \text{(A–30)}$$

The probability of higher state occupancy is relatively less here for the same ρ than in the $M/M/1$ case since the additional servers brought in clear the system out more rapidly. We compare this queue discipline (multiple servers) with the $M/M/1$ case in the following table:

Parameter	Multiple Server Case		M/M/1 Queue
1. Probability queue is empty p_0	$=$	e^{-p} $>$	$1 - \rho$
2. Probability queue is nonempty (server is busy) $1 - p_0$	$=$	$1 - e^{-p}$ $<$	ρ
3. Average queue occupancy $E(n)$	$=$	ρ $<$	$\rho/(1 - \rho)$

Note that the average queue occupancy rises only linearly with ρ in this case and does not show the rapid increase with ρ as $\rho \to 1$ in the $M/M/1$ case (Figure A–7). In fact, here $\rho > 1$ is allowed since more servers are simply brought in to accommodate the increased demand as λ increases.

Another example that leads to the identical result as the many-server case is the so-called queue with discouragement. Here the model used is $\mu_n = \mu$, $\lambda_0 = \lambda/(n + 1)$. Thus, as the queue size increases, the arrival rate drops accordingly. The server discipline remains the same, however. (The number of links does not increase.) It is left to the reader to show that the equation for p_n is exactly that of equation (A–27) from which equation (A–30) again follows. The previous table thus applies here as well with the multiple server case replaced by the queue with discouragement.

Consider now a finite birth-death, or state-dependent, queueing system. Let the maximum queue size again be taken as N. The throughput, in terms of average number of packets or customers delivered per unit time may be obtained in terms of the probabilities of state by focusing on either the input or the output of the system. Thus, consider the input first. Given the system operating at state n, the arrival rate is of course λ_n. This must exclude state N, however, since at that state the queue is full, and no arrivals are allowed. Summing over all states, from $n = 0$ to $N - 1$, while appropriately weighting the arrival rate at each state by the probability of being in that state, one gets as the overall throughput the following expression:

$$\sum_{n=0}^{N-1} \lambda_n p_n$$

Note, as a check, that if λ_n is a constant value λ the expression becomes $\lambda \cdot \sum_{n=0}^{N-1} p_n = \lambda(1 - p_N)$, since the sum of p_n over all the states is just 1. But $p_N = P_B$, the blocking probability, and the throughput is exactly that of equation (A–24).

Now consider the output of the queue. Calculating the throughput here by summing the weighted service or departure rates over all the states, except for $n = 0$ (why is that state left out?), one gets as the throughput $\sum_{n=1}^{N} \mu_n p_n$. As a special case, let the service rate be the state-independent or constant value μ. One then gets the value $\mu(1 - p_0)$, just the value obtained previously for the state-independent, single-server $M/M/1$ queue. Equating the two values of throughput, one obtained by focusing at the input, the other at the output, we get as the throughput expression generalizing equation (A–24),

$$\sum_{n=0}^{N-1} \lambda_n p_n = \sum_{n=1}^{N} \mu_n p_n \qquad \text{(A–31)}$$

The multiple server queue and queue with discouragement, just discussed, are examples of queueing structures where equation (A–31) can be used to find the average throughput. (Note that calculating either side of the equation, whichever is simpler, suffices to find the throughput.) Another example is a queue with two servers or packet transmission links. For this case it is left for the reader to show that $\mu_1 = \mu$; $\mu_n = 2\mu$, $n \geq 2$. For Poisson arrivals and a finite buffer, this gives us the $M/M/2/N$ queue, for which the throughput equation may then be written, using equation (A–31), as

$$\lambda (1 - P_B) = \mu p_1 + 2\mu (1 - p_0 - p_1) \qquad \text{(A–32)}$$

Details are left to the reader. Note that this equation enables us to calculate the blocking probability in terms of the probabilities p_0 and p_1, if we so desire.

■ M/G/1 QUEUES: GENERAL SERVICE TIME DISTRIBUTION

We now extend the queue analysis to one involving a general service time distribution. In the data transmission context this implies packets with nonexponentially-distributed lengths. We shall show that the average buffer occupancy and hence, by Little's formula, the average time delay expression may be found for this case quite generally. The resultant expression is called the *Pollaczek-Khinchine formula.* It enables us to see how different choices of statistics affect the average time delay determined on the basis of exponentially distributed (*M/M*/1) packet lengths.

To handle the general packet length (or service time) case we approach the problem quite differently than in the previous section. We shall handle general service time first, independent of the arrival distribution, then focus on the *M/G*/1 case, with Poisson arrivals. The approach here is to focus on the times (randomly-distributed) at which service on a packet is completed. (Transmission of the packet in question is then concluded and the packet leaves the buffer.)

Thus, assume a sequence of packets arrives at a buffer, each with randomly varying length (or service time). The server works on one packet at a time (that is, the transmission link handles one packet at a time) until completion. Then service begins on the next packet, first-come-first-served. Let n_j be the queue length *after the departure* of the jth packet (j is the running time index). We can write a simple equation relating n_j to the queue length n_{j-1} after the departure of the $(j-1)$ packet. Specifically, we have

$$n_j = (n_{j-1} - 1) + v_j \qquad n_{j-1} \geq 1$$
$$= v_j \qquad\qquad n_{j-1} = 0 \tag{A-33}$$

Here v_j is the number of messages arriving during the service time of the jth packet (or jth customer). This is itself of course a random variable. The times involved are diagrammed in Figure A–10. Equation (A–33) simply states the obvious fact that the queue length decreases by 1 after departure of a message (*if* there was a message in the queue) and increases by the number of arrivals.

The equation may be written in an alternate fashion as

$$n_j = n_{j-1} - U(n_{j-1}) + v_j \tag{A-34}$$

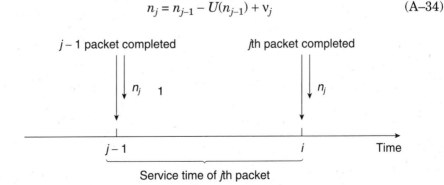

$j-1$ packet completed jth packet completed

n_j 1 n_j

$j-1$ i Time

Service time of jth packet

FIGURE A–10 ▪ General service time distribution.

with $U(x)$ the unit step function defined by

$$U(x) = 1 \qquad x \geq 1$$
$$= 0 \qquad x < 1$$

Let $j \to \infty$ and assume equilibrium has set in. Taking expectations on both sides of equation (A–34) and replacing variables by their equilibrium values, one gets

$$E(v) = E[U(n)] = P(n > 0) \equiv \rho \qquad \text{(A–35)}$$

Note that $E(v)$ represents the average number of arrivals in a service interval. It is left for the reader to verify that this is precisely the utilization ρ as indicated in equation (A–35). (This will be shown to be the case for Poisson arrivals shortly.)

To proceed we now square left- and right-handed sides of equation (A–34), simplify, and let equilibrium again set in with $j \to \infty$. (Note that there is method to our madness, as will be apparent shortly!) Again, taking expectations of both sides, we find that we get the following equation for $E(n)$, the average number of packets in the queue:

$$E(n) = \frac{E(v)}{2} + \frac{\sigma_v^2}{2(1 - E(v))} \qquad \text{(A–36)}$$

In obtaining this result, use has been made of the fact that $U^2(n) = U(n)$ and $E[nU(n)] = E(n)$. Since packets arrive independently in adjacent service intervals under the Poisson assumption, we must also have $E(n_{j-1}v_j) = E(n_{j-1}) \cdot E(v_j)$. Finally, the term σ_v^2, yet to be calculated, is the variance $E(v^2) - E^2(v)$ of the arrivals in a service interval.

To find σ_v^2 we now specifically invoke the Poisson arrival assumption. The service-time (packet-length) distribution is left general, however. To proceed, we define $P(v = k)$ as the probability that k packets (customers) arrive in a service interval. The average number of arrivals $E(v)$ in a service interval and the variance σ_v^2 may then be written in terms of $P(v = k)$, respectively, as

$$E(v) = \sum_{k=0}^{\infty} kP(v = k) \qquad \text{(A–37)}$$

and

$$\sigma_v^2 = \sum_{k=0}^{\infty} [k - E(v)]^2 P(v = k) \qquad \text{(A–38)}$$

We now let the general service-time distribution be given in terms of a probability density function $f_\tau(\tau)$, with τ the random packet length or service time.

The conditional probability $P(v = k|\tau)$ that there are exactly k arrivals in a specific time interval τ is, for Poisson arrivals, just the Poisson probability

$$P(v = k|\tau) = \frac{(\lambda\tau)^k e^{-\lambda\tau}}{k!} \tag{A–39}$$

(See equation (A–1).) The probability $P(v = k)$ is then found by averaging over all values of service time τ:

$$P(v = k) = \int_0^\infty P(v = k|\tau) f_\tau(\tau) d\tau \tag{A–40}$$

Inserting the Poisson probability of equation (A–39) in equation (A–40), then, in turn, using the resultant expression to calculate, first, $E(v)$ from equation (A–37) and then σ_v^2, from equation (A–38), one gets, after interchanging the order of integration and summation, the following values for these two quantities:

$$E(v) = \lambda E(\tau) \equiv \rho \tag{A–41}$$

with

$$E(v) = \int_0^\infty \tau f_\tau(\tau) d\tau \tag{A–42}$$

and

$$\sigma_v^2 = \rho + \lambda^2 \sigma^2 \tag{A–43}$$

Here $E(\tau)$ is the average packet (service-time) length and σ^2 is the variance of the packet-length distribution. For exponentially-distributed lengths, the case assumed initially in this Appendix in discussing the *M/M/*1 queue, we had $E(\tau) = 1/\mu$. The variance $\sigma^2 = E^2(\tau) = (1/\mu)^2$ in this case. For the *M/D/*1 queue, with fixed-length packets, $\sigma^2 = 0$. Note that $E(v)$, the average number of arrivals in a service interval, does turn out to be the utilization ρ in this case, as suggested earlier. As indicated by equation (A–41), it is the product of the average arrival rate λ and the average service time. This extends the definition of ρ to more general service-time statistics than the exponential case. With $E(\tau)$ the average service time, $1/E(\tau)$ is the average service rate, or the capacity, of the queueing system, and ρ quite generally is defined as the ratio of load to capacity.

We are now almost at the final desired result! We insert equations (A–41) and (A–43), obtained for the case of Poisson arrivals, into the general expression (A–36) for the average number of packets (customers) in the queue, and obtain the average number for the *M/G/*1 queue, that is, a queue with Poisson arrivals and *general* service time (packet-length) distribution. We choose to write the resultant expression in the following form:

$$E(n) = \left(\frac{\rho}{1-\rho}\right)\left\{1 - \frac{\rho}{2}\left[1 - \sigma^2 / E^2(\tau)\right]\right\} \tag{A-44}$$

Note how this expression compares with the corresponding expression for the average number of packets in the *M/M/1* queue given by equation (A–16). The first part of equation (A–44), shown within the parentheses, is precisely the *M/M/1* result. This is obtained for the special case $\sigma^2 = E^2(\tau)$, just the case of the exponential distribution, as expected. This *M/M/1* result is then modified by an expression that depends on the ratio of the variance of the packet-length (service-time) distribution to the average length squared. The variation with link utilization ρ is still principally determined by the denominator term $(1 - \rho)$. The resultant average number of packets in the queue is, however, modulated by the expression in brackets. The number increases above the case for exponential packets if the variance increases. It decreases if the variance is less than that of the exponential case. In particular, if the variance is zero, that is, all packets are the same length, as in the ATM case, one gets the following *M/D/1* result:

$$E(n) = \left(\frac{\rho}{1-\rho}\right)[1 - \rho/2] \tag{A-45}$$

The average number in the queue is reduced somewhat from the *M/M/1* result, depending on the value of the utilization ρ. For $\rho = 0.5$, for example, $E(n) = 1$ for the *M/M/1* case and 0.75 for the *M/D/1* queue. As ρ increases to 0.8 (the beginning of the region of congestion) the average number equals 4 in the *M/M/1* case, 2.4 in the *M/D/1* case. For $\rho = 0.9$, the two numbers are, respectively, 9 and approximately 5. For even larger values of utilization, the *M/D/1* result is one-half that of the *M/M/1* result.

We now readily obtain the expression for the average delay through the queue, including transmission (service) delay, by applying Little's formula. This gives us, finally, the celebrated Pollaczek-Khinchine formula mentioned at the beginning of this section. Dividing $E(n)$ by the average arrival rate λ we get

$$E(T) = \frac{E(\tau)}{(1-\rho)}\left\{1 - \frac{\rho}{2}\left[1 - \rho^2 / E^2(\tau)\right]\right\} \tag{A-46}$$

The comments made above about the relation of the *M/G/1* result to the special case of the *M/M/1* queue clearly apply here as well. The average delay through the queue for the *M/D/1* queue, for example, found by setting the packet-length variance σ^2 to 0, is just

$$E(T) = \frac{E(\tau)}{(1-\rho)}\left[1 - \frac{\rho}{2}\right] \qquad (A\text{–}47)$$

Note also that this equation is easily obtained from equation (A–45) by applying Little's formula directly to that result.

It is of interest to conclude this section and tutorial on queueing by obtaining a second form of the Pollaczek-Khinchine formula. This expression is one for the average *waiting time E(W)* of the *M/G/*1 queue. This is the average time spent waiting for service. Since the average service or transmission time is just $E(\tau)$, or $1/\mu$ in the exponential case, we simply subtract $E(\tau)$ from $E(T)$ in equation (A–47) to obtain the desired expression for *E(W)*. Doing just this, one obtains, after some simple algebraic manipulation,

$$E(W) = E(T) - E(\tau) = \frac{\lambda E(\tau^2)}{2(1-\rho)} \qquad (A\text{–}48)$$

Here the term $E(\tau^2) = \sigma^2 + E^2(\tau)$ is the second moment of the packet-length (service-time) distribution. Note how simple the form of this expression is. In particular, for the *M/M/*1 queue, with $\sigma^2 = E^2(\tau) = (1/\mu)^2$, $E(\tau^2) = 2E^2(\tau)$. For the *M/D/*1 queue, with the packet length constant, $\sigma^2 = 0$, and $E(\tau^2) = E^2(\tau)$. Equation (A–48) simplifies correspondingly in these two cases. This form for the waiting time is particularly useful in calculating delays in queues with priorities [SCHW 1987].

References

[AHMA 1982]   Ahmadi, H. and W. E. Denzel, "A Survey of Modern High-Performance Switching Techiques," *IEEE JSAC*, 7, 7 (Sept. 1989): 1091–1102.

[ANSI 1991a]   *American National Standards for Telecommunications Digital Hierarchy Optical Interface Rates and Formats Specifications*, ANSI T1.105–1991. New York: American National Standards Inst., 1991.

[ANIC 1982]   Anick, D., et al., "Stochastic Theory of a Data-Handling System with Multiple Sources," *Bell System Tech. J.*, *61*, 8 (Oct. 1982): 1871–1894.

[ATKI 1980]   Atkins, J. D., "Path Control: The Transport Network of SNA," *IEEE Trans. on Commun.*, *COM-28*, 4 (April 1980): 527–538.

[ATM 1994a]   *Closed-Loop Rate-Based Traffic Management*, Document Number ATM Forum/94-0438R2 (Sept. 1994).

[ATM 1994b]   *Credit-Based FCVC Proposal for ATM Traffic Management* (revision A2), ATM Forum/94-0632 (July 1994).

[BALA 1990]   Bala, K., et al., "Congestion Control for High-Speed Packet-Switched Networks," *Proc. IEEE Infocom '90*, San Francisco (June 1990): 520–526.

[BAIO 1991]   Baiocchi, A., et al., "Loss Performance Analysis of an ATM Multiplexer Loaded with High Speed On-Off Sources," *IEEE JSAC*, *9*, 3 (April 1991): 388–393.

[BARN 1994]   Barnwell, A. W., "Baseline Performance Using PRCA Rate-Control," ATM Forum/94-0597, Traffic Management Sub-Working Group, ATM Technical Committee (July 1994).

[BELL 1990]   Preliminary Report on Broadband ISDN Transfer Protocols, Special Report SR-NWT 001763, Issue 1, Bellcore, Morristown, NJ. Dec. 1990.

[BENE 1964]   Benes, V. E., "Optimal Rearrangeable Multistage Connecting Networks," *Bell System Tech. J.*, *43* (July 1964): 1641–1656.

[BERG 1990]   Berger, A. W., "Performance Analysis of a Rate Control Throttle Where Tokens and Jobs Queue," *Proc. IEEE Infocom 90*, San Francisco (June 1990): 30–38.

[BOLO 1990]   Bolot, J-C, and A. V. Shankar, "Dynamical Behavior of Rate-Based Flow Control Mechanisms," *ACM SIGCOMM Computer Communication Review*, (April 1990): 35–49.

[BONO 1995]   Bonomi, F., and K. W. Fendick, "The Rate-Based Flow Control for the Available Bit Rate ATM Service," *IEEE Network*, *9*, 2 (March/April 1995): 25–39.

[BRAD 1969]   Brady, P. T., "A Model for Generating On-Off Speech Patterns in Two-Way Conversations," *Bell System Tech. J.*, *48* (Sept. 1969): 2445–2472.

[BUCK 1990]   Bucklew, J., *Large-Deviation Techniques in Decision, Simulation, and Estimation*, New York: John Wiley, 1990.

[BUTT 1991]   Butto, M., et al., "Effectiveness of the 'Leaky Bucket' Policing Mechanism in ATM Networks," *IEEE JSAC*, *9*, 3 (April 1991): 335–342.

[BUZE 1973]   Buzen, J. P., "Computational Algorithms for Closed Queueing Networks with Exponential Servers," *Comm. of the ACM*, *16*, 9 (Sept. 1973): 527–531.

[CAMP 1976]   Campanella, S. J., "Digital Speech Interpolation," *Comsat. Tech. Rev.*, *6*, 1 (1976): 127–158.

[CCITT 1992a]   Recommendation I.121, Broadband Aspects of ISDN, CCITT, Geneva 1992.

[CCITT 1992b]   Recommendation I.362, Adaptation Layer (AAL) Functional Description, CCITT, Geneva: 1992.

[CCITT, 1992c]   Recommendation I.363, Broadband ISDN Adaptation Layer (AAL) Specifications, Geneva: 1992.

[CCITT 1992d]   "Traffic and Congestion Control in B-ISDN, I.371," Recommendation, CCITT Study Group XVIII; Contained in Temporary Document 62 (XVIII), CCITT, Geneva: June 1992.

[CCITT 1992e]   Recommendation Q.922, ISDN Data Link Layer Specification for Frame Mode Bearer Service, Annex A, Core Aspects of Q.922, for Use with Frame Relaying Bearer Service, CCITT, Geneva: 1992.

[CHAN 1992]   Chang, C-S, "Stability, Queue Length, and Delay, II: Stochastic Queueing Networks," *Rpt. RC 17709*, IBM Research, Yorktown Hts., NY, 10598, Feb. 1992.

[CHAN 1994]   Chang, C-S, "Stability, Queue Length, and Delay of Deterministic and Stochastic Queueing Networks," *IEEE Trans. on Auto. Control*, *39*, 5 (May 1994): 913–931.

[CHIA 1994]   Chiang, T., and D. Anastassiou, "Hierarchical Coding of Digital Television," *IEEE Commun. Mag.*, *32*, 5 (May 1994): 38–45.

[CHOU 1993]   Choudhury, G. L., et al., "Squeezing the Most out of ATM," AT&T Bell Labs. paper, May 28, 1993.

[CIDO 1993]   Cidon, I., et al., "The plaNET/ORBIT High-Speed Network," *J. High Speed Networks*, *2*, 3 (Sept. 1993): 1–38.

[CLOS 1953]   Clos, C., "A Study of Nonblocking Switching Networks," *Bell System Tech. J.*, *32*, 2 (March 1953): 406–424.

[COPP 1992]   Coppo, P., et al., "Optimal/Cost Performance Design of ATM Switches," *Proc. IEEE Infocom 92*, Florence, Italy, May 1992: 446–458.

[COST 1991]   *Performance Evaluation and Design of Multiservice Networks*, J. W. Roberts, ed., Final report, Cost 224 project. Luxembourg: Commission of the European Communities, Oct. 1991.

[COUD 1987]   Coudreuse, J. P., and M. Servel, "Prelude: An Asynchronous Time-Division Switched Network," *Proc. IEEE ICC 87*, Seattle, WA, June 1987: 769–773.

[COUR 1977]   Courtois, P. J., *Decomposability: Queueing and Computer Systems Applications*, Academic Press, 1977.

[COVE 1991]   Cover, T. M., and J. A. Thomas, *Elements of Information Theory*, New York: John Wiley, 1991.

[COX 1965]   Cox, D. R., and H. D. Miller, *The Theory of Stochastic Processes*, London: Methuen & Co., 1965.

[CRUZ 1991]   Cruz, R. L., "A Calculus for Network Delay, Part I: Elements in Isolation," *IEEE Trans. on Info. Theory*, *37*, 1 (Jan. 1991): 114–131; "Part II: Network Analysis." Same journal, same issue: 132–141.

[DAIG 1986]   Daigle, J. N., and J. D. Langford, "Models for Analysis of Packet-Voice Communication Systems," *IEEE JSAC*, *SAC-4*, 6 (Sept 1986): 847–855.

[DAIG 1992]   Daigle, J. N., *Queueing for Telecommunications*, Reading, MA: Addison-Wesley, 1992.

[DECI 1990a]   Decina, M., et al., "Bandwidth Assignment and Virtual Call Blocking in ATM Networks," *Proc. IEEE Infocom 90*, San Francisco, June 1990: 881–888.

[DECI 1990b]   Decina, M., and T. Toniatti, "On Bandwidth Allocation to Bursty Virtual Connections in ATM Networks," *Proc. IEEE ICC 90*, Atlanta, GA, April 1990.

[DECI 1990c]   Decina, M., et al., "Shuffleout Switching for ATM Interconnection Nets," *7th ITC Specialist Seminar*, Morristown, NJ, Oct. 1990.

[DEME 1989]   Demers, A., S. Keshav, and H. Shenker. "Analysis and Simulation of a Fair Queueing Algorithm," *Proc. ACM SIGCOMM 89*, Sept. 1989: 3–12.

[DEVA 1988]   Devault, M., et al., "The Prelude ATD Experiment: Assessment and Future Prospects," *IEEE JSAC*, *6*, 9 (Dec. 1988): 1528–1537.

[DIXI 1991]   Dixit, S. S., and P. A. Skelly, "Video Traffic Smoothing and ATM Multiplexer Performance," *Proc. IEEE Globecom '91*, Phoenix, AZ, Dec. 1991.

[DZIO 1990]   Dziong, Z., et al., "Admission Control and Routing in ATM Networks," *Computer Networks and ISDN Systems*, *20* (1990): 189–196.

[ECKB 1979]   Eckberg, Jr., A. E., "The Single Server Queue with Periodic Arrival Process and Deterministic Service Times," *IEEE Trans. on Commun.*, *COM-27*, 3 (March 1979): 556–562.

[ECKB 1990]   Eckberg, Jr., A. E., et al., "Bandwidth Management: A Congestion Control Strategy for Broadband Packet Networks—Characterizing the Throughput-Burstiness Filter," *Computer Networks and ISDN Systems*, *20* (1990): 415–423.

[ECKB 1991]   Eckberg, Jr., A. E., et al., "Controlling Congestion in B-ISDN/ATM: Issues and Strategies," *IEEE Commun. Mag.*, *29,* 9 (Sept. 1991): 64–70.

[ELWA 1991]   Elwalid, A. I., and D. Mitra, "Stochastic Fluid Models in the Analysis of Access Regulation in High-Speed Networks," *Proc. IEEE Globecom 91*, Phoenix, Dec. 1991: 1626–1632. (A more detailed version appears in *Communication Systems*, Special issue of *Queueing Systems*, D. Mitra and I. Mitrani (eds.), *9* (1991): Basel, Switz.: J. C. Baltzer A.G., 29–63.)

[ELWA 1993]   Elwalid, A. I., and D. Mitra, "Effective Bandwidth of General Markovian Traffic Sources and Admission Control of High-Speed Networks," *IEEE/ACM Trans. on Networking*, *1*, 3 (June 1993): 329–343.

[ENG 1992]   Eng, K. Y., et al., "A Growable Packet (ATM) Switch Architecture: Design Principles and Applications," *IEEE Trans. on Commun.*, *40*, 2 (Feb. 1992): 423–430.

[ENG 1995]   Eng, K. Y., and M. K. Karol, "State of the Art in Gigabit ATM Switching," *Proc. 1st IEEE International Workshop on Broadband Switching Systems*, Poznan, Poland, April 1995: 3–20.

[FEND 1991]   Fendick, K. W., et al., "An Approach to High-Performance, High-Speed Data Networks," *IEEE Commun. Mag.*, *29*, 10 (Oct. 1991): 74–82.

[FEND 1992]   Fendick, K. W., et al., "Analysis of a Rate-Based Control Strategy with Delayed Feedback," *Proc. ACM SIGCOMM 92*, Baltimore, MD, Aug. 1992: 136–148.

[FERR 1990]   Ferrari, D., and D. C. Verma, "A Scheme for Real-Time Channel Establishment in Wide-Area Networks," *IEEE JSAC*, *SAC-8* (April 1990): 368–379.

[FORE 1992]   *ForeRunner™ ASX-100 ATM Switch Architecture Manual*, Release 2.1. Pittsburgh, PA: Fore Systems, Inc., 1992.

[GARR 1994]   Garrett, M. W., and W. Willinger, "Analysis, Modeling, and

Generation of Self-Similar VBR Traffic," *Proc. ACM SIGCOMM '94.* London, (Aug. 1994): 269–280.

[GECH 1988]   Gechter, J., and P. O'Reilly, "Standardization of ATM," *Proc. IEEE Globecom '88*, 4.3.1–4.3.5, Dec. 1988.

[GIAC 1990]   Giacopelli, J. N., et al., "Sunshine: A High-Performance Self-Routing Broadband Packet Switch Architecture," *Proc. XIII Internatl. Switching Symposium*, ISS 90, Stockholm, May 1990.

[GIBB 1991]   Gibbens, R. J., and P. J. Hunt, "Effective Bandwidths for the Multi-Type UAS Channel," *Queueing Systems*, 9 (1991): 17–28.

[GOLE 1990]   Golestani, S. J., "Congestion-Free Transmission of Real-Time Traffic in Packet Networks," *Proc. IEEE Infocom 90*, San Francisco, June 1990.

[GOLE 1991a]   Golestani, S. J., "Congestion-Free Communication in High-Speed Packet Networks," *IEEE Trans. on Commun.*, *39*, 12 (Dec. 1991): 1802–1812.

[GOLE 1991b]   Golestani, S. J., "A Framing Strategy for Congestion Management," *IEEE JSAC*, *9*, 7 (Sept. 1990): 1064–1077.

[GOPA 1983]   Gopal, I. S., and T. E. Stern, "Optimal Cell Blocking Policies in an Integrated Services Environment," *Proc. 17th Conf. on Info. Sciences and Systems*, Johns Hopkins Univ., Baltimore, MD, 1983.

[GOPA 1987]   Gopal, I. S., et al., "Paris: An Approach to Integrated Private Networks," *Proc. IEEE ICC 87*, Seattle, WA, June 1987: 764–773.

[GUER 1991]   Guerin, R., et al., "Equivalent Capacity and Its Application to Bandwidth Allocation in High-Speed Networks," *IEEE JSAC*, *9*, 7 (Sept. 1991): 968–981.

[HAND 1994]   Händel, R., M. N. Huber, and S. Schröder, *ATM Networks: Concepts, Protocols, Applications*, 2nd ed. Wokingham, England: Addison-Wesley, 1994.

[HAJE 1982]   Hajek, B., "Birth-Death Processes on Integers with Phases and General Boundaries," *J. Appl. Prob.*, *19* (1982): 488–499.

[HEYM 1992]   Heyman, D. F., "A Performance Model of the Credit Manager Algorithm," *Computer Networks and ISDN Systems*, *24* (1992): 81–91.

[HLUC 1988]   Hluchyj, M. G., and M. J. Karol, "Queueing in High-Performance Packet Switching," *IEEE JSAC*, *6*, 9 (Dec. 1988): 1587–1597.

[HSIN 1994]   Hsing, D. K., and F. Vakil, "A Discussion on the ATM Forum Flow Control Proposals," TM-24456, Morristown, NJ: Bellcore, Sept 19, 1994.

[HUI 1988]   Hui, J. Y., "Resource Allocation for Broadband Networks," *IEEE JSAC*, *SAC-6* (Dec. 1988): 1598–1608.

[HUI 1989]   Hui, J. Y., "Network, Transport, and Switching Integration for Broadband Communications," *IEEE Network*, *3*, 2 (March 1989): 40–51.

[HUI 1990]   Hui, J. Y., *Switching and Traffic Theory for Integrated Broadband Networks*, Boston: Kluwer Academic Publishers, 1990.

[HYMA 1991]   Hyman, J., et al., "Real-time Scheduling with Quality of Service Constraints," *IEEE JSAC*, 9 (Sept. 1991): 1052–1063.

[HYMA 1992]   Hyman, J., et al., "Joint Scheduling and Admission Control for ATS-Based Switching Nodes," *Proc. ACM SIGCOMM 92*, Baltimore, MD, Aug. 1992: 223–234.

[IEEE 1989]   *IEEE J. on Selected Areas in Communications*, Special Issue on Packet Speech and Video, 7, 5 (June 1989).

[IEEE 1991]   IEEE Standard 802.6, Distributed Queue Dual Bus (DQDB), Subnetwork of a Metropolitan Area Network (MAN), New York: IEEE, 1991.

[ITU-T 1993a]   "Frame Relaying Service Specific Convergence Layer (FR-SSCS)," Draft Recommendation L365, COM 13-10-E, ITU-T. Geneva, March 1993.

[ITU-T 1993b]   Section 6 of Recommendation I.363-Framework of AAL Type 5, COM 13-9-E. ITU-T, Geneva, March 1993.

[JACO 1988]   Jacobson, V., "Congestion Avoidance and Control," *Proc. ACM SIGCOMM 88*, Stanford, CA., (Aug. 1988): 314–329.

[JENQ 1983]   Jenq, Y. C., "Performance Analysis of a Packet Switch Based on a Single-Buffered Banyan Network," *IEEE J. on Selected Areas in Commun.*, *SAC-1*, 6 (Dec. 1983): 1014–1021.

[KARO 1987a]   Karol, M. J. et al., "Input vs. Output Queueing on a Space Division Packet Switch," *IEEE Trans. on Commun.*, *COM-35*, 12 (Dec., 1987): 1347–1356.

[KARO 1987b]   Karol, M. J., and M. G. Hluchyj, "The Knockout Packet Switch: Principles and Performance," *Proc. 12th Conf. on Local Computer Nets*, Minneapolis, MN, Oct. 1987: 16–22.

[KARL 1975]   Karlin, S., and H. M. Taylor, *A First Course in Stochastic Processes*, 2nd ed. San Diego: Academic Press, 1975.

[KELL 1991]   Kelly, F. P., "Effective Bandwidths of Multi-Class Queues," *Queueing Systems*, 9 (1991): 5–16.

[KESI 1993]   Kesidis, G., J. Walrand, and C-S Chang, "Effective Bandwidths for Multiclass Fluids and other ATM Sources," *IEEE/ACM Trans. on Networking*, 1, 4 (Aug. 1993): 424–428.

[KLEI 1975]   Kleinrock, L., *Queueing Systems, Vol. I: Theory*, New York: John Wiley, 1975.

[KLEI 1976]   Kleinrock, L., *Queuing Systems, Vol. II: Computer Applications*, New York: John Wiley, 1976.

[KOST 1984]   Kosten, L., "Stochastic Theory of Data Handling Systems with

Groups of Multiple Sources," *Proc. 2nd Internatl. Symp. on Performance of Computer Commun. Systems*, North-Holland, 1984.

[KOZA 1991]   Kozaki, T., et al., "32 × 32 Shared Buffer Type Switch VLSIs for B-ISDN," *Proc. IEEE ICC 91*, June 1991: 711–715.

[KRAI 1984]   Kraimeche, B., and M. Schwartz, "Circuit Access and Control Strategies in Integrated Digital Networks," *Proc. IEEE Infocom 84*, San Francisco, April 1984: 230–235.

[KUNG 1995]   Kung, H. T., and R. Morris, "Credit-Based Flow Control for ATM Networks," *IEEE Network*, 9, 2 (March/April 1995): 40–48.

[KURO 1992]   Kurose, J., "On Computing Per-Session Performance Bounds in High-Speed Multi-Hop Computer Networks," *Performance Eval. Review*, 20, 1 (June 1992): 128–139.

[LAZA 1983a]   Lazar, A., "The Throughput-Time Delay Function of an M/M/1 Queue," *IEEE Trans. on Info. Theory*, *IT-29*, 11 (Nov. 1983): 914–918.

[LAZA 1983b]   Lazar, A., "Optimal Flow Control of a Class of Queueing Networks in Equilibrium," *IEEE Trans. on Auto. Control*, *AC-28*, 8 (Aug. 1983): 1001–1007.

[LEGA 1991]   LeGall, D., "MPEG: A Video Compression Standard for Multimedia Applications," *Comm. of the ACM*, 34, 4 (April 1991): 305–313.

[LELA 1994]   Leland, W. E., et al., "On the Self-Similar Nature of Ethernet Traffic (Extended Version)," *IEEE/ACM Trans. on Networking*, 2, 1 (Feb. 1994): 1–15.

[LITT 1961]   Little, D. C., "A Proof of the Queueing Formula: $L = \lambda W$," *Operations Research*, 9 (1961): 383–387.

[MAGL 1988]   Maglaris, B., et al., "Performance Models of Statistical Multiplexing in Packet Video Communications," *IEEE Trans. on Commun.*, 36, 7 (July 1988): 834–844.

[MAND 1983]   Mandelbrot, B., *The Fractal Geometry of Nature*, New York: Freeman, 1983.

[MITR 1988]   Mitra, D., "Stochastic Theory of a Fluid Model of Producers and Consumers Coupled by a Buffer," *Adv. Appl. Prob.*, 20 (1988): 646–676.

[MITR 1990]   Mitra, D., and J. B. Seery, "Dynamic Adaptive Windows for High-Speed Data Networks: Theory and Simulations," *Proc. ACM SIGCOMM 90*, Philadelphia, PA, Sept. 1990: 30–40.

[MITR 1992]   Mitra, D., "Asymptotically Optimal Design of Congestion Control for High-Speed Networks," *IEEE Trans. on Commun.*, 40, 2 (Feb. 1992): 301–311.

[MUKH 1991]   Mukherjee, A., and J. C. Strikwerda, "Analysis of Dynamic Congestion Control Protocols—A Fokker-Planck Approximation," *Proc. ACM SIGCOMM 91*, Zurich, Switz., Sept. 1991: 159–169.

[NEUT 1981]   Neuts, M. F., *Matrix-Geometric Solutions in Stochastic Model-*

ing: An Algorithmic Approach, Baltimore, MD: Johns Hopkins University Press, 1981.

[NOBL 1977]   Noble, B., and J. W. Daniel, *Applied Linear Algebra*, Englewood Cliffs, NJ: Prentice-Hall, 1977.

[PANC 1994]   Pancha, P., and M. El Zarki, "MPEG Coding for Variable Bit Rate Video Transmission," *IEEE Comm. Mag.*, *32*, 5 (May 1994): 54–66.

[PAPO 1990]   Papoulis, A., *Probability, Random Variables, and Stochastic Processes*, 3rd ed., New York: McGraw-Hill, 1990.

[PARE 1993]   Parekh, A. K., and R. G. Gallager, "A Generalized Processor-Sharing Approach to Flow Control in Integrated Services Networks: The Single-Node Case," *IEEE/ACM Trans. on Networking*, *1*, 3 (June 1993). Also, same title, The Multiple-Node Case. *Proc. IEEE Infocom 93*, San Francisco (March 1993): 521–530.

[PATE 1981]   Patel, J. H., "Performance of Processor-Memory Interconnections for Multiprocessors," *IEEE Trans. on Computers*, *C-30*, 10 (Oct. 1981): 771–780.

[PAXS 1994]   Paxson, V., and S. Floyd, "Wide-Area Traffic: The Failure of Poisson Modeling," *Proc. ACM SIGCOMM '94*, London, Aug. 1994: 257–268.

[PENN 1975]   Pennotti, M. C., and M. Schwartz, "Congestion Control in Store and Forward Links," *IEEE Trans. on Commun.*, *COM-23*, 12 (Dec. 1975): 1434–1443.

[PRYC 1991]   de Prycker, M., *Asynchronous Transfer Mode Solution for Broadband ISDN*, Chichester, England: Ellis Norwood, (1991).

[RAMAK 1990]   Ramakrishnan, K. K., and R. Jain, "A Binary Feedback Scheme for Congestion Avoidance in Computer Networks," *ACM Trans. on Computer Systems*, *8*, 2 (May 1990): 158–181.

[RAMAM 1990]   Ramamurthy, G., and B. Sengupta, "Modeling and Analysis of a Variable Bit Rate Video Multiplexer," Paper 8.4, 7th ITC Specialist Seminar, Morristown, NJ, Oct. 1990.

[RATH 1991]   Rathgeb, E. P., "Modeling and Performance Comparison of Policing Mechanisms for ATM Networks," *IEEE JSAC*, *9*, 3 (April 1991): 325–334.

[ROBE 1994]   Roberts, L., "RM Cell Format Proposal." ATM Forum/94-0973R1, Traffic Management Sub-Working Group, ATM Forum Technical Committee, Nov. 10, 1994.

[SCHW 1970]   Schwartz, M., *Information Transmission, Modulation, and Noise*, 2nd ed. New York: McGraw-Hill, 1970.

[SCHW 1982]   Schwartz, M., "Performance Analysis of the SNA Virtual Route Pacing Control," *IEEE Trans. on Commun.*, *COM-30*, 1 (Jan. 1982): 173–184.

[SCHW 1987]   Schwartz, M., *Telecommunication Networks: Protocols, Modeling, and Analysis*, Reading, MA: Addison-Wesley, 1987.

[SCHW 1990]   Schwartz, M., *Information Transmission, Modulation, and Noise*, 4th ed. New York: McGraw-Hill, 1990.

[SHAI 1989]   Shaikh, S. Z., et al., "Performance Analysis and Design of Banyan Network-Based Broadband Packet Switches for Integrated Traffic," *Proc. Globecom 89*, Dallas, TX, Nov. 1989.

[SHAI 1990a]   Shaikh, S. Z., et al., "A Comparison of the Shufflenet and Banyan Topologies for Broadband Packet Switches," *Proc. IEEE Infocom 90*, San Francisco (June 1990): 1260–1267.

[SHAI 1990b]   Shaikh, S. Z., et al., "Analysis, Control, and Design of Crossbar and Banyan-Based Broadband Packet Switches for Integrated Traffic," *Proc. IEEE ICC 90*, Atlanta, GA, April 1990.

[SHRO 1995]   Shroff, N. B., "Traffic Modeling and Analysis in High-Speed ATM Networks," *Ph.D. dissertation*, Columbia University, 1995.

[SIDI 1989]   Sidi, M., et al., "Congestion Control Through Input Rate Regulation," *Proc. IEEE Globecom 89*, Dallas, TX, Nov. 1989: 1764–1768.

[SKEL 1992]   Skelly, P. A., et al., "A Histogram-Based Model for Video Traffic Behavior in an ATM Traffic Node with an Application to Congestion Control," *Proc. IEEE Infocom '92*, Florence, Italy, May 1992.

[SKEL 1993]   Skelly, P. A., et al., "A Histogram-Based Model for Video Traffic Behavior in an ATM Multiplexer," *IEEE/ACM Trans. on Networking*, *1*, 4 (Aug. 1993): 446–459.

[SKEL 1994]   Skelly, P. A., et al., "A Cell and Burst Level Control Framework for Integrated Video and Image Traffic," *Proc. IEEE Infocom 94*, Toronto, June 1994: 334–341.

[STER 1983]   Stern, T. E., "A Queueing Analysis of Packet Voice," *Proc. IEEE Globecom '83*, San Diego, CA, Dec. 1983: 2.5.1–2.5.6.

[SUNS 1977]   Sunshine, C. A., "Efficiency of Interprocess Communication Protocols for Computer Networks," *IEEE Trans. on Commun.*, *COM-25*, 2 (Feb. 1977): 287–293.

[SZYM 1989]   Szymanski, T. H., and S. Z. Shaikh, "Markov Chain Analysis of Packet-Switched Banyans with Arbitrary Switch Sizes, Queue Sizes, Link Multiplicities, and Speedups," *Proc. IEEE Infocom 89*, Ottawa, April 1989: 960–971.

[THOM 1984]   Thomas, A., et al., "Asynchronous Time Division Techniques: An Experimental Packet Network Integrating Video Communication," *Proc. ISS 84*, paper 32C2; Florence, Italy, May 1984.

[TOBA 1990]   Tobagi, F. A., "Fast Packet Switch Architectures for Broadband Integrated Services Digital Networks," *Proc. IEEE*, *78*, 1 (Jan. 1990): 133–167.

[TURN 1986]   Turner, J. S., "New Directions in Communications (or Which Way in the Information Age?)," *IEEE Commun. Mag., 24,* 10 (Oct. 1986): 8–15.

[VERB 1989]   Verbiest, W., and L. Pinnoo, "A Variable Rate Code for Asynchronous Transfer Mode Networks," *IEEE JSAC, 7,* 5 (June 1989): 761–770.

[VECI 1994]   De Veciani, G., and G. Kesidis, "Bandwidth Allocation for Multiple Qualities of Service Using Generalized Processor Sharing," Tech. Rpt. SCC-94-01. U. Texas at Austin, March 1994.

[WONG 1988]   Wong, L-N, and M. Kramer, "A Performance Analysis of a 'Leaky Bucket' Access Control Scheme for Broadband MANs," unpublished paper, Nynex Science and Technology, Aug. 1988.

[WONG 1990]   Wong, L-N, and M. Schwartz, "Access Control in Metropolitan Area Networks," *Proc. IEEE ICC 90,* Atlanta, GA, April 1990.

[YATE 1993]   Yates, D., et al., "On Per-Session End-to-End Delay Distribution and the Call Admission Problem for Real-time Applications with QoS Requirements," *Proc. ACM SIGCOMM 93,* San Francisco, Sept. 1993.

[YE 1991]   Ye, J., "Analysis of Multimedia Traffic Queues with Finite Buffer and Overload Control—the Folding Algorithm," *Ph.D. dissertation,* Columbia University, 1991.

[YEH 1987]   Yeh, Y. S., et al., "The Knockout Switch: A Simple, Modular Architecture for High-Performance Packet Switching," *IEEE JSAC, SAC-5* (Oct. 1987): 1274–1283.

[ZEGU 1993]   Zegura, E. W., "Architectures for ATM Switching Systems," *IEEE Commun. Mag., 31,* 2 (Feb. 1993): 28–37.

[ZHANH 1991]   Zhang, H., and S. Keshav, "Comparison of Rate-Based Service Disciplines," *Proc. ACM SIGCOMM 91,* Zurich, Switzerland, Sept. 1991.

[ZHANL 1980]   Zhang, L., "A New Architecture for Packet-Switched Network Protocols," Ph.D. dissertation, MIT, July 1980.

Index